By the same author…

Solidarity: Poland's Independent Trade Union

François Mitterrand: A Political Odyssey

*Power! Black Workers, Their Unions and the Struggle
for Freedom in South Africa*

International Labour and the Origins of the Cold War

Britain's Steel Industry in the 21st Century

Heath

Globalising Hatred: The New Anti Semitism

Why Kosovo Still Matters

PRISON DIARIES

PRISON DIARIES

DENIS MACSHANE

Biteback Publishing

First published in Great Britain in 2014 by
Biteback Publishing Ltd
Westminster Tower
3 Albert Embankment
London SE1 7SP

ISBN 978-1-84954-762-8

10 9 8 7 6 5 4 3 2 1

A CIP catalogue record for this book is available from the British Library.

Set in Adobe Garamond Pro by five-twentyfive.com

Printed and bound in Great Britain by
CPI Group (UK) Ltd, Croydon CR0 4YY

CONTENTS

CAST OF CHARACTERS

Rt Hon Sir Kevin Barron MP – MP for Rother Valley. Chairman of Commons Standards Committee, 2010 to present. According to the *Daily Telegraph* he made a large profit from selling property in London, bought with the help of the MPs' expenses system. Employed, and employs family members, on taxpayers' payroll.

Darren – in Belmarsh for knife crime.

Julian – involved in criminal gambling, sentenced for murder.

Robert Ekaireb – London property owner and manager sentenced to twenty-two years after being found guilty of murdering his Irish-Chinese lap-dancer wife of a few weeks, even though no body, weapon, DNA or any evidence linking him to the crime was ever shown to court.

Detective Chief Supterindentent Matthew Horne – Scotland Yard Specialist Crime unit, who informed MacShane in 2012 that he would not face prosecution.

Douggie – cellmate in Brixton. Edinburgh businessman, chef, jailed for VAT carousel fraud.

John Lyon CB – lifelong Whitehall bureaucrat 1969–2012, Parliamentary Commissioner for Standards 2008–12.

Mumble (Clifford Hobbs, who agreed I should use his real name) – professional criminal specialising in security van robberies.

Mole – professional criminal awaiting sentence after shooting someone.

Father Edward Okon – Catholic Chaplain, Belmarsh.

Alan – ex-Royal Marine sentenced to twelve years for bringing drugs to wealthy drug users in Dorset.

His Honour Sir Nigel Sweeney QC – educated at Wellington and Nottingham University. Golfer. Known for his keenness on custodial sentences.

Bennie – east Londoner awaiting trial after he voluntarily confessed to mercy-killing his terminally ill mother.

Tahrir – Algerian who has lived in England since 1991, detained (not convicted) on grounds of links with Islamist terrorism.

Mr Henderson – thoughtful Scottish prison officer.

Ms Greer – energetic can-do wing manager.

Edmond Tullett – Governor, Brixton Prison.

N.B. The names of most prisoners have been changed.

INTRODUCTION

This book was written out of necessity. I did something foolish, no, let me rephrase that, I did something wrong in the way I sought reimbursement a decade ago for parliamentary expenses networking in Europe on behalf of the government and as an MP.

I admit my wrongdoing. I was guilty of breaking the Commons rulebook. I can only blame myself. That is why I long ago paid back all the £12,900 claimed over four years a decade ago. I apologised time and again. But I accept that I am the author of my own misfortunes, and when you do wrong, you must accept the consequences.

In 2009, the press published details of MPs' expenses. Formal complaints were laid against 317 MPs. I was one of them. The Law and Order spokesman of the British National Party submitted a complaint about me. As a pro-European, anti-racist MP who had written a book on anti-Semitism, which exposed the obnoxious anti-Jewish remarks by the BNP, I was not overly bothered by the BNP complaint.

I read jaw-dropping newspaper reports about what fellow MPs had done – the speculation in the London property market using taxpayers' money, expensive renovation work, the purchase of furniture or expensive TVs, the double claims on council tax or direct payment of rent to partners, monthly payments of £250 under so-called petty cash, without receipts, going straight into MPs' personal bank accounts. I learnt for the first time about many of the abuses that so outraged the public. But I was guilty myself and this I now fully accept.

My crime was to have submitted invoices for my European travel, newspaper, book and journal purchases, and other research work, using a small policy institute set up in 1992. The money had been expended. The expenses forms were filled in usually at midnight or later, at the end of a tiring day's work. There was no intent to commit a crime, just a quick way of being paid back for all the money I had spent. No one at any stage has suggested I did anything for personal gain or profit.

But I accept that it was a form of self-billing and thus utterly wrong. I should not have done it, though without some covering of costs I could not have been one of the best-informed MPs on Europe, which I was, even if my views were not popular with the prevailing Euroscepticism.

The parliamentary office charged with investigating the complaint never interviewed me to seek an explanation. Instead, in October 2010, the Parliamentary Commissioner, John Lyon CB, sent my dossier to the Metropolitan Police with the support of Kevin Barron, the MP for the neighbouring constituency to mine in South Yorkshire, who was chairman of the Commons Standards Committee. The heavens fell in. From October 2010 to July 2012 I was suspended from the Parliamentary Labour Party. I stood down from parliamentary committees and delegations. All the press coverage implied I was a bad man.

For twenty months, a Detective Chief Superintendent, a Detective Chief Inspector and an acting Detective Sergeant investigated my case. I was questioned orally and in writing with supplementary questions. Others linked to me or the policy institute were interviewed and bank accounts were examined.

In July 2012, Detective Chief Superintendent Matthew Horne wrote to inform me that the case was being closed and, after extensive consultation with the Crown Prosecution Service (CPS), then headed by Keir Starmer QC, there would be no prosecution.

I was mightily relieved, as were many friends in the Commons. I was welcomed back into the Parliamentary Labour Party. I was set to resume my work as a Council of Europe delegate, which had been suspended. Conservative and Liberal Democrat colleagues expressed satisfaction that my ordeal was over.

I had spent my modest life savings on legal fees but this seemed small change now that the nightmare of the BNP complaint had been lifted.

However, the Metropolitan Police and CPS verdict was ignored by those in the Commons who had the power to destroy me. The parliamentary bureaucracy and certain MPs decided to use the Commons procedures to condemn me. They ordered that I be suspended for a year in November 2012 – a verdict which they knew meant the end of my life as an MP. I resigned and faced life as a disgraced MP without work, salary or future. Some right-wing opponents of mine insisted that the police case should be re-opened. The police and CPS agreed to this and then, in July 2013, without ever interviewing me – I had never faced arrest or detention until after I left the Old Bailey Court Number 9 on the day before Christmas Eve 2013 – I was charged with a single charge of false accounting.

The CPS under Keir Starmer did not produce any fresh evidence to justify the reversal of the decision to clear me the previous year. In court, the CPS QC admitted there was no fresh evidence, simply a change of mind.

But however much that may rankle, there is no point in moaning. What I did was wrong. I want to underline that it was my fault, my fault, my most grievous fault and if it was decided I should go to prison, so be it.

Like other politician prisoners I expected to be transferred to an open prison after an initial few days in a reception prison in London. Instead I spent all of my sentence in Belmarsh and Brixton. There I met people I had not, and would never have, encountered in my previous life.

I reverted to being a reporter, a note-taker, and wrote down what I heard, saw or was told. I cannot vouch for the verity of all the stories I came across. In two decades as an MP, I cannot vouch for the verity of everything ministers and fellow MPs told me, and still less for the accuracy of what I was told by journalists.

All I can say is that anything between quotation remarks is a contemporaneous record. I have weaved into this account some reflections on why I ended my political career in one of Europe's toughest prisons and why Members of the House of Commons do not enjoy the public confidence that the hard work and dedication of so many of them merits.

Readers uninterested in the politics that led me to prison can skip over these reflections. Voltaire noted that the only way the English knew how to encourage their admirals was to shoot one from time to time. Sending a politician to prison from time to time is intended to have the same impact.

My main purpose is to reveal what life as a prisoner is really like. To be sure, I was incarcerated for only a short time. However, as we grapple with the problem of a hugely expensive prison system that sees most leaving to return to crime, the witness I record from other prisoners serving much longer sentences in Belmarsh and Brixton may be of use to those in charge of public policy. They know that the English prison system does not work but do not know how to reform it, or perhaps do not even want to.

Denis MacShane
Belmarsh and Brixton, December 2013–March 2014

DECEMBER 2013

MONDAY 23 DECEMBER 2013

So far, the grub is OK. As I come down the stairs from Court Number 9 at the Old Bailey, at about the time I would be making my morning cup of coffee, I don't know what to expect. I have just been sentenced to six months in prison. I go down the narrow flight of stairs from the dock and I am handed over to a polite woman who handcuffs me to her wrist. Prison life has begun.

The Homebase-looking wooden panelling of the court quickly gives way to the old institutional cream stone and concrete wall of schools, hospitals and police stations from my schooldays in the '60s. I am marched, no, accompanied, along a narrow corridor. Doors open and shut. The clanging sound of doors is the most common sound in a prison. Heavy doors and noisy keys tell me I have left freedom and entered captivity.

There is no hostility or even interest. I am being processed. It will take time to get used to who is who. With a mixture of Irish and Polish blood, my default personality setting is anti-authority. After experiences of being arrested in political demonstrations in Britain, Europe, even South Africa, I know the correct posture: be polite, head-down, cooperative. Inside, you may be boiling over with injustice or your own idiocy, but there is no point in fussing once in the hands of men and women in uniform.

There is a first time for everything and my natural curiosity and journalistic instincts take over as I try to make a mental note of what is going on. The first stop is a counter where my details – name, address and date of birth – are entered in a register. This is the world of ledgers and big, bound books. Computers have no place.

In my anorak, over a formal suit, there is a thriller in the pocket. A friend who has done time inside warned me to make sure I had books with me. My suitcase, which always amused the press as I trundled backwards and forwards off the number 11 bus to the Old Bailey, is full of books. I am taken back to a small cell where I get out the thriller and start reading.

After a short while, the door opens. 'Legal visit,' I am informed. I follow the guard down the long corridor to a cream-painted interview room. I was never really sure of the point of having lawyers at the end of a long process that began with the BNP making a complaint about me in 2009. Martin Rackstraw, my solicitor, comes from Bindmans, the wonderful King's Cross firm founded by the great Sir Geoffrey Bindman decades ago. It has been the left-liberal reference point for so many people in trouble with the police. I have been using them for forty years and have always liked the different solicitors there.

Martin had found a barrister, Mark Milliken-Smith QC, who had done his best. I suspect he knew, as I did, that my case was never to be about truth or justice or proportionality, but was intensely small p and big P political.

Like a journalist, or perhaps a politician, the judge had the facts wrong in his sentencing statement. My QC is dismayed that a 65-year-old first time criminal who had not profited from the offence, whose case file had already been closed by the CPS and the Metropolitan Police, and where the contested moneys were nugatory, is now to spend Christmas in prison.

I calm him down. The judge who insisted on sentencing me is already a part-timer on the court of appeal and destined for full-time appeal court work. So appealing against his sentence to his own friends, all from the same background and political outlook, is pointless.

Moreover, the legal costs of dealing with the BNP complaint have drained most of my savings. I have four children and my main concern is helping them. Paying out even more money to my learned friends has lost all attraction.

I agree that my pathetic hopes that someone, somewhere would actually read the facts of the case and the double jeopardy of being cleared of a crime, and then, without fresh evidence, sent to jail, were unrealistic. This is English justice at its finest. Get a grip, MacShane. Get your life back. Get over the next few weeks. Get on with a new life post-BNP, post-Parliament, post-CPS, post-Old Bailey. I say goodbye to my lawyers, shake their hands to thank them for their diligent work, and wish them a Merry Christmas with their families. They leave and I am taken back to my little cell.

1150H A kindly lady warder opens the door and gives me two boxes of an all-day breakfast, piping hot from the microwave, and a welcome cup of tea in a Styrofoam beaker. I blow on the cheap sausage, bacon and beans, and eat both boxes. It is the last bacon, indeed the last cooked breakfast, I am to enjoy before being released.

I sit with my feet up on the hard wooden bench against the wall in my cell. My folded up anorak from Decathalon is a cushion. No BlackBerry, no iPad, no more messages, or tweets, or emails, or calls to distract me. It is relaxing, even if I have no idea what the future will hold.

1615H The door opens. 'You're off, MacShane.' I follow obediently down the corridor. I notice my suitcase out of the corner of my eye and long to get to work with the pads of paper inside and a long book review I have planned. There are half a dozen other prisoners. We are told we are going to Belmarsh.

Belmarsh! Hang on a second. Isn't that Britain's hardest prison? A maximum security jail for the worst criminals – murderers, gunmen, terrorists? What am I doing going to Belmarsh? The other politicians who have been sentenced have gone to Wandsworth and quickly transferred to rural open prisons.

Suddenly the future looks bleaker. It is made worse by the dark December weather on one of the shortest days of the year. I am led to a curious upright white van, about the size of a small lorry. Inside are six compartments. They are like upright coffins. There is a small ledge as a seat and a tiny slit window with darkened reinforced glass. You can stand up but not move. I am not claustrophobic but this tiny vertical enclosed space is oddly unsettling.

I watch London, my city, go by. I do not know where we are. I cannot even work out which bridge over the Thames we are taking. Once on the other side of the Thames, the streets go by without any sense of where we are heading.

1700H The van slows down and turns off the main road. A giant set of doors opens and we are inside the Belmarsh complex. I later learn that there are in fact four prisons here, the main one for hardened criminals like me. There is also a youth offenders' prison and a maximum security block for terrorists or the worst murderers on remand, though given the numbers of gates and walls we have gone through, I am not sure how anyone can escape. Finally, there is a private prison called Thameside. The Belmarsh Prison complex opened in 1991, the first new prison to be built in London since 1885.

It has its own magistrates' court on the site. There is an underground tunnel from Woolwich Crown Court to Belmarsh. According to my friend, John Austin, who for many years was the MP for Belmarsh, senior judges refuse to hear cases at the Crown Court, as there is no decent restaurant to hand.

I have some sympathy with the judges, as I am indeed feeling peckish and could do with a decent bottle of chilled Chablis as I wait around with other prisoners to enter Belmarsh. We are in a dirty room with the biggest steel bar gate I have seen so far. We wait our turn to be called. I hear two men talking in Albanian and three in Romanian. They are rough, brutish men drawn to Britain by employers who do not want to pay fair wages to British workers.

There is a tall friendly man who I see later. He just tells me to keep my head down and I'll be OK. Prison is no stranger to these men.

'MacShane,' barks a voice. I go to a counter. I give my name, date of birth and address. I notice they have written me down as 'Ian McShane'.

'Excuse me, Sir, but my name is Denis MacShane, not Ian.'

The officer takes no notice and so, as I enter prison, I have a new identity. I hope the actor, Ian McShane, whose robust performances I have always enjoyed, is not too upset that Her Majesty's prison service has bestowed his name on me.

First names don't exist for prisoners. You are known, called for, shouted or barked at, by your surname. So I am McShane. Ian is just for the prison records.

'Right, over here. Take off your clothes.' This is a first. When imprisoned in communist Poland I was not subjected to a strip search.

As you take off your top garments, you are given a prison T-shirt and sweatshirt. These are robustly made with strong thick warm cotton, not the gossamer thin garments you buy in Primark or H&M.

'Right, trousers and underpants and socks off.'

I begin to feel like Mr Godfrey in *Dad's Army*, wanting to go to the loo as the prison officers stare disinterestedly at my genitals.

'Right, put your trousers on.'

Not my suit trousers which, along with my suit jacket, shirt and tie, hang on hooks as I pull on prison underpants. These would pass the Jeremy Paxman test after the *Newsnight* presenter rightly sent a cross email to the Marks & Spencer boss, Sir Stuart Rose, complaining that M&S knickers were so poorly made with such weak elastic that they were forever slipping down Jeremy's bottom and thighs.

In fact, I feel warm and homely in the prison trackies and pants, and am quite happy to say goodbye to the formal attire of dark suit and striped shirt. During my court hearings I wore a striped blue and white tie I had bought at Heathrow.

The Chancellor, George Osborne, spotted it once in the Commons and said, 'Denis, isn't that a Bullingdon Club tie?' Sadly, I was never invited, when at Oxford, to join the legendary club whose brightly coloured tail suit costs £2,000.

I loved Laura Wade's play, *Posh*, when I saw it at the Royal Court. Almost all the events depicted in it are based on what David Cameron and Boris Johnson got up to when in the Bullers at their time in Oxford. If carried out by a black or working class man in south-east London, such drunken loutish smashing up of property would guarantee a swift trip to Belmarsh from a magistrates' court.

But there are different rules for Old Etonian members of Oxford's Bullingdon Club who go on violent drunken destructive rampages in bars and hotels. And judges, often from the same background, are there to keep the lower orders in check, not to require ruling elites to behave.

My suitcase suddenly appears and I reach out to take some books and writing pads and pens.

'No, they stay in there. You can't take any books into Belmarsh. You'll be given prison writing paper to write letters,' says the guard.

He holds up a retractable biro I had bought in Staples yesterday. 'That could be a weapon,' he says, as he clicks the pen on and off and tosses it back onto the suitcase.

I ask why on earth I cannot take in a book or two, even if a biro is classified as a dangerous weapon.

'You'd better ask Chris Grayling,' came the reply. 'We're just doing what he tells us.'

My prison-experienced friend had told me to take warm clothes with me. So my suitcase has some shabby cashmere jumpers with holes in them, suitable for gardening or going to prison. I had also gone to Primark and for £40 bought thermal vests, a neat pair of tracksuit trousers, as well as some pyjamas, which I haven't worn in bed for fifty years. From home I brought a couple of Berghaus mountain tops and a pair of trainers.

One by one all these garments are lifted out and recorded.

'One pair of Clare Rayners. Two T-shirts, Cedar Wood. One new set of pyjamas, Primarni,' intones the shaved-head guard, who now and then pauses to suck on an electronic cigarette.

Later I am told that one of the Belmarsh reception prison officers was the police officer who was paid £40,000 by the families of the murderers of Stephen Lawrence to remove key evidence relating to the killing of the black teenager before the trial began.

According to this prison gossip, the best way to protect the policeman was to hide him away as a prison officer in Belmarsh.

True? Untrue? I cannot tell. I decide I will simply record what I am told, what I see, what I hear. Reader, dear reader, please bear in mind that everyone in prison has almost certainly told a lie at some stage of their lives.

I would love to pretend that my former profession of being an MP, minister and privy councillor, and before that a BBC journalist, meant that every word I had ever uttered was pure unvarnished truth. But I would be telling a lie if I said so. Politicians and prisoners have their own relationship with truth, but then, so do journalists, QCs and judges.

So I cannot weed out what is untrue from what is fact. In prison, as in life, *se non è vero, è ben trovato*.

My suitcase is shut and that is the last I will see of my books for four weeks. This removal of reading and writing material has been ordained by Chris Grayling. Jeffrey Archer was fortunate to have had a different Justice Minister at the time of his incarceration. He records how, when going into Belmarsh, his son had already sent him David Niven's autobiography and several A4 writing pads and pens.

The minister now in charge of prisons thinks such mollycoddling of prisoners should end. Chris Grayling, about whom much more anon I am sure, is keen to prove that prisons are for punishment, and depriving newly arrived prisoners of the right to read and write will be a suitable reminder that they are wicked people who must be punished.

It certainly works. *Scribo ergo sum*. Descartes will have to forgive me. If I don't write, I don't exist. Right now I am adjusting, but shutting away my writing material hurts. I had read three quarters of my thriller in the Old Bailey cell but this too is taken off me and shut in my suitcase.

I empty my wallet of credit cards, which are sealed in a small plastic bag. I had been told to take plenty of cash with me, and £340 pounds and a few coins are carefully counted out and noted. They are then pushed through a narrow slit in the counter, like paying for the *Catholic Herald* or *The Tablet* in church.

My keys and the rest of my wallet, with its Oyster card, driving licence and national identity card, which for a few blissful months in the summer of 2010 allowed passport-free travel around Europe, are all placed in the suitcase.

I am not allowed to handle anything. I can only respond to instructions or reply to questions. I have lost my name, my books, my clothes, my notebooks and my pens. Most worryingly of all, my toothbrush, dental floss and dental brushes (like many of my generation, my teeth are a mess. Aneurin Bevan may be a saint for founding the NHS but it didn't do teeth!) are confiscated, as is the nightly supply of aspirin my doctor brother says I should take against strokes and heart attacks.

Welcome to Planet Grayling. I say nothing other than the odd 'Can I take this with me?'

'No.'

'Why not?'

'Orders from Chris Grayling.' The prison officers spit out his name with venom. He does not appear to be a popular man with the prison officer class.

I just go with the flow. I enter Belmarsh for Christmas.

1710H My first stop is with a nurse. She rattles through the illnesses or conditions I might have.

'Suicidal? Ever considered self-harm?' There are a few people I would like to self-harm, but life is for living not leaving, and luckily I have enjoyed good health so far.

I ask her to take my blood pressure. It is high, 190/86. I look at the notice offering Hep B injections. My Twitter inbox has been full for weeks of blood-curdling invocations on what will be done to me in prison. The tweet trolls, egged on by the better known names who support the BNP–UKIP line on Europe, have been promising me a rough time in prison. My Twitter fans are delirious in their congratulation of Paul Staines, who runs a right-wing blog under the name of Guido Fawkes. He boasts about persuading the CPS to prosecute me and about his closeness to the Commons Standards and Privileges Committee. Several tweets warn me what to expect in prison.

@RantyPantz_: @MoodySlayerUK: Big day for @DenisMacShane. Hope he's packed his lube. #Porridge

@BrockSamsonUK: Wonder if @DenisMacShane will be swapping his lovely goulash for gob porridge and spunk semolina later today

I reckon a Hep B injection cannot harm in case I scratch myself or pick anything up from the showers. The nurse gives me the first one and tells me to come back for the next shot in ten days. Ten days? Will I still be in Belmarsh?

1725H The rest of the first evening is uneventful. I am in a large room, almost a small hall, with an office behind partitioned walls. The woodwork is painted white. Behind a large table is a food trolley. Two men wearing green trousers are 'Listeners', trained by the Samaritans to be available to any prisoner who needs a shoulder to lean, even cry on.

'I am Darren, this is Will,' says the smaller of the two. 'Do you want some food?'

'Yes, please.'

'There's only chicken curry left.'

It is not chicken curry as I know it, whether from Asian restaurants or from my own rich curried chicken legs and thighs that I make with the help of Mr Patak's corner-cutting Madras paste at home.

Instead, these are tiny square pellets of a faintly yellowing material in a weak, light brown gravy that has a very remote link to curry. It comes with a generous heap of plain, boiled, tasteless white rice.

I sit quietly, eating. Darren explains that this is the induction wing and I will be allocated a cell shortly. He points to a heap of plastic bags which, close up, have some green sheets and orange-yellow blankets in them.

I take one. He asks if I smoke. I shake my head and he gives me a 'Non-smokers pack'. It has a bar of chocolate, some biscuits, a carton of mixed fruit juice, a pack of dried noodles promising a tomato and onion flavour and, most welcome of all, a box of tea bags.

I am given a tiny plastic bag with some Weetabix, sachets of sugar and three tea bags, as well as a small carton of UHT milk. Things are looking up. Providing I can get boiling water and a cup in which to make tea, I can survive.

I sit on the padded benches against the wall. There is a small bookcase on wheels. There is nothing I want to read. Several bibles and korans, a Jeremy Clarkson autobiography and ghosted autobiographies of sports heroes I have barely heard of. There is one large-print murder mystery written by a woman writer I have just about heard of but never read. I look round to make sure no one is looking and shove it under my sweatshirt. The sweatshirt is generous of size, so the hidden book makes little difference.[1]

1750H Finally, a woman officer with neat, short-cropped blonde hair and a kindly, if no-nonsense smile, comes to take me through to the 'spur' where my cell is. She reminds me of the headmistress of St Joseph's, my north London primary school, run by nuns of an indeterminate age and variable temper.

I ask the prison officer if I can make a phone call. Although everything was taken off me when I came in, I have managed to keep a tiny bit of paper with key phone numbers on it. Again, important advice from an experienced convict.

The woman officer explains that tomorrow I can send in a list of numbers to be approved and I will get some phone credit to make calls. Tonight she allows me to make one call using her own PIN number. I get through to the voicemail of my eldest daughter and assure her that all is well. I am OK. In an earlier life, I didn't really have anyone to call when arrested or detained in communist Poland or at political and trade union events in Britain. Or perhaps I was just too insensitive to the worries that nearest and dearest might then have had.

---

1   I never got to see the prison library in Belmarsh though I was told that Greenwich Council operates one there.

Now I need to hear a friendly voice. I make the call and hearing 'Hi, this is Sarah. Leave a message and I'll get back to you' makes me feel much better.

More steel barred doors open and shut. I am by now quite disoriented. An elderly Scottish officer, Mr Henderson, leads the way. (I encounter so many officers that unless I note down their names, which is hard as I have neither notebook nor pen, I cannot remember their names. Mr Henderson and I had several good chats and he treated me with fairness and some sense of the dignity of humankind.)

Already I am famous here. The judge, as I explain below, had obtained maximum publicity with his decision to delay the sentence until the eve of Christmas. I was the third item on the TV news. As I left the dock, I had turned to the press bench just beside and said, '*Quelle surprise.*' I was being ironic, I hope. No one knowing this judge could possibly have been surprised at his incarceration sentence.

Prisoners are not allowed to speak from the dock. My comment was to try and indicate that I knew what was going on. To my surprise, the TV reporters all picked up on it, and the prison officer asked me if I had really spoken in French to a judge.

Another warder joins in the discussion. 'Why are you here? You should have claimed for a duck house.' I cannot be bothered to explain that the duck house claim was a cute journalistic invention. There is even a theatre play running in the West End based on the myth that some MP got a duck house paid for on expenses. MPs put many more expensive items on expenses, with a very tenuous connection with parliamentary duties. But the duck house is now official parliamentary mythology legend, and will be as long as the Commons exists.

Years of dealing with constituents who believed something to be true when it wasn't had taught me that it is a waste of a time for a politician to try and correct error, so I simply smiled and said I preferred to eat ducks, not house them.

I am told I will have no visits for at least a week. This is in contrast to a friend sentenced and imprisoned earlier in the year, who was allowed a family reception visit within two days.

Is this a Belmarsh rule? Or one of Chris Grayling's get-tough measures? I don't know. And no one can tell me. I am learning the most important thing. Information in prison is a fluid, easily evaporated concept. I will spend the next weeks never really knowing what, when, or why anything is happening, has happened or will happen.

1755H I am in my own cell on the ground floor. It has a narrow steel metal bed, a sink and a toilet. It's about half as big again as a sleeping compartment on a British Rail sleeper train – do they still exist? I dump my things.

I have been allowed to keep my watch so I know the time. A bit before six, the door clangs shut. I make my bed. The mattress is hard but over the years I have slept rough, on wooden floors, slumped in a cramped airplane seat or lolled half-dozing during a late-night Commons debate. The pillow seems like a lump of wood. There is no give at all in the hard, blue, plastic-covered head rest. I fold over a tracksuit bottom to soften the hardness of the pillow. If ever I was to write a *Prison for Dummies*, I would advise bringing in your own pillow – if the officers and Mr Grayling allowed it.

There is a small kettle and I have a blue plastic dinner plate, bowl and mug, and a blue plastic knife, fork and spoon. I make a cup of tea, nibble on a bit of chocolate and eat a biscuit. There is a small table and a white plastic moulded chair. On the table is a pre-flat-screen small TV set – the kind students might have had thirty years ago. I can get the first five channels, Film 4 and a couple of other channels. There is no remote. It has been so long since I've watched TV, other than for news, I have no idea what is on or what to watch.

I watch until half ten, the longest continuous watching of television since I became an MP. I cannot sleep without a few pages of reading and start on my stolen book, which seems a complicated thriller about a self-obsessed violin prodigy. None of the characters make sense. There is a police superintendent who is a Lord. Surely they don't do Peter Wimsey detective stories any more.

Yet it calms me down. The cell is warm enough. I sleep as I always have in just a T-shirt. The years of uncertainty since the BNP submitted its complaint are over. I fall asleep as gently as ever I have. But first I relive the events of the day, and try to make sense of what happened.

His Honour Sir Nigel Sweeney looks like a kindly Santa Claus in his red dressing gown and ribbed white hijab over his white hair. He is about to send me to Belmarsh Prison as a Christmas present for the British National Party. I know exactly what he is going to say and do. He is notorious as a judge deeply in love with prison.

A few weeks ago, Lord Neuberger QC, the President of the UK Supreme Court, our highest judge, announced that short prison sentences of six months or less were pointless. In 2013, 43,880 people were sent to prison for sentences of six months or less. As Lord Neuberger noted, 'A short prison sentence can be disruptive for the prisoner's job, home etc. And on the other hand, if an offender needs help for any reason, such as substance abuse or training for a job, there is no point in her being in prison for much less than six months.'

Judge Sweeney has no truck with such wishy-washy nonsense. My QC, Mark Milliken-Smith, made a valiant plea for a non-custodial sentence. As Jenni Russell wrote in *The Times*, 'MacShane didn't seek personal gain and could have claimed the same amounts from Parliament had he filled in the proper forms. Sending him to jail … was a triumph of judicial retribution.'

I am sure that's not how Sir Nigel sees it. He brushed to one side appeals from various of the great and the good – ambassadors, Labour and Conservative politicians, former TUC general secretaries, leaders of the Jewish and Muslim communities – who politely pointed out that no one in the Commons or who knew me thought I was a crook.

I was never interviewed by anyone in the Commons on the substance of the BNP complaint, which is quite odd for a so-called disciplinary hearing. Instead, my file was sent with massive publicity to the police, on the decision of political opponents. The Metropolitan Police and the Crown Prosecution Service investigated the BNP complaint against me for twenty months after October 2010.

The police did a thorough job, headed by Detective Chief Superintendent Matthew Horne. Unlike those in Parliament, the police interviewed me and asked for an explanation. It must have satisfied them, as Mr Horne wrote to me in July 2012 to say the case was closed. I had long ago paid back the disputed money, including every penny I was entitled to.

But for a reason that has never been explained, the CPS, headed at the time by a lawyer named Keir Starmer, who many friends described as a liberal, decent man, reversed the decision not to prosecute after various right-wing politicians wrote and demanded that I be charged.

I took advice from top legal chums – former Lord Chancellors, an ex-chair of the Bar Council, a senior crown court judge who sat with Mr Justice Sweeney at Southwark Crown Court. Their verdict was unanimous and without appeal. In their view, there was no jury to be found without bias and prejudice against MPs, given the massive publicity about my case and others, including those of MPs such as David Laws or Maria Miller. No criminal charges were involved in these cases, but the continuing fury of the public over MPs and their expenses was fuelled by newspaper reporting. Hoping for a fair jury trial was an utter waste of time and effort.

It left a rather bitter taste in my mouth to be told that the pillar of the British justice system – a trial by an open-minded jury of fellow citizens – was not available to me. Ah, well, surely a fair-minded judge wouldn't think jail was necessary. I had told my lawyers I was happy to be dealt with by the magistrates' court. I made it clear that I did not contest the facts – namely that I had submitted improper claims for reimbursement for what I considered proper MP's work – and I had never denied my guilt. So I was not going to waste time and money with a not-guilty plea. However, the chief magistrate at Westminster Magistrates' Court was not keen to save public money; he insisted on my case going to Southwark Crown Court.

But again, for some inexplicable reason, His Honour Judge Sir Nigel Sweeney insisted he wanted to deal with me at the Old Bailey, the nation's number one court for the worst criminals in the land. I was flattered, intrigued and worried.

In the end, I appeared in front of Sir Nigel Sweeney three times: once in November 2013, and twice in December. I assumed that, as I was not changing the position I had held for more than four years – that of accepting my responsibility and guilt – the matter would be disposed of quickly.

Before the first hearing, the CPS QC told my lawyers that the CPS accepted that I had made no profit or personal gain and that they 'were not looking to be severe'. The CPS QC was as good as his word. He barely looked up as he read out the charge sheet. He admitted there was no fresh evidence to justify the Director of Public Prosecutions Keir Starmer's change of mind. The old doctrine that a man was free to go about his life once a police inquiry finished with a *nolle prosequi* had now been binned. A DPP could flip and flop once under pressure from politicians. In my case, given that a jury trial was out of the question, to charge was to convict.

The question in my mind was whether the instant guilty plea, with all the other mitigating factors, might lead to a non-custodial sentence. One look into Sir Nigel's eyes told me all I needed to know. In November, he sent me away with my suitcase full of books, to wait for my sentencing in December.

He brought me back the Friday before Christmas and I arrived with my books, ready to go to jail. It was the day the trial of Nigella Lawson's assistants ended. The only court case likely to have any publicity was about Nigella, an old friend from the days when she was married to Johnny Diamond, a wonderfully warm and witty lefty journalist, sadly taken away far too young by throat cancer. Nothing Sir Nigel might say or do that Friday would get any publicity, so he sensibly deferred his sentence until the Monday just before Christmas.

So, on the Monday before Christmas, for the third time, I trundled into the Old Bailey with my suitcase containing books, including a long study of the 1944 Warsaw Uprising by Alexandra Richie and the latest Michel Houllebecq in French, which I thought would take longer to read than the average English novel.

This time Judge Sweeney, by now dubbed Judge Meanie by my children, who had flown in from Toronto, Córdoba and Edinburgh, or caught the tube from Fulham, to see their papa behind the glass wall of the dock, had the news agenda to himself.

It is an old newsroom adage that Christmas is a news-free time, so a rotund denunciation by a judge, of a here today, gone tomorrow ex-minister, makes marvellous copy. As a former journalist, I was amused at how often 'cheat', 'disgraced', 'shamed', 'fraud', 'deceit' and 'fiddled' could be worked into the same sentence. Sir Nigel gives good copy. He sentences in clichés, and reporters like clichés. He had got some facts wrong and clearly had not read or understood the police evidence.

He said, for example, that the policy institute had stopped work in 1994, which was when it began publishing books and reports. He implied that my name, which has been spelt differently over decades, may have been deliberately mistyped in order to confuse the House of Commons Finance Department. On the contrary, as it functioned at the time, the Finance Department helped and advised MPs on how to maximise expenses and never bothered with the spelling of Denis with one 'n' or two, or Mc- versus MacShane.

In fact, the department was utterly uninterested in the spelling of any name on any expense form it received. Their job was to pay out the cash, provided it was within the permitted limits, and not query any claim, whether for installing a new kitchen, buying an £8,000 television set, or taking out massive interest-only mortgages by MPs who were already well-housed and rich. One of my daughters moaned to me, 'What on earth was Judge Meanie doing banging on and on about how you spelt your name? I spell my name differently from you and so does Uncle Martin.'

Sir Nigel was also worked up about a different business name I used. I have flown under so many names in a life of writing for other people. Like the Conservative Party chairman, Grant Shapps, exposed by Channel 4 for using a fake business name, Michael Green, to advertise his business, I had been using for decades a business name for the administration purposes of the small think tank I set up in Geneva in 1992 called the

European Policy Institute, and which still functions today. I thought nothing of it, but for Mr Justice Sweeney it allowed more denunciations to flow from his mouth.

He went to a minor public school, Wellington, which used to specialise in taking boys destined for the army. There is something about the adjutant in Judge Sweeney as he peers with disinterested eyes at the bolshy squaddie up on a charge in front of him. A spell in the guardhouse and then it's time to get in nine holes of golf, about which his colleagues tell me the good judge does talk rather a lot in best 19th-hole-bore fashion.

In the days when I did court reporting, you had to have a good note to get down the judge's condemnations. Today, the Old Bailey press office puts out a press release with the judge's words of wisdom ready to go straight onto the screen and the next day into the papers.

Sir Nigel, like many judges, had clear views. My background and life story were the very antithesis of his life, dedicated to the most conservative of professions. I do not know if he read the appeals for clemency from Muslim women I had helped, steelworkers I had gone to bat for, my parish priest, and others from my constituency who testified to their belief and knowledge that I do not have a criminal cell in my body. Their support will stay with me forever. But, having done my research on His Honour Sir Nigel Sweeney QC, I expected no mercy. I got none. But, dear reader, I forgive the learned judge. He was simply the last link in a long chain that began a decade ago when I did wrong. I repeat, I did wrong. I am the author of my own misfortunes and I have only myself to blame that I am now about to spend Christmas in one of Europe's most feared prisons – HMP Belmarsh.

CHRISTMAS EVE, TUESDAY 24 DECEMBER

Sorry to hear your fears confirmed. Horrible Xmas present. 'Worst case they had come across'? There is still not one banker behind bars for destroying the world's economy in the years leading up to 2008.

– Sir Peter Westmacott, HM Ambassador to the United States

0650H I sleep peacefully. I fear it is the first time in years I have gone to bed without having had at least a glass (or two) of wine but the absence of booze is no problem.

In my bedroll bag I find a threadbare white towel, a small square of thin flannel, a tablet of soap, some toothpaste and a white toothbrush with a thin, soft brush – just about the cheapest, nastiest toothbrush I have ever seen. I wash myself like Elvis Presley, the so-called whore's wash of a wet flannel over face, armpits and groin. Cleanliness does not seem a Belmarsh priority.

I make a breakfast of Weetabix, an apple which was in my welcome bag, and a cup of tea. I examine my cell more closely. The loo is disgusting with ingrained dirt in the bottom of the bowl. The bin for waste is even filthier. I dare not look too closely at the encrusted muck at its bottom.

I wash my breakfast bowl and tea mug using my hands and the bar of coarse prison soap I provided with last night.

I had made a point of having a no. 1 haircut on my sparsely covered head, in my confident belief that the mitigation plea was a waste of time given the good judge's views, so I don't need to worry too much about washing my hair.

There is no radio so I put on BBC Breakfast TV. Every story seems repeated fifteen or twenty minutes later. I remember working on the first BBC TV current affairs lunchtime programme called *Pebble Mill* after the Birmingham BBC TV centre it was broadcast from. It was unremittingly boring, a sad hunt for soft feature stories without bite. Although I learnt some of the rudiments of TV production there, the dullness of the journalism edged me more and more in the evening into political and trade union activity or at weekends hunting down real stories to write for the *New Statesman* or *Tribune*. The rest is my history.

BBC *Breakfast Time* or whatever it is called seems little different from *Pebble Mill*. This time it comes from Manchester. But whether it is Birmingham or Manchester, the plain fact is that all news comes from London. The poor presenters have to twist their back to interview people in London. I long for the *Today* programme and some real edge.

0900H The door opens and I am told to go to an induction session. This means climbing green metal stairs to the next landing where there is a small queue. My name is checked off followed by a search. Arms out, a quick pat on my burgundy-coloured sweatshirt, followed by a swift flick down my tracksuit bottoms, a turn round for the same from behind and then I move on.

Then it is down more metal stairs and into the area I arrived in last night. The wings in Belmarsh are formed like a plus sign or Maltese cross with four spurs, as they are called, going off the centre. Each spur has a ground, first and second floor with twelve cells on each side. Most appear to have a bunk bed and some have a third, single bed. I wonder if I will have to share.

There are three shower cubicles and one bath on each floor. Nothing is private and at any time a prison officer can see who is in the shower or bath. The phrase I will hear more often than any other in Belmarsh is: 'You're in prison now. Get used to it.'

Each moment is a reminder that, in addition to loss of liberty, you also have to fold your human essence into what the prison dictates. Perhaps for longer-term prisoners there is some effort to restore individual humanity but for now I am a prisoner, stripped of who and what I am, and must accept the regime I now exist in and submit to the will of its custodians.

Each floor has a big black dustbin to dump cell rubbish in. On the ground floor there are two BT telephone cubicles fixed to the wall but I later learn that only one of them works properly. There is small pool table and some cheap easy chairs against the wall, such as those in a cost-conscious GP's waiting room.

I am back in the waiting area I arrived in last night and, together with a dozen or so new arrivals, I am ushered into a room set out classroom style with chairs equipped with flip-up tablets to write on.

Not all the new arrivals are new. 'Brown, not you again,' says the induction officer.

'Yes, Miss,' grins a thin, gaunt looking man of about thirty-five with lank hair and missing most teeth. 'I need my meth, Miss, and fast. When can I see the nurse?' he asks. The drug addict looks as if he should be in a secure medical unit. Throughout the induction sessions he badgers the woman officer with questions which I don't understand. There is a whole prison vocabulary I will quickly learn. But right now it is like being in a foreign country where the language seems familiar but nothing makes sense.

I fill in the forms and skim through a simple reading and arithmetic test, presumably to identify the illiterates. I still have a deep shame that, after thirteen years of a Labour government committed to 'Education, Education, Education' in Tony Blair's famous 1997 mantra, our primary schools are still sending children to secondary schools unable to read and write and our secondary schools decant too many children without core numeracy and literacy. Why are our teachers so unable to inculcate the core citizenship right of the three Rs? And why do we have such third-rate civil servants and Education Ministers that they don't seem to think this is important?

I say I would like to do an education course, especially IT. I fill in a form to go to the gym. For decades I have been trying to go out for a decent morning run every second day and go for a swim or do a gym on the other day. When I was defenestrated from Parliament in November 2012, I was without any income and had to cancel all subscriptions including, sadly, to the excellent Bannatyne gym and swimming pool opposite the Palace of Westminster.

I was made welcome by the Parliamentary ski and tennis clubs whose members knew exactly what they thought of the hypocrisy and double standards applied to force me out of the Commons. Now I have hours to spare in prison I hope some of that time can be spent in a gym. My hopes, at least in Belmarsh, will come to nothing.

We are shown how to fill in our menu sheets. On a single side of A4 in fine print is a choice of five dishes each day. Three meat, one vegetarian, and one halal. The induction officer says you have to declare yourself a Muslim to get the halal option. This seems a bit hard. Some curries listed look better than the non-halal choice. You also have to choose a main vegetable – rice or mashed potato. For lunch there seem to be endless baguettes.

Each choice is made by a black line against the preferred option, I assume to make it easier for a scanner to read. I vaguely thought a communal canteen was an important part of prison life. As well as queuing up to choose between different foods, prisoners can indulge in some banter with the server or negotiations to get extra helpings. But the Belmarsh food ordering system is all on paper.

The proof of the pudding, as ever, will be in the eating. I am not confident. Tomorrow is Christmas. It must be a special day as there is an entry for a half-chicken in the middle of the turkey and roast pork and curry. I go for the half-chicken as a Christmas treat.

Most of the newcomers barely listen to the guidance on filling out the menu sheet. They have been there before and know how to do it.

1000H Back in my cell. The door slams shut. I can look out of the window to a small playground or exercise yard area surrounded by high wire fences. And 'the little tent of blue which prisoners call the sky' as Oscar Wilde put it. I memorised the *Ballad of Reading Gaol* at school. As I lay in the communist prison cell in Warsaw in 1982 and now in Belmarsh, Wilde's description of what the prisoner feels and fears is as true as ever.

In the induction session we were given a cheap blue half-length ballpoint pen, like the ones in Argos, to fill in the forms. I hid it under my sweatshirt. On the ground floor there are racks full of all sorts of forms to fill. They are only copied on one side and no one seems to mind my taking a few. This is Belmarsh's Christmas present to me – pen and paper. As long as I can write I know I almost won't notice being inside. I scribble a few notes and start on the outline of a political thriller based on a deal between Putin and David Cameron.

1130H Dinner as the midday meal is called. It is a small plastic box with cold chop suey. Obeying a deep instinct that says 'Eat', when you are not sure what and when the next meal will be, I slowly munch the food, dreaming of Me Me, the Vietnamese restaurant at Fulham Broadway. My children are a quarter Vietnamese, a quarter French, a quarter Polish and a quarter Scottish-Irish. That gives them a good start in the global cuisine stakes. They have been scoffing Viet food and using chopsticks since they were in nappies. I would prefer a bowl of pho but chop suey will do. And as long as I have a cup of tea, I am fine.

1215H There is a noise at the door. The observation slit cover is pulled back and I hear a voice with a foreign accent saying, 'Mr MacShane. Mr Denis MacShane?'

A strong broad face with a good nose, blue eyes, grey hair and a kind smile is looking through.

'I am Father Edward Okon, the Catholic Chaplain in Belmarsh. Father Pat phoned me up and asked me to make sure you were OK.'

Bless, bless. Father or Canon Pat Browne is parish priest at my local church in Pimlico, the Holy Apostles. A small, quick, deeply smart Irishman with a wonderful singing and chanting voice, he has made the church into one of the liveliest in London.

Although brought up a Catholic, I have never been a good one. But I think belief is important and can be a massive consolation. It certainly was for my mother. Having seen the power of faith and religion in action in Poland under Communism, and having got into trouble with my political masters as a Foreign Minister by pointing out that ideological Islamism was a pernicious danger, I have always thought religion was important and should be handled with care.

One of my best friends, Christopher Hitchens, as well as many others, was a devout atheist. They are right to denounce many of the foolish and at times evil things done in God's name. But to make the twenty-first century work, an understanding of the power and hold and reach of religion is a political-intellectual requirement.

My children all went through Fr Pat's hands for first communion or confirmation. While many Sundays were spent in my constituency or on European work, I enjoyed, when I could be bothered, the coming together on one day a week for a moment of reflection and common communion.

Pat Browne was also appointed Catholic chaplain to Parliament. The full-time chaplain there has her office almost opposite mine, just under the Chamber. So if Pat was coming along that corridor, he would pop in to say hello, enjoy some craic on politics and discuss what latest silliness the Pope had got up to.

'I am from Poland,' said Fr Edward through the door slit. 'Fr Pat says you have some Polish connection.'

'*Tak, tak,*' I stutter. '*Dzien dobry, dzien dobry, czesc,*' I greet him, using my few words of Polish. I explain that my father was a newly commissioned second lieutenant in the Polish army in 1939 from a poor farming background. He was wounded in the first battles with the Germans in September. He ended up in Scotland, where he met my mother, and died when I was ten.

'Well, my father was a Spitfire pilot and a Wing Commander in the RAF, so we have something in common,' said Fr Edward. 'I'll see you at mass tomorrow. Is everything OK? – given the circumstances,' he added.

I could think of all the things that are not OK but what's the point. This is a ray of humanity in what has been a bleak twenty-four hours.

'I'm fine, Father, just fine. Please thank Pat and wish him Happy Christmas. I'll see you tomorrow at Christmas Day mass.'

1300H The cell door opens. 'MacShane you're moving. Get your stuff.'

Wow, am I off to an open prison already? Will I spend Christmas Day in the fresh air, with a library with real books? Maybe Chris Grayling isn't such a prick after all.

Dream over. 'We're putting you in with another prisoner. He's a nice guy, you'll like him', says the screw. Dear reader, you will read the term officer, screw, guard, warden and other references to prison staff all mixed up. Prison officers call themselves screws, so the term is colloquial not derogatory. But when a prison officer does something nasty, then he or she is definitely a screw.

Mike, my new cellmate, is a chatty, friendly, white-haired Irishman who seems half his seventy-four years. He is being held on remand in Belmarsh over a dispute with the tax people. He says HMRC want £500,000, which he has offered to pay, but they want to see this septuagenarian Irishman in prison.

As with every other prisoner I will meet, I can only note down what I am told. I cannot check if the story I am given is true, half-true, a titchy bit true or just plain lies. He is due for a court appearance early next year. He and his wife are ready to pay any bail demanded. They are ready to be tagged, report daily to police stations, deposit their passports with the court and offer any surety for what Mike says is a mistake by his accountant, which can be cleared up with the help of a cheque made out to the taxpayer.

Instead, another prison-junkie judge has sent him, at an average cost of £1,000 a week, to waste his time in Belmarsh. Perhaps I have got it all wrong. Perhaps Mike is a murderer, rapist and gunman in addition to making HMRC unhappy. Still, looking at this gentle, chatty soft-spoken Dubliner with three quarters of a century behind him, I don't see him as even reaching the standards of the determined killers we let out of prison in order to make the Northern Irish peace process win acceptance. I cannot work out why the taxes I pay are wasted on keeping him in Belmarsh.

Mike has a house in Blackheath and, to judge by his well-stocked cell, is not short of cash. I explain that I write a lot and hope to read a bit. He reaches under the bed and gives me a John Grisham.

He says I can have the top bunk where the light is a bit better for reading. In a two-man cell, the loo is behind a thin partition wall so you don't have to do your business in front of a cellmate. But the door doesn't quite shut, and private it isn't.

I say I would like to have a shower and Mike reaches into another box under the bunk bed. He gives me a decent three-blade razor and some shampoo. I haven't yet learnt the ropes of buying these extra treats in prison but as Christmas presents go, they are as welcome as any I have had in recent years.

The advice flows. 'Don't trust or confide in anyone here.' 'Just keep your head down.' 'Don't get involved in trading burn (tobacco), just say you don't smoke.' 'Never believe what a screw tells you. They don't lie, they just don't care and will say anything.'

I go off for my first shower and wash off the lingering smell of the Old Bailey's red dressing gown and wig aroma. If I could just have some fresh air, life would be OK. The children are with their mother and *papi* (grandfather) in Brittany. The French celebrate Christmas on Christmas Eve. I can see the plateau of fresh oysters, foie gras, smoked salmon and other Christmas Eve delicacies served up in France.

My Christmas Eve supper is served at 4 p.m., the last meal of the day. I climb up the green stairs with Mike. We wait on the first floor landing to be allowed down, six at a time. The food is served by prisoners in whites with little chef hats. It is a vegetable stew with boiled rice. No pepper or salt or anything to give it taste.

'You won't get this on expenses,' says one wag.

'It's free here so you don't need to fiddle it,' jeers another. It's jokey not menacing or insulting. The prisoners enjoy someone they have seen on television and read about in the papers. I am their Christmas celebrity, even though not one would have had the faintest idea of who I was before Judge Sweeney did the business.

A screw tells me: 'MPs are the lowest of the low.'

'As low as paedophiles?'

'No, a bit above that. Maybe on the same grade as estate agents.'

I don't bother to ask him where he ranks prison officers, policemen and judges.

1610H I finish my Christmas Eve dinner and wash the plate and plastic fork. The cell door opens.

'MacShane, get your stuff. You're moving.'

I bundle sheets, blankets, toilet gear into a plastic bag with profuse thanks to Mike for his kindness in giving me a razor and shampoo. Our relationship lasted all of about four hours. I would have been happy to stay with him and I think he was disappointed I was going.

Who you share your cell with is part of the key to surviving in prison. The wrong age, a smoker, a need for loud pop music or a particular kind of television programme, a bad snorer, a man who doesn't make his bed or is untidy and dirty or takes drugs, and the cell becomes hell, not a temporary home.

The screw explains I am being moved to Spur 3 where I will have a single cell. 'There's loads of Muslims here and the high-ups are worried about your security, so they think you are better in a ground floor single cell close to the officers' desk,' he says.

It's true that my political work exposing and denouncing Islamist ideology, especially the rancid Jew-hatred of the Hamas Charter has earned me no end of hate and condemnation at the radical end of Muslim identity politics. My 2008 book *Globalising Hatred: The New Anti-Semitism* and my work chairing the All-Party Inquiry into Anti-Semitism also aroused the ire of many Muslims for whom any discussion of the return of anti-Semitism is just evil Zionist propaganda.

I did receive death threats from Muslim extremists, sufficiently worrying in their language to require police investigation. Young Muslims affiliated to the extremist MPAC (Muslim Public Affairs Committee) outfit attacked me verbally outside a local mosque close to my house in Rotherham during the 2010 election. They repeated the BNP lines of attack on my expenses that had been doing the rounds since 2009. However, they rather lost the plot when they urged their fellow Muslims to vote BNP and not Labour in order to remove me as an MP.

Most of the hate tweets against me come from either the BNP or George Galloway, who I once described in the Commons as Saddam Hussein's 'Lord Haw-Haw', as Hansard records. I wonder if George and the BNP swap notes on what abuse to amuse me with.

Islamists spent tedious efforts getting into my Wikipedia entry to insert as many Wikilies as possible to blacken my name. They liked to denounce me as a 'secret Jew', which I found flattering.

I had also got into trouble in 2003 when, as a minister, I denounced the promotion of terrorist ideology in the British Muslim community. My remarks followed the death of a young South Yorkshire Muslim who blew himself up in a Tel Aviv bus station. What kind of ideology, I asked, was driving a British citizen to travel to the Middle East and, thanks to a mistimed explosive device, end up blown to bits? Surely it was better to promote British or European values.

My remarks made the front page of *The Guardian* and *The Observer* with denunciations by Trevor Phillips, then chair of the Equality and Human Rights Commission, and some venomous remarks by Shahid Malik, a Labour MP from Dewsbury, who saw himself as the spokesman of the British Muslim community.

I was branded as an Islamaphobe in left-liberal circles. My boss, Jack Straw, was very angry and said I might well be fired as a minister. He spent a great deal of time cossetting his Muslim constituents in his Blackburn constituency. His private secretary complained to me once that he could not get Jack to focus on his Foreign Secretary work, as Straw spent all the time talking to dissident Muslim councillors in Blackburn, to bring them back to the Labour fold.

I wanted to keep my ministerial job and genuinely did not intend to insult Muslims in general or their religion in particular. But, unlike most MPs, I was already reading myself into Islamist texts. As a daily reader of French newspapers, I was aware of the concern in France about Islamism and its propagandists like Tariq Ramadan.

So, against my judgement, I signed some cringe-making half-regret drafted by Jack's special adviser and the row faded away. Two years later, when Yorkshire Islamist terrorists killed scores in London tube trains and on a bus in July 2005, the tone changed. Ministers and MPs competed with each other in their denunciation of what I had tried to draw attention to.

It didn't matter. In politics, timing is everything. Conservatives tried to de-select Winston Churchill when he warned about Nazism and the threat of Hitler in the late 1930s. I make no comparison but I wish Jack Straw and Trevor Phillips had thought a little harder and earlier so as to use their voice and authority to warn the Muslim community about the evil ideology hidden in their midst and mosques.

But in the wider scheme of things I had never encountered the slightest hostility from Muslims. A bonkers Romanian had threatened to kill me years before in Rotherham when I refused to back his phoney claim for political asylum.

Still, someone somewhere had put on my prison file that I could face threats from Muslims if someone sent a message into prison that I was a legitimate ideological target. Prisons are not safe places. A jug of boiling water filled with sugar can easily be poured over a face. A chat in a cell can turn ugly. A prison razor melted down with its blade turned into a stabbing instrument can do damage. Ultimately, just suffocating a prisoner under a mattress is a quick, noiseless murder.

As I wait to be transferred to Spur 3, which, according to Jeffrey Archer, was known as 'Beirut' when he was there, I find myself chatting to a Muslim chaplain. The young Imam comes from Nuneaton. He talks about visiting the prison within the prison, where all the Islamist terrorists are detained. As always when talking to British Imams, I feel I am with a decent, thoughtful man whose main purpose is directing his faithful to live by the five entirely honourable pillars of Islam.

It is the politics of faith, the use of a god to justify violence, that is the problem. I can never forget that the three biggest mass murderers and torturers of the last 100 years – Stalin, Hitler and Mao – had nothing but contempt for religion and tried to expunge it from their nations.

I don't mention the reason for being moved to a single cell to the Imam. I never felt the slightest sense of fear or threat all during my time in Belmarsh. But I am glad to be in my own cell where I can control my own timetable and space.

1700H The cell door is locked and that's the last sight of another human being I'll have for Christmas.

I inspect my new lodgings. The same iron bed and the same hard pillow. A filthy loo and dirt encrusted waste bucket. Or perhaps something worse. There is congealed dark muck staining the door which looks suspiciously like dried blood. So I was wise to start my Hep B injections. There is no mirror so I don't know how I'll shave. A white plastic chair and cheap table, half of which is taken up by a small television set which looks as it was bought in a car boot sale twenty-five years ago.

On the wall there is a noticeboard but no notices or pins to put anything up.

There is a cheering poem written on a board.

> It soon be over
> Freedom is on its way
> Just hold on
> Brov
> However please don't come back here
> Learn from the past
> Only a fool makes the same mistakes

Another previous inmate has left a slightly harder message on the wall.

> You've got years of not having a shag, having no beer or going to clubs or having nice meets. Shit ain't it?
> PS. On the out your bird is getting fresh cock. Ha, ha, probably mine.

No sex then, but I now have a John Grisham thriller.

I settle down to write a few notes on the purloined prison forms. I make a cup of tea and combine a square of chocolate with a biscuit as a Christmas Eve treat. Between the nine TV channels, there's usually a passable film to watch.

My second night in Belmarsh. I'll survive.

CHRISTMAS DAY,
WEDNESDAY 25 DECEMBER

Oh, the inmates and the prisoners
I found they were my kind
And it was there inside the bars
I found my peace of mind
But the jails they were too crowded
Institutions overflowed
So they turned me loose to walk upon
Life's hurried tangled road

– Bob Dylan

0215H I am woken in the middle of the night by screams of delirium. A man is banging hard on his door and the noise would wake the dead. He bangs and shouts and shouts and bangs. I cannot make out a word.

The racket is dreadful. Surely all of south-east London must be awake? Dogs arrive, barking like something out of a film about Nazi prison camps. I feel sorry for the prison officers who have to turn out in the middle of the night to deal with a seriously deranged man. Should our judges and Crown Prosecutors have to rely on these low-paid public employees to deal with one of the victims of the way we organise society, which offers no hope or purpose to these failures?

I lie awake, thinking how the rich and powerful rely on police, judges and warders to deal with the social deprivation, lack of families, well-run schools and, above all, decent jobs, which spew out these wounded, disabled creatures and leave them shrieking and head-butting in the darkness of Belmarsh, so that Christmas night is undisturbed in Notting Hill, Islington and Kensington.

0730H There's nothing to wake me up and nothing to wake up for. I don't have to sneak in the middle of the night to fill stockings or get up to put a big turkey on. My window consists of two narrow panes of thick glass, which can be pushed open about five inches. Then there are steel bars and a grid. If I stand right up to the window and push my mouth to the aperture, I can at least breathe in some of Woolwich's fresh air. There is no curtain, no way of darkening the cell if there is light outside. The cell seems warm enough, though I cannot work out the source of heating.

I eat my cereal and an orange Mike kindly gave me in our brief togetherness of yesterday afternoon. In the rush to move cells I forgot to bring my mug with me. I make my tea in the bowl after cleaning the remains of rice crispies from it. I use my flannel to wash face and armpits. Like in a Soviet-era hotel, there is no plug in the sink. I improvise, using the top of my prison issue roll-on deodorant.

I am fairly fastidious about keeping clean, changing clothes every day, but so far I have not broken into a sweat or even gently perspired, not even glowed, in prison. I pull on the T-shirt, pants and tracksuit I have been wearing since my arrival on Monday. I am very impressed with the boxer shorts, strong of cotton and elastic. Maybe whoever is now running Marks & Spencer should give a contract to the British prison that makes them, instead of to the slave labourers of Asia most British textile firms (ab)use.

As it's Christmas Day and I will go to mass, I decide to shave. In my prison issue toiletries there is a tube of green slime. It is called shave gel but not the kind of gel you rub together to make a mousse. This is just smeared cold over the stubble. I squat down to use the TV screen as a kind of mirror and scrape away. It's not the best shave I've had in my life but the ritual of renewing my cheeks and chin cheers me up.

However, the absence of dental floss reminds me where I am. This must be the nastiest, least effective toothbrush I have ever used. I could clean my teeth better with a finger. I want no special treatment but surely a decent toothbrush and floss won't get Chris Grayling negative headlines in the tabloids about going soft on convicts?

I watch BBC TV but there is a Putin-style obsequious narration of how marvellous the royal family is. On and on it goes in a manner that would have made one of Stalin's propagandists blush.

0950H My door opens and a screw barks, 'Catholic service.' There are seven inmates from my spur. Again up the stairs to have my name checked off on a list by a screw standing outside the central glass-walled control room, which oversees all four spurs.

'McShane, Ian,' he ticks off the list. I assume all this checking and preparing of lists is to make sure no one escapes, though I haven't the faintest idea how anyone could even begin to plan to get out of here.

I wait in a small room with a bench fixed to each wall. It fills with men from other spurs waiting to go to Christmas Day mass. Some wear rosaries around their necks. I guess prison is where you come back to your God, though most are here for not following one or more of the Ten Commandments. Judeo-Christian morality seems keen on crime and punishment, especially the latter.

There is the usual joshing about my political status.

'What party you from, then?'

'Labour.'

'That's alright then. We're all Labour here,' says a prisoner with a rosary around his neck. I hear an Irish accent, some Polish and Romanian, though I thought Romanians were Orthodox. There is no check on your religious belief and for many men it is just a good hour or ninety minutes out of the cell. But for those who go fishing for God, it matters little what motive brings a man in front of the cross, as long as he is there.

'You're that MP who must be the most fucking stupid of the whole lot of them,' says an *EastEnders* voice. There is no aggression in it, so I nod politely.

'Yeah. You're the one what didn't make any money, so that's why you're sent here. When are they are going to send the real thieves in Parliament to jail?'

Luckily, the nice Scottish officer, Mr Henderson, appears to take us to mass, so I don't have to answer the question.

We set off past offices and a nurses' surgery and then turn into a long corridor with a warder standing at each junction. It is the usual mid-century style cream-painted brickwork, anonymous and institutional. I had vaguely hoped that there would be some prisoners' artwork up to see but there is no relief from the depressing dullness.

I have no sense of Christmas. No tree, nor decorations, or warders wearing a Christmas hat. There are people who are crackers here but not a Christmas cracker to pull. I suppose a sprig of holly might be a weapon.

It all changes as we enter the religious centre of Belmarsh. It has a large chapel with meeting rooms and offices for the chaplains, the nuns and lay people who minister tirelessly to the prison population. There are bookshelves with books for Catholics and other Christians, a great deal of Muslim literature and of course bibles and korans for the taking.

But we remain prisoners. There is a pat-down search entering and leaving and the escort officers sit at the back, usually with a head buried in a paperback. As I enter, one says very loudly, 'Be careful, Mr Henderson, or he'll call you a pleb. Oops, sorry, wrong party.' No Christmas crackers but no shortage of jokes.

I have already met Fr Edward and he makes a point of coming up to greet me again. The mass is brisk and to the point with a talk rather than a homily. To my surprise, Asil Nadir reads one of the lessons. I only know his story vaguely as the Polly Peck tycoon who gave hundreds of thousands of pounds to the Conservative Party in the 1980s. I remember he went back to his native Turkish Cyprus, where he avoided extradition after his company went bust, leaving shareholders penniless.

I cannot help but think of all the bankers, including the RBS managers who raised £11 billion from investors in the summer of 2008 when the bank was already technically insolvent and heading for the massive taxpayers' bail-out to keep trading. So far there has not been a single prosecution against a British banker. But they are not Turkish Cypriots.

Nadir came back voluntarily and paid over £5 million to those who claimed they had lost money. I have lost money on duff investments. It is called caveat emptor. What on earth is Asil Nadir doing in Belmarsh? Surely, if someone should be an open prison, he should? As I learn, his return has caused no little embarrassment to many high in the British establishment. At least in Belmarsh he is shut away. It is not quite *The Man in the Iron Mask* but not that far off.

After the blackish hole I have been in since I was sent here, it is a relief to be out and about in a normal if unusual church service. I doubt if I shall ever hear 'Silent Night, Holy Night' sung with the intensity it is in the Belmarsh Chapel.

Fr Edward tells a lovely story about the handsome cruets used to bring the water and wine to the altar.

In the summer of 2012, an Italian tourist came to London for the Olympic Games with his wife. He bought a ticket, which turned out to be a fake one. When he presented it at the Olympic Stadium turnstile, he was arrested. He spoke not a word of English and found himself in front of a judge at one of the instant courts set up to deal with miscreants during the festival of sport in London. Unable to explain himself and faced with a monolingual police and judicial system, he was sent to Belmarsh for fifty days.

Fr Edward described the man's despair, loneliness and at times suicidal misery at expecting to come for a holiday in London and finding himself in one of Europe's harshest prisons.

'All the prisoners rallied round the Italian gentleman and gave him extra food. I was able to help a bit with interpretation, and eventually he found a lawyer and was allowed contact with the consulate and to be reunited with his wife and go home. Two months later, a package arrived for me at Belmarsh. It contained these two beautiful cruets with their silver-plated handles and a thank you from the Italian,' Fr Edward explained.

It was cheering story on a bleak Christmas Day but a tribute, not just to one prison chaplain, but to the whole network of Catholic and other faith chaplains who work tirelessly to help prisoners.

I chat briefly to Asil Nadir as we mill around after the mass is over. He says he has read abut my case and shrugs his shoulders as if to say, 'British politics, what do you expect?' He tells me he is in the middle of a complicated appeal and that the Foreign Secretary, William Hague, has refused to allow British courts to use key evidence Nadir believes will clear him. There are thirty-six Public Interest Immunity Certificates (PIICs) that deprive the courts and the defence of key information, which ministers are withholding in the name of national interest. Nineteen of these PIICs are about secret documents relating to the informants used by the police against Nadir or about the trial judge, Sir Richard Tucker.

With the public, press and defence lawyers refused access to key documents in the hands of the state, justice becomes a secret affair with trials, and now an appeal, taking place without lawyers being allowed to use or even see evidence. For me, Asil Nadir was just another dodgy businessman from the Thatcher get-rich-quick era. I knew he had given half a million pounds to the Conservative Party. I remember when he came back in 2010 to clear his name there were Labour calls for the Conservatives to pay back the money. But, like the £2.4 million given by a fraudster called Michael Brown to the Liberal Democrats, once money is in party coffers it never gets returned.

But in our brief talk after mass I find in Asil Nadir an elegant, intelligent, articulate man who makes no complaint about being in Belmarsh and clearly enjoys the company of Catholics, although born a Muslim.

I had some experience, as No. 2 at the Foreign Office, of Security and Intelligence problems, especially in terms of dealing with Islamist grooming of young kids to be suicide bombers and killers. No one has an answer to bringing to open courts men about whom intelligence clearly indicates their criminal intent, when to reveal the source of that intelligence would condemn to death someone prepared to break Islamist omerta codes and reveal details of evil death plots against innocents.

But this 72-year-old was no terrorist. Whatever he had done in the heyday of Thatcherism, he had made loads of money for many in that era of greed and corruption. But what was happening to British judges and prosecutors that they were acting as collaborators with a state that was terrified some truth might come out about Nadir that might embarrass those in power?

I remember being shocked when a top Swiss diplomat told me he had been called by a Labour minister and asked if the Swiss authorities could go easy on a bribery case against the Hinduja brothers, two fabulously rich Indians, who had been generous in donations to British politicians. My Swiss friend was deeply worried that a British government official was seeking to urge the Swiss government to drop a case which had been properly launched and was being conducted by the independent Swiss prosecution and investigation authorities.

Was this approach an official one by the British government, my Swiss friend wanted to know? I checked as cautiously as I could and of course the junior minister had been freelancing on behalf of the Hindujas. I still don't know to this day whether I should have denounced him and destroyed his career.

Now I had Asil Nadir talking quietly to me in the five or so minutes before we were sent back to our respective spurs. I was powerless to help. I could imagine that no Conservative MP would speak up for him, and concern about abuse of justice had withered away amongst Labour ranks. As we parted I did not tell Nadir that I thought his chances of finding a judge brave enough to challenge secret justice was also zero.

1045H Back in my cell, locked in. I write some notes and watch a cookery programme.

1120H Cell door unlocked for the midday meal. 'Dinner,' barks the screw. I grab a plate, go upstairs and downstairs, and wait to be given some food. Each prisoner is listed on sheets and I see the prisoner ticking off the names, looking for mine.

I glide my finger down to my name and he snaps at me, 'I can spell.' It's the first and about the only unpleasant remark I get from a fellow prisoner in Belmarsh. Later I overhear two screws complaining about the man's 'attitude'. This is bad news for him. The one thing a prisoner mustn't have is 'attitude', as I will soon find out the hard way.

I get a sandwich. Christmas lunch it isn't. But I ask for a mug as there are plenty of spare plastic utensils behind the serving counter, so at least

I do not have to make my cup of tea in a bowl. I walk back through the barred gate to my cell on the ground floor. The door slams shut.

1415H The key in the door turns. 'Exercise' is the one word I hear. I go out and see other prisoners queuing to leave the spur and be searched. I join the line. The search is completely perfunctory. I hardly feel the officer's hands as I face him and then turn about.

I join the other prisoners as we go out through the laundry room, to judge by the big washing machines and tumble dryers.

The exercise yard has the outline of a half-size basketball court on it. There is a high fence with wire netting over the top. No one has ever managed to escape from Belmarsh. All I can see are walls and other buildings.

It is December cold. My anorak was confiscated when I entered Belmarsh so I have only a sweatshirt to keep warm. I spend some time just running around the yard. One or two other prisoners do the same. This is the first exercise in three days. I filled in the gym form yesterday but nothing has come back and I have no idea of when, indeed whether I can use it.

Then it's just falling into conversations with other prisoners. They seem to enjoy having a politician in their midst.

'You're the idiot who didn't make any profit, aren't you? So whatcha doing here?' says one, using a refrain I'll hear again and again.

I spot three Vietnamese men and since I have some connections with the country via the mother of my four children I join their group. One claims they were just selling kit used in a dope farm. Hmm. The real point, surely, is that I have lost count of friends from Oxbridge, from journalism, from the BBC, from political activism, for whom rolling a joint was as normal as uncorking a bottle.

Why is it a crime to produce a commodity – marijuana – the middle and ruling classes consume but not a crime to buy and consume that commodity? Demand creates supply. If the middle classes did not smoke pot as casually as they drink a beer there would be no drugs business.

These entrepreneurial Viets should be paying tax to HMRC rather than taxpayers paying to keep them in prison.

There is a man in a wheelchair moving very slowly around the yard. Benny is a lifelong east London Labour and trade union activist. An utterly secular Jew, he is well read on all aspects of labour movement history. He says that during his teenage Young Socialist days he went out with Lyn Brown, the delightful MP for West Ham, one of those radiant woman Labour MPs that make being in the Commons fun, in addition to being a privilege and an honour. I'll check with Lyn when I get out.

Benny was a shop steward, representing his fellow dustbin men employed by Newham Council. He is inside because he surrendered himself to the police after ending the life of his 77-year-old mother who was dying in agony from cancer.

'She only had a few weeks left, six, maybe two months. All she said to me was, "Please end this, please let me go, please." So I kissed her goodbye and put a pillow over her head.'

I don't like euthanasia, though if ever I got to some terminal agony I hope the morphine button would be there to press away at. I am not sure why Benny has to be in Belmarsh. He phoned up the police and told them what he had done. I cannot imagine a judge and later a jury will convict him of murder. He is not well and lists his ailments, which mean he spends a lot of time in a wheelchair.

Surely bail or a home tag would make more sense? But our prison-obsessed judges obviously think Belmarsh without a full contingent of prisoners over Christmas would be letting down the side. His case has dragged on for months. He is full of contempt for the upper echelons of lawyers. 'They all know each other, have dinners together, scratch one another's backs.'

I would like to leap to the defence of the legal profession, but Christmas spirit only goes so far. If I meet another lawyer who boasts about swapping speeding points, which led to eight-month jail sentences by Sir Nigel Sweeney for a former MP colleague and his ex-wife, who simply did as she was asked to by her husband, I shall yawn.

Prison rules stipulate thirty minutes of exercise a day. In Belmarsh it will be the only fresh air I get. If it's raining, there is no exercise. I pray to the weather god to let the rain fall elsewhere in England.

On the way back in through the laundry I see a pile of washed, clean sweatshirts. I am now freezing, so I grab an extra-large one and shove it up the one I am wearing and hunch forward so it doesn't look too conspicuous. The screws aren't paying attention as the prisoners troop back inside.

Not yet seventy-two hours in prison and I have become a criminal, purloining prison property.

My cell door stays open for what is called 'Association' in prison jargon. Prisoners are free to leave their cell, though not the spur. It's a time to shower, to make a phone call, play pool, clean out your cell, fill in forms, ask prison officers about an issue or just chat with other inmates. The Association period is in the gift of the officers, who can allow it to run for up to two hours or cut it back to thirty minutes.

I want more than anything to call my children and my partner. But there is only one properly working phone on the spur. One phone for eighty prisoners. I queue but there are too many in front of me and most give up in despair. I assume this is part of the punishment but I really do wonder if any Prison Minister actually knows what it is like on Christmas Day when you cannot even say Happy Christmas to your children.

1529H I am locked away, or banged up, to use prison jargon. It's only a short bang-up because it's soon the final meal of the day. On my menu sheet I opted for a half-chicken, which was special for Christmas. When I arrive with my plastic plate I am told all the chickens have gone – in other words, the servers have given the half-chickens to their mates.

Instead it is two thin slices of industrially produced turkey. But at least there is a tiny cocktail sausage with a bit of bacon round it and a smidgeon of stuffing. And the Christmas pudding with custard bears some resemblance to the real thing. All in all, a Christmas meal that at least makes an effort to resemble what the rest of the country, except those dependent on soup kitchens and food banks, are enjoying.

I eat by myself locked in my cell. Christmas Day TV has the greatest movie ever made, *Casablanca*. I watch Bogie and Bergman and Sam playing it again and the Marseillaise drowning out the Nazi war song, and everything is OK.

BOXING DAY, 26 DECEMBER 2013

Good luck, old friend. This vindictive sentence really is appalling. It contrasts remarkably with the gallery of decent and committed people who have spoken so eloquently and honestly for you. I hope this message gets through and that we will see each other soon.

> – Aidan White, General Secretary,
> International Federation of Journalists 1987–2011

0830H A long sleep. Yes, the steel bed and thin mattress are hard, but maybe the absence of booze reduces the nocturnal pee. I am sleeping really rather well. When picking up food for the final meal, you are given pieces of white sliced bread. I don't bother with it and push little bits through the bars and grill to feed the birds outside.

Yesterday was Christmas, so as a treat we are given a croissant. It's the worst kind of plastic industrial one but a croissant is a croissant. It comes with a plastic sachet of strawberry smear – jam or preserve would be to over-honour the red goo – but it's a change from the rice crispies and cornflakes.

The screws leave the cell door open so I wander out onto the bottom floor and chat. Benny, the mercy-killer, sits in his wheelchair talking to Paul, who needs a walking frame to get around. He is well-spoken, with a strong, black beard and has his head buried in Richard Dawkins's paean to atheism, *The God Delusion*.

Paul says he is in Belmarsh for attempted murder. He tried to kill his wife. He tells me is sixty-eight and he looks rather frail to be a wife-killer.

I wondered if his interest in the non-existence of God was linked to his murder attempt.

'No. She just made me mad when she threw out all my books, so I just picked up a carving knife.'

'Oh dear, I'm sorry to hear that. So I guess you're now divorced.'

'Good Lord, no. She wants me back,' Paul explained, adding that he was sure he would get out on probation.

I suppose there is a rhyme and reason why these no-longer-young men have to be banged up in Belmarsh, a maximum security prison, but it escapes me.

The prison population in England and Wales has almost doubled from 44,000 in 1993 to 89,000 today. A succession of Home Secretaries have gone potty encouraging judges to throw people into prison. Judges in England and Wales in the past twenty years cannot hand out prison sentences fast enough, so that now we have the record of jailing the largest number of people in Western Europe.

Did any of this work? It seems not. Despite the massive increase in prison population, a report by the think tank Civitas noted that, halfway through the last Labour government, a European Union Crime and Safety Survey looked at eighteen countries and found that the UK was a 'crime hotspot', and in 2007 the Eurostat figures for the twenty-seven EU members found that England and Wales had the third worst crime rate.

Under Labour, with its prison-obsessed ministers, England and Wales came near the top of the league table of thirty-four European countries for crime. Looking at the most serious crimes, we were third for assault, fifth for rape and seventh for both robbery and burglary. As Civitas laconically noted in 2011, 'Compared with our peers, the report shows that we are a high-crime society with a particular propensity to violence short of intentional homicide.'

The useful idiots of the right like to point out that crime has fallen since the increase in prison numbers under Michael Howard and his Labour successors took off. But crime has fallen faster in most other modern democracies, where prison numbers have been kept low.

So prison clearly doesn't work, and the lie from so many politicians and tabloids that more prisoners equals lower crime is simply not true. But why did Home Office civil servants sign off on this nonsense? Why do judges surrender their intellectual capacity on opening the papers they like to read, which clamour for ever more people to be sent to prison?

A little bit of me is to blame. I never took the slightest interest in prison matters in my two decades as an MP. There were committed MPs, like Jean Corston (who later produced a very important report on women in prison as a peer) and Paul Goggins, who were concerned about prison reform, and all credit to them. I think there is an All-Party Parliamentary Group on prisons, as there is on all subjects under the sun. And I do not wish to disparage any former colleague who may have challenged the ever rising number of prisoners sent by the CPS and judges to our jails. But I just cannot recall any prison reform MP making a mark or changing policy on prisons. And there was certainly no force field of MPs able or willing to push back against the policy of successive Conservative, then Labour, and again Conservative ministers, with the help of supine judges, to keep increasing the prison population.

The prison budget now runs at a colossal £3.4 billion a year. This is more than the budget of the Department of the Environment, Food and Rural Affairs, or the Foreign and Commonwealth Office. The estimates vary from prison to prison, but it can cost over £100,000 a year to keep a prisoner in jail – the rough average normally given is £1,000 a week.

So the sad old men I am talking to are already costing you, the reader and taxpayer, thousands to keep them hanging around Belmarsh waiting for a trial instead of being out on bail. I wouldn't know it from the quality of the food, bedding and conversation, but I have already cost the taxpayer £500 plus whatever the judge and CPS earned while taking their time sending me here.

It's not that prison officers are well paid. The starting salary is £18,000, well below the national median earnings for a full-time employee, which stand at £26,000. Some are tempted to earn extra. In Belmarsh, a prison officers' union official is suspended as part of an investigation into newspapers paying police and prison officers for information.

Other prisoners repeat without end: 'You can get anything in prison. Mobiles, an iPad, and as much drugs as you want.' The smuggling is done by prisoners' friends and families, but also by prison officers.

I have seen no evidence of this so far and in any case will keep a million miles away from anything so dumb. But wherever and whenever there is prohibition of a desired commodity, someone will take money to bring it in. After all, we were all taught to celebrate the great English tradition of smuggling by Kipling:

> Five and twenty ponies
> Trotting through the dark –
> Brandy for the Parson,
> 'Baccy for the Clerk;
> Laces for a lady, letters for a spy,
> And watch the wall, my darling, while the Gentlemen go by!

Prison officers are just being true to Kipling's celebration of smuggling. The inhabitants of our prisons turn to watch the wall as the smuggling goes by.

1125H Lunch is two cold samosas. Far from my favourite, but I am craving taste. The lack of salt or pepper or anything to add taste to the dull, bland food is driving me mad.

1140H One of the perks of prison is clean laundry. You are given a bag made from netting with a label to write your name on. Twice a week you put all your dirty clothes in and they come back thoroughly washed and dried. Not all prisoners take advantage of this excellent service. There are some grubby people about. Some cells are Brigade-of-Guards-garrison spick and span, with sheets and blankets boxed. Older prisoners tell me that used to be routine, especially in borstals. I just make my bed as tidily as possible.

1430H Exercise is long today – nearly a full hour. A Christmas Day present from the officers. Again I half jog, half walk around the yard. The jokey calls never stop. 'Order! Order!' they call out. They ask shyly if I have met Tony Blair, the only politician they know. This is a post-Thatcher generation on the whole. 'Yes, I worked with him as a minister and have known him for more than thirty years.' The Blair connection gives me good Belmarsh credit.

I never quite made it to the high-profile recognition stakes as an MP or minister. But here everyone seems to know me and wants to talk. Most confess bafflement at my presence given both the small amount of money and, most bizarrely of all, the fact that I didn't get rich. They listen as I list all the other ways MPs abused and abuse the expenses scheme. I sketch out the main naughtinesses.

Using the mortgage interest payment to speculate in the London property market really took off after 2001. You could see the new boys and girls at the Tory end of the tea room getting tutorials. They were told to designate a modest flat in their new constituency as the main family home and then they could take out an interest-only loan on their existing London house. MPs could claim up to £2,000 a month in mortgage interest payments which meant a loan of up to £800,000 to spend as you liked, providing you showed a statement from the Halifax or a bank that you were paying £2,000 a month in interest. My neighbouring Rotherham MP, Kevin Barron, talked openly about buying a ritzy flat using this system and when he sold it the *Daily Telegraph* and *The Guardian* reported he made an estimated £500,000 in profit. All this was perfectly within the rules, and he should know. He is the chair of the Commons Standards and Privileges Committee.

Then there's buying a large house in your constituency using a substantial mortgage interest payment from the taxpayer and then enjoying the accrued value. David Cameron bought his home in the wealthy Chilterns town of Witney. With an estimated family wealth running to £20 million or £30 million, he had no need to be subsidised by the taxpayer. But month by month he claimed a steady £1,081 in mortgage payments as his investment increased in value. This was all perfectly within the rules as they existed, but my exercise-yard prisoners are stunned at just how rich the expenses system allowed MPs to become.

They loved hearing details of the petty cash diddle. MPs could claim £250 a month under a heading 'Petty Cash' without producing a single receipt. It would be nice to believe that this consisted of tenners stuck in a tin box for use by constituency employees but the regular claim month by month was transferred straight to the MP's bank account. It was all perfectly within the rules and George Osborne pocketed his monthly £250 with gusto. He also claimed back for interest rate payments for a mortgage worth more than the value of his house. He probably wishes getting money into the Treasury coffers was as easy.

Then there was the council tax help-yourself. MPs would claim back reimbursement for the full value of the council tax on their constituency homes but would only pay 50 per cent of the tax, as was permitted on second homes. Poor Jack Straw could be seen scrambling to pay back £1,500 in over-claimed council tax for his Blackburn home for the years 2004–09, when the details were exposed.

I had never heard of the John Lewis list – some guide to furniture that could be bought that would be accepted by the House of Commons finance officials. State-of-the-art TV sets, sofas, or paintings for walls were all paid for by taxpayers.

There are stories about mileage claims and MPs sharing a car going home to Scotland or the far north of England and each claiming the mileage as his own. Occasionally, the claims got so wild – one story told of an MP claiming 100,000 miles a year – quiet words would be exchanged between finance officials and the whips, and the naughty MP would be secretly warned to ease off.

One of the biggest sources of extra income for MPs was to employ wives and children. In most modern democracies – including the

United States, Australia, New Zealand and the northern EU states – this practice is simply banned as corrupt and illegal. Not so here, where even today MPs employ family members. The Tory MP Peter Bone gets the taxpayer to pay his wife £45,000 a year. Kevin Barron has had both his wives salaried by the taxpayer as well as other family members. Of course, this is within the rules, I explained to my jaw-dropping Belmarsh fellow convicts. After all, Kevin Barron chairs the Committee that defines and upholds the rules. His predecessor up to the 2010 general election was Sir George Young, a Tory MP who presided over the Standards Committee. Sir George employed his daughter, who was paid by the taxpayer.

I told them of the MPs who gave big monthly salaries to their children while said children were studying full-time at university, and of the £40,000 paid to the boyfriend of David Laws, the Lib Dem MP. This latter was nominally paid as rent but the Commons rules explicitly forbid any such payment in rent to partners or spouses. Naturally, this was looked upon kindly by the Whitehall civil servant entrusted with defending taxpayers' money paid to MPs for expenses. He and the Standards Committee applied a minor sanction to Mr Laws, who quickly returned to David Cameron's Cabinet.

In theory, MPs are meant to travel second class, but I regaled my prisoner friends with stories of how many MPs ordered carnets of first-class tickets, which cumulatively came in within the limit of full second-class tickets and thus allowed them to travel by train as they used to.

The new oversight regime, brought in with great fanfare after the 2010 election, has turned out to be farcical. It allowed one Tory MP to claim £5,822 for heating the stables where he kept his horses. The MP, Nadhim Zahawi, said he was 'mortified' at his mistake and promised to pay back the money, just as I had. The cost of running the new MPs' oversight system has risen to £6 million – three times the cost of the old system, which came to an abrupt end in 2009. MPs were given much more money to rent out London flats than they had previously been paid in mortage help. They promptly started renting to each other, with Kevin Barron renting a flat from a fellow Yorkshire Labour MP who benefitted from the taxpayer-paid rent.

As I explain the details of the MP expenses system, there is one shrewd observation from Darren, the 'Listener' who received me with sympathy on my entry into Belmarsh. 'Yeah, but it's all perks isn't it? Everyone has those don't they, even judges I'll bet.'

Darren is perfectly right. Unlike MPs, judges can claim first-class rail travel and have a much more generous mileage allowance. They can even claim if they stay overnight with members of their family, a perk that no MP would have dared claim. They can claim a flat rate of £1,700 a year without any invoices – a bung agreed with HMRC. Perhaps judges should come and give tutorials to MPs on arranging expense systems.

The abuse of the expenses system by MPs goes back decades. David Howell, a Tory grandee and former minister under Mrs Thatcher, told me how in the '60s the Inland Revenue (now HMRC) came to the Commons and suggested a flat-rate tax-free payment to cover the costs of MPs living in two places at once.

According to Howell, wealthy, land-owning Tory MPs had been claiming against tax the cost of their London homes in Belgravia. Rather than dealing with each individual claim, the tax authorities suggested a common allowance, which evolved into a monthly maximum payment for rent or for just the interest payment segment of a mortgage.

By the early 2000s this had been seized on by some MPs as a way of getting massive loans from mortgage lenders, which they used to purchase top-end flats in London's rising property market or to take out mortgages on existing homes to use as they pleased.

Peter Snape was a newly elected Labour MP in 1974. He told me how, as a former railway worker, he could hardly survive on his then salary as he tried to be a full-time MP in Westminster and maintain a home in the West Midlands.

'There were a number of us new MPs in similar positions. We went to see Harold Wilson, who told us, "Don't worry lads, I've told the Chief Whip to put another £1,000 on mileage."'

Mrs Thatcher, John Major and Tony Blair also turned a blind eye to arrangements made by whips with the full agreement of the Commons authorities to augment salaries which were held down despite the recommendations of outside independent bodies. Instead, successive Prime Ministers improved MPs' salaries with these differing forms of expenses.

The public is right to be outraged, but the fault lies with the top political leadership, and none of today's senior Cabinet ministers made any protest at the time as they trousered every allowance they could.

As prisoners pepper me with questions, I feel at times I am back in an MP's surgery or a constituency *Any Questions*.

'Why is cannabis illegal? Alcohol is far worse,' asks one prisoner. I have no answer.

A young plumber tells me he is in Belmarsh for twenty-eight days after a banal punch-up. 'I shouldn't have done it. First time, last time here.' He promises to come round and fix my ageing boiler. Belmarsh mates rates. But wait a second. Didn't the President of the Supreme Court say that prison sentences of six months or under were pointless? Why is this young man here over Christmas?

1610H Evening meal of rice and mince stew. No salt or pepper. Locked up. *Harry Potter* on the television.

FRIDAY 27 DECEMBER 2013

When I got to the street, I walked boldly. But I was always accompanied by an agonising thought: the fear that honest people may be thieves who have chosen a cleverer and safer way of stealing.

– Jean Genet

0755H Wake up to breakfast TV. Please can I have *Today* and the ever young John Humphrys sharpening himself on politicians' pomposities? I shave bent down in front of the switched-off TV. Breakfast is rice crispies, which I have always disliked. I get a piece of fruit a day instead of a pudding, so I eat an orange, which cheers me up.

0830H Exercise. I pull on two sweatshirts to keep warm. A pat-down search, back and front. I jog around the exercise yard. A tall, bulky prisoner who came in with me from the Old Bailey joins in the run, as well as two cheerful black guys. It's a sedate pace. If I really ran I would do a circuit in twenty seconds, so small is the space. The screws huddle against the wall, close by the door. We are under constant supervision, though where we can go or what wickedness we can get up to is not clear.

Different groups form. Muslims, some with long robes and heads covered, assemble and lean against the fence. Remand prisoners can wear their own clothes. It is new-boy convicts like me who have to use prison clobber, though I am warm and comfortable in my prison-made trackies and two sweatshirts.

I could do with the beanie shoved in my anorak pocket as, given my lack of hair covering as the years have passed, I tend to feel very cold on the top of my head. Younger, sad-looking men, younger than my own children, walk about. Middle-aged professional criminals, who clearly know each other from the outside, form a small conversation group. Benny in his wheelchair and Paul on his walking frame edge slowly around the yard, grabbing the precious ration of fresh air that is all we are allowed.

As I go by, a very tough-looking man, burly and not one to be messed with in his smart, thick woollen jacket, which would look good in a bar in Davos, silently hands me four envelopes with first-class stamps. 'You can use these, I reckon.' I shove them up my sweatshirt and am deeply grateful as I have no way of writing letters to my children. I don't even know him and he is not from my spur. A small gesture of solidarity and a generous Christmas present.

An inmate of Spur C, Phil, says, 'I hope the screws didn't see that.' My envelope donor had timed the exchange when we had our backs facing the wall and door where the screws were standing, so I don't think there's any chance.

I jog some more and everyone joshes me by crying, 'Order! Order!'

0910H The cell door is not closed so I grab soap and a thin towel and head for a shower. On the ground floor the shower is a single cubicle without a door, next to a bath. A prisoner is running a bath, which seems to take ages.

I swapped baths for showers when I went into exile in Switzerland when Margaret Thatcher was elected. I couldn't get a job as a journalist anywhere in England in 1979 thanks to my reputation as a hot-headed NUJ militant, forever taking journalists out on strike. I had got into trouble when a BBC producer asked me to fake a caller on a late-night local radio phone in and I got carried away and made rude remarks about a Tory politician. The BBC bigwigs had made it clear they disapproved of my political activities, so out I went. Perhaps there is some bad gene in my DNA that just gets me into trouble.

At the time I just thought I was trying to get fair pay for the journalists. But fair pay for some is extremist radical ideology for others, and in the tiny world of newspapers and broadcasting I was blacklisted as a strike-happy militant. I took what I thought was a temporary job with an international trade union organisation based in Geneva. I stayed there fifteen years until my election to the Commons in 1994.

In hard-working Switzerland and Germany there was no time for baths. So I left behind the English wallow and began to enjoy the strong-pressured showers of continental Europe.

In Belmarsh you are strictly enjoined to go to the shower fully clothed. Notices on the wall warn prisoners always to wear shoes, not flip-flops, not to be seen in shorts or vests, and not to walk around with our hands stuck down the front of our tracksuit trousers.

I place my clothes on the wall outside the cubicle with my prison-issue deodorant, take the soap and enter the cubicle. The floor is dry, though I wish I had some flip-flops in case of picking up athlete's foot or some other fungal infection.

The back wall is covered with tiny black flies but I just ignore them. The shower itself is a nightmare. There is a button to press, which offers a thin squirt of water that lasts about fifteen seconds before suddenly turning off.

The water is cold to begin with and then warms up but never really gets hot. There is no force but, with enough pushing and re-pushing of the shower button and turning round and about, I have a decent wash and feel much better.

On my way back to my cell, a prisoner says, 'My mum told me about you. She said all the MPs were at it but they had to find a scapegoat.'

Another, who knows I am using up the tiny three-inch ballpoints used in prisons, slips me a full-length biro. I was hoping to use the phone to talk to the children, who are in France or maybe now en route to the Geneva branch of the family. But only one phone works and the queue is too long.

0945H Bang-up. About twenty minutes later the observation slit opens and it is Fr Edward on a pastoral tour. 'You should stay in Belmarsh. It's better than many prisons.' I guess I have to take his word, though I cannot think of how things could be any worse. Perhaps no television, nothing but bread and water, cold showers and fresh air only every second day? I can live with my own company, with tasteless, thin food, but surely even in eighteenth-century prisons you were allowed books and paper to write on?

1130H The quick ten-minute outing for lunch. The queue of Spur C prisoners shuffles forward on the 'twos' – landings are called 'ones', 'twos', 'threes', 'fours' and so on. The 'ones' are the ground floor, so when I go up one flight of stairs I arrive on the 'twos'.

Six of us are allowed through at a time to go downstairs to join the queue for food. I get a soft, puffy 'baguette' roll with tuna paste in it. I think of the baguettes of France, surely the best single bread ever invented, even if I prefer the dark breads further east in Europe. This prison 'baguette' is about a third the length of the real thing. It has no crust and could be eaten easily by a toothless baby.

I watch TV, with programmes like *Colombo* from another era.

1620H Doors open for supper. In theory it is fish and chips with mushy peas. The mushy peas are OK. The chips are lukewarm and made of powder. The fish is a toilet-paper-thin slice of some utterly tasteless white fish squeezed between two thick slices of Polyfilla batter. Ugh. No salt and no chance of vinegar, tomato ketchup or HP sauce, let alone pickled onions or a wally – a gherkin, to the uninitiated – which makes fish and chips one of the world's greatest treats.

It's boring but I just get on with it. I am running out of paper to write on even though I have a full-length ballpoint. I will have to go out tomorrow and half-inch some more prison forms and hope the screws don't notice. Actually, I don't think they care.

2230H Bang, bang, bang. The prisoner at the end of the ground floor is smashing himself into his door. He is clearly in the grips of some demon. Is this a case of cold turkey, the agony of withdrawal from skag (heroin) or Charlie (cocaine), or just the need for some burn – tobacco for a smoke? His door is always closed during the Association period. He stares forlornly with wild, staring eyes set in a skeletal, unshaven face through the cell bars as we march past during exercise.

Bang, bang, bang and even more shouts. In each cell there is a call button but with a large notice stating that it is only to be used for real emergencies, not just to call the duty guard for some minor reason. I can hear the screws shouting at the mad man, though I cannot make out what is being said.

It is the closest I will get to Bedlam in clever modern England, which talks 'compassion' and 'care' as if these words have meaning. I wish Chris Grayling could see what prisons are really like.

SATURDAY 28 DECEMBER 2013

Thinking of you. You have so many friends who are wishing you well, admiring your courage and waiting for your return.

All the very best,
Charlie Falconer QC

0750H Cornflakes and tea. Amused to hear on BBC morning TV that Keir Starmer is to advise the Labour Party on rape victims. Certainly the successful prosecution of rapists and the prosecution of victims of domestic violence in our country in recent years has been amongst the lowest in Europe. He sounds just the chap to help women.

It's a sunny Saturday. My cell is heated but I don't have enough blankets to keep warm at night. Should I ask for more? Better not. Just find where they are stored and help myself.

0925H Association is a bit longer today, a full two hours, presumably a weekend treat. I had an appointment to see the nurse to check my blood pressure, which was high on Tuesday, my first day in Belmarsh. It has now come down a bit but remains higher than it should be.

'Why didn't you come and see me the second day you were here for another blood pressure check?' asks the nurse, a middle-aged Afro-Caribbean woman.

'I wasn't told to.'

'I told the officer to get you.'

'Well, someone knocked on my cell door and said did I want medication.'

'Yes, that's right, medication, a blood pressure test.'

'Sorry, I'm not on medication and he didn't mention a blood pressure test.'

'Well, you should have come.'

I gently explain that prison officers are all-powerful. She seems annoyed and I watched my blood pressure soar into a danger zone. I say I don't think it is a good idea to get a patient all stressed up before taking blood pressure.

She glares at me and then lightens up and, as the stress subsides, so my BP on a second try is down a bit and down further on a third try, standing up. It's always a good idea to take two BP tests, one preferably lying down.

Back on the landing, I talk to a young prisoner who is in Belmarsh for four weeks for breaking a window. I wonder what world the judges who sent this boy to Belmarsh live in. Nick Clegg was arrested and convicted for breaking into a greenhouse and setting it on fire when he was a teenager, and who knows what damage David Cameron, Boris Johnson and George Osborne did in their Bullingdon Club days. But my Belmarsh friend is black and didn't go to Eton, Westminster or St Paul's.

Finally, my prison PIN number works so I try to make calls. But, predictably, all the mobiles of family and friends are on voicemail, so the £1 phone credit, which is all Chris Grayling allows a new prisoner in his first two weeks, as part of his punishment regime, is exhausted.

I write a letter for a hapless, tall, skinny Iraqi. He is forty-eight years old and fled to Britain from Saddam Hussein's terror in 2002. He has leave to stay here. At least then we accepted some refugees escaping war, terror and torture.

Now Britain will not accept a single Syrian refugee fleeing from the war between Assad and his opponents, whom Britain encouraged with blithe promises earlier this year from William Hague to arm jihadis. The excuse is that we divert development aid money to pay for refugee camps. I wonder whether, if the Department for International Development had been around in the 1930s, a Conservative Prime Minister would have sent cheques to Jewish asylum seekers fleeing from Hitler, as long as they did not seek to come to Britain.

My Iraqi friend tells a curious story. Like many refugees with poor English he decided to rent out rooms in the Greenwich property he occupied to make a little money. He let out rooms for £50 a week to Romanian workers. They had paid no rent for two months. When he went to ask for the rent he was owed, the Romanains attacked him, smashing in his mouth. He opens it and I can see a gaping, bloody gap in his upper jaw where some teeth have clearly been knocked out.

The Romanians called him a 'dirty Arab', though his slight, thin middle-aged frame seems perfectly clean to me. When he called the police, they had a choice of arresting him or his European assailants. Naturally they opted for the Arab. He was bundled off to Plumstead police station. He was not allowed to make any phone calls to try to find a solicitor and instead was given one by the police.

Although he insists to me that he has a house he lives in and pays council tax on, the police refused him bail, which was upheld by a local judge. Instead he was charged with grievous bodily harm. The Romanians showed the police the broken skin on the back of their hands where they had hit him and knocked out his teeth. Now, more than a week later, he is helpless and hapless in our top security prison.

Of course, as he told me his story in poor, broken English, he could have been making it all up. Perhaps he is a violent, vicious landlord who assaults defaulting tenants. Yet, looking at the frail, confused creature, I could not see him as a GBH merchant. Of course, it looks good for the local police to add a GBH arrest to their checklist of targets, and if he is convicted then the CPS can show it is getting tough with violent crime.

Several people thought I should be given a community service sentence rather than costing the taxpayer money with a custodial sentence. I had done my research on the judge and knew that was unlikely. I had done two decades of community service as an MP. I like helping people – who doesn't? For many MPs, as they realise that power and position will never come their way, it is easy to relapse into being a constituency social worker.

The great Labour politician and creator of the NHS, Aneurin Bevan, used to get hundreds of letters a week. Each day he put them all into a little cupboard MPs have lining the corridors leading away from the Members' Lobby. Once a month, Nye Bevan would get a mailbag from the Commons Post Office, just off the Members' Lobby, put all his letters in it and throw them away.

Times have changed. Nick Soames, the Tory MP who was my pair when pairing existed, said he had to spend two hours a day just dealing with constituents' emails. Bit by bit, MPs have given up national and international politics as they turn into a rather better-paid version of local councillors, trying to deal with every local moan and complaint.

Many MPs take very little interest in political questions. Several Conservative MPs, for example, earn more than £1 million a year from outside directorships and consultancies.

I hope I was assiduous and attentive to my constituents – regular surgeries, home visits, street surgeries, coffee mornings, town centre public meetings when anyone could come and attack me or ask questions. But after two decades I had done enough.

Now I revert to being an MP again as I write out a letter for my Iraqi friend and send it to his MP. I warn him it will have little impact but it is better than nothing.

Again and again, prison officers tease me when I ask where to leave a form or what time exercise will take place.

'Oh, you think we plebs have an answer.'

'I'm only a pleb, what do I know?'

If the 2009 expenses scandal Chernobyled the Commons, leaving it contaminated for years to come, the Plebgate row is going to poison relations between the political class and the police as well as the other uniformed ranks of the judicial apparatus, including prison officers.

I protested Andrew Mitchell's dismissal from government because, like Chris Mullin or David Davis MP, I can smell a stitch-up over Mitchell, even if it was a Cabinet Secretary, Sir Jeremy Heywood, and ultimately, David Cameron himself, who destroyed Mitchell by forcing his departure from the Cabinet. According to Belmarsh Prison officers, Tory ministers and, by extension, all other politicians see them as plebs.

When the *Daily Telegraph* paid a reported £250,000–£300,000 to a thief for the stolen data disc that allowed the expenses details to be published well beyond the requirements of the Freedom of Information legislation, Parliament was dealt a blow from which it has yet to recover. Whoever put the word 'pleb' into national political discourse has widened and deepened still further the crevasse of contempt between many voters and the political elites.

1050H Whoops, another crime to confess. It's turning cold and the two thin blankets I have been allocated are not really holding off the chilly air. Saturday is bedclothes change day. I go up with sheets, blanket and towel to the first floor, where there is a folding table set up with fresh bedding but, oddly, not a clean pillowcase.

I am given back my towel. 'You'll just have to wash out your towel yourself. You only get one for the duration,' says a guard. Hoping he won't notice, I just throw down one blanket on the heap of dirty bedclothes and take two clean blankets to give myself an extra layer.

The screws take no interest in this minor larceny. But I have cheated the system, broken the rules, and helped myself to something paid for by the taxpayer to which I am not entitled. I hope the BNP don't find out and another half-decade of investigation and condemnation doesn't open up.

I am given a strip of a green scourer torn in half, so now I can wash my plate and cup without using my hands. There is also a giant container of washing-up liquid but I have no container to pour some of it into, so will have to keep using my soap tablet to wash dishes.

I borrow a brush, mop and bucket and clean up my cell as best I can. The waste bin under the sink is filthy, encrusted with muck, old tea bags and what looks suspiciously like dried blood at the bottom. The loo is filthy. Can it be hygienic to eat food so close to a dirty bog and mucky waste bin?

I ask a screw for some something to clean and disinfect the loo. 'We used to give bleach to prisoners but some of them swallowed it,' he says bleakly. The warders must be as fed up as the prisoners sometimes at the number of small things they can no longer provide because at some stage in the past they have been abused.

I use loo paper to blow my nose or clean around the sink.

I write at my small table, looking through bars at the blue winter sky. 'Stone walls do not a prison make nor iron bars a cage,' rhapsodised Richard Lovelace, the Cavalier poet of the seventeenth-century Civil War. Sorry, but they are doing a good impression here. They're helped by 25ft-high wire fences with razor wire on top.

There's a prison myth that the European Union, or, more likely, the European Court of Human Rights, has banned razor wire as it is so dangerous to humans and that the Ministry of Justice pays a fine rather than adjust the fearsome razor wire. I'd like to know an example of a prisoner throwing himself on or over it. From talking to men here, I know such scarpering as does go on – it happens in transfer movements or when out on some kind of supervised leave.

One terrorist suspect, Mohammed Ahmed Mohamed, simply cut off his tag, donned a burka, as worn by pre-modern Muslim women, and walked out of a London mosque. I suppose if I saw all Belmarsh Prisoners wearing burkas I might guess a mass escape was being planned but the idea of launching oneself over razor wire seems unlikely.

There are steel hawsers over the exercise yard in case anyone wants to call the Addison Lee helicopter service. My bed is bolted to the floor but, for all that, the cell is far more luxurious than most mountain dormitories I have overnighted in when climbing in the Alps. At times I think I am back in my rooms in Oxford, waiting for the scout to wake me up, though in Belmarsh the screw does the office of wake-up man and I have to make my own tea. Do Oxford undergraduates still have an adult servant bringing them a morning cuppa?

Someone slips me a pink sheet with a tiny printed list on both sides. It is called 'Canteen' in prison jargon and if your eyesight is good you can just about read the list of extra goodies that can be bought. These include food like tins of tuna or baked beans, hot chilli sauce, tobacco and roll-up cigarette papers, an enormous choice of chocolate, biscuits, instant coffee, all sorts of toiletries, and to my frustration, A4 pads and pens.

The frustration arises because I only have £5.62 to spend. Prisoners 'earn' money by working or following education classes. This doesn't seem open to me and so I have only the basic allowance, which the guidebook to Belmarsh says is £4. Apparently, the £340 in notes I stuffed into the Belmarsh cash box doesn't count. I put all my money into buying phone credits. BT runs a racket, with the calls to mobiles being very expensive and landline calls more costly before 6 p.m. Since bang-up depends on the whim of the screws and can be as early as 3.30, the calls are consequently more expensive. I assume at some stage the block on my talking to my children will go, and I want more than thirty hurried seconds.

The remaining 60p I spend on tomato ketchup. The food would benefit from a little pepper and flavour but my favourite brown sauce – like Harold Wilson I can drown most food in HP or Daddies' sauce – costs £1.50 so I opt for ketchup. The guard looks at my choice.

'Tomato ketchup,' he says scornfully. 'Surely that's only for the plebs, not for MPs like you.' It's odd. Even though I have been defrocked for more than a year, everyone still assumes you stay an MP forever.

1140H Lunch is a jacket potato with beans. Watch some sport on TV but it seems to consist of men in open-necked shirts talking to each other.

1505H Cell door unlocked. Twenty-five minutes' welcome fresh air walking round and round. I arrange a deal: the noodle soup packet in my welcome bag against a full-length ballpoint. There is endless swapping and dealing going on. The screws know it but wisely turn a blind eye. Everyone calls them 'Guv', like old-fashioned taxi drivers addressing a middle-class fare. I don't know their names and usually begin with a 'Sir', since for some reason that comes more naturally than 'Guv'.

1610H Supper is fish and chips again – but this time with not one but two oranges. I think I've been given an extra one by a friendly server. He slipped them into my bowl under the slices of bread which I will feed to the birds. So that's one for tonight and one for tomorrow. The cell door key is turned and that's me locked up for the next seventeen hours. I hope there's something worth watching on TV.

1650H Bang, bang, bang from the end of the row of cells. Benny, the man next to to the clearly ill banger and shouter, is on so much medication he needs a wheelchair to move around. It seems torture to place him beside the banger-shouter. On the way back to my cell there was a signed notice from the Governor saying he would not tolerate anti-social behaviour. Yet the Belmarsh boss-man seems oblivious to the anti-social behaviour of the man at the end of my row of cells.

1700H *Guns of Navarone* on BBC2, so I shove away the pile of hidden forms, the back of which I use to make these notes. I arrange my pillow against the wall and half lie on the bed, which I am not keen to begin doing because once you lie down during the bang-up hours, will you ever get up? My plastic mould chair is OK for writing but just not comfortable. I try and pretend I'm on a flight to Toronto to see my daughter Laura and lean back to allow David Niven and Anthony Quayle to take me away for two hours.

I am watching so much TV perhaps I should apply to be a TV critic. But, to be honest, British television just isn't very good. A BBC costume drama called *Atlantis* is sheer drivel. And a two-part murder mystery set in Georgian England is just low-quality soap with agonising slowness of acting, as if endless shots of some rented Palladian mansion and its gardens was a substitute for drama.

SUNDAY 29 DECEMBER 2013

Beast says 1.35 p.m. Strip him of his pension, snap all of this teeth with pliers, castrate him and stuff his scrotum into his mouth, kill of [*sic*] his family before his eyes, flay him alive then roll him down a heap of salt. Call me medieval but that would be justice
Jeremy Clarkson says 1.37 p.m. Steady on, a bit much!
   [Exchange of tweets after MPs decided to ignore the decision of the
      Metropolitan Police and Keir Starmer not to prosecute me]

0140H More banging and screaming during the night. It is now a bedtime chorus and I get used to it. I am not even sure any longer what time it happens but I am usually woken from my sleep by the noise.

0805H Get up and shave. I eat my orange slowly, savouring each segment. Normally I quarter an orange each morning and just suck out juice and fruit as a start to the day. Now the orange is my main treat of the day and is taken slowly before getting down to the boring cereals – coco pops, sugar flakes, rice crispies – which I have never liked, even as a child. Kippers with toast, now that's a breakfast, but only one to dream about in Belmarsh.

0850H The cell door is unlocked for Association. This isn't fair. I aim to go to mass today and now part of the mass time coincides with Association so less time to chat with fellow prisoners, or try to make phone calls. I rush out and grab a shower to wash my hair. The early Sunday morning water is tepid at best.

I hope my friend, Jock M, who lives close to my Pimlico house, is happy. He is a fat, big, brutish Scot who for years has been shouting at me whenever he passes by in the street. It's not just the BNP complaint. For years before he was ranting at me about Europe. It's actually been quite threatening as he plants himself in my path to make me stop and listen to his obscene insults. No fist is raised but his big stomach nudges into me.

I remember the journalist Peter Oborne using the same aggressive paunch technique after I pointed out in public an untruth he had written about me. Like most political pontificators, Oborne loves dishing out criticism but hates it when someone exposes his casualness with facts. At a Labour Party conference in the press centre, Oborne came up red-faced, angry and shouting, 'How dare you accuse me of telling lies!' I walked backwards as he launched his well-lunched stomach at me. I had never been stomached before and just retreated as fast as I could to the sanctuary of the conference floor before the cross Peter fell over on top of me.

Pimlico Jock had clearly been at the same school of paunch-pushing. Like Oborne, he was obsessed with Europe. While Peter wrote his Europhobe diatribes in elegant English, Jock just started shouting UKIP or BNP slogans about the European Union. When John Lyon CB decided to convert the BNP complaint into a criminal investigation, Jock's cup ran over. Every time he saw me he shouted out to the baffled passers-by in peaceful Pimlico, 'Oh, it's prison for you, you fucker. Behind bars, you dirty wee criminal. Don't bend over in the showers. You'll be where you belong.'

Jock was quiet for a bit when Detective Chief Superintendent Horne and Keir Starmer decided not to prosecute me. But when John Lyon CB and Kevin Barron MP decided to end my parliamentary career, Jock was exultant and loved nothing better than to bellow insults at me if ever our paths crossed as I was scurrying to Victoria Station or just shopping in Lupus Street in Pimlico. He got even more hysterical when Keir Starmer reversed his earlier decision, and when I announced I was not going to bother with a trial and would plead guilty, his ecstasy grew and grew.

A neighbour came out as Jock – I know his name and address, as his obsession with stalking me extended to sending me postcards full of abuse – banged on my car roof top and rattled its door. 'Oh, I hope you go to Barlinnie. Only Barlinnie is good enough for you. They'll sort you out, you fucking thieving criminal.'

I don't know how Barlinnie – Glasgow's notoriously hard jail – compares to Belmarsh. As I have my shower the only thing I seek to dodge is the growing number of tiny black flies, which, like my tweet trolls, seem to be pullulating. I am glad it is not summer, as I assume the winter cold keeps down the fly population. One prisoner spent Christmas in hospital after he had been bitten by some noxious insect. Prison guards wear blue plastic gloves when handling or searching prisoners, and the kitchen duty prisoners also look properly clothed.

But this is not a healthy environment. I would give anything for some bleach or disinfectant to clean out my cell and the shower I use. The screws who are friendly just hide behind the rules. One of the rules of prison life is that within a day or two a prisoner should be allowed a 'family reception visit' before he settles down to the rhythm of normal social visits. It's important for partners and children to see their loved one is OK after the trauma of seeing the disappearance into the bowels of the Old Bailey.

But whenever I asked why, a week into being incarcerated in Belmarsh, I have been denied the family reception visit, they shrug their shoulders and say, 'It's the Governor's decision.' As with the confiscation of my books, I never got an explanation of why I was not allowed the family reception visit. It's easier for the officers to blame Chris Grayling or the Governor.

0910H The Catholics on Spur 3 assemble on the second-floor landing to go to mass. Again, the search, back and front, the checking of names, the waiting in a small room and then the walk along disorienting corridors to the religious centre. As I go in, Father Edward asks me to read the second lesson. It's odd to be on my feet again speaking, if not quite in public, at least to more listeners than attend most debates in the Chamber of the House of Commons or come along to political party meetings.

Asil Nadir also reads a lesson. After the mass he tells me he is helping prisoners. 'I think I have done more good here than in any previous existence.' He looks and sounds much younger than his erstwhile Tory chums, the Michaels Heseltine and Mates. I ask him about Turkish politics as, in the midst of the endless yawn that passes for TV news in the midst of the holiday season, it is clear something big is happening in Turkey.

Protestors in Istanbul are again being clubbed by the police. They are calling for the Prime Minister and strongman in Turkey, Recep Tayyip Erdogan, to go. He has been in power too long. As at the end of the Major or Brown years, a party too long in power rots from within. 'Erdogan has lost the support of too much of the military, 75 per cent of the judges and there is too much corruption,' Nadir says. He adds that Washington has told Erdogan to go – peacefully and democratically, before Turkey turns to its dark side.

I have been fascinated by Cyprus and Turkish politics since first visiting both countries after the 1974 invasion and occupation of northern Cyprus. Here in Belmarsh is a man who knows an awful lot and from whom I can learn. But we only get to talk if he, an indifferent Muslim, and I, a bad Catholic, meet at mass. The screws hover around the mass-goers as the more religious turn to the Madonna to whisper a bit of rosary, but their basic duty is to get us back to our cells and not to let any fraternisation take place.

Nadir gets the *FT* delivered so knows what is happening in the world. All I have is BBC TV news.

1040H Back on C Spur, Association is drawing to an end. But I finally make a phone call and talk to someone. Vicky answers a call and explains that Sarah has not been able to pick up her mobile as she dropped it down the loo! Everything was taken off me when I arrived at Belmarsh, even a Kleenex, at the moment of the first strip search. I have no memory for phone numbers and if the ones I had noted down don't work, I am sunk.

I am trying to see how how it might be possible for my second daughter, Laura, to visit me before she returns to Toronto, where she's been working since graduating from McGill University. Vicky says Laura is frantic at the lack of communication with her papa. I explain I sent her a first-class letter using the stamped envelopes passed to me by a prisoner on Friday during exercise. The Belmarsh guide booklet states: 'When you post out mail, the envelope must be unsealed as all your outgoing mail will be censored.' I wonder if the Governor is saving up my letter to Laura so he can get a thrill out of reading it? Why am I being held so utterly incommunicado?

1130H The duty officer signals to me that I have to end my call as it is time to be locked away again for the rest of the day, save a short exercise period assuming it isn't raining. When I as politely as possible suggest it is a bit inhumane to keep people incarcerated in their cells for such long periods, he shrugs and says, 'You were out to church this morning. You'll get half an hour of fresh air this afternoon. What more do you want?' What more indeed?

1149H Lunch is two thin slices of industrial processed ham with white bread slices but no marge (forget butter. It doesn't exist in prison) and a plate with some salad leaves and one or two cucumber slices. Blessedly – perhaps because it's Sunday – there is some piccalilli, and I spoon as much as I can on to my plate so that there is some taste in my food. I wonder how many decades it is since I ate lettuce leaves without vinaigrette or mayonnaise.

A black prisoner asks forlornly if there is any salt. I assume some Whitehall warrior has removed salt from the prison diet to help George Osborne obtain savings in the prison budget so that he can cut taxes for his rich pals.

I am feeling very low, almost at breaking point. A week in prison. One phone call and no chance to hug my children. I am content with my treatment and I have learnt more about English prisons in six days in Belmarsh than in two decades in Parliament. But I write to the Governor, a Philip Wragg, and remonstrate that his denial of visits – for whatever jobsworth, staffing reasons – are unworthy of a public service in a democracy. I know I write in vain and if anything my complaint will only please those who enjoy punishing me. But I write it anyway. *Scribo ergo sum.*

1433H It's not raining so we get twenty-seven minutes of a brisk walk in the winter sun. The exercise yard is about half the space of the centre court in Wimbledon, I reckon. My friend Julian, who arrived from the Old Bailey with me, runs round and round. He is early forties, about two metres tall and big of body, with long floppy black hair and a Tottenham accent. He had made a fortune in betting on horses. I ran a small bookies' ring as a sixth-former but have kept away from betting ever since.

Julian is in for murder but doesn't talk about it. Another Spur C inmate says he was not involved but just picked up as an associate. Guilt by association is now built into the policing and criminal system. The criminal law has been extended to allow accusations of 'joint enterprise'. This means anyone just standing on the edge of a scene of violence or unwittingly lending his car or mobile phone to someone who later commits a crime can be found guilty of joint enterprise. It's a modern catch-all version of conspiracy and allows judges to send any number of people to prison.

In Julian's case, the killer walked free but Julian's QC was less silver-tongued, so he was found guilty. In anger at the CPS's failure to nail the killer, the judge took it out on Julian, who was sentenced to eighteen years. Last night I watched a silly BBC drama in which an eighteenth-century judge, resplendent in red dressing gown and wig, sentenced a wholly innocent if unpleasant man to hang.

I don't want to believe such miscarriages of justice can happen today. It means the end of belief in British justice. Yet if I look at how some of the biggest profiteers of the MPs' expenses scheme opened the door for me to Belmarsh or how two QCs with prosecution and judicial power over freedom and unfreedom kicked me into this hellhole, how exactly am I to believe that we have the most honest Parliament and the most fair criminal justice system in the world?

As ever, I don't know the details of Julian's case. It wasn't he but a worldly wise fellow prisoner who described to me how he had to become the scapegoat for a judge's fury as the presumed killer walked free. It will cost the taxpayer £1 million or more to keep Julian inside. Money well spent?

He stops in his endless jogging round the yard. 'You shouldn't be on this spur. It's full of really bad guys, real hard men, murderers.' Maybe, but they seem much nicer than the Commons bureaucracy or the hard men of the CPS and the Old Bailey who sent me here.

I explain that I am on this spur in a single cell because – so I was told – there were fears a message might have been sent in to hardline Islamists amongst the 190 Muslims in Belmarsh with orders to get revenge for all my public attacks on Islamist ideology and especially on the Islamist obsession with Jew-hating.

In fact, I would love to engage with Muslims here in Belmarsh and try to explain that while their faith should have the same status as other faiths, if they insist on adding -ism to Islam they will encounter problems, just like every other faith in history that has sought to convert belief into political control. But as far as I can see, such talent as I have for political debate and dialogue will not be put to use other than in informal discussions.

I would love to do political education classes with my new colleagues here, just as Asil Nadir might have interesting things to say about the interface between rich businessmen and Tory politicians.

Might I do an *Any Questions* session for those prisoners that wanted to come, in order to alleviate their and my boredom at the dehumanising enclosure behind an iron door with iron bars in the window? I suppose Chris Grayling would demote Governor Wragg if he showed any such initiative.

Curiously, so far no one has asked me about votes for prisoners, which sent Tory and tabloid blood pressure through the roof in the last two years. In fact, other than jokes about my politician status, no one seems much interested in who governs the nation or what policies a government applies.

Another prisoner slips in beside me as I walk.

'You that MP, then?' I have given up explaining I am no longer an MP, but in prison it is a status title not an actual job.

'Yes.'

'Which party?'

'Labour. Who do you vote for, the BNP?'

'Nah. UKIP. That's the one, that's who you vote for.'

I don't bother explaining Nigel Farage's £2 million expenses, revealed at the 2009 European Parliament election. In fact, although I am an object of friendly curiosity there is no interest in politics. One or two of the prisoners mention UKIP, not the BNP, but no one ever breathes the name of a political leader of any sort. Cameron, Miliband and Clegg do not exist. And, sad to say, I do not know the name of the Prisons Minister who serves under the odious Grayling. Is it Helen Grant? Simon Hughes?

Although I consider the 2010 intake on Labour's front bench, especially the women, to be of high political calibre, I cannot think of anyone on the Labour side who speaks on prison. There is Yvette Cooper, of course, who upset Charlie Falconer by implying on the *Andrew Marr Show* in November 2012, after I was forced out of the Commons, that the police should re-open their investigation into me.

It was a throwaway line on those Sunday morning political programmes watched by politicians and political editors, but no sane human being. Charlie was very cross with Yvette even though, when it was reported to me, I assumed they were just unguarded words. Careless talk costs votes and, in my case, perhaps freedom. The other shadow minister in this area is the amiable Tooting immigration solicitor, Sadiq Khan. I just cannot recall anything he or Yvette has ever said on prisons.

The man who slipped me the stamped envelopes comes from another spur. His name is Cliff and he is in prison for twenty years for security van robbery.

'No violence. Never harmed or touched anyone in my life. I'm old school.' He tells me his nickname is Mumble though I can hear clearly what he's saying.

I tell him there were 317 complaints against MPs over expenses in 2009 and I was the only one pursued through different mechanisms to end up here.

'So, if you don't mind me asking, I suppose you're a Conservative?'

'No, Labour.'

He takes in the political affiliation without comment.

I watch an athletic Afro-Caribbean do handstand push-ups in the yard. I filled in the form to go to the gym at the induction last week but nothing has happened.

A gentle eighteen-year-old English-Turkish boy from Haringey with a few wisps of beard beneath a handsome filmstar face tells me he too is in prison for murder. 'I'm not in a gang or anything. I went to a friend's house and there was a fight there – some kind of feud – and I was arrested for just being there. Now I have to go on trial for murder.'

He is younger than my youngest child, my son at Edinburgh University. I shudder to think of Benjamin finding himself on the edge of some dreadful row or fight in a house when someone pulls a knife out of the kitchen drawer and, with one stab, ends a life. Perhaps again I am having the wool pulled over my eyes. I ask the boy if he will scarper to Turkey if convicted and condemned to some long sentence in an English prison.

'No, man. I was born here and I want to live here.' He hopes he will get a fair trial. But the *Evening Standard* is always warning Londoners about the terrors of knife crime and gang culture as well as – to be fair – campaigning to get kids out of gangs and into work. I think of the average London jury, the avarice of the CPS and its QCs for convictions, and the judges who love imprisoning for long sentences as many people as possible, and I feel for this lad's future.

Another inmate, Don, joins me on my *tournée* around the yard to tell me how he met John Stonehouse in Wormwood Scrubs. 'He was a real gent. We sat in what we called the bathhouse. He said to me, "Look at these walls. That's not to keep me in, but to keep out those who want to get me out."'

I vaguely recall the Stonehouse sensation. Stonehouse was a Labour and Co-Op MP from the West Midlands who got into a financial mess in the '70s and staged a bizarre disappearance by leaving his clothes neatly folded on a beach in Miami as if he had gone for a swim and never come back. He went to Australia, which is the last place on earth to go if you are a British Cabinet minister hoping not to be recognised.

I know MPs, and the idea that they can stop gassing and hide away forever is implausible. He was brought back to London and is another Old Brixtonian, where he was remanded before getting a seven-year sentence.

My friend said Stonehouse was very helpful to fellow prisoners, filling in forms for the – then as now – often half-literate prison population. 'His secretary was waiting for him outside the gates when he left. He dumped his wife, married his secretary and they made a go of it. I admired him, real gent.'

Sounds as if Stonehouse was a typical MP. Careless with cash. Confused about truth. Trading in his wife for an assistant. I tease my exercise *confrère*, 'Now you can say you've met two MPs in prison.'

'Yeah. I know. I've got to stop meeting politicians like this.'

1502H We are marched straight back in from exercise to be locked away for the rest of the day. Before I settle down to write, the cell door opens and in comes a nurse to take my blood pressure. It was far too high last week but now is a reasonable 147/85. At least, I hope it's reasonable. Apart from a few kilos too much in weight, I have enjoyed good health and been reasonably fit all my life. But now I am in sniper's alley – the period from about age sixty to seventy-five when illnesses arrive, some with a deadly suddenness. It doesn't keep me awake because I've enjoyed just about every day of my life, which has passed with brutal speed. But I'd rather not be ill in prison.

The only thing I really, really miss is Google. It has become second nature to check everything on Google. Is blood pressure of 147/85 OK for a man of my age? I cannot be sure unless I call my doctor brother or hit Google. Neither is possible. I watch a bit of a tedious Tom Hanks film called *Castaway* about a FedEx plane crashing in the South Pacific and Hanks living as Robinson Crusoe for three years. Did it really happen? I'd like to know. But no Google, no check.

1603H Let out for food. A warder shouts at a man who is talking to his friend.

'Keep away from the door. Move!'

The prisoner ignores him. Across the landing, the warder starts bellowing, 'Move! Get to the back of the line.' He runs around to where we are queuing on the second-floor landing and screams in the man's face. 'I asked you nicely. NOW I'M TELLING YOU. MOVE TO THE BACK!'

Julian is next to me waiting and says the stress is just too high on our spur, due to the number of murderers waiting for their trial or sentence.

Supper at teatime is a slab of chicken looking plaster-of-Paris-white, as if both extra hormones and special whitening were applied to the poor bird in its cage. There are peas and potatoes and gravy so I assume this is a Sunday dinner. But still no salt or pepper or anything to give the food taste. We are given packets of sugar with our cereal and tea bags so why not, at least, some salt?

1614H Bang-up for the rest of the day. I watch *Porridge* on BBC2. Like *The Shawshank Redemption* a couple of nights before, prison dramas now take on a different meaning for me, though neither the cruel brutality of the US prison system nor the jokey familiarity and cunning of Ronnie Barker seem to have any connection with Belmarsh or my prison life so far.

Given my current residence, I am as enthused by prison movies as I might be by an airplane disaster movie if flying across the Atlantic. Of course many survive in prison and there are some Ronnie Barkers full of schemes to outwit the screws. But the prison experience I have so far is more about misery and despair and pointlessness. Not, I assume, material for a sitcom like *Porridge*.

MONDAY 30 DECEMBER 2013

One of my favourite operas is Beethoven's *Fidelio*, music which in Byron's words makes an 'appeal from tyranny to God'. When imprisoned in communist Poland, the song of the prisoners as they were briefly freed to see the sun and breathe fresh air each day never left my head. Now, in Belmarsh, that prisoners' hymn to freedom kept coming back.

Chorus of Prisoners
Oh what joy, in the open air
Freely to breathe again!
Up here alone is life!
Oh Freedom! Will you be given us?

0740H Up to munch my rice crispies. I am not getting to like them. I wish Weetabix would return to the breakfast menu. I watch a minister, Owen Paterson – surely someone promoted above his abilities? – tell viewers they should stay in touch with the Environment Agency by computer to hear about flood alerts. Given that the power cuts caused by the flooding means there is no electricity in affected areas, I am not sure how this can be done.

The BBC *Breakfast* news lady doesn't pick up on this and other flaws in the hapless minister's responsibility-ducking answers. She has to look down at the questions prepared by researchers and starts each one with 'Eh', 'Well', 'Y'know'. And to think *Today* is losing Jim Naughtie. As far as I am concerned, John Humphrys or *les frères* Dimbleby can go on until age eighty or ninety, as the next generation of news presenters do not know how to ask questions. Or maybe it's crusty old me. The BBC *Breakfast* woman and her male partner are fluent, calm and probably just right for the audience. I wonder why I have a TV but not a radio?

0812H I have not finished my tea in its cheap plastic cup when the cell door is unlocked for exercise. As an early morning jogger around Battersea Park or Clapham Common, this is more like it. I get into a good pace, though not as fast as a trim black guy who isn't young but is very fit.

A few weeks before I went to the Old Bailey I did a charity fundraising run for the British Heart Foundation in Hyde Park. My reward for the four-figure sum I raised was the usual medal and a handsome red T-shirt with the BHF logo on it. It was confiscated when I arrived at Belmarsh.

Taking a pause in my run, I end up chatting again to Mumble and his mate Gary, whose nickname is Mole. They're two men in their fifties who both accept that they are professional criminals and that doing time is part of the profession. We form a little symposium as I try to enquire into the nature of the philosophy of crime. We are joined by Jack. Two are in for murder and the other, in for security van robbery, had been on Scotland Yard's most wanted list. I didn't know that concept still existed.

Jack, the younger man, was mentally unstable and his condition brought him to Belmarsh. He was under the care of his local mental health trust. 'I was out of my head but the only treatment they gave me was Prozac. I told them I had blackouts and if I didn't get better treatment, stronger drugs, I would either kill myself or kill someone. But they insisted on sending me out in the community and the inevitable happened.'

I asked if his condition and his appeal to local doctors to be treated in hospital, or at least prescribed more appropriate drugs than Prozac, were taken into consideration at his trial.

'Nah. The CPS could have charged me with manslaughter but that would have opened up the mental health trust to investigation and they didn't want to risk that. I was tested by a psychiatrist who said I had diminished responsibility. But the police psychiatrist who spent just forty-five minutes with me said I was perfectly normal, so the judge sent me away for thirty years.'

So our incompetent NHS sent this semi-mad youngster out into the community where he killed someone. One life snuffed out. Now Jack's non-life stretches into the future as the state takes its revenge and, with the help of Keir Starmer's CPS, avoids any court-room examination of the mental health trust officials who have some share in causing this double tragedy.

0840H Other prisoners are going out to work or to education courses. I remain locked in my cell. There's a knock on the door. 'Excuse me, sir, do you have any sugar for me tea, please?'

Each evening I am given a small plastic bag about the size of a sandwich bag. It contains the morning cereal, three tea bags, and sugar which I never use. I am happy to push a couple of sachets of sugar under the bottom of the door for him.

The book situation is a little better. In between the iron bars of the partition that separates Spur 3 from the other spurs, prisoners leave books they have read and it's possible to take one.

So, for the past day, I have been reading a well-written picture history of the First World War. I don't think I can take four more years of WWI history. It's not even a hundred years since the Archduke was shot and we are already in the trenches of endless histories in books and on television. I have decided to be a conchie and take the white feather of cowardice in the face of incoming from Sir Max Hastings and Jeremy Paxman. I wonder how many of those producing WWI tomes can read German or French – or do they rely only on published documents and books written in English?

Then, through the cell door I hear the worrying words, 'The library is shut. There's no Librarian in.' This means the trickle of books that arrive in Spur 3 will now dry up. The exchange must have been between a screw and one of the prisoners out working as a cleaner, or maybe one of the Listeners, who have the freedom to roam the Spur. If they are just outside my door I can overhear a little of what they say. But otherwise I am in my enlarged coffin.

One of the confiscated books waiting to be read is Michel Foucault's famous study of prisons and punishment, the opening pages of which are surely amongst the most horrifying in any language. I had fondly assumed a spell in prison would be the perfect moment to get on top of Foucault's thesis, to move from theory to fieldwork, as it were. But I am glad to have an easy-to-read picture history of WWI, with a John Grisham as a fallback if reading too much slaughter on the Somme gets me down.

0926H The cell door is unlocked. In comes a new prison guard I haven't seen before. He is of Chinese origin. The prison service must be the most multinational of any public service. I am losing count of the different nationalities or ethnicities I have come across.He looks at my wall, where a previous inmate has squeezed out toothpaste to write a name or word – 'KYZE'.

'Can you clean that off,' he half-asks, half-orders.

'Why? I didn't put it there. I have no cleaning liquid, no brush, cloth, bleach, disinfectant. How do I clean it off?'

He scowls, turns on his heel and slams the door shut.

A minute later it opens again and I go with other prisoners who arrived a week ago to what is grandly called the lecture room. It is just a small room with about two dozen chairs with flip-down writing tablets.

There are two women who hand out a sort of eleven-plus exam. Much of it consists of spotting grammatical or spelling errors. I notice one on an official HMP notice about racial discrimination tacked to the wall of the room. 'Commited' is spelt with one 't'. The notice looks quite old and will have been written by some Home Office official, perhaps even the good John Lyon CB himself before he was shunted off somewhere else in Whitehall.

The test papers have A4E stamped on them. The outfit has seen its managers charged with fraud as they helped themselves to taxpayers' money. But it still seems to operate in prisons. I ask if I can keep the pen I used to do the A4E tests. 'Sorry, luvvie, prisoners aren't allowed pens,' the nice woman doing the induction says. Of course. Silly me. I go back to my cell now, worried that, although I have paper from the purloined prison forms, I may not be able to write.

1112H Another mistake. I like tuna sandwiches and ordered one on the menu order form last week for lunch today. Quite the smallest roll I have ever seen in my life is what I get for lunch. Other prisoners tell me they are starving and I have already given a precious noodle soup to a hungry prisoner who looked as if he had stepped out from behind the barbed wire of the Serb concentration camp where they kept Bosniaks in the '90s.

So do I use up my last packet of noodles or keep it in reserve? I resolve to stay a little hungry – after all, I am a full stone over what I weighed before I became an MP. A tomato or a bit of celery or carrot or even a slice of red onion with the tuna would help.

In our symposium walkabout this morning, Mumble complained bitterly about the Belmarsh cuisine. 'It's pure stodge. Disgusting white processed bread. You get no fibre, no roughage, not enough fruit. You can't cook anything in your cell,' he complained. I remember visiting, as Minister for Latin America, a women's prison in Sao Paulo, Brazil, to talk to women from Britain and Europe who were being held on drug mule charges. They lived in small dormitories of about eight women prisoners and there was a small kitchen corner where they could make their own food. It certainly smelt and looked more nourishing than the white blob I am holding in my hand for lunch.

A week now in prison and I am still determined not to give the BNP or my tweet trolls the satisfaction of allowing my morale to lower. But as

I look at the smallest tuna roll with the most minimum amount of fish imaginable, I can imagine how easy it is to break a man's spirit.

Benny rolls out from the server queue in his wheelchair, clutching his roll. 'You OK?' I ask.

'I would be if I had my medication. I need painkillers badly.'

I stop a big, bulky blonde woman officer and say, 'Excuse me, Miss, why has this man been denied his medication?'

She glares at me for daring to ask the question.

'The nurse has been round. She must have missed him,' she snaps.

Given Benny is in for an end-of-cancer mercy death and is in a wheelchair I am not sure how he was able to disappear during the nurse's medication round.

I just look at the officer, allowing a little hint of authority to enter my eyes and she turns on her heel and goes off to phone the medical office to see if painkillers can be found.

Benny's cell is next door to the Iraqi with a smashed mouth after Romanian rent dodgers attacked him. The Iraqi's cell is a pit, with papers and bits of food strewn on the floor and the sheets and blankets lying askew.

Benny's cell is spick and span. He's one of those who box their bedding, which I learnt to do when in the school's Combined Cadet Force (CCF), where I rose to the serried rank of Company Serjeant Major – early training for telling people what to do in a loud voice.

'You have to keep your bed neat otherwise it looks so sloppy and you're temped to lie in all day,' Benny explains. 'And if you box your bedclothes you also get a better view of the cockroaches.'

Roaches have never bothered me, though for some women friends, especially American women, it is the ultimate horror, like snakes for Indiana Jones or rats for Winston Smith in George Orwell's *Nineteen Eighty-Four*. I haven't seen any roaches or bugs and my only contact with the Belmarsh insect population is the tiny black flies in the shower.

My bog is beginning to smell a bit. I try to keep it clean with loo paper and my tablet of prison-issue soap. But without disinfectant it isn't easy. I open the cell windows to its maximum 4 inches. That gives on to bars and a grill, so getting anything in or out is not easy.

I break up and push some stale, hard white bread broken into morsels through the grill for the birds. I enjoy the open windows even if the cell quickly gets very cold.

The rain is pelting down and the wind is getting up. Two of my children are flying home from seeing their aunt, cousins and a new generation of babies and toddlers in Geneva. Half the films I have watched locked away in Belmarsh have been plane disaster movies.

I am sure the girls will be fine, but having lost my eldest daughter in a skydiving accident in Australia in 2004, a little bit of me lives in permanent terror of another phone call. The moment Clare's mother, Carol Barnes, came on the line I knew before she said 'It's about Clare…' what had happened. Parents should die before their children. But when the reverse happens, you know – you just know without being told.

My four other children are all alive and well. I have not been able to see or speak to them since they sat in the gallery of the Old Bailey watching their father. I have tried to phone but if all you get is voicemail you go back to the end of the queue and, with only one good phone for all the Spur prisoners, that means if you lose your chance to talk you've lost it.

The man in charge of French prisons, Monsieur Delarue, is recommending that French prisoners – far fewer per head of population than here in Britain – be allowed to have mobile phones. It seems sensible. Of course, in France as in Britain there will be a hue and cry about molly-coddling prisoners. But the same noise was heard when prisoners were allowed landline phones, soft toilet paper, a loo rather than a bucket in cells, and the chance to wash more than once a week.

I am not sure if we all sat naked chained together in an open yard whether the politicians who decide ever more stupid prison policy would get any extra votes.

My friend Manuel Valls is France's former Interior Minister – the equivalent of our Home Secretary; in French the post is nicknamed *le premier flic de France* – France's top cop. As Interior Minister, Valls was tough on criminals and won a reputation for supporting working-class communities in particular against social delinquency. He has won this reputation, propelling him to the office of Prime Minister, without having to throw so many people into prison in the fashion of his opposite numbers in Britain over the last two decades.

1345H I am doing nothing but sitting in my cell behind a locked door. I can just see one of the phone cubicles on the wall opposite if I look through the slit of space between the door's edge and the frame. It is forbidden fruit. I cannot talk to my daughters to know that, despite the howling gale outside, they have arrived home safe and sound.

I have saved my tuna roll and now eat it in small bites to make it last. There is no difference in the textures of the vaguely fishy sludge and the soft, gummy bread roll.

I wonder what I will get in a few hours time as the main last meal of the day? It is now a week since I was sent here. Do I feel punished? No. Do I feel more contrite than I did four years ago when I apologised for my actions and repaid all the monies in dispute, even though it was all expended from my own pocket for proper reasonable parliamentary and political and government work? Again, not really.

Do I feel any bitterness? No. I am curiously grateful to be here and to meet in such an intense manner men whom in my normal life I would never have encountered.

To be sure, I would rather be with children. My own and also Vicky's grandchildren. Playing with little ones and making them laugh has been a joy all my life, ever since I was put on nappy-changing, bottle-feeding and story-telling duty by my mother when suddenly, aged forty-one, she was a widow with two boys under ten and a baby. Laughter and love of friends have been at the heart of my existence – especially laughing at stupid rule books and the jobsworths who enforce them.

Outside, I expect my friends and family are more worried about me than I am about myself. He who travels fastest, travels alone. I enjoy my own company. I can read books, even if not those confiscated by silly Chris Grayling. For the first time in years I can watch as much television as I want.

It is hard to understand why the BBC puffs and preens itself on being the best broadcaster in the world. Maybe it deserved that reputation back in the late '60s, when I was recruited as a trainee at Oxford. But now I flee from the dross and dreary sameness of BBC1 and BBC2. To be fair, I have no radio here. Presumably making convicts and guards think by exposing them to the better programmes of Radio 4 and Radio 3 would cause all sorts of unhealthy stirrings.

Do I regret not staying at the BBC? Had I polished a seat, sniffed the wind and kept firmly in the centre ground, pro-market but not ultra-Thatcherite in the 1980s, compassionate but not crudely Campbellish under Blair, I could have seen out my time and become boss of an opera company or master of an Oxford college once my pension was secured.

As a producer on Radio 4's *World Tonight* in the '70s, a smart woman, Jenny Abramsky, was my studio technician. When she retired in 2008 she was earning £316,000 and had a pension pot of £4 million, all paid by the poorest in the land via the regressive BBC tax. She added to her £190k annual pension with a nice little earner of £45k as chair of the Heritage Lottery Fund.

Her boss, the BBC Director General Mark Thompson, was paid £800,000 a year. He went to the same Oxford college as I did. I never recall debating in Parliament this massive transfer of public money to a single public servant. The sheer greed of the top echelons of the BBC, as they rewarded each other with ever increasing salaries, was one of the most demoralising aspects of the get-rich years of so many top public sector bosses in the Major and Blair eras.

So yes, I gawp in awe at how much money I might have made had I stayed as a BBC lifer. But no, I would not have swapped my life with its crazy ups and downs, its insane adventures, its abrupt changes in direction, for all the money in the bank that a BBC man of my generation might have tucked away.

When my mother died in 2006, she left me £65,000, which I invested with an independent financial adviser called Mark Bentley-Leek, someone I had known for more than a decade. He put it into his own property business, offering a guaranteed rate of 10 per cent per annum.

I don't exactly know what happened. I liked and trusted him, but he walked off with my money and, as I later learnt, he took millions from hundreds of other clients. Some had put their entire pension pot into his Ponzi-esque property scheme, for which he kept collecting funds, even when it was clear after the 2008 crash that everything was heading south.

The man working to clear up the mess reckons Mark walked off with £20 million–£30 million of investors' money. The Financial Conduct Authority has struck him off and their press release gave his address as Koh Samui in Thailand. I remember it as a beach hut paradise from a holiday nearly thirty years ago, when it was undeveloped.

There is an extradition agreement between Thailand and the UK. But Mark is sipping his Tiger beer on a Thai beach while I am stuck in Hellmarsh. The amount of money he helped himself to from me alone, as well as infinitely more from other decent, hard-working people who had entrusted him with their savings, dwarfs the paltry sum I was accused of improperly claiming and even the much bigger amounts from David Laws and other MPs who have faced no sanction.

I reflect on the money spent investigating me and sending me here for Christmas and wonder why Keir Starmer or the Metropolitan Police do not seem remotely interested in bringing Mark to justice. The Financial Conduct Authority has fined him more than £500,000. So, for some, a fine. For others, Belmarsh. Ah well, that's the luck of the draw. If you get to read this Mark, you know my address and I'd love to have my money (or some of it) back, please.

I do miss my December in the Alps, as it is boring to go through a few consecutive months without climbing a ridge or skiing off-piste. And then the news that the racing driver Michael Schumacher is lying in a coma, seriously injured after a ski accident. He was wearing a helmet, as I shout at my children to do.

I mean no rudeness to those I have sat beside at many a dinner party in the last 360 days but the conversations in Belmarsh are richer, denser and full of a life and warmth that we self-regarding, self-important, self-ignorant English-educated men are rarely capable of.

Do I miss reading the papers? Again, no. I have kept a weather eye on all the reporters who have written about me. On the whole the

Westminster political editors avoided the story as they know the truth of the whole case. Instead, newbies who don't know or understand the procedures are happy to repeat the lurid lines and accusations of the Commons bureaucracy.

The older hacks know I know every expense trick the journalists of my 1968 generation got up to. When I hear or watch or read famous names I knew forty years ago and know how eagerly we discussed how we could put this or that on 'exes', I am amazed at how effortlessly they can pitch their tone into denunciatory mode about MPs doing exactly what they did.

In any case, news has moved off-print, off-page. I love to read the newer columnists like Owen Jones and Rosamund Urwin, but why are there so few of them? Most columnists seem to have been there since Margaret Thatcher was PM. The news business, like the business of politics, just doesn't seem to be working.

So while I still love papers and spend too much time reading them to very little profit, no, I cannot say I miss them in Belmarsh. And no one wants to discuss politics. If the subject comes up, prisoners ask me the name of the Prime Minister. Ed Miliband means nothing to them, still less Nick Clegg. The only minister they can name is Christopher Grayling.

I don't have to worry about what clothes to wear, what time I put out the light, if and when I shave. I am master of my fate as long as I am here.

1437H Unlocked and told to go for gym induction. It takes place not in the gym, wherever that is, but in the multi-use classroom. The gym warder arrives in shorts, with his keys, a taser and other black bits hanging off his belt. He is well-built, a no. 1 haircut, not fully shaven, a tough London voice, several grades lower than *EastEnders*.

He distributes forms with the titchy blue pens. I tick all the boxes about being in reasonable health. My first gym was in the '80s in Geneva. It was part of the extraordinary Swiss Migros supermarket chain. It began as a do-gooding venture in Zurich in 1925. The founder sold staple foods at wholesale prices to poor people.

There's a great myth that Switzerland has always been rich and stable. On the contrary, in the 1920s and 1930s there were giant strikes and occupations of Nestlé plants, and a massacre in Geneva in 1933 when the Swiss Army opened fire and killed and wounded a hundred people demanding work and food.

In 1938 the Swiss employers and trade unions brokered what they called a peace treaty, agreeing not to strike in exchange for fair wages and proper treatment of workers, via their unions in the workplace. It was that plus Swiss neutrality that laid the foundations of Swiss wealth. British trusts and City lawyers hide far more money from scrutiny than all the Swiss banks combined.

In addition, Switzerland opened its doors to foreign workers and today, at 15 per cent, Switzerland has the highest proportion of immigrants in its population of any European country.

The Migros do-gooders grew into the Alpine confederation's biggest supermarket chain and is in the world top forty of food stores. It refused to sell alcohol or tobacco and the profits went into night schools, holiday centres for poor people, cafeterias where you could eat cheaply and well, and gyms.

The Commons also had a gym tucked away in a basement in grim, dingy conditions. Jack Straw was a regular, appearing perspiring at 'morning prayers', as the 0900h meeting for FCO ministers and top officials was called. Robin Cook could be found there after he left the government, dressed in a baggy white tracksuit like a football manager in the '60s. Paddy Ashdown worked the climbing stairs, ferociously pounding up and down to maintain his legendary military fitness. It was a great place to catch locker room gossip and negotiate political deals.

Later I joined a Bannatyne gym in 4 Millbank, almost opposite the House of Lords. It had the inestimable advantage compared to the gym in the Westminister Palace precincts of having a swimming pool, steam room, sauna, Jacuzzis and newspapers, which I could read on the exercise bike at seven in the morning. There seemed to be more Tories there and in the mists of the steam room there was a chance of trading some cross-party gossip.

Gloria de Piero, now a rising Labour star, was a young reporter who would put her feet up on the bench in the steam room and enjoy a good political discussion. When the Standards Committee orchestrated my removal from the Commons in November 2012, I was plunged into an income-free existence with three children at university and all my bills going up under George Osborne's stewardship of the economy. So I had to cut out every subscription and discover the joys of Lidl and Iceland. The gym went and I got my exercise from running or swimming in public pools in the hours reserved for over-60s.

Now, thanks to the taxpayer, I can start to go to a gym again. We are each given a gym card on a piece of stiff paper. The gym screw is unclear when we might go or what we will do. 'It's all a bit hit and miss. We don't control it. It's decided elsewhere. It's not that great a gym but that's what we've got.'

This is a constant refrain from prison officers – the 'it's not me, it's not us' line which allows them to abdicate responsibility or to do whatever they want in the name of what is ordained from above. I vaguely thought that at some stage I and other new boy inmates would get some kind of pep talk from the Governor, but he exists only as a name on tatty orders pinned here and there.

I had hoped that after a week's incarceration I might be able to do some exercise in addition to my paltry stretching and sit-ups on the dirty linoleum of the cell floor. But it appears it will be another week before I can enjoy the pleasant stretched sense of a proper workout.

'No drinks, no food, no tobacco and no weapons are allowed in the gym,' intones the gym screw. 'No weapons!?' And I thought Belmarsh was a secure, safe environment. He gives us all a sheet with 'Ten Simple Steps to Achieving a More Balanced Diet'. It's like something out of the *Daily Mail* health pages, the best part of the paper. The top bit of advice is 'Stick to Whole Food Products'. In Belmarsh? If only.

'Fibre should also be gained from eating plenty of fruit and vegetables, roughly eight to ten servings a day.' Quite so. The sheet adds, 'Eating healthily doesn't have to be difficult.' No, just impossible on the Grayling diet in Belmarsh.

1525H Taken back to the cell and locked up. No chance to make a phone call. I hope the children have got back OK. I remain stoic but so far today I have not been able to have a shower or even get close to a phone call. This time last week all my fellow arrivals at Belmarsh assured me I would be out and sent to an open prison within a few days. Oh well, just another day.

There is a knock on the door. It is thin Phil, who seems to be a cleaner or something and has the freedom to roam a bit.

'Got any sugar, mate?'

I slip some sachets under the door.

'Thanks. I can't drink tea without sugar.'

'And I can't drink tea with sugar.'

'Yeah, we should share a cell,' and I can see the grin with so many teeth missing.

1700H Still banged up. I hope I get to make a phone call.

I have a pinboard on my wall, which is painted a neutral sky-blue. I don't think I have any pet peeves other than a dislike of racism, xenophobia and bad manners. But I do like a little order, especially a running order in my day, week, year. Each day in Belmarsh is a mystery. I don't know when I will eat, when the cell door will open, when I can shower, or when I can talk to other prisoners, let alone make a phone call. So putting up a time-table to gym sessions is the first sense of order I have had since arriving here. Alas, the pinboard lacks one thing. Pins. So I stare at my pinboard and imagine the gym timetable up there, giving me some fixed points in this life without order, sense or rhythm.

1740H Lots of voices chattering outside. I don't know what's going on. For the last three days I have eaten my final meal of the day two hours earlier, at about half past three. Now I can hear women warders cackling away. But what's it all about? I don't know.

1812H The doors open for the last meal of the day. There is a chance to make a phone call, which I grab. I talk to Vicky. She says there is no chance of a visit before 5 January in the New Year – two weeks after Sir Nigel did his business.

Laura, daughter No. 2, is apparently very upset she cannot see me before she has to go back to Toronto. Suffer the little children not to come unto their papa is the prison system's New Year motto. But it is lovely to hear a voice from outside, not the barks and sneers of the screws or the estuary-speak of most of my fellow inmates. Vicky sounds clear, calm, in control. She has sent my prison email address around but so far not a letter or email has arrived. This is my second conversation with someone outside.

I try to call Sarah but get voicemail only. There is no one else waiting to call as I am dangerously close to missing my food as I delay going up and then down the stairs to get my supper. You have to wait ten minutes between calls which makes it even more nail-biting as you watch the queue upstairs get smaller and smaller and work out if another phone call can be squeezed in.

I give up and go and get my chicken, boiled rice and industrially diced carrot. It has an ersatz jerk sauce which at least, at last, provides a little taste.

Still fifteen minutes to be outside the cell. This is now Association and the warders decide how long it will be, so they can tell when it will end. The officers sit at their desk at the end of the spur and prisoners come up to ask for information or have a modest moan. A new prisoner comes up and asks for something to clean his loo with. The woman screw shrugs her shoulders.

Little Buzz, who buzzes around me imparting information as if it was his sacred duty, overhears the exchange and says, 'They can't give you bleach or anything that can be used in making explosives.'

'Well, what about sugar then?' I ask, remembering school holidays in Ireland where my cousin, whose father had some historic connection with the IRA, taught me to make pipe bombs with sugar and sodium chlorate, bought and used as weedkiller.

'Shut your gob. Do you want to be really popular?' as he goes on to point out that taking away sugar would be blamed on me.

Buzz points to the short, slight man with a dark, well-trimmed beard who regularly pushes a mop around the single bath and shower cubicle area. 'He did the Soho nail bomb. He's in for fifty years. You don't know who's in here. You could be chatting to Ian Brady but unless you know what he looks like it's just another geezer in prison. That Soho guy hates blacks. His head flipped. You wake up after a drink and a snort with a black guy and pull a condom out of your arse. You hate them forever after that.'

I don't tell Buzz there was a bit more to the Soho nail bomber. He belonged to the BNP, who began the process of sending me to prison, as well as other right-wing outfits. He hated gays and ranted about 'ZOG' – the 'Zionist Occupation of Government' – a term used by anti-Semitic racists as shorthand for their claim that Jews control Western governments, media and capitalism.

Modern anti-Semites like to claim they are simply anti-Zionist, not anti-Jewish. I was regularly accused of being a Zionist simply because I refused to support the demands in the Hamas charter for the elimination of Israel. Hate ideology scrambles the brains of modern citizens.

The killers of the off-duty soldier, Lee Rigby, will soon be sentenced and, like the Soho nail bomber, will get a sentence measured in decades not years. I wonder if they will end up in Belmarsh and come across the Soho nail bomber to sit down and discuss their views on Zionism and Jews.

A man comes in with a pair of hair clippers. There is a little seat at the far end of the spur ground floor where you can get your hair done. Another free service. Buzz, however, warns me: 'There's no disinfectant, so don't touch it – you could pick up something really nasty.'

Half-listening, the woman duty officer says there ought to be a spray disinfectant. She tells us she was a hairdresser before she joined the prison service. 'The Governor always says it's the cuts when we can't get anything but there's loads of money around.'

Buzz eagerly takes up the theme. 'There's millions still coming into prisons. But it's all privatised. Look at the medical services. That's private, so if they don't want to treat you because it costs money, they don't. Last time I was in here I had a tooth problem and my face swelled right up. But they weren't interested in the medical unit until a screw just marched me down to the dental unit and demanded I be treated.'

The former hairdresser turned warder has been ear-wigging and says that this morning a man had his jaw broken on another spur. A feud or an old score was being settled but 'half his jaw was out of kilter with the other half. I offered to hit the side of his jaw that was displaced to put it all in the middle again,' she jokes, sort of. 'I took him down to see the doctor but he wasn't really interested. "Come back and see me in the morning," the GP said.'

A quick shower between hot and cold. It's a juggle soaping myself and finding a hand to push the button to get some flow of water, with no certainty as to the temperature of the water that will emerge. I should have flip-flops but, again on Grayling's order, everything is taken away. If I get athlete's foot I shall know who to blame.

I call my brother and, thank God, he is not on voicemail. I tell him I am having the best Christmas–New Year break of my life – well, I have to boost the morale of those worrying for me outside. I tell him to tell the wider family and that I am OK and will come out with so many tales to tell. He says the general reaction is that it must be like boarding school. No, I say. I expect Eton was much more violent with much more buggery. After all, his and my school is now famous as a centre of Benedictine monastic paedophilia.

1925H I have a biscuit and little bit of chocolate with a cup of tea. *Dad's Army* is on and the timelessness of Captain Mainwaring and his team defying Hitler is still much more enjoyable than any modern BBC comedy series.

MONDAY 31 DECEMBER 2013

Throughout the eighteenth century … one sees the emergence of a new strategy for the exercise of the power to punish … not to punish less but to punish better … in order to punish with more universality and necessity; to insert the power to punish more deeply into the social body.

– Michel Foucault, *Discipline and Punish: The Birth of the Prison*

0305H Wake up with my head full of worry. Before Belmarsh I would have blamed a glass too much or my bad habit of eating little all day and then gorging on a big dinner late in the evening.

Now I wake up with my head full of interrogations. Should I have limited my trips to Europe to the maximum of three under the formal Commons regulations? Of course.

Should I have politely declined the invitation from No. 10 to go to Europe to see ministers, editors and MPs and then report back without asking No. 10 to cover costs? Of course I should have.

As I begin wallowing in self-pity, I remember one of my oldest friends in Manchester, the writer Clarissa Hyman, who is full of insights into politics and public opinion, saying, 'The BNP are complaining about you after all your work exposing their anti-Semitism. You haven't pocketed any money. There's no way anyone can take this seriously.'

She was wrong. The parliamentary functionary John Lyon was very proud of his honour, Companion of the Order of the Bath, a gong which is given to all senior Whitehall officials after two or three decades of seat polishing. He always put CB after his name on his letters to me. I worked with numerous decent civil servants who had gongs galore. Lyon was the only one I came across so pleased with his ribbon and medal that he put it after his name on every letter.

In Whitehall no one ever gets sanctioned, just moved out of sight. So the four-day week, £105,000 a year job as the parliamentary official in charge of complaints was given to John Lyon CB to see out his days before retiring on the generous Whitehall pension civil servants award themselves.

Normally in a disciplinary hearing the person accused has a chance to appear in front of the disciplinary officer to state his case. I remain baffled to this last day of 2013 why Mr Lyon CB never interviewed me. Instead, he created the maximum publicity by referring the matter to the police. He was clearly disappointed when Detective Chief Superintendent Matthew Horne and Keir Starmer decided not to prosecute in July 2012.

Damn! What am I doing? Am I mad to be lying on a Belmarsh mattress at three in the morning thinking about what some second-rate interior ministry discard did to me? It was my fault anyway. In the wonderful letters between Philip Larkin and Kingsley Amis there is an exchange in which Larkin, stuck in his house in Hull where he was Librarian at one of the best campus universities in England, writes to Amis about waking up in the middle of the night to stare at the ceiling full of worry and apprehension at the problems life throws up. What, he asked Amis, should he do?

Put on the light and read Dick Francis is the reply from Amis, of Garrick Club bar fame and author of *Lucky Jim*, still England's finest post-war comic novel. So that's what I did. Light on and I turn to the rather dense crime novel by Elizabeth George I 'borrowed' from the induction centre. It has a slow, obvious plot with McGuffins scattered in the reader's path. One police detective is an Earl who drives in his Bentley to interview witnesses. But he does conceal evidence compromising a fellow officer, and his side-kick, a woman detective, agrees to keep mum. 'I don't grass,' she says in the book. Heavens! Metropolitan Police officers tampering with evidence. I am sure Commissioner Sir Bernard Hogan-Howe would never allow that to happen.

As I read for a few minutes to settle down, the slide over my window slit in the cell door opens. I don't look up but am reassured that the night watch of prison guards is keeping an eye on me. One of the warders, a gentle man who had seen it all, and didn't need to throw his weight around, told me the worst job in Belmarsh was suicide watch – hour after hour throughout the day and night, keeping an eye on some poor wretch who might take his life.

A few weeks before I arrived, an eighteen-year-old killed himself in Belmarsh. More than a hundred prisoners kill themselves each year – about fifteen times the rate of suicide in the general population. No one seems to care.

What happens behind the gates of Belmarsh and other prisons doesn't worry MPs, editors or the public. How animals are killed in conformity with Muslim or Jewish religious dietary rules arouses far more interest and passion.

There is an easy way to reduce the suicide rate in prisons – treat the men and women inside as human beings. But that won't happen on Grayling's watch or as long as our off-shore owned press lust after punishment and pain to be inflicted on anyone sent to prison.

0820H Cornflakes for breakfast. It's a really small thing but I miss dental floss and inter-dental brushes. The Labour politician and *New Statesman* editor, Richard Crossman, thought you went to the dentist to have your teeth cleaned. In Peggy Noonan's book about her time as Ronald Reagan's speechwriter, she describes a Senator dying of cancer coming for his last visit to the Oval Office. On the way in, he passed the White House press corps. 'How's it going, Senator?' asked one reporter solicitously. 'Put it this way boys,' said the near-death politician, 'I've stopped flossing.'

The cheap soft toothbrush issued to me after my own was confiscated doesn't do the business. Can dental floss be used as a killer weapon to strangle or garrote someone? I asked a screw why there was no pepper to help make the bland food palatable. 'Pepper can be thrown in some-one's eyes,' she told me.

Yes, and my rickety B&Q table in my cell can be smashed over some-one's head, a mouth can be stuffed with loo paper to stop breathing and a few savage blows in the semi-privacy of the shower room can injure for life. Anything can be a weapon. Not to worry. Pepperless food is all we Belmarshites need and deserve.

The door opens and I'm told to get ready to go to a Catholic discussion group. I fear I maybe overdoing the faith stuff but anything to get out of my cell. My second week and all the assurance from my lawyers and others that I would be in an open prison in a jiffy have turned out to be false. I still haven't the faintest idea what Chris Grayling and the prison service have in mind for me.

I ask the woman guard who unlocks if I have time for a quick shower. The single shower is only two cells down from mine and since I am the fastest showerer in Britain I can shower myself in under two minutes.

'Sorry, MacShane, flannel wash only,' she says.

Naturally, it's a further fifteen minutes sitting in my cell before I move out. I cannot work out if the guards are obtuse, don't know their own timings, or just have a built-in reflex of saying No to any request from a prisoner to try and keep clean.

Before I leave she comes back. I see in her hand letters. For me!? Can it be?! Yes. Two envelopes. The first one is stamped 'Censors 3'. What is this? Colditz? Censors? A censors department just for Spur 3? Is this a secret POW camp? No, it is a letter I had sent out to my daughter that was being returned to me by this mysterious 'Censors 3' *Abteilung*. Because of the Grayling policy of not being allowed my writing pads and pen I have been using the back of prison forms to send out letters.

Apparently, this is *Verboten*. I cannot use the back of a Visitors Order form, on which I had written my children's names, to scribble a few lines. It is Day 8 and I have still to hear the voice of one of my children, let alone see their faces. Now the hopes of a visit are put off still further.

But in the second envelope I get some emails from friends; www.emailaprisoner.com is a wonderful charity set-up, which allows anyone from anywhere in the world to email prisoners. The emails only cost 30p and are printed out by prisons cooperating with the charity and delivered to the prisoners' cells like other mail.

One might have thought all the high-paid civil servants running the prison service in Whitehall could have come up with this simple idea. Instead it took a former prisoner, Derek Jones, to dream up the idea and persuade the first prison in 2006 to allow its inmates to receive emails. He has sold his firm for a six-figure sum and moved on to create another charity to help prisoners back to work. Mr Jones, I owe you a drink, as your genius idea allowed me to write to a friend when in prison and allowed her to write to me, which is a blessing, as the Rosetta Stone is easier to decipher than her handwriting.

So I get news from friends and family, from America, Australia, France and Switzerland. They send me the orgy of troll tweets celebrating Judge Sweeney's sentence. I doubt if I will ever have time but I would like to publish somewhere the social media trolling of me, initiated and organised by the far right between 2010 and 23 December 2013.

Contempt of court theory is based on what newspapers publish. Today, newspapers are almost irrelevant as jurors get their information from other sources, principally social media. But judges do not live in the world of jurors.

So many messages from so many who know the truth. Sadly, one daughter is so distraught that she has not spoken to me. Another, scheduled back to Toronto, has been told that Belmarsh visiting rules are inflexible there is no chance of a visit. The sins of a father should not be visited on the child is clearly a biblical injunction unknown to Chris Grayling.

I wonder if he has children. He certainly has form on expenses, claiming £5,000 to tart up a flat near Westminster as well as thousands in mortgage payments from taxpayers, even though he had a big house in his Surrey constituency in London's commuter belt. He also claimed mortgage help from the taxpayer on two properties with the blessing of the Commons finance supervisors. Dear, oh dear, why didn't I claim my expenses like other profiteering MPs?

Dear quaint Sir Nigel with his belief that the Commons officials needed to have the wool pulled over the eyes in order to be reimbursed for European travel! They never batted an eyelid at any claim of any sort as Minister Grayling can confirm. I wonder if Grayling has sold his central London property at a huge profit, like Kevin Barron, or has kept it.

The emails cheer me up immensely. Christopher Hitchens once told me that it was always worth writing to someone ill, in hospital or grieving and, I would add, in prison. I hope I won't have any friends finding themselves in the same predicament as me but if so, I promise myself I will write, write and write again, as each letter that comes in boosts morale.

0930H I put my name down for a talk on faith but when we get to the chapel we are told it is cancelled. Not enough prison officers to supervise, apparently. There are three screws on my spur not exactly doing a lot. The cuts again.

I wish Asil Nadir Happy New Year as we hang around before being sent back to our spurs. I would like to explore his story more and talk to him about Cyprus and Turkey. But the *Shawshank Redemption* or *Porridge* vision of prison, allowing all inmates to meet and mingle over food or exercise, does not correspond to Belmarsh where, unless a prisoner is on your spur, you only have fleeting contact after mass or going out to do something.

On the way back I pop into the medical room where a Nigerian woman nurse looks a bit surprised but agrees to take my blood pressure which is an acceptable 147/85.

0945H Taken back to my cell. Before lock-up I talk to a small slight young man with a trim black beard. He is busy brushing the floor of the common space on the ground floor between the two rows of cells. We are alone and I say, 'Gosh, I never realised there is so much dirt and dust on the floor,' as I watch the pile of grey fluff and dirt grow beside the dustbin in which we dump our waste.

'It's asbestos, isn't it?' he says in a matter-of-fact manner.

'Asbestos! Surely not. They can't allow asbestos in prison!'

'Don't be silly. There's asbestos in the air here. Look, they need people to get cancer. It's simple economics. You put a guy here for fifty years at fifty or eighty thousand quid a year. Work out what it costs. The sooner we die, the less the taxpayer has to fork out.'

All this was said quietly, without emphasis or anger. I didn't have the heart to tell him that Belmarsh was opened after 1990, long after asbestos has been exposed for its danger to health and banned for use in any building.

But the reference to fifty years struck home, as this was the Soho Nail Bomber Dave Copeland who had been sentenced to fifty years in prison. A friend had been in a bar in Old Compton Street the night of the explosion and I remember the fear in her eyes as she recalled that night of death in the narrow streets on Europe's most vibrant capital. What made this insignificant little man do something so wicked? I am getting used to talking to fellow inmates about their crimes. But I just don't want to go there with him and am glad to be locked away.

1110H Lunch is a soft pliable white 'baguette'. Can anyone explain to the Ministry of Justice that a baguette should have a crunchy, crispy crust, otherwise whatever it is it isn't a baguette. There are two hardboiled eggs with it and two sachets of runny, tasteless 'mayonnaise'. I know we cannot have pepper in case it is weaponised but is salt a potential lethal instrument of aggression? With it there is a small plastic bag of 'cheese puffs'. The ingredients include 'cheese flavouring, whey powder, flavour enhancer, monosodium glutamate (I thought that had been banned?), dextrin, colour, whey protein, colour and paprika extract flavouring'.

I am so hungry, I eat this revolting chemical cocktail. This seems far more likely to set off cancer than the Soho Nail Bomber's imagined asbestos. There is a widespread view amongst prisoners that someone is on the take, given the miserable quality and quantity of food. If it is costing £1,000 of taxpayers' money to keep me here, not much of it is going on food.

1415H Out for Association. The woman guard is getting a hard time from prisoners who are expecting letters but none have arrived. She says it's not her fault. The mail is handled by outside contractors. I gently join in the conversation saying that when I did Christmas work in the Post Office as a student it was no problem to sort out letters for delivery to a community the size of Belmarsh.

She shifts her ground. 'All the letters in and out of Belmarsh have to be opened and read.' This is bullshit, though I don't use the word to her face. I received two emails in French and I doubt if there is a French reader on duty in the Belmarsh censors' department.

'Look, as an MP I would get fifty to a hundred letters a day,' I explain. 'You open them fast and quickly can see those that contain a problem or which need a closer look. I just don't believe it is so hard to get the mail to people more quickly.'

She loses interest in discussing mail delivery. I just see screws sitting around much of the day without a lot to do. There is no excuse for keeping letters from prisoners.

Apparently there will be no exercise today because there is a hint of rain in the air. The woman screw couldn't care less. 'If the weather is bad you stay inside. You have the right to thirty minutes' fresh air a day. Any other time outside your cells to associate with other prisoners is not a right. It's what we allow you if we want to,' she states.

So, New Year's Eve without fresh air. I call Sarah. I get voicemail though the kids have left little messages. Benjamin says they had great skiing but his mother tells the truth that most Mont Blanc slopes were shut due to thin snow cover. Snow can fall as hard in April as any month so, who knows, maybe I'll get some skiing in.

Julian is fed up with being cooped up in the spur without a chance to do his daily run around the yard. I belt up and down the metal stairs a few times, which produces more sweat and heart beating than a standard jog outside. I walk along the top landing doing stretching and John Cleese silly walks just to keep my legs alive.

It is so easy to vegetate. No books, no physical movement, no intellectual stimulus. Clearly, once settled in, a different rhythm would impose. But I have no sense of anyone here being a) improved or turned into a better person as a result of incarceration or b) being in any sense punished beyond the only punishment that matters – loss of liberty. Grayling's conceit that making life harder for prisoners by reducing what they can do inside will make the slightest difference is pure persiflage.

I have a tepid shower. I think I need about eight presses of the button to get wet, soap myself, wash it all off. I live a simple life in my tracksuit tops and bottoms. I don't miss my own clothes and, if alone of a day with writing ahead of me at home, will happily pass it in tracksuit bottoms and a T-shirt plus sweatshirt if cold. Some are made for suits, ties and cufflinks. Not me.

Abdul, the handsome Turkish boy, comes up to talk. Buzz, as ever, hovering and keen to impart information and his point of view, joins in. He says that bystanders, not main protagonists, get sucked into arrest nets and pay a terrible price. He tells us a story of a man who dumped his wife to go off running after fresh meat.

'His wife blew her top,' recounts Buzz. 'She picked up a jack-hammer, grabbed her 22-year-old son and stormed round to the replacement woman's house. When she opened the door, the dumped wife swung her jack-hammer and killed the mistress. In court she pleaded diminished responsibility and went free. But her son, who was simply present but played no part, was sent to jail for twenty years for taking part in a murder.'

Now I cannot check this story and am simply recording what I am told. The Turkish lad also had been part of a group where someone else had wielded the knife that had done the damage. Again, that's his story. But he tells it with such a sad conviction that I tend to believe him. Our jails need to be filled and the police and CPS need to meet targets.

1510H Bliss. I call Vicky and not only does she answer but she has Laura and Benjamin with her as well as their mother. At last I can hear my children's voices. Better still, perhaps my letter of complaint to the Governor about being denied a family reception visit has done its trick or perhaps pressure from outside, as they tell me I will get my family visit on Thursday.

Hooray! Eleven days after Sir Nigel sends me down and I will be able to see my children. Better still, I go to the back of the phone queue and wait patiently and Sarah is there picking up her phone. It's just lovely to hear her voice. She starts to rail against Judge Sweeney but I tell her one or two stories to head her away to calmer waters.

Of course children love and support their parents. But they quite independently know what's right and what's wrong and the difference between justice, injustice and fairness. They know I did wrong, made a stupid mistake, but they also know their papa and nothing will persuade them that the decision of Sir Nigel to imprison me was fair, just or proportionate, even if it was within his legal power.

That's over now and we all have to move on. I do so by wishing everyone a Happy New Year, *Bonne Année*. I used to like taking friends to the Commons Terrace for the New Year fireworks. But it got taken over by too many Tories with rich business associates and just became another money-fest that can be seen any evening in private dining rooms of the Commons where big business schmoozes with MPs. So I stopped going.

In truth, I am not a great New Year person, though I always enjoy the moment of cheer. I spent too many New Years as a boy in Scotland not to feel a twinge of nostalgia when Auld Lang Syne is sung and for a brief moment the untactile British are allowed to hold each other's hands. But the end of this *annus miserabilis* is not one to celebrate.

1525H I hand in some laundry to be washed – sweatshirts, a trackie, underpants and socks. At home I would be manipulating the washing machine and drying rack. Here it is all done for me, in fact the first time someone has done my laundry in years. I brush the floor of my room and find a mop and bucket of water – but no cleaning liquid – to swab the floor. The blood stains on my door look nasty. Will they ever be removed?

Benny has a chat and gives me a drawing he has made of my cell. All the cells on this row are the same. He is a bit nervous as apparently it is a major breach of prison rules to make a drawing or diagram of anything inside Belmarsh in case it can be used to facilitate an escape. It would be nice to think they didn't want to see what living and eating twenty-four hours a day with a stinking loo looks like but, for most of the public, even convicts having a flush lavatory shows what a luxurious life we enjoy.

1629H *Mon dieu!* Did I really order this? A tasteless thin slice of white fish – Whiting? Coley? Vietnamese catfish? – with even more tasteless white rice and chopped swede. What has HMP Belmarsh got against seasoning?

2300H Banged up for six and a half hours on New Year's Eve. I am watching *Hot Fuzz* when I smell the sweet, cloying, consoling aroma of dope. No, it can't be. Or has someone saved a little weed or hash for New Year. Well, good luck. This is the first New Year in more than half a century without a glass of something. But I am sure this abstinence is doing me no end of good.

2400H The roar of fireworks over the Thames can be heard. There is a great banging of cell doors – rather like demonstrators I saw in Venezuela banging their pots and pans on balconies in protest against the idiocies of Hugo Chávez. Belmarsh sees in 2014 with as much noise as it can manage. I join in, giving the cell doors a thump. It is not Princes Street, Edinburgh, where my son, a student at the university, is out with his mates but it is a Hello to the New Year and I do not feel at all alone.

JANUARY 2014

NEW YEAR'S DAY, WEDNESDAY
1 JANUARY 2014

One should respect public opinion insofar as is necessary to avoid starvation and keep out of prison, but anything that goes beyond this is voluntary submission to an unnecessary tyranny.

– Bertrand Russell, Old Brixtonian

0425H Someone has the television on very loud. I can't sleep, so sit down to write a bit. A guard told me I could be of use in the education classes, helping prisoners with low literacy. I know about that from my constituency. To encourage voter turnout, I spent hours trying to get Rotherham citizens on the electoral register. Even though it is a safe Labour seat, rarely do more than half its citizens vote. Just 34 per cent could be bothered to vote in the by-election that followed my ousting from the Commons.

I went to see some mothers in a community centre in one of the poorest areas of the constituency. I helped them fill in the electoral registration forms by writing in names and addresses but they had to sign the form. 'You sign for me, love,' more than one said. They could not write their own names.

I left the paper with the woman to avoid the humiliation of her signing X in front of me. It would have been wrong for me to sign and I preferred to go without the vote than put her or me in the wrong. I remain puzzled that, after the huge amount of money we pour into our schools, they disgorge so many denied the human right of being able to read or write. Votes at sixteen is a modish demand. How about being able to sign your own name at sixteen first?

0850H I had gone back to sleep and it turned into a delicious late lie-in. A quick flannel wash and I have just put in my tea bag and looked miserably at my portion of rice crispies – what does Chris Grayling have against muesli, All-Bran or for pity's sake some fruit? – when the door is opened and we are ushered out for exercise.

I cheerfully offer Happy New Year to the prison officer searching me but get a grunt in return.

0905H Some fast jogging round the yard today. This is the longest period of time since my early twenties when I have not done serious exercise. In between bursts of running, I link up with my symposium friends – the serious professional criminals. Mumble gives me a New Year present of some more stamped envelopes. I asked about the sweet smell of marijuana from last night.

'Yeah, could be. You can get anything in here. Someone probably saved it up for New Year,' said Cliff.

Dave, who is doing a stretch for possession of a firearm – in other words a gunman – butts in. 'Don't forget everyone in here is a criminal. Except you. You're innocent.'

I ask him to give me a signed statement to that effect and tell them if not telling the truth is the criterion for being categorised as a criminal then I fear that the DNA of most of my former MP friends might not pass the test.

'Did you hear the cries this morning?' I am asked.

'No, not really, I was dozing until quite late.'

'There was a prisoner moaning and groaning and crying out, "Don't leave me, don't leave me."'

Gosh, is there a secret love affair going on? Some of the women warders are very attractive and many of the prisoners extremely fit. A prison is a bit like a party political conference – full of intensity, lies, showing off, preening, seeking to dominate and conquer. Many affairs start at party conferences, some of which can be real shagathons as the Lord of Misrule takes command. The rules of fidelity are fluid or in suspense as the nocturnal frolics of a political party conference unleash themselves.

To be fair, the only overtly sexual comment I heard in Belmarsh was a sad screw in his fifties who was discussing the number of political sex scandals and said miserably, 'My wife is dead from the waist down.' But every now and then there are reports of prisoners and their jailers having sex and so I imagine, or is it fantasy, the New Year's Day vision of a prison bunk bunk-up. Bonking Belmarsh can almost take on a human allure.

The symposium on prison life continues.

'Why do we have to call them "officers"?' asks Buzz. 'They're not officers. They're guards, screws. I wouldn't dignify them with the term "officers". You don't need any qualifications to work in prisons. People who need an exam or an NVQ don't bother applying to work here.'

I don't like the turn of the talk. Some warders have been curt, cocky, without care or much humanity. Others seem more gentle and even compassionate. But more than one has promised to get me some paper or a pen, or told me I can go and get my blood pressure checked, and not kept their word.

Another symposium member in for attempted murder, and a professional criminal since childhood, is Mole. Mole is fifty-four, stocky, shaven headed, chatty and talks mainly about getting his daughter Anna into university. 'She is brilliant at photography and art. She does fusion camera work,' he tells me as if I had the faintest idea what that means. I suggest a couple of London university colleges that do art and photography. I give him my email address and promise to help his daughter if I can.

Mumble tells me about his life as a security van robber. 'I did a couple of big jobs – a BBC payroll of £800,000,' – I assume that was just for senior BBC executives' expenses – 'and then a £1.3 million Heathrow job. I was on the run for seven years, South America, all over Europe but my wife was pregnant in Alicante and I really had to see my daughter and that's when they must have picked up the trail and I got arrested in Germany.'

He didn't sound enamoured of the life of a fugitive abroad. He is pure south London and would be a fish out of water away from his local haunts. I doubt if anyone messes with Mumble and the fact that he has stretched out his protective arm to me as we walk and talk is noticed by all the other prisoners and screws.

He has nothing but contempt for what he clearly considers amateur, yobbish criminals.

'There was one kid who thought he was it because he did a bit of drug delivering. He turned up to see me one day and parked his Lamborghini outside the house. A fucking Lamb-bore-gheenee! What a little cunt. I told him, "What are you driving that stupid car for, you cunt? You want everyone in the street to know what you're up to? Get rid of it and get a normal car like a Beamer or a Merc." Stupid git. Kids like that make you sick and give crime such a bad name.'

0928H After exactly twenty-three minutes a woman warder tells us to get back inside, 'You've had your half-hour, back to cells.'

I eat my rice crispies and drink my now tepid, almost cold tea. Again the cell door is unlocked.

'Association,' says the warder. I finish the boring, unhealthy rice crispies quickly and go to the shower to wash off the faint film of sweat from the jogging a few minutes before.

Under the half-cold shower, watching the black flies march up and down the cream wall, I hear my name called. 'MacShane, chapel,' bellows a woman warder.

I had wondered what happened to the New Year's Day mass Father Edward has promised. Services are normally at 9.30 but now it's a quarter to ten. I desperately rinse off and pull a tracksuit bottom onto my wet legs as there is no time to dry. I take a risk by going the few yards back to my cell half-naked. It is strictly against the rules to be out of one's cell other than fully clothed and shod, but no one notices. I get a sweatshirt and thrust my wet feet into town shoes and run upstairs to go through the searching process. The corridors to the chapel area are cold and chilly and I shiver in my wet state.

Three masses in one week! My mother would have been so pleased. She died in 2006, two years after my daughter Clare was killed. I was on a trip to meet key French politicians and editors for the Prime Minister when I got the news from my brother that she was dying. It was one of the trips I improperly claimed reimbursement for.

Fr Edward says this mass is dedicated to the mother of Christ. His homily, which I can see he has written out himself in neat black ink on small cards, is all about the role and importance of motherhood. My own mother, widowed at forty-one, sacrificed a lot for her three sons. She had to wait until her sixties to become a grannie and was very kind to Clare.

I was in the French Alps skiing with Bernard Kouchner, soon to be France's Foreign Minister, when my doctor brother phoned up to say, 'You'd better come back. Mother's in her final days.' I raced back in my car and was stopped for speeding on the autoroute to Calais. I explained I was returning urgently to be at my dying mother's bedside. The normally unforgiving gendarmes let me off without a ticket and on-the-spot fine. '*Sur votre parole d'honneur, Monsieur le Ministre* – On your word of honour, Minister.' I was no longer a minister in 2006, having been moved to do other European political work by the Prime Minister but, in France, once a minister you are '*M. le Ministre*' forever.

I joined my brothers at my mother's bedside. She could no longer speak and was taking a little nourishment from a toothbrush-sized sponge dipped in orange juice and placed between her lips to suck. There was no pain and her mind was still there, though the body and will to live was fading.

We told her all the news about the children and what they were up to. By now she had nine grandchildren. Her eyes lit up with a mother's and grandmother's deep satisfaction that the next generations were coming along fine.

She beckoned to me but could not formulate words. Instead she reached for a pad and a pen and with great force of concentration slowly wrote something down. She held up the paper on which in capital letters had been written her last words to me: 'DON'T DRINK.'

Ah, dear mother, if only, if only. We left, but three days later I returned with her eleven-year-old grandson, Benjamin. By now she was in a coma, breathing slowly but peacefully. We held her hand but there was no grip back. We waited quietly, just looking at this lined face of a woman who had been born in the middle of the Battle of the Somme and spent her young woman years as German bombs fell on Glasgow. She had a brief decade with her husband before he died as a result of a war-wound-induced illness. The rest of her life was devoted to her sons.

One reason I cannot give in to the fashionable contempt against European construction is perhaps because I had two parents stemming from the bookends of Europe – Ireland and Poland – whose countries have become whole and free and much richer as a result of membership of the European Union. I do not know why so many of the political-media elites who control Britain want to throw this away.

We gave a final kiss to her gentle, lined, at-ease face and left. The next day she died. There is an opera duet 'Your tiny hand is frozen' in *La Bohème* that I cannot hear without tears rising to my eyes as the memory sweeps in of holding Clare's tiny cold hand as she lay in her coffin in Melbourne in 2004. Father Edward's invocation of motherhood has the same effect as I remember my mother's almost gone body.

I am glad she isn't there to see me in prison, though she took all the other vicissitudes in my life in her stride. And as someone from a strong Irish background she would not have had much confidence that an English bureaucrat, an English MP, an English prosecutor and an English judge would ever treat fairly her beloved unEnglish son.

Behind me in the chapel sit two Polish newcomers, one from Warsaw, one from Lodz. I rise in their estimation when I tell them I was arrested, convicted and spent time in Polish cells in the communist era.

A young Russian came up to say '*Dobry den!*' He was in for a VAT fraud. I think of all the Russian oligarchs and other Russian who have stole their nation's assets in the post-communist years, with full complicity of the state apparatus, and were brought to London to be hidden away with the help of the gentlemen of the City. A Russian lawyer told me that 30 per cent of the money City lawyers make comes from handling dubious Russian money.

The young Russian says he was close to Boris Berezovsky, the exiled Russian billionaire who was Vladimir Putin's sworn enemy. I ask him if Berezovsky really committed suicide.

'No, MI5 killed him,' he replies as if it was an undisputed matter of fact.

This has to be absurd. Except Asil Nadir told me that senior Conservatives told him to do a runner to Turkey and northern Cyprus because there were elements in the British state security services ready to off him. And current ministers are ready to sign Public Interest Immunity Certificates so that Nadir's lawyers cannot get access to key documents that would help his appeal.

Have we all been seeing too much James Bond on TV over the festive season? And yet we know Putin's tax police put to death Sergei Magnitsky, the harmless legal accountant who was investigating a $230 million tax robbery carried out by Putin's tax police as they stole from a British firm. And we know Putin's agents came to London to kill Alexander Litvinenko with polonium. And we know that David Cameron and William Hague have given up bothering Putin on Litvnenko and have rejected a unanimous vote of the House of Commons for visa bans and asset freezes to be imposed on Magnitsky's killers. No wonder our capital is called Londongrad by Russians.

The Russian says he would like to do business with me once he gets out. 'You can get anything Britain needs in Russia and sell it here at a profit.' I think I'll keep my distance. '*Spasibo*, thanks,' I tell him but I doubt we'll meet again.

So many of the men in Belmarsh simply feel they have been unlucky. In the detective novel I am reading by Elizabeth George, one of her characters, an East European living in London, has had a nasty brush with the police. 'In her experience the police couldn't be trusted with anything. Indeed no one in the whole legal system could be trusted if it came down to it. In the legal system, plods settled on a story and bent the facts to fit it, presenting those facts to magistrates in such a way that bail was deemed foolhardy, and a trial in the Old Bailey followed by a lengthy prison sentence was the only cure for social ill.'

Ms George is a novelist and so what she writes is of course pure fiction and far removed from the facts.

After mass, I tell Fr Edward that this may be the last time I see him as I cannot believe that, in contrast to all the other politician prisoners, this is now my second week in Belmarsh surrounded by my fellow criminals – murderers, drug dealers, and gunmen. I enjoy their company and from every conversation I am learning more as I realise that the world of MPs, civil servants, editors, and other professionals knows as much about what happens inside our judicial-security-prison world and its denizens as they – or I – know about the internal politics of North Korea.

1047H Back on the spur I get to hear Vicky's voice on voicemail. Other phone numbers of close friends I have listed on an official form to be allowed to call don't seem to work. One of the two phones is at a child's height so I have to bend double to use it. The other one is a normal stand up phone but seems sensitive and breaks off calls abruptly. Phones are on a use it and lose it basis as once a call has been made, even for twenty seconds, you have to wait ten minutes to make another one.

I am now gagging to know what is going on. The TV news programmes are ridiculous in the shallowness of their non-reporting of the world. Poor Michael Schumacher, who is at death's door after his skiing accident, is the only European news story. What is happening in Turkey? Do the terror bombers in Volgograd threaten the Sochi Winter Olympics where British security outfits, with Cameron's help, have negotiated a juicy contract or two? Is there no news out of Germany, France, Brussels?

Are the protests against the wretched Yanukovich going on in Ukraine with the intensity of the Orange Revolution ones I witnessed as a minister in 2004? Might he and his kleptocratic regime be in real trouble?

What is happening in Iran? The US foreign security 'expert', Richard Haas, has failed to get the ultras in Northern Ireland to a lessening of the old Republican-Unionist hates. Perhaps the EU foreign policy chief, Catherine Ashton, who got the Serbs and Kosovans to cut a deal, should be sent over to Belfast to tell the two sides that Ulster will be booted out of the EU unless they rise above their hates.

Minister Grayling has ordained, as part of his punishment regime, that I cannot have a newspaper in Belmarsh, though Julian tells me that even if I did order one it would take three weeks before it began to arrive. Again and again I hear the lament: 'There is no rehabilitation here. They just let you rot.'

1105H Jacket potato and baked beans for lunch. 'Beans!' bellows out the prisoner after you give him your name and he looks down the single-spaced typed list and finds 'Ian McShane'.

I take the food to my room. Actually, I like jacket potatoes and baked beans, though I am not sure where these beans come from as the 'sauce' they come in coagulates into a kind of orange glue on the plastic plate. And without salt or pepper they are tasteless. The warders don't seem to be banging up so, as soon as I have finished, I nip out to try and make a phone call.

I just hear the BT voice saying 'Connecting you now' when a woman warder snaps at me, 'MacShane, cell!' and I have to put down the receiver and retreat to my hole.

I long for a salad, anything green. This food is much as was served in my primary school, St Joseph's in Wealdstone, in the '50s. It is not bad, just tasteless stodge. I watch prisoners go by with a long sausage and a soft baguette on their plate. I love sausage and beans, which was one of my Tea Rooms staples over the years. But here there is no mixing and matching.

Ah well, as hundreds of thousands of my fellow citizens will have little or no food this New Year's Day, as poverty rises remorselessly, I am getting a filling if boring meal courtesy of the taxpayer.

Thirty minutes of bliss on TV as the Vienna New Year's Concert is shown. I am disappointed at the dress-down style of the Vienna Philharmonic and their conductor, the great Daniel Barenboim. Gone are the white tie and tails of classical Vienna, to be replaced by an open-collared Barenboim and suit, white shirts and boring grey ties of the orchestra, which seems entirely composed of men.

The music carries me away as I remember the polkas and mazurkas I used to dance in order to be in the same Polish dancing group in west London as my first girlfriend. The wonderful music of the *Blue Danube* – a very dirty muddy brown every time I've seen it – lifts me out of my seat. I grab a sweatshirt, extend its sleeve and, before I can stop myself, I am waltzing with my sweatshirt partner up and down, round and round in my cell. *Prosit* 2014! as I whisk myself to a café on the *Stephanplatz* to enjoy a *Brauner* and a *Schnapps*.

1420H Out for Association. There is a half-size pool table, which seems to be bagged by competent pool players and since childhood I have never been much good at pool, snooker or billiards, despite dutifully applying myself. That's it. No chess or cards, nothing to do to raise the spirits and pass time.

I go up and down the thirty-nine steps of the red and green metal stair-case connecting the three landings. Anything to keep moving, have some exercise.

There are three airport lounge-type armless blue easy chairs beside the phones and opposite the pool table on the ground floor. I sit beside a new arrival, Terry. He tells me he is forty years old and his wife is forty-eight. They have a child and she has five children by previous partners. She works as a health-care assistant.

Terry is here because his wife accused him of domestic violence. He works, or worked, as a fork-lift driver and they own their own house.

'I was lying in bed with the flu. I couldn't move when the police arrived I was so flued up. They arrested me and before I knew it I was in Belmarsh.'

'But did you hit her?'

'Look, we both took cocaine but when we woke up in the morning to go to work there were real rows, bad ones. Charlie gives you a high of euphoria but when it's over, a few hours later both she and me were not fit for each other.'

'So what's the evidence against you? Marks? Bruises?'

'None. Her word. My word. If the police had just spent a few minutes listening they would have realised what's going on.'

'Yes, but there is real concern about domestic violence now. The DPP guy, Starmer, who's just moved out, was given real grief because of the low charging and conviction rate for domestic assaults. The new DPP is a woman and is presumably taking it all a lot more seriously.'

'Look, she says she'll withdraw the allegations if I drop charges against her son for assault.'

'What?!' I exclaim as the story takes this new turn.

'A week before I was arrested, her son came round and smashed me in the face and attacked my little daughter. You just don't know what impact Charlie has on people. But I won't drop the charges, even if that's the only reason she called the police about me. I reckon five out of six lads who are in here on domestic violence aren't really guilty but the police can say whatever they like and the judges send you straight to prison.'

He sat there disconsolate. I suggested a trade with his partner. But there was no response. Clearly I am hearing only his side of the story. And there is rightly more pressure on taking action against domestic bad behaviour. I remember Keir Starmer telling MPs that domestic violence should now be extended to psychological pressure and coercion.

Yet is there a danger this extends into becoming a tick-box exercise? The *EastEnders* world adapts quickly to changes in societal rules. If the word goes out that all that is needed to get revenge for whatever reason is to phone the police and make accusations of domestic violence, in the certainty that police will arrest without bothering with too many questions because that is what those in power now want, then our jails will quickly fill up with those accused of domestic violence but not much will actually change.

'Look,' said Buzz earlier, in one of our symposium walk-talks, 'they have to fill the prisons. The judges and QCs have to justify their jobs and pay. If you actually targeted the causes of crime, and that's mainly no-hope poverty, or if you stopped sending people here who had a moment of madness or stopped sending people to prison for crimes that aren't violent or don't cause harm, the prisons wouldn't need filling and judges would have to be laid off. Can't have that, can we?'

Later, during Association, I was distributing my sugar rations of sachets – usually to those on anti-depressant or calming medication – when Buzz sidled up to me.

'You wanna know the best story in Belmarsh?'

Always up for high-class goss, I nodded, of course.

'You remember the Stephen Lawrence murder?'

Another nod of assent.

'Well, the families of his killers paid forty grand to a plod to remove the knife that killed him from the evidence. Everyone in south London knew what had happened and who this bent guy was, as did the cops. But they were all covering up for each other. Because if the cops did one of their own who was bent, he would know so much on other cops who had been naughty it would all collapse. So they eased him out of the police service and gave him a job here. He works in the reception unit where you arrived from the Old Bailey. Now there is a new investigation and he knows, and the rest of Belmarsh knows, the net is closing in.'

Again, I relay what I was told. Certainly in Whitehall sinecures are always found for redundant civil servants who are not wanted by their superiors. Why should the police service be any different? As with the bankers of 2008, no police officer seems to have been held to account for the cover-ups of the police investigation of the murder of the Stephen Lawrence.

I chat to Benny, who says Thameside, the privatised prison on the sprawling Belmarsh estate, is very different from the HMP we are in.

'The cells are nicer. You have a shower and a phone in each cell. You can take the back off the television, stick an aerial in and hang it out the window and get 120 channels. (Please may I be spared that!) But I never really felt safe there. The guards weren't properly trained. They allowed the Muslims to form controlling groups and any Muslim prisoner who wanted to feel safe had to become ultra-religious and take their line. They allowed prisoners to play fighting games and that could go wrong. Maybe I'm old-fashioned but I think prisons should be run as a public service, not profit centres for Serco.'

1610H Dinner. A beef curry with white rice. Not as utterly tasteless as last night's fish but only Belmarsh can serve a curry that tastes of anything but.

I watch *The Dam Busters* and am amazed that all the references to Wing Commander Guy Gibson's dog 'Nigger' are still audible in the film. Surely editing technology allows a quick change of syllables of this profoundly offensive racist epithet? That apart, the film is so much better than all the other war-related modern movies I have watched in Belmarsh, with their computer-generated military whizz-bangs. The reason is very old-fashioned. Good acting. A quick look at BBC1's flagship *Sherlock*, which has fine actors comprehensively sacrificed to pointless camera and computer trickery, proves the point.

THURSDAY 2 JANUARY 2014

No, no, no, no! Come, let's away to prison.
We two alone will sing like birds i' the cage.
When thou dost ask me blessing, I'll kneel down,
And ask of thee forgiveness. So we'll live,
And pray, and sing, and tell old tales, and laugh
At gilded butterflies, and hear poor rogues
Talk of court news, and we'll talk with them too,
Who loses and who wins, who's in, who's out;
And take upon's the mystery of things,
As if we were God's spies. And we'll wear out,
In a wall'd prison, packs and sects of great ones,
That ebb and flow by the moon.

– *King Lear*

0819H Again, a good sleep. I think the fact that the BNP shadow over me for nearly five years has gone is a help. The fact that I don't have to face finding fresh thousands on lawyers' fees and can build a future partly outside Britain with its complex hypocrisies also helps. Despite Hellmarsh, I am more at ease with myself than in a long time. I think I have lost weight. I sleep better despite the hard mattress and rock-like pillow.

0823H I hardly have time to put the kettle on before the cell door opens and it is exercise time. It is a gloriously sunny morning. I start by running as hard as I can round and round the exercise yard.

I then wait until core symposium members form up to walk and talk. The morning sun has made everyone cheerful. Mumble says a screw told him to stop smiling. 'You look too happy. Get that grin off your face!'

Mumble thinks he'll be here until August. 'Can you get me a job as an MP on the outside, mate? How about a job as an MP?'

'Well, the two main requirements of a successful politician are an ability to talk and keep talking non-stop and never be too honest with voters as you will get caught out.'

The symposium bursts out laughing. 'That's you, Cliff. You'll go straight into the Commons!'

I want to explore the reasons they are all here but after barely twenty minutes the guards announce that exercise is over. Sometimes exercise doesn't happen because it is raining. Today it is curtailed because it is sunny. Most of my symposium members are on a different spur so I only see them during exercise sessions. The spur I am on has a number of remand prisoners as well as a great number of drug dealers or youngsters sent to Belmarsh by south-east London magistrates who stupidly think that a short sentence in Belmarsh will make a difference to someone who lost his cool and threw a punch he should not have.

0846H I would love to have a shower but it's back to the cell where I sit in my sweaty clothes to eat my cornflakes, the worst of all the industrial cereals and an apple I have carefully kept for down moments. It is half rotten and I hack away at the bad bits with my blue plastic knife but even a small taste of fruit at breakfast is heaven.

Before I can pour hot water on last night's tea bag, my cell door clangs open and a screw snaps, 'Medical care.' I have no idea what this is for but, on the principle of never turning down an opportunity to be out of your cell, I go up the metal stairs, am searched, get my name checked off a list and go for a wander through corridors to the medical wing. I have to go through a scanner to get in and am directed to small surgery.

'Name?'

'MacShane.'

'No. I've only got first names here.'

'Denis.'

'No Denis down here.'

'Try Ian,' I suggest. I smile as I remember Judge Sweeney tying himself in knots over various ways my name is spelt. This name business has got hilariously out of control.

Apparently I am seeing the nurse to have a Hepatitis B injection. The burly prison medical orderly has a dreadful blotchy skin condition on his forearms and face – psoriasis? – and does not look like a good advert for healthy living. But he is polite enough and asks me if I know what a Hep B injection is for.

I nod but I add I hope I won't be in any dangerous situation – a fight, being bitten, sodomy or injecting myself – the usual blood transmission mechanisms for hepatitis.

'You can't be too careful. You may just accidentally be in contact with someone's blood,' he says wisely.

'The only blood I've seen is all the dried blood on my cell door.'

'Yours?'

'No, it's old and dried but does anyone ever clean anything in Belmarsh?'

Of course, there's no answer. There never is. Prison officers or orderlies are trained not to have intelligent exchanges with prisoners making reasonable points.

The injection is done professionally, unnoticed and I go back through the security scanner and stroll down the chilly corridors to try and find my spur. I suppose if I wanted to try and escape this would be the moment. But I have no idea of where I am, which corridor leads where, how close I am to a wall or exit, or even where north or south is or which way lies the Thames and which way central London.

Jeremy Bentham, the founder of utilitarian philosophy – roughly, policy should deliver the greatest good for the greatest number – invented the 'Panopticon' – prison with just one warder at its central hub who could keep an eye on the prisoners in cells radiating out in spurs. Bentham, a late eighteenth-century reformer, thought this would reduce the cost of supervising prisoners. He obtained land on Millbank on the site of the present Tate Gallery, and Britain's first National Penitentiary was built there, though not to the Panopticon design. It was there the prison ships destined to transport prisoners to Australia would moor to pick up the convicts sentenced to transportation. The Aussie term 'Pom' to designate someone from England is said to come from 'Prisoner of Millbank'.

There is a hint of the Panopticon in the glass-walled office at the centre of the four spurs and by which all prisoners must pass to enter the rest of the prison. Hopes that smart design could reduce costs foundered in the eighteenth century as they founder today by the sheer number of prisoners to be dealt with and the growing understanding that, if re-offending was ever to be brought under control, having too many prisoners and too few staff made this impossible.

Even without supervision, I am lost as I wander the corridors of Belmarsh, to the amusement of the guards stationed at key points, who kindly set me off in a new direction until I recognise the outlines of my spur and almost with relief I am glad to be home.

I have to return to my spur passing the food counter in the central hub for the four spurs in my wing. I find the prisoner who was offensive when I tried to show him my name on the list for food, having a row with a woman guard. He is wearing green trousers – the sign of a prisoner authorised to do prison tasks like sweeping floors, preparing food and handing out bedding to new arrivals.

He is complaining that he never moves off the task of checking prisoners' names and then shouting out what they are entitled to eat. 'Meat, beans, fish, chicken,' he calls out as we shuffle down the counter line to hand over our blue plastic plates to get food.

The woman guard looks at him with contempt. 'You're getting ideas above your station, Mallory,' she says, turning her back on him and walking away. He throws down a brush and pan and stalks off.

I wait in front of the bars that form the barrier into Spur 3 with a gate on the right-hand side. I notice a toaster on a little ledge sticking out from the wall. It is an industrial one with a revolving grill rack you find in hotels where you make your own toast. I switch it on and no one pays attention. I have never seen it being used. Toast at breakfast, does that still exist outside Belmarsh? Certainly there is no honey for tea.

1011H Back in the spur I tell the guard that I hope today to be seeing my children for the first time since the judge glanced briefly at them as he sent their daddy away for Christmas. Could I please have a two-minute shower before I see them?

'No, you should have had a shower yesterday,' he says as he slams shut the cell door.

I did shower yesterday, Mr Screw. Believe it or not I try and clean myself every day and sometimes shower more than once if I have done exercise.

This surly, unhelpful contempt does make me depressed. Of course, Laura and Benjamin have seen their father unshaved, unwashed, sweaty, but as a family we are keen on cleanliness. I spent happy hours bathing or showering my children until they were old enough to wash themselves. Now I find myself shouting at my son who seems to spend hours in a shower while others wait.

So Grubby Grayling and his minion warder want me to see my children in a less than pristine state. As a small act of resistance I open the window its full 4 inches and breathe in fresh air while breaking up stale dry bread to push through the grill to feed the birds. It is strictly against the rules and John Lyon CB, if he reads this, will certainly feel justified in ending the parliamentary service of this wicked rule-breaker. But having wallowed in *Gone with the Wind* over the holiday TV, I don't give a damn. Two birds flutter down in the January sunshine and feed happily, and instantly my good humour returns and I feel content.

I finish my half-apple and wash – a flannel over face, armpits and groin. The cell door opens and a guard comes in and starts inspecting the cell. He says nothing and does not seem to notice the dried blood or black-rimmed loo. I make my final appeal.

'Any chance of a shower so I can see my kids nice and clean?'

'No. You're in prison. Get used to it.'

1109H Emails and two letters from France arrive. The letters are just pushed under the door. It is important to Belmarsh that I remain locked up. One French friend, who I was working with for decent money before my incarceration, emails to say that the word in Paris and Brussels is that my case is '*ridicule*'. 'And the sentence is totally disproportionate to your wrongdoing – by this yardstick there are a few hundreds of national politicians and thousands of local ones who should go to jail once in a while for sure in France yet hardly anyone goes.'

Mon cher ami, hardly any politicians go to jail in England. If the MPs who paid boyfriends rent, or their university student children salaries, or helped themselves to petty cash without receipts, or plundered taxpayers' money to speculate in London property were treated on the same basis, Belmarsh would have to open an extension in SW1.

British politicians and journalists are always smug and superior about their French counterparts. Michael Cockerell, the BBC political documentary film-maker, was once interviewing Jack Straw as Foreign Secretary, when Jack made the then commonplace remark that if the then French president, Jacques Chirac, was a British politician, he would be in prison because of illicit party fundraising.

The BBC team retold Straw's comments, which whizzed straight over to the Elysée, and French officials protested privately to me that Britain's

Foreign Secretary should control his tongue. But Straw has a point. It's true that French party financing is dodgy and the former French Prime Minister Alain Juppé was sentenced to eighteen months – suspended – for fictitious employment of party hacks. But Juppé came back to be Mayor of Bordeaux and Foreign Minister.

At least Juppé suffered some sanction as did Chirac, though his status as an ex-president and hint of early dementia prevented a jail sentence. His successor Nicolas Sarkozy is still under investigation over political finances during his term in office. Contrast that with Britain, where we are the only 'democracy' where a party leader can make someone a law-maker in exchange for a large cheque. Or where political parties can take six-figure donations from criminals and not hand the money back.

Since most editors and senior journalists are gagging for a knighthood or, better still, a peerage there is no media discussion of the profound corruption in our legislature's make-up. The BBC has a legislator as its chairman and another legislator as its Director-General. So much for separation of powers and so much for the chances of the excellent Michael Cockerell making a programme challenging the way party leaders exchange the right to be a legislator for big money. Britain also allows MPs to divert taxpayers' money to pay for party political offices in constituencies, a practice outlawed in most democracies.

As far as I can see, no French president has enriched himself in, or on leaving, office. Giscard d'Estaing came from a wealthy family and spent the three decades following his loss of power in 1981 being active in politics and making a considerable difference to French and European politics, even if he never again achieved high office.

François Mitterrand died owning just a small house in Paris and a cottage in a remote part of the south-west Atlantic coast. Jacques Chirac has been well paid over decades as a high state servant in France but has not gone off to enrich himself on leaving office. Contrast that with Ted Heath who was paid handsomely by communist China, or John Major who monetised his premiership by going off for a fabulous salary as European chairman of the US-owned Carlyle Group. And Tony Blair has not done badly either.

In short, the interface between British politics and politicians and money is every much as corrupting and corrosive as in France. But we love to believe everything is rosy in the British political garden, and weed-choked and full of dishonesty across the Channel.

One of the saddest aspects of the whole MP expenses affair was the seediness of the greed. A quick glance through the claims sees pathetic instances of money-grabbing. When trying to work out why John Lyon CB singled me out but ignored nearly all other MPs who had question marks over their expenses claims, I spent a little time researching parliamentary colleagues.

Jack Straw, as Foreign Secretary, had two official residences as well as his home in south London, a country place in Oxfordshire and his constituency home in Lancashire. As a minister in the Foreign Office you rarely if ever had to buy a meal or food, as dinners, lunches, sandwiches, buns and as much tea or coffee as you could wish for was always on hand. And your constituency accepted that being a foreign minister meant a lot of time outside the UK on business. Yet there is the neat round sum of £1,000 claimed for food eaten in his Blackburn house while Jack was on the top salary of a senior Cabinet minister.

As with claiming full reimbursement for council tax on a constituency house when in fact only 50 per cent was paid because it was classified as a second home, it is important to stress that all these claims were defined by the Commons bureaucracy as being within the rules. But it was an arbitrary definition of what the rules were and how they should be interpreted, and when the details were published there was a collective shudder of horror throughout the nation that has yet to subside.

I talked to another prisoner, not on my spur, while waiting in the holding room before going for my Hep B injection. He expected to be held in Belmarsh until June. The police had arrived in his street after a night-time burglary was reported by the owner of the house where my Belmarsh colleague lived. He had been previously sentenced and was wearing a tag anklet. If he so much as opened his door and put a foot outside after 7 p.m., the beep would go straight to Serco or the tagging company and he would be straight back to prison.

Although, as was later found out, there were no fingerprints, no sign of breaking or entering, the house-owner opposite insisted he had had property stolen.

'Ah, you mean an insurance job,' said Buzz, who as usual was ear-wigging.

The police, as keen fans of *Casablanca*, rounded up the usual suspects including the tagged man now telling me the story. He did, it's true, have a criminal background and, as a tagged prisoner on provisional release, was listed as such. It was an easy job for the police to arrest him and tie the burglary to his previous crimes.

Now he might be lying and he has a criminal record, as do I and more than nine million fellow citizens according to official figures, but it seems surreal to break your tag curfew by walking across the road and, without leaving a fingerprint or any trace of breaking into the house, manage to commit a burglary. But for the police and CPS another box has been ticked, a target met. If it was an insurance job and the claim is not too high, it will be paid out and our insurance premiums will edge up slightly. Meanwhile a judge and the public get the satisfaction of seeing a working class young man put in prison for several months, at great cost to the taxpayer, until the court system can find the time to deal with him.

1112H I barely have time to glance at my mail when there is the call for lunch. OMG. I ordered a tuna baguette. This unpleasant white cotton wool bread and fishy slush fit for someone eating with their gums is horrid. My mistake. I would give anything for some wholemeal bread. I walk to the end of the counter and see a metal serving tray heaped with lettuce and tomatoes. I reach out for a tomato.

'No,' says a prisoner with a guttural East European accent. 'Not Kommuns hier. Kant haf.'

To think of the hours I spent on the BBC arguing with the Nigel Farage and William Hagueites saying that we were right to open the UK to workers from new EU member states. This is my reward. *Vd'aka*, as you might say in Slovakian. Better still, fuck off.

1120H More emails and letters are shoved under the closed cell door. From Orcas Island off America's north-west Pacific coast near Seattle, Don sends me his family news and then has the genius idea of adding the BBC World News online summary.

Colin takes three emails from Tuscany to report on the slaughter of a pig and how, after an epic struggle to lasso the Italian porker, it was suspended, its throat cut with blood splashing all over the famous professor before it became salami, prosciutto, sanguinaccio, pork chops and roasts. I am already on the plane to Pisa, the bus to Florence for lunch and can feel the chilled glass of Gavi in my hand on a terrace overlooking the incomparable hills of Siena. A little later, Orcas.

One of the best novels last year was Robert Harris's rendering of the Dreyfus affair. It has been nearly as long since the BNP complaint and although I make no comparison, none at all, I cannot wait to be free of having to worry about John Lyon CB, Kevin Barron, Keir Starmer and Sir Nigel Sweeney. They can send the whole world to prison if that's their pleasure but I shall be free without a care in the world.

Back to earth or rather back to my sodden white bread fish paste concoction. Tuna has been one of my favourite fishes since forever. In a *salade niçoise, vitello tonnato*, a sandwich, a tuna and bean salad, as ceviche or grilled. But tuna à la Belmarsh is coming close to killing my fondness for the fish.

An email from one of my former private secretaries at the FCO who was a joy to work with. He has been offered one of the best embassies in one of the most fascinating countries in Latin America. But his second son, just born, has severe cystic fibrosis, a wretched ailment that clogs up lungs and is miserable for child and parents. He needs to stay close to the NHS and has to decline a prize ambassadorship in order to stay in London so his boy can get proper treatment. My worries are as nothing compared to a child's chronic illness and how much strain it causes parents.

Children never come into prison except for visits. But they are constantly present. Prisoners talk more than anything else about the absence of contact with children and grandchildren. A phone call a day – if both phones are working, and the queue is not long, and you have phone credit (mine is down to £7.14) – is all you are allowed. Will your children be taken into care? How will your current partner or wife live without income and a man?

Again and again, as I jog past prisoners in the exercise yard, I hear snatches of conversation. 'And now the slag's gone off …' or 'That cunt is seeing her.' Others appear to have stable family homes and no fear of family break-up. But the obsession of turning the sausage machine of policing and justice into a conveyor belt for sending hapless, stupid people into prison – often for months before they face trial – seems as good a way of breaking up families and rotting the foundation of partnership to care for and nurture children as could be devised.

A terrific email from Tom Harris MP:

> I took to the airwaves the day you were sentenced to say what a raw deal you'd had and consequently (inevitably) I invited a degree of criticism from the lovely users of Twitter. As a New Year Resolution have decided to abandon Twitter altogether – what a waste of time and effort it is.
> It would be lovely if you came back to the Commons to see some old friends. Remember you have the love and support of a lot of people who know you are a good man and are prepared to say so.

We'll see. Tom has been incredibly brave, as has Michael Connarty MP, who tried to defend me in the Commons in the face of Kevin Barron's lurid denunciation, written for him to echo the language of John Lyon CB. Connarty was shut up by the Speaker, John Bercow.

Bercow had been genuinely friendly and supportive during the long period of the police investigation. He encouraged me to play a full part in the Commons despite the suspension of the Labour whip. But when I asked Speaker Bercow or the Clerk of the House, Robert Rogers, why John Lyon CB never interviewed me or sought any face-to-face explanation why I had sought reimbursement in the way I did, both the Speaker and the Clerk shied away.

I understood John's reticence, as he had been criticised during the expenses scandal and had paid more than £6,000 to the taxman after accusations by political opponents. The Clerk of the Commons, Sir Robert Rogers, expressed sympathy but kept saying, 'We cannot do anything with Lyon', echoing Kevin Barron's assertion that 'we (the Standards and Privileges Committee) have no control over him'.

At the time, I was surprised that the Speaker of the House of Commons – a personage before whom Winston Churchill bowed when the then Speaker visited Chartwell for lunch, because the Speaker is the third person in the unwritten constitution after the monarch and the Lord Chancellor (dear me, is Chris Grayling really the second person of the land?!) – was so fearful of a middling Whitehall parliamentary bureaucrat. At the time, and especially after the David Laws finding, I assumed common sense would prevail. If the police and CPS found no reason to prosecute, surely John Lyon CB could not overrule that decision?

Throughout the period from the BNP complaint being referred to the police to my defenestration as an MP, I received endless private messages of support, affection and best wishes from MPs who knew I was not a crook. But no MP dared to turn private good wishes into public support, except Tom Harris and Michael Connarty. Many were, and remain, fearful that any support for me would turn the media spotlight on their own expenses. Harriet Harman led a distinguished team of parliamentarians including David Blunkett, Peter Hain, and Lords Brookman, Falconer, Jordan and Monks, who sent powerful testimonials based on decades of close knowledge of me, all of which were brushed aside by the judge.

I was foolish to trust to the honour and integrity of the Parliamentary system after the police and CPS cleared me. I should have counter-attacked against the personal obsession against me of one man, and got more MP friends to speak up. But how many times did I walk on the other side of the road when a political colleague was under fire and being torn apart by the media witch-burners? Having been a political coward myself I should not have expected head-above-the-parapet bravery from other MPs.

1530H Hooray. My first visit after eleven days. Laura and Benjamin come in with Vicky for a so-called family reception visit which is meant to happen shortly after arriving in prison. I write some email instructions on a small scrap of paper. The paper and pens different guards have said they will provide have still not arrived. In the first day or two I met some kindness and courtesy from the guards. Now the tone has hardened and I just don't feel I can trust any of them.

I shove my scrap of paper down my sock into the sole of my New Balance trainer. A long walk to another search point and then a yellow bib over my tracksuit top.

As I wait in the holding room before going in for the visit, I talk to Mel, a man about fifty, neat and trim. He is waiting to see his wife of thirty years. He has lived at the same address and worked successfully as a chauffeur or courier, even at times sub-contracting to other people.

He was hired by a man from Liverpool to chauffeur him around London. All the payments were made in cash – the preferred no-receipt, no-VAT, no-tax method of remuneration of the self-employed. He was told to take a car up to Liverpool and there asked to run a package down to Bournemouth.

'I knew what was in it. I didn't want to do it. I was half leaned on and half needed the cash. On the M6 I was pulled over by the cops as someone had grassed.'

Mel was quite happy to admit he had done wrong, would plead guilty and take his punishment. But, he protested, he had been in Belmarsh for six weeks and would have to wait another five months for his trial.

'Look, I've lived in the same house for thirty years with the same wife. The police went through everything and found no evidence of funny money. All they could find was furniture twenty years out of date and two £10 Rolexes I'd bought on holiday in Turkey. The detective who found them got excited at first until a wiser sergeant said they were worthless fakes.'

His passport has been confiscated. He had offered to be tagged until his trial, report twice daily to the local police station and with the help of family and friends had put up £15,000 in bail. To no avail.

'I know I did wrong. I admit that. But I have not been in trouble with the police since twenty-seven years ago. I have worked hard. I haven't moved house. I lead a stable life. I don't know why I am here', he said miserably as he waited to see his wife, a neat, good-looking blonde lady.

'I am ready for a sentence. Murderers and violent criminals are granted bail, why not me?'

I have no answer but again feel that the Old Bailey and Belmarsh are like being on the *Titanic* in an era of space travel. Surely modern surveillance technology can tag or chip someone who is waiting for a trial where he will plead guilty, without all the dehumanising treatment dished out in Belmarsh?

The prisoners' visiting room is a large lecture hall with a low soft seat for me and a three-seat low sofa for my two children and Vicky. I am searched and then sit waiting in my yellow bib to further highlight that I have to be marked out as separate from all decent citizens.

In they come with the biggest hug from Laura, who feels my absence the most strongly as she lives and works in Toronto. They have all queued up to be finger-printed. The sniffer dog, there to look for smuggled drugs, licked Vicky's hands. I guess electronic finger printing is no big deal today compared to the old ink roller system but it seems hard for children's finger prints to enter national databases forever on record.

A tea counter provides drinks and snacks and sweets but I am only hungry for their presence. They give me news of scores of friends who have phoned, sent texts and emails as well as friendly supportive articles by Michael White, Chris Mullin and John Walsh – thanks, comrades.

They listen goggle-eyed to stories of murderers and the employment of unpleasant, deliberately designed language of humiliation used by one or two guards. They cannot understand why I have not gone to an open prison like all the other politician prisoners.

'What? No word from the Governor on a transfer?' asks Vicky and then sweetly adds, 'Well, believe me, Belmarsh will be a lot more interesting than the prisoners you'll meet in open prison.'

Laura has clearly been doing some research. 'Dad, they've closed four prisons in Sweden, as they can keep people under control better by letting them live at home. But I guess that nasty Judge Meanie had it in for you. They all think you're Ian McShane here. The judge went on and on about how your name is spelt. But I never use a capital S, Uncle Martin spells it differently. I couldn't believe such nonsense from a supposedly intelligent man.'

Benjamin says the *Huffington Post* had an article: 'Denis MacShane. Tragic Hero.' *Merci*, Mehdi. So at any rate these two of my four children are finding the prison sentence to be pure Theatre of the Absurd. Their mixture of laughter and indignation cheers me up no end.

We chat about a talk I have to give in Quebec after the tag anklet comes off, which will give me a chance to see Laura in Toronto. I make Benjamin, off shortly on a university skiing trip, promise to wear the helmet I bought him.

The four of us try to work out how to accommodate all the editors and journalist friends as well as other friends who want to visit me in Belmarsh.

I guess it's not often they have a hardened criminal – me – to visit, and coming into Belmarsh will amuse dinner tables of the London intelligentsia and political chattering classes in the weeks ahead. Ian McEwan, an old friend, has sent a warm email, as apparently his nephew is also in Belmarsh, though how I could find out and make contact I have no idea.

We try to plan future visits but information in Belmarsh is the most preciously husbanded and guarded of all commodities. I have no idea when anyone can come. You are given no control over your life, so as to feel permanently at the mercy of the prison system.

There is a black guy beside us sitting by himself. His promised visit had not happened. We offer coffee and chocolate flake. He shakes his head sadly.

It is an easy, relaxing hour. I don't know what they think of their father sitting in his bright orange bib over dull tracksuit gear. The children have been au fait with my problem ever since the BNP sent in its complaint. They know how much time I spent travelling in Europe as part of my parliamentary work, how much time on the phone gassing in French or German, how many books and magazines I would bring back from each trip to pile up on chairs and tables as I tried to make sense of what was happening in Europe, since most of my fellow MPs just relied on what the Eurosceptic press told them.

In fact, I am sure I have been a crap father, as all that time spent on European affairs I could have spent being a better father.

There is no suggestion of reproach in their voices, just concern that their poor old papa will survive these surreal few weeks. They leave to pat the drugs dog on the head and get out of the stale air of Belmarsh, and I hand back my bib. Mel has been cheered up. 'The wife was really down to begin with. But she was great today. Really strong and positive.'

I am meeting more and more people accused of non-violent and minor crimes just decanted into Belmarsh on remand. I cannot begin to compute the cost in pay and overtime of all the officers who stand silently as I go by, or search me, or supervise my visit, or finger-print my children. I trust the sniffer dog gets better food than inmates and then there is the investment and running costs of a large visitor centre. Surely home detention is a more sensible alternative?

1645H I go back to my cell and put out my laundry, especially the sweaty clothes from my morning jogging. The warder refuses to let me put out my bag.

'It's only in the morning,' he says indifferently.

'Hang on. The notice over there says Tuesday and Thursday. I put out my laundry bag on Tuesday afternoon and it got done.'

'Morning only. I told you that at induction.'

He didn't and, although not telling a lie, is no longer able to know the truth. I turn away in disappointment at his cheap meanness and say, 'You wouldn't let me have a shower today and now you won't let me wash clothes.'

The guard is an ugly bully with thin turned-down lips snaps, 'I told you. You should have washed yesterday. You're in prison. You don't like it. Get used to it.'

I am getting used to it. The guard doesn't have a CB or QC after his name and doesn't wear a red dressing gown to work but at long last, after many decades, I am getting used to it.

1750H The cell doors open for dinner. There is a long queue on the first floor where we all have to go to leave the Spur and access any other part of the prison including the serving counter just outside the Spur's barrier of iron bars. The one exception is for exercise when the spur gate is opened and we don't have to traipse up and down stairs. I take my chance while the unpleasant guard's back is turned and dart into the shower for a quick wash. The water also takes time to move from cold to tepid. I don't want to miss dinner so a cold shower will have to do.

Julian is beside me in the food queue. 'You still here? Most of those who came in the same day before Christmas with you and me have already been moved. There's something wrong that they're not moving you to an open prison.'

I talk to Nathalie to get a full report on how the trip to France went and the state of the children's grandfather. Just good to hear a friendly voice. My phone credit is down to £6.27.

Another bizarre tale. A well-spoken British citizen of Indian descent, about forty I would guess, tells me his story. Ran is a university graduate who works, amongst other jobs, as an IT consultant for banks in the City. He had a regular contract with a minicab driver. The driver was found with a packet of cocaine in his car. This presumably was for delivery in the City whose denizens snort cocaine as casually as I drink Chablis.

Ran was arrested and charged with conspiracy. The police searched his house and took away his computers. There was no evidence of any cocaine or any transactions suggesting dealing. His bank statements corresponded to his stated earnings. He paid his taxes. The police say they observed him having a coffee with his driver and money changed hands. According to the police the value of the cocaine seized amounted to £350,000. As Ran noted drily, 'That's quite a lot of notes to stuff into your jeans' back pocket.'

The driver has confirmed that his IT consultant had nothing to do with any crime and was blameless. Nevertheless the police and CPS are seeking to press conspiracy charges. Ran has already been held in Belmarsh. He has offered to put up £150,000 bail which the police and

CPS oppose. Naturally, the judge sided with the police, and the taxpayer has been paying £1,000 a week (costs are higher in Belmarsh, with an average per prisoner annual cost of £65,000) to keep Ran in prison. Once again I enter my mental proviso that Ran, who struck me as being on the level, may well be a cunning liar and the purveyor of all the cocaine the City hedgies, traders, and bankers need to consume in order to carry out their vital work in the national economic interest.

Am I allowed to believe that the police, CPS and judges just throw people into a hellhole prison like Belmarsh in the hope that they will break down and sign anything to move on? No, these are unworthy thoughts. Our police are the finest in the world. The CPS is a byword for meticulous unbiased charging decisions. Our judges are fair and all men of depersonalised unprejudiced integrity.

Another prisoner hanging around after the meal asks if I took any interest in prisons and justice when an MP. I confess No. He asks who might be an MP that could take an interest in what happens to prisoners. I am tempted to say Keith Vaz, high-profile chair of the Home Office Select Committee. Should I tell my Keith stories? No, it's in the past and Keith is Keith. I cannot think of the name of the chair of the Justice Ministry Select Committee. In fact I cannot think of a single high-profile forceful MP who I associate with reforming what I am finding out to be a profoundly rotten, useless, stupid justice and custodial system.

I am happy to accept what has happened to me. I did wrong. It was my fault. I could have behaved differently and I accept the punishment meted out. But I will be out shortly. Meanwhile, other men, whose guilt I am not sure I believe in, are thrown in here. Their families, homes, income and status are turned over. Perhaps the police will find no evidence and the CPS will drop charges. Perhaps – unlikely, but perhaps – a judge will not roll over for the prosecutor. Perhaps a jury will not convict. But nothing will ever return to them the lost seconds, minutes, hours, days, weeks, months of rotting in Belmarsh.

1823H Lock-up. I wash out a sweatshirt and T-shirt the screw refused to let me send to the laundry. On the TV News David Cameron is proposing 100-year sentences. Goodness me! Why so liberal and soft? Why not 200- or even 1,000-year prison sentences, to show the world that Britain isn't a soft touch with criminals. Thus the state of my country, New Year 2014.

1915H Thank god for *Channel 4 News*. It is streets ahead of the BBC News shows. Matt Frei challenges a smug UKIP spokesman, Patrick O'Flynn, who works for Richard Desmond, the newspaper and porn magazine mogul. 'Why is it OK for 400,000 Brits to take advantage of Spanish healthcare but wrong for a few hundred Romanians to use our hospitals if they fall ill? Why is there no press campaign against Brits in Spain compared to the British press hostility to Europeans here?'

The UKIP man who I vaguely recall as a puffy, cheery right-wing political reporter [Paddy O'Flynn was Chief Political Commentator for the *Daily Express* before becoming UKIP's Director of Communications] in the Commons splutters that the new EU entrants are poorer than Britain. So was Ireland, Spain or Greece when they entered the EU. I think I'd rather stay in Belmarsh than re-enter a Britain where the poisonous xenophobia and corrupt misogyny of UKIP MEPs is treated as serious politics by the BBC and *The Guardian*.

I wanted to watch the BBC2 documentary on the wartime convoy, *PQ 17*, as my uncle, Neil MacShane, was killed as a sailor while on convoys to wartime Russia. Then I saw it was presented by the unpleasant and often blatantly racist Jeremy Clarkson and the thought of his crude tabloid reflexes surfing over the memories of those brave sailors made me unable to watch the programme.

FRIDAY 3 JANUARY 2014

@thevoice of sense: An official award for Guido from a grateful nation and a lengthy prison sentence for MacShane.

@gramma: 'Most would love to see him hung, drawn and quartered.'

0810H Another good night's sleep. This no booze, final meal by five o'clock regime is working well.

Does the North Face pay the BBC for product placement? Every single BBC *Breakfast* TV report seems to be promoting the American outdoor clothing firm. Surely there is a British anorak company that is just as good, so that BBC reporters can fly the flag?

I start to do my cell stretching and get down on the floor to work my legs when the shout goes out: 'Exercise!' I had sliced the remainder of half a banana very thin to go into my cornflakes but there's no time to eat before I have to go outside.

The same pat-down search routine, which just adds a few minutes as we wait in turn to be beckoned forward for the back and front hand rub on our outer garments.

I do a little jogging before settling down with the symposium. When Cliff gave me the second batch of stamped envelopes he sent a little note in one of them saying, 'Yes, Minister! Your stamps and envelopes. 3 x 1st, 3 x 2nd. See you soon. Keep ya chin up! Your friend, Cliff.'

I asked one of my children to Google him and apparently he is one of England's most notorious gangsters; he was on Scotland Yard's most wanted list after some spectacular security van robberies, escapes from detention, years on the Costa del Crime and even some unclear connection to nobbling the jury in the famous Ernest Saunders case, when the boss of Guinness got his sentence for insider dealing reduced by claiming he had Alzheimers – an idea put to him by his fellow inmate Gerald Ronson, who I later got to know because of his immense contribution to combatting anti-Semitism.

Anyway, the Cliff I know is a gentleman, more Michael Caine than Ronnie Kray. He keeps insisting he has never used violence, lifted his hand against anyone or touched a weapon.

So, since he addressed me with 'Yes, Minister', I breeze up and call him 'Sir Humphrey'. He looks at me sadly and says, 'You know, we've all been talking about you and we all agree you shouldn't be here.'

Thanks, Sir H, but I am really getting far more out of this Belmarsh experience than I would ever have imagined. If I'm not careful I will begin to look on Judge Sweeney as a friend.

Instead, the symposium discusses the ethics of the criminal class, the profits of crime and the difference between attempted murder and grievous bodily harm. Mumble and Mole are awaiting a visit from a friend who has just agreed to pay £650,000 to SOCA – the Serious Organised Crime Agency – to get them off his back.

'They shut down all his accounts, seized his house with its big swimming pool inside like a Roman villa, but in the end they couldn't prove anything so they are just taking his money.'

I thought back to the repayment I made years ago of the money I had actually expended. It made no difference to the obsession of those who wanted my skin. The symposium agreed that it made more sense for the police to get all, most or even some of the money out of their targets and call it quits. Well, they would, wouldn't they.

In the case of their friend who had swollen the state's coffers to the tune of £650,000, 'Of course he had been up to this and that but he's doing £7,000 a week off his investments so he's OK.'

Legitimate earnings of £7,000 a week helps keep you on the straight and narrow. But the ethics of criminals keeping in touch with each other and lending support is important.

'It's the old school rules, really,' explains Mumble. 'You never go and visit the wife of someone inside without taking your wife or a woman with you. You have to be very careful. Any woman whose old man is doing time is vulnerable so you should never see her alone, even if you're an old friend. Mind you, them's the old rules and maybe they'll go out with us.'

I am tempted to discuss the history of the concept of the chaperone, which certainly has never been of revelance in my lifetime. Still, it's rather touching that this concept of never being alone with a woman whose man was not in the room, which dates back to the Middle Ages, is upheld today by long-service professional criminals.

Mole, by now a valuable contributing member of the symposium, told us, or rather me, why he was here. 'I was trying to sort out a problem, a row between two groups. I arranged a discussion meeting in a house. But four guys turned up, all carrying. I could see the guns. I said, "Are you mad? You gonna kill me?"'

'Well, one got out his gun so I got mine out faster and shot him. It was pure self-defence. If I hadn't moved first, it was four against one and I would have been killed.'

'Did you kill him?' I asked.

'Nah, I hit his shoulder. He was out of hospital in two weeks and now he's over there.' Mole pointed in the direction of the ultra high security block, the prison within the prison at Belmarsh.

'He's in there for kidnapping. Not a nice geezer.'

Mole explained that if you shot someone below the belt the charge was GBH – grievous bodily harm. Above the waist even if it was only a slight flesh wound it is attempted murder. 'I'll plead self-defence because it's true,' he said, but without much hope that a judge would take any notice given he had a gun-using criminal in the dock.

Later I was chatting to Mel, who said he reckoned there were professional criminals in Belmarsh and other prisons for whom doing a stretch was just part of the *cursus honorum*, as the Romans called the various stages of the career of an important person. 'If you've got £30 million stashed away, what does it matter to spend a few years? You keep your head down, read the papers, watch television, lose weight and then off you go to enjoy your money.'

So far I haven't met a single banker in prison. Yet our bankers have been shown to be stealing money through fake insurance scams and, in the case of RBS, trading insolvently, in the sense that the bank did not have assets and income in order to cover its obligations. If a corner shop behaves like that, the manager has committed a crime and may go to prison. If a mother on benefits keeps claiming tax credits and other means-tested benefits while earning a little money while stuffing envelopes, judges send her to prison.

They talked about Ross Kemp, the *EastEnders* hard man who married Rebekah Wade, now Brooks, the editor of the *News of the World* and *The Sun*. 'He did some TV series about the SAS and came down wanting to talk to us and meet some ex-Army men.'

I told them how I was called up last January while skiing at St Moritz by a detective from the Met. He asked me if I was prepared to be a prosecution witness in the trial they were planning against Rebekah Brooks.

'You see, Dr MacShane, your phone was hacked by News International when you were a senior minister engaged on an important confidential government business,' explained the detective. 'You're in a very different category from all those celebrities and film stars who were hacked just to get a cheap headline about who they were sleeping with. You're viewed in Scotland Yard as a much more serious witness.'

It was a hilarious moment under the bright blue Alpine sky. One bit of Scotland Yard had been told by the CPS under political pressure to find new evidence to justify charging me – an unsuccessful mission as it turned out – while here was another unit wanting me to be a star witness in the forthcoming 'trial of the century' as the proceedings against Rebekah Brooks and Andy Coulson, David Cameron's closest media adviser in Downing Street, were dubbed by their fellow national newspaper editors.

I replied cheerfully to the detective, 'Of course, officer, you know me. There's no greater pleasure in my life than helping the wonderful Metropolitan Police.'

When I reported this conversation to my legal team, my solicitor, one of the most senior and respected in the business on white-collar crime, reacted furiously. 'No, no, you never help Scotland Yard. They are utterly cynical and have no interest in the truth. Never, ever trust them.'

I was shocked at his vehemence. At the time I was placing my faith in the 2010–12 Scotland Yard investigation, which ended in no action. My lawyer knew better. The police and CPS can do what they like, irrespective of truth and evidence. They can destroy Andrew Mitchell or the Deputy Speaker of the Commons, Nigel Evans, or send me to prison. I am glad not to be involved in the Rebekah Brooks trial, and anyone who has had any dealings with tabloid editors knows that the idea that she alone indulged in dubious practices to get stories is simply laughable.

The symposium session ended with a warning from Cliff. 'You'll be off soon to an open prison. Be careful there. You've made friends here. People like you. They think it's quite out of order that you're in Belmarsh. It'll be a different type of person in a Cat D prison. Even if you've done serious time they are on the way out. They can phone who they want and see their mates. Don't talk to them. They'll all want to sell some stupid story to the tabloids. All the screws earn money that way. Anything you say can be twisted. They sneak in cameras and take pictures of you. The press will love any story about you. So just be very, very careful who you talk to and what you say.'

Cliff sounded like my friend Michael White of *The Guardian*, a Westminster political editor who everyone trusted because everyone knew he cared about the truth. Poor Michael was always telling me to shut up, to be more serious, to stop making people laugh if I wanted to get on in politics. He was right. But I am me. I watched ambition turn decent men and women into speak-your-weight machines, cauterising wit and thought as they scratched and clawed their way up the greasy pole.

This time I shall try to heed Cliff's advice and guard my counsel if ever I get as far as an open prison. But when will that be? Here I am on the twelfth day of my prison Christmas. My fellow MP convicts spent just a few days in a 'hard' prison before leaving for a soft one. I am still in my unwashed clothes. The loo pongs.

My towel is unwashed so, as the route into the exercise yard goes through the laundry, I watch to make sure a screw isn't looking when exercise ends and stuff a fresh towel under my sweatshirt. We are not searched on the way back into the spur so I can get it into my room or, if he did notice, the screw, one of the humane ones, couldn't care about my minor prison pilfering.

A plastic envelope is lying on the floor of my cell. It tells me that my canteen order has been processed. I have £5 phone credit but the tomato ketchup I had ordered has not been delivered because of 'insuffcent funds.' Yet it stated quite clearly that I had £5.62 to spend under the new Grayling rules. £5 went on phone credit. Tomato ketchup cost 60p. But my condiment, so much desired to add taste, any taste, to the bland food, has not arrived. At some stage in the future I shall see salt, pepper, garlic, vinaigrette, chilli, mustard and brown sauce. But not in Belmarsh.

0843H Locked back in my cell. As I am making my cup of tea, a folded-over stapled piece of paper is pushed under the door. It is addressed to

'Dennis MacShane' so one bit of the prison has stopped calling me Ian even if they cannot spell my name correctly. The paper is titled rather grandly 'Prisoner Movement Slip – HMP Belmarsh'. My heart leaps! Am I finally getting out of here? Then I read the small print. It was the confirmation of my appointment yesterday for the Hep B injection.

I see through the door observation slit that one of the more humane guards is going by. I knock hard on the door to try and attract his attention. There is a call button next to the sink but it is to be used only in a real emergency – death, for example – and we were told never to use it on pain of some punishment like being sent to the isolation block.

The nice guard opens the door. I show him the 'Prisoner Movement Slip'. He looks at it. 'That's dated yesterday. They probably forgot to give it to you.' I ask if he knows anything about my move out of Belmarsh. He shrugs and shakes his head as he relocks the door.

0912H The cell door opens. Not with movement news but for a monthly Catholic service on Fridays. Again I grab it – anything to get out of the cell and the spur, even if my daily ration of fresh air is over. 'It's only time', someone has scrawled on the noticeboard but time is going by so slowly. I soak some dried bread in water and push it through the window bars and grill for the birds outside. A search and a check that I am on a list to go to the religious centre. I am back listed as 'I. McShane' I am glad to note.

We are carefully counted in. Twenty-two of us. A guard checks us against a list and then, as in previous services, retires to the back of the chapel to read a paperback. It is the first time I have been searched going into a religious service. Outside priests and ministers are desperate to get anyone to attend church. Here, we are searched back and front in case we might be taking anything into a house of God except a desire to be there.

I am sat beside a prisoner apparently wearing a tracksuit from Ikea in garish yellow and blue Swedish national colours. His trackie bottoms have vertical blue and yellow stripes and his sweatshirt has blue and yellow squares like a variation of the Harlequins rugby shirt. He says he has to wear this colourful gear because he once ran away from an open prison. He seems to be able to say thank you in as many European languages as I can.

After absconding from his open prison he ran away to the continent. His crime wasn't heavy – low profit burglaries – but life on the run wasn't fun. He returned to his native Leeds, met a woman, and settled down, still hiding from the law. The inevitable happened and someone told the police, so here he is in his striking Swedish colours on the basis, I assume, that if by some freakish miracle he could escape from Belmarsh he would stand out in the dull landscape of south east London.

'In the end it's not worth it. You worry. You never sleep. You are always looking over your shoulder. I feel better now. I'm sleeping more than in years. I'll do my time and make a new start,' my Harlequin friend told me.

I am absurdly jealous of Mel, who tells me he has another visit today and a double visit tomorrow. I am keen to see my closest, oldest friend before he returns to Pittsburgh this weekend, where he is a professor of English. But there is no help to make contact and the entire Belmarsh regime is based on humiliation and crushing of the human spirit.

It is a smaller service with a table doing office for an altar. Asil Nadir and I read lessons. After the short mass, a prisoner comes up and asks, 'You an actor or something? You know how to speak, not read, look us in the eye, make it sound convincing.'

Mass ends with a cup of coffee and a chance to talk. I am at the end of my second week and have not been allowed to get close to a gym or see the inside of the library, run by Greenwich Council. Short conversations at exercise time or waiting in the queue to phone is the most human contact I am allowed.

So ten minutes of talk with a cup of Nescafé with Fr Edward and Asil Nadir is bliss. Asil claims that he persuaded the Turkish Cypriot leader's longtime leader, the Inner Temple lawyer, Rauf Denktash, to stand down to pave the way for a settlement on the divided island.

He invites me to visit him in Turkey or northern Cyprus and it's true that the Cypriots, Greeks or Turks remain the most hospitable people in the Mediterranean. But like Serbs and Bosniaks, or Unionists and Nationalists in Ulster, they do not know how to rise above their political leaders, who always stoke up identity hate rather than communal compromise.

He says he could have stayed in northern Cyprus or Turkey forever but believed he had put together enough evidence to demonstrate the corruption he believes was involved in his original prosecution.

'So I came back confident that English law would give me a fair hearing. But ministers have signed thirty-six Public Interest Immunity Certificates' (a mechanism used by government to stop documents relating to a criminal case or a coroners' inquiry being made available to courts. They are very rarely used as, in effect, it means the state denying evidence that can help a court come to a correct decision. In my eight years at the Foreign Office I cannot recall a PIIC being signed. That today's ministers have signed thirty-six in the single case of Asil Nadir, which goes back thirty years, is very unusual) 'so I don't know where I am.'

I don't know the details of his case but if current government ministers have really signed thirty-six PIICs – which is a massive state interference by the executive in supposedly separate administration of justice – then they must be very worried about what would be revealed going back to Nadir's financing of the Conservative Party and allegations of corruption involving police and court officials.

As we talk, I say I am getting emails coming in.

'I've had none for two months. There seems to be a block on all my mail.' Nadir is a controversial figure. But is he getting justice?

It is a working day for the courts and they are spewing out the usual conveyor belt of victims into Belmarsh and some of them have arrived at this service. There is one young man who is waiting to go back to court in a week. His story is that his partner had serious mental illness problems, including major schizophrenia fits. He tells me he tried to help her, calm her, watch out for when she would leave full normality behind and enter the disturbed world of those whose mental stability can instantly disintegrate without warning.

'In the end it got so bad that when she started screaming and kicking out I had to restrain her. She didn't like that and, to get her own back, she called the police and said it was domestic violence, even if I was more marked from her scratching and biting than she was.

'The cops came and sussed what happened but they still took me in and have charged me with common assault, the lowest of the domestic violence charges. What they and she don't know is that I recorded the entire scene on my phone and if I can show that to court next week I don't think they'll think there is a case to answer.'

Domestic violence again. He does have scratch marks on his face and obviously I cannot tell how much he is saying is true, though he is fluent in his story and confident that the recording will vindicate him.

1102H Lunch is another tasteless soft white bread 'baguette' with two half-inch wide slices of corned beef. No mustard, no pickle, no nothing to give it taste. Bang-up.

1600H Locked away until four o'clock when the cell doors open for Association. I dart out for a shower. The hot water is off and washing hair in cold water is less than fun. Outside there has been flooding, gales and too much rain but in Belmarsh I could be in outer space. I try and call Vicky but, just as she says 'Hi!' in the voice that does so much for my morale, the prison phone cuts me off. I have to wait another ten minutes to make the next call. When I dial the number a prison warder, a woman, shouts at me to go and get my food. I am clutching my plate between my knees as I try to call Vicky after the Belmarsh BT system broke the communication. Do I phone and go without food for the rest of the day or do I make the call as I expect Vicky will be waiting for me to make a second call after the first one was cut off?

The woman warder keeps snapping about getting food so I put down the phone and go sadly up the metal stairs, angry and depressed. As I get to the landing, the woman guard is standing arms akimbo glaring at me.

I lose it. 'So that's it,' I say between clenched lips. 'Either I talk to my close ones or I starve.' It is a stupid, pointless remark but I am at the end of my tether. She begins shouting at me, almost out of control, and I walk on down the landing as I do not want to miss my food.

'MacShane,' she screams. 'Turn round when I'm talking to you.' I do so. She begins a rant. I look her full in the face as I always do with bullies and say, 'I'm sorry, Miss, but you told me I had to stop using the phone after I was cut off or go without food. That's not fair.'

She glowers at me as if auditioning for a role as a warder in Ravensbrück, the Second World War Nazi prison camp for women. 'You've had your Association. Now you have to get your food,' she snarls back at me, utterly missing the point about the broken phone system and that the warders have allowed so little time to make calls today and I had taken the first and only opportunity I had.

I go and get my fish and chips and at least eatable mushy peas and put them in my cell to congeal while I desperately wait in a new queue to call my eldest daughter, Sarah. I want to talk to Vicky and to Colin before he leaves for Pittsburgh but if you place a call and it goes to voicemail you have to wait ten minutes even if there's no phone queue.

Thankfully, Sarah is there but frustrated she has received none of the Visitors' Order forms I have sent her. After the Censors returned one Visitors' Order form because I had written on the back of it, I gave another form to a warder, who promised to send it out. But nothing has arrived and poor Sarah is almost crying in frustration at not being able to visit her father. One of the nicer guards is counting down to bang-up. 'Two minutes.' Then 'Thirty seconds,' so I have to put down the phone with nothing resolved.

For the first time I go back to my cell in sheer misery after the encounter with the bullying woman guard. Outside my cell on the wall is a printed notice about 'Anti-bulling Policy' in Belmarsh. I think Governor Wragg means anti-bullying, but if you cannot spell, the chances of having good policy are slim.

1633H Bang-up. I eat my cold fish and chips and for the first time am really quite down. Suddenly the door is flung open and in comes the nice warder with the Ravensbrück bully.

'MacShane, I am making a negative report about you to the Governor.' God, what a pathetic creep. I just don't care. Minor self-important bureaucrats – the John Lyon CBs of the world and bullies like the bulky woman who seems to spread out to fill the cell, with the nice screw looking shamefaced by her side – have been the bane of my life. Perhaps being on the Governor's report list may means I finally get to meet this shadowy figure.

'Left, right, left, right, halt. About turn. Hat off! MacShane, sir. On report for wanting to talk to his children.'

'Now, then MacShane, here in the Wellington School CCF we can't have that kind of behaviour. What would England be if chaps with foreign backgrounds like you imported funny continental habits, eh?'

I snap out of my reverie as the door is slammed shut. Fuck them all. The evening is passed writing out my journal. I have a selection of forms I use the back of to write my daily log. This is a Belmarsh Gymnasium Application. It allows me to choose between:

- Basketball
- Cricket
- Circuit
- Fitness
- Over-fifties
- Enhanced
- Volleyball
- Spinning
- Astro Football

It sounds a wonderful range of sport but I have no evidence that any one of them happens and I cannot see any outdoor area where cricket or volleyball might be possible. I filled in the gym form two weeks ago, opting for the over-fifties slot, but so far haven't seen a weight or running track.

Another form is the Visitors' Order. This allows a visit by three adults and three children under age ten. The form demands name and address of visitors and date or birth. Oh dear. I have no idea of the dates of birth of the many friends who want to visit. The visitor has to bring ID like a passport and there is a stern list of banned clothing for visitors:

'Designer jeans which contain tears or rips.'

'Short skirts.'

'Big belt buckles.'

'Watches.'

'Any uniform that resembles a prison officer's uniform.'

Given that the latter consists of a white shirt, dark trousers and black shoes I am not sure how any visitors are allowed in.

There is an 'Application for free monthly five-minute phone call for foreign national status prisoners'. This reads: 'PSO 4400 states "Foreign national prisoners or those with close family abroad will be permitted a five minute phone call at the prisons expense where the prisoner has had NO domestic/social visits in the preceding month."' I wonder if I could get a free call to Laura in Canada or Emilie in Spain, though I did have a visit yesterday, so would not be eligible.

I feel nervous at using the back of all these forms – sixty pages so far – but what can I do if under the new Grayling regime I cannot have the A4 pads I specifically brought into prison with me? To be fair, the screws seem quite uninterested as I help myself to sheaves of forms, although a cursory glance at my desk will see the written pages mounting up.

1912H Wash out some underwear. My final food of the day – a cup of tea and a biscuit. Outside, I usually try and wait until seven-thirty or eight before a glass of wine as a reward for a day's work as I settle down to cook and talk to whoever's around. Belmarsh is a reversion to childhood, where the evening meal was prepared by my mother on return from school and eaten at four-thirty or five. A biscuit and hot milk later on in the evening. Perhaps I have got Belmarsh wrong. It is not out to dehumanise but to infantilise, and the warders are just bossy governesses without a Mary Poppins in sight.

After my daily write-up I watch TV. I am seriously longing for the books confiscated twelve days ago. Watching the pap that is Friday evening television is torture. A few pages of Elizabeth George before lights out at 11.30.

SATURDAY 4 JANUARY 2014

Prisons are built with stones of Law, brothels with bricks of religion.

– William Blake

0820H Another long sleep after the usual middle-of-the-night What Am I Doing Here auto-interrogation. The problem is I can only interrogate myself and all the other questions I want to ask – why was I never interviewed in the years-long disciplinary process? Why did a High Court judge get simple facts wrong? Or why did Keir Starmer reverse his decision to close the case file? – will never be answered. What you don't know shouldn't keep you awake. What you cannot know does.

Normally if I cannot sleep I put on the light and read. But my books are still confiscated. Has Governor Wragg got a secret passion for reading modern French novelists? Is he fascinated by the uprisings in Warsaw in 1943 and 1944? Has he quietly taken away my books for his own pleasure? I don't mind. I have given away nearly all the books I have bought over the years. I want to see them in circulation, not lined up in dusty rows on my bookshelves. Can Chris Grayling seriously believe he will improve the chances of prisoners leaving prison as better putative citizens by limiting their chance to read?

This is the first two weeks in nearly half a century without my buying a book, opening its pages, smelling the binding, feeling the texture of the paper, or enjoying the cover. I turn down corners to mark pages and scribble in margins or make notes in front covers. Sacrilege to some bookies; for me a book is just a tool and here I am without one. Each country has different ways of producing books. The English hardback with its neatly cut pages. The American softback with heavier absorbent paper and rough edges to its pages. French books are never hardback, as the assumption lingers that you get your books bound yourself with your initials on the spine. German books have footnotes and comprehensive indexes, unknown in French publishing.

By every bed I have slept in, on every kitchen table, in every loo of a house or flat I have owned, in every room, in every brief- or suitcase I go out with, there have always been books, books, books. I don't Kindle, and I cannot get on a bus, a train or plane without a novel and a non-fiction book. I wonder what Belmarsh Prison Library is like and if I will get to see it.

After the unpleasant experience with the woman screw who got her prison officer diploma from the Ravensbrück Academy for training female prison guards I meet a friendly screw who sees me looking with longing at the four or five books stuck between bars. 'Help yourself,' he said when I glanced at the books last night. There is nothing I want to read. An old Jeffrey Archer, which I am pretty sure I read years ago. I'd love to read his *Prison Diary*. Like a Gideon's Bible in hotel rooms, maybe it should be placed in every Belmarsh cell.

I've asked friends to Amazon me the masterworks of prison literature but Grayling's anti-books policy may not allow them to arrive.

I do ski calisthenics on my cell floor. I have given up worrying about the dirt. I just need to move my muscles, myself. It is raining hard so there will be no exercise, no fresh air. Instead, the screws open the door to allow some association. It is Saturday so perhaps the bang-up norms are relaxed a little.

I phone Vicky after yesterday's aborted effort thanks to Frau Ravensbrück. She is surprised that I have no information of any sort on a transfer.

I cannot face cornflakes with their chemical, sugary additives, so just munch an apple for breakfast, carefully cutting out the rotten bits. A sheet is shoved under my cell door. It lists all the things I can buy from a central depot in Long Lartin, which despatches what prisoners order all over the country. It is called 'Canteen' – a name which holds from the time when each prison did indeed have its own canteen where prisoners could use their weekly earnings to buy extras.

This friendly local service, tailored to each prison's needs, was centralised as part of some outsourcing policy. Now I have to look at an endless list in what appears to be six-point print, so small that even with glasses I can hardly read it. The amount you have to spend that week is at the top of the page. I have £12.31. I haven't earned any money as I have not yet been allocated or allowed to work or go to any education classes, which are the two main activities rewarded with payments. I did hand over more than £300 in notes when I arrived and I assume this £12.31 is what I am allowed from my kitty to spend on my heart's desire.

There are dozens of different types of biscuit I can order and twelve types of card: I Love You, Mum, I Love You, Nan, Son, Dad etc. At the end there is a 'special offer' of Valentine cards but I hope I am out by the time that amorous day arrives.

I put most of my money into phone credits. I order some Heinz chilli sauce and I hope it turns up, as the *sans* taste blandness of the food is depressing. I spot a Mr Patak's lime pickle but until I know these goodies will actually arrive I am not sure if I dare order it.

I scan the miniature print of the single-spaced list of three columns over two sides of the same pink sheet but can see nothing remotely healthy to eat – nothing fresh, no fibre, above all, no fruit.

On the third floor landing there is a bedding change. I take up my sheets to get fresh ones. The last bed-sheet had little brown spots on it as if sprayed with blood droplets but today's washed sheet looks newer. A prisoner-worker stands up with a large industrial container of diluted washing up liquid. But I have no Fairy Liquid Bottle, no other container to pour it into. I wonder, if I cup a hand, whether some would remain as I went downstairs. But into what would I pour it in my cell?

I will have to keep washing the plastic plate and bowl, with their greasy residue of food cooked in cheap oil or glutinous sauces, under the tap, or boil a kettle and pour boiling water over the dirty dish and cup. Come to think of it, the most dangerous weapon I have in the cell is a small, half-size electric kettle such as can be found in cheaper hotel rooms, but scalding water can be as nasty as any blade if you want to hurt and damage someone. I pour boiling water into my loo but the browned porcelain just says to me, 'You're in prison, get used to it.'

A shower, but this time the water never gets above cool to tepid. This pleases the black flies who seem more numerous than a week ago. I talk to Sarah, who is upset that the last time she saw her father was in a past year when I was Sweenied to Belmarsh. I sent her a Visitors' Order form but it was sent back to me. So I sent another one. I also gave one to the guard on Thursday. The post does not seem to work.

Before Christmas, Vicky sent me a letter and stamps, including those needed to write to friends in Europe (I hope the BNP or UKIP don't know I am in communication with Europe) but they have not yet arrived. No. 3 daughter, Emilie, who is spending a year in Córdoba as part of her university course, has yet to visit me.

On the TV news I watch a minister called Norman.[2] At least I think he is called Norman. He is a Liberal Democrat. Quite a lot of them are called Norman but I forget which is which. He is saying the government will launch a £25 million programme to try and bring more mental illness awareness to police stations and courts. I wish him well, even if this sounds like a New Year government spin announcement at a time when there is no news.

Yet, unless a psychiatrist has the power to say to the police or to the Sweeneys on the bench, 'This person is mentally unstable and should not be charged and sent to Belmarsh', nothing will happen. Which of us is not disturbed, distressed, not in control of his or her faculties at some stage? The government is cutting care, cutting help for the most vulnerable, booting the poor out of social housing if they have a tiny spare bedroom to house a carer.

For many of my former poor constituents racked by no or low income, broken marriages, limited education, multiple children by different fathers, alcoholism, no family or friendship networks, drug addiction,

2   Norman Baker is actually a Home Office minister. Jeremy Wright, a Conservative, is Prisons Minister at the Ministry of Justice.

disability and prey to all the fears and worries that burn the mind, there is little hope or help in today's Britain. Two of my closest friends have siblings who have spent their lives in varying degrees of mental illness.

The police arrive at the scene of a fight or dispute involving violence to property or person. Their first reaction is to arrest, detain, charge, tick the box to meet a target, and move on to the next problem in the community. The judges are obsessed with sending people to prison. In Belmarsh I hear the screams and shouts and bodies crashing into metal doors of people who are clearly in severe mental trouble. But a judge has sent them to prison and a prison governor, let alone an unqualified prison warder, cannot heal society's mentally walking wounded.

The minister, I am sure, is a decent chap and means well. At least he is not Chris Grayling. Before his interview on TV he will have been given a well-written report with bullet points on the first page to explain why this is an important initiative. Twenty-five million sounds a lot but it will be spread over nearly 100 crown courts, several hundred magistrates courts and 2,000 police stations, to make sure that people with mental disabilities are not conveyor belted through the police-judge-prison system and instead are given appropriate treatment. His big money announcement will amount to little more than a few posters, a training course and money for the contractors and evaluators who will report back in twelve or twenty-four months' time.

It isn't until judges are made to understand that prison should be the last not first option and turn around public opinion to understand that police and prison cells are not where we put the troubled minds of our divided, broken society, that progress will be made.

Benny is out of his wheelchair with towel and soap and waits for a shower. They require a punch on a button every few seconds to keep the water coming. Benny cannot manage that. So he has to wait for the one shower that has a continuous flow of water, but it seems occupied all the time by just one man. Since he is big, black and young, the old, frail, small, unwell Benny just has to wait and to hope bang-up won't be called before he is clean.

Ali from Iraq comes up to me again with his long sad face and shows me letters from a solicitor about the charges he faces after his face was smashed in by his Romanian tenants. He has to appear in court on Monday. I look at the letters. They are computer generated pro-forma letters and worthless. His solicitor has not been to see him. The police state that there is CCTV evidence but Ali insists there is no CCTV in his cheap, low-rent dwelling. One of the Romanians involved in the fracas did hold up a mobile camera to film the exchange. This man has disappeared and I wonder what evidence the police lawyers can have.

I tell Ali he has to present documents showing he has a legal contract to rent the house, that he was paying utility bills and council tax and he could show receipts from his tenants. Documents, documents, documents might help the judge move away from simply rubber-stamping the police arrest.

'But I only have all this paper in house. I go court Monday,' he wails mournfully. For heaven's sake I am not his solicitor, not his MP. Some lawyer will make money from legal aid out of Ali's case. I have written one letter for him. I write out some notes on the back of his solicitor's letter. They constitute a sort of 'To Whom It May Concern' memo on what Ali needs to do by way of evidence, and questions the police need to answer.

'Do I show this to judge?' he asks.

'No the judges are Conservatives and won't like a Labour guy telling them facts they prefer not to hear. It's for your solicitor and maybe he should ask for an adjournment so you can get all your documents together.'

Yet an adjournment is absurd. Ali should never have been sent to Belmarsh at such wasteful cost to the taxpayer. He is not going back to Baghdad to be killed. He can't do a runner. Why on earth is he here?

Ran also wants me to look at his case file and the police evidence. He says he was kept under observation for three months while doing his IT work in the City. A full police search of his house, the stall he has in a local market, his car and the house of his driver reveal no trace of drugs. The only evidence is Ran giving £180 to his driver – also here in Belmarsh – and the purchase of a pair of Ugg boots for his niece, which the police said was a handing over of a bag full of cocaine.

Again I cannot judge if he is telling all the truth but I promise to look over his papers. What does seem odd is the need to keep him in Belmarsh for week after week. If he is a criminal he has clearly cleaned his property, bank and so forth of any evidence. Why does the taxpayer have to fork out so much to keep him here?

He has been here some time and I moan about the Ravensbrück screw. Ran knows who she is. 'She was only doing a relief shift or two. She doesn't know anyone here. They all think they have to bully and treat you like shit even if some of the screws are OK. Be careful about complaining or writing about them. If you go anywhere else the prison officers' network will let your new place know that you are a problem prisoner.'

The two green-trouser prisoners who are spur trusties seem surprised I am still here. 'You should have been given a Category D by now and shipped out to an open prison,' says Darren. 'I'm astonished they've left you here so long. Normally they don't want people like you to see what a shit-hole Belmarsh is. Those books written by MPs on prison life are all about open prisons. You'll like it. You're pretty much your own boss. There's one near Aylesbury where you can visit Bicester Village, the shopping outlet place, at weekends. These are the places the papers write about when they say prison is too soft. The journalists ought to come here to see what it's like. Belmarsh is meant to be a flagship prison. But look at it. Everyone leaves here worse than when they came in. Bang-up for most of the day and nothing to do.'

Apparently I should have been categorised, had an interview about release date and being tagged. However this is Graylingstan and I have lost my name. But not yet my mind.

1100H Lunch. The best offers look like sausage and beans, which of course I haven't ordered. I watch endless James Oliver and Gordon Ramsay clones cooking up dishes which I can only dream of. They all seem to have enormous kitchens, chest-level cookers, a complete *batterie de cuisine* and the finest ingredients, fresh herbs, spices and obscure bottles to make their dishes comes to life. Who on earth do they think has hours or money to spend finding the best, freshest produce and *matériel* to learn from them? Still, I will have some tagged weeks ahead of me and since I like cooking and can sort of cook, I will see if I can do some TV chef dinners at home before off and away from this country which has sent me to Belmarsh.

I have ordered a baked potato and tuna but it isn't available and the servery prisoners give me some chicken confection instead. When I say I'll swap that for a spoon of baked beans or a sausage, everyone looks at me as if I were Oliver Twist asking for more. I take my chicken muck and return to be locked in the cell.

1430H Other prisoners are exercising in the yard as the rain has stopped. I hope my spur gets out today.

I examine the bed and mattress before I make up the bed with clean sheets. The metal bed is 6 feet (1.82m) long. That's OK for my 5 feet 9 inches (1.75m) height but Julian who is 6 feet 5 inches (1.95m) tall has real difficulties, he tells me. The mattress has odd white stains all over it like an abrasive powder rubbed into the hard plastic coating on it. There are some other white marks and, more ominously, some brown stains half-way down. Oh well, put the sheets on and try not to imagine where the dark stains came from.

1505H Out for exercise. It is really cold but under Grayling's rules my anorak was confiscated so unless I run hard, even with a double sweatshirt layer I shiver.

My symposium comrades of senior criminals don't seem to have been let out of their spur. Instead, I try and console Don who was in court yesterday. He was in Wormwood Scrubs with John Stonehouse, another Labour MP who did time, and spent his last decades in Thailand. He told me coyly last week he had worked all his life 'in chemicals'. It doesn't require a knowledge of Thai to work out what he was up to.

He is enthusiastic about his adopted country. 'Thailand exports more rice than any other country and supplies KFC with most of its chickens. Bangkok has got more skyscrapers than London,' he enthuses. He is articulating the shift of world economic activity to Asia and the rise of a giant Asian middle-class, whose consumption patterns have altered global economic relations.

Last week when we talked, he was confident there wasn't enough evidence to convict. After his court day yesterday he is not so sure. 'My lawyers are basically saying I should plead guilty and I'll get five to six years. Plead not guilty, risk a trial and it's seven to ten years if I am found guilty. So my wife is coming in next Wednesday and we'll make the decision together.'

He explains the arithmetic of sentences. 'Five years, of which I'll do half, and I've done six months since my arrest. That's what the system wants, as they like guilty pleas or risk ten years if the jury doesn't like me. We'll have a talk and decide. I just want to get back to Thailand. This is a country going nowhere. Britain is rubbish. I don't want to live here.'

Don is sixty-one and I expect has made a sort of living in and out of legality for years and perhaps got attracted to one lucrative deal which has resulted in his arrival in Belmarsh. It is his choice to cop a plea or risk a trial. Luckily, I never had to make that choice as every senior judge and QC told me that, as an MP, there was no chance of finding an unbiased jury given the media hate campaign against MPs and expenses. Of course I will be out soon but there is something not quite right about a justice system not based on truth, evidence, reason and facts, but on whether or not a jury trial can be held with the bribe of a lower sentence so the prosecution has to do no work.

1635H Last meal. I ask to make a one-minute phone call as the queue for food is long and will take a while to go down as prisoners are only allowed down to the serving counter six at a time. I would like to talk to Laura as she disappears back to Canada tomorrow and I know all the children will be together.

'No,' says a different woman warder.

Thanks, Governor Wragg. Your petty Saturday cruelties do have an efficiently depressing, demoralising effect. I suppose that's why they're there.

At least there's a doughnut and a banana so it's not that grim in Belmarsh on a Saturday night in January.

A guard shouts 'Put your shoes on!'

I can't work out who he is barking at. There is a Muslim in a long flowing robe and his feet in slippers but they look OK.

No, it's me. I am wearing black town shoes into which I have shoved my feet as I don't bother with shoes in the cell. The back of the shoe is bent down so my heel is showing. I put them on fully before going up the stairs.

'Elf 'n safety,' guffaws another guard at the pleasure of seeing me forced to bend down and obey a pointless order. 'We don't want you falling over, do we?'

After dinner a nurse takes my blood pressure. It is down to 137/85. My pulse is 81. Thanks, Belmarsh Health Club. I notice my fingernails are getting rather long. Nail clippers and emory boards are in my washbag, taken off me when I arrived two weeks ago. They are not yet claws or long Charlie Chan fingernails but I wonder what purpose is served at not being allowed to maintain normal levels of personal neatness and hygiene?

1647H Cell door locked for the next seventeen hours. I notice a graffiti I hadn't seen before, left by a previous occupant. 'To be a black man in the UK is very hard.' I wonder if there are any black judges or CPS senior prosecutors

SUNDAY 5 JANUARY 2014

But a punishment like forced labour or even imprisonment – mere loss of liberty – has never functioned without a certain additional element of punishment that certainly concerns the body itself: rationing of food, sexual deprivation, corporal punishment, solitary confinement … There remains, therefore, a trace of 'torture' in the modern mechanisms of criminal justice – a trace that has not been entirely overcome, but which is enveloped, increasingly, by the non-corporal nature of the penal system.

– Michel Foucault

0810H Wake up to strong winter sunshine. Good. We should get some fresh air today. I had no idea that prison life was so devoid of fresh air. I can open a window a few inches and the spur and corridors are large and airy. There is some kind of ventilating system which also provides heating, I think. I wonder, if there is a total all-out riot, whether they push some calming gas into cells.

I don't know who decided that television sets should be provided in each cell instead of fighting over which channel to watch in communal TV rooms – and in Belmarsh I cannot imagine where such common rooms might be as the whole object of the geography of this *cité carcéral*, to use Foucault's words, is to atomise, stop togetherness, and suppress community. All power to the screws is the watchword.

The downside is that a prisoner has had his TV on full blast since five o'clock this morning. Can't he be like the rest of the nation and wait obediently for Andy Marr to spend a full hour without getting a straight answer from anyone?

I sleep through the noise. I wake with a slight headache. On most previous mornings in my life I might have put that down to a glass or bottle too much the night before. Now what's the reason? Does a cheap doughnut give you a headache? I must ask for some aspirins. I brought some in with me but of course they were taken away a fortnight ago under the Grayling régime.

I do cell exercises based on my old ski ones. They are all based on strengthening legs, especially thighs, for off-piste skiing so I can manage a mini leg and thigh workout in the tiny space between my bed and the wall.

I crouch down in front of the TV screen and shave ahead of mass. According to the wording on its tube the green shaving slime is a gel, but it's not the kind of gel you work into a mousse to soften the bristles. Better than nothing, as I crouch down in front of the reflection of the TV screen and shave. Naturally, blobs of slime and bristles fall on the floor. I clean the mess up as best as I can with loo paper.

I watch Andy Marr. His wife, Jackie Ashley, wrote in her *Guardian* column in November 2012 that what I had done was 'unforgiveable'.

I assume she was taking her facts from the dishonest, partial *Guardian* news report, not written by one of their political journalists who knew the facts and background. I remember her line as it struck me as an oddly judgemental adjective to use about politics. All the more so, as Jackie has had to do some major forgiving in her recent life.

Andy has always been one of the best journalists, fair, penetrating and tough. David Cameron tells Marr that the state pension will go up in line with inflation, or in line with pay increase, or by 2.5 per cent, whichever is the greater. Prince Charles who has just started to draw his pension having reached sixty-five will be delighted. But it is so crudely a voter bribe. Pensioners turn out to vote at twice the rate of other age groups. Surely someone will see through the bribe. Probably not.

0920H My cell door has been opened while I was shaving. I went out and heard a woman warder tell a cheerful Irishman to stop whistling tunelessly.

'Why?' he asks.

'We have whistles in case of trouble and we cannot allow any confusion over the signal by allowing prisoners to whistle.'

I cannot believe my ears. I tell the Irishman to hum his tunes instead.

I go up the stairs to go to mass. I walk along the landing to the central control unit for all four spurs. There are two officers lounging at the desk discussing their pension, and I ask when the mass will begin.

'RC or C of E?'

'Catholic.'

'It was called from the middle landing.'

'When? I didn't hear it.'

'Go and see the nurse and get your ears tested,' says a screw with a smirk on his face. It would have been easy to let me go through, and the mass isn't due to start for a few minutes. But the pleasure of seeing a prisoner denied his rare chance to be out of his cell is their Sunday treat.

They know me by now and have seen me troop off to spend time with Fr Edward. It would have cost nothing to shout out my name, which they are keen enough to do for other appointments and they do for any prisoner going off the spur for whatever reason. No, that would have meant treating us as humans and the tabloids would have got very angry.

I go miserably downstairs. The pool table has no clatter of balls. I ask why.

'The screws say the cue is broke,' says one of the regular players.

'Punishment Sunday,' observes Benny in his wheelchair.

In the phone queue I see that my credit to make calls is down to £4. Where is all the money I brought in with me?

I talk to a Kosovan who is in Belmarsh with his son. He comes from Peja – Pec in Serbian. It is a beautiful city on the edge of a mountain range with a twinkling river running through its midst. It is home to the Serb patriarchy. His eyes gleam as I tell him I know his city well and enjoy its Peja beer, the best in the Balkans. Momentarily, I think of all the trips I made to Kosovo, the book I wrote in 2011 on its politics, and the articles and talks I have done on behalf of the people of Kosovo in their struggle to escape from the shadow of Slobadan Milosevic and his genocidal militias.

Again, I kick myself for taking such an interest in Europe, especially its awkward corners and contested nations. If only I had focused on prison reform, or maybe national forests inside the UK, I could have spent far more under the expenses regime than I did, without any sanction at all. MPs could claim what was called 'extended travel' to go anywhere inside the UK. If an MP wanted to become an expert on universities, or motor parts manufacturers, all trips would be reimbursed. MPs can speak anywhere in the country and get travel costs reimbursed if the subject they are speaking on is being discussed somewhere in Parliament – as most subjects are. My mistake was to assume my parliamentary interest in Europe meant my travel costs should be reimbursed – though I did it in a wrong way. Since Europe has landed me in Belmarsh, should I join UKIP?

The Kosovan is here with his son, a pale, slim, barely bearded boy. Again, it's woman trouble. His story is that his son married a Kosovan girl here in London. The marriage turned into a permanent row. The Canon of Lek, the centuries-old code by which Albanians were ruled, is, shall we say, pretty clear on the superior role and authority of the man and duty of the wife to obey, submit to and service her husband.

They lived in 2014 Lewisham not 1914 Pristina but, as he explains the row, I can see all sorts of Albanian DNAs acting out. The fight extended from the son and his wife to wider family clans as honour was at stake, and the screams escalated to 'I'll kill you, I'll kill you', some of which were recorded.

So the police were called and, again, what choice do they have? Honour killing is a Kurdish rather than a Kosovan speciality in Britain. I once heard Inayat Bunglawala, spokesman for the Muslim Council of Britain, at a public meeting where he refused to call for the outlawing of stoning to death of a woman accused by her husband of adultery because the MCB man said he couldn't go against the Prophet's teaching.

When you get this kind of reactionary nonsense about killing women from an educated British citizen, why should we expect Albanian-Kosovan villagers who now live here to behave with polite tolerance of marital upheavals and disputes?

The Kosovan father explained the call from the angry wife to the police conveying the 'I'll kill you' threat, which the father had shouted while his son was in a different part of the house on the phone. It's his story and I am sure there is more to it. Somehow, we have to drill into people who come to Britain from far away that some, many, not all, but some, of their customs have to be left behind.

I was always worried in Rotherham by the extent of patriarchal attitudes in the Muslim community. Go to a public meeting for British Kashmiri citizens and the women sit on one side and the men on the other. Some Muslim girls at a local comprehensive formed an Asian dance group. When the school laid on an evening of folk and other dancing and listed the Muslim girls on the bill, a leaflet was circulated saying they should all be killed for the crime of appearing on the same stage as white girls and exposing a tiny part of their legs and bodies in their dance routines. My Labour friends and I knew, or at least had good suspicions, about who was behind the death threat – he later became a pillar of the Rotherham Muslim community – but chose to say nowt.

Just before the Parliamentary Committee decided to accept without challenge or amendment the lurid language John Lyon CB used to end my parliamentary career, I had an unpleasant row with the committee chairman, my fellow Rotherham MP, Kevin Barron. We were together in a committee room in Rotherham Town Hall with leaders of the council. Barron was aggressively denouncing, in front of the local municipal grandees, the reporting of the prize-winning *Times* journalist, Andrew Norfolk. He had exposed in *The Times* the cover-up by the South Yorkshire police and Rotherham Council of the extent of grooming of young girls by local Asian men. Taxi drivers and others befriended vulnerable girls barely into secondary school age and showered them with presents, rides and promises of love. Many of these children were in care or from dysfunctional families. Barron objected to Andrew Norfolk's reporting in *The Times*, which painted Rotherham in a black light.

I blew up. 'For heaven's sake. He's a reporter. He reported what happened. We should be asking how it happened under our noses, not blaming the reporter.' Barron glared at me angrily. We never spoke again and a few days later he sentenced me to political death.

I feel ashamed that I too, like so many MPs, preferred to keep silent on some of the dirty secrets about bad practices in the Kashmiri Muslim community. The suffocating blanket of political omertà was thrown over a grave scandal. Many communities of incomers into Britain provide vast reservoirs of votes, which MPs ignore at their peril. In their day, this was true of constituencies of Irish or Jews, just as today MPs look to Muslim voters from the sub-continent.

One of my Commons heroines was Ann Cryer, the MP for Keighley a little further north in the West Riding. Time and again in the Commons or in the media she would denounce the scandal of forced-arranged marriages that reduced many women to chattel status or obliged a British-born and educated youngster to accept as his bride a girl from a peasant community, with no English and no chance of integration as she became a slave to her in-laws.

To be sure there were marriages that worked or settled into mutual support and stability. But too many left men sexually frustrated and keen to enter the shadowy world of prostitution and internally trafficked girls, groomed into becoming sex slaves. The police and CPS refuse to use their powers under a 2009 act of Parliament to challenge men who pay for sex with coerced or trafficked girls.

So while I listened carefully to my Kosovan fellow inmates, lamentations, I was far from sure all the right was on his side. The sad record of Albanian criminality – more from Albanians proper or Albanians seeking to pass themselves off as Kosovans – is clear and well-known. As a minister, I persuaded the then Kosovan Prime Minister to say on the record, in public, that all Kosovan asylum-seekers should return home from Britain as their country was no longer under Serb threat.

But Serbia, supported by well-known democracies like Russia and China, still refuses to allow Kosovo to join the United Nations and thus obtain the full international legitimacy which brings credit, investment and commerce. So Britain and its justice system will have to live with Kosovan and Albanian incomers for some time yet. More effort, including confronting cultural bad behaviour, is needed before women, in particular, are treated on an equal basis with men in many of Britain's new communities

1015H Miserable after missing the hour away for mass and the chance to continue the conversation with Fr Edward and Asil Nadir, I mooch around the spur. I go up and down the thirty-nine steps two at a time. The sun seems to have gone in but no fresh air so far today.

I talk to Darren, who greeted me when I first arrived. He is waiting for his trial on a knife offence and spent the first six months on remand at Thameside, the neighbouring privatised prison on the Belmarsh estate.

He didn't like it. 'The cells are nicer with individual showers and phones and but being banged up twenty-three hours a day is dreadful.'

Here in Belmarsh he has the status of a 'Listener' and is out of the cell during much of the day. I know the long bang-up syndrome.

'There is so much violence in Thameside. It's where all the gangs go and they re-create their gangs inside. They'll go for someone or start a fight just if you have the wrong postcode,' explains Darren.

Apparently, the privatised prison guards cannot control the restless angry energy of the young London gang members poured into Thameside Prison from the courts.

'They're let out to eat all at the same time and all it needs is a flare-up over getting food and a fight starts and then it's complete lock-down. You can wait two or three hours to get your dinner.'

Thameside, however, is profitable under the iron law of the last three decades, namely that almost any part of the public service can become a profit centre for investors if staff are cut, pay is lowered, and training is reduced. Much as I am now depressed at the lack of human contact via visits or phone calls, it sounds as if I am better off in Victorian Belmarsh than Holiday Inn Thameside.

More prisoners come up asking for advice on their cases. What do I know? I took advice from top lawyers and pleaded guilty, as they said (but could not guarantee) that no reasonable judge confident in his intellect and judgement could jail me given all the circumstances. But here I am.

I sit in a cell on the threes (third floor landing) looking at the police evidence against Ran. It is all utterly circumstantial. A man he used regularly for taxi rides around London was caught with two blocks of heroin in his car on the M6. Two years ago Ran had his first brush with the police. After a heavy party he returned home drunk to sleep off the booze. Later the next day, after eight hours in bed, he was stopped in his own car and found to be over the limit.

Idiot. I remember a BBC boss in the Midlands breathalysed taking his daughter to school but he could always rustle up a taxi on expenses thereafter. The '70s drinking at the BBC with Oddbins-size drinks cabinets in editors' rooms was quite extraordinary.

Ran has a 2.1 in computer science from De Montfort University in Leicester. Ran reminds me of Private Pike in *Dad's Army* – a bit of this and a bit of that. A gambler and occasional stallholder in a local east London shopping centre, he operates in cash rather than bank transfers and credit card payments.

The local police in Romford clearly think he is a no-good and have turned over his house and previously detained him without charge. But now they clearly see him as a drug-dealing godfather sitting at his shopping centre stall web, sending out minions to do the business.

According to the police evidence, a team of half a dozen detectives spent three months keeping him under observation. He is recorded leaving his stall, which he tells me he set up to give his girlfriend something to do.

The police noted that: 'He went out of the shopping centre, lit a cigarette and with his other hand used what appeared to be a mobile phone to make a call,' records one of the Metropolitan Police's finest. He is seen having a coffee and giving 'what appeared to be a sum of money' to his driver.

In their own report the police have to admit they can find no trace of drugs on him. There is no money at his home. No evidence of high living or expensive holidays. No trace of drugs on him or anything belonging to him.

Yet a for a clever QC, with a jury told each day about the dangers of drugs and dazzled about the so-called street value of drugs, usually beefed up by the police to sums with at least six zeroes, it will be child's play to weave a tissue of circumstantial detail that will invite the jury to deliver a guilty verdict. Add in a judge keen to keep his imprisonment record high in order to win promotion and it is almost game, or freedom, over. Ran, after all, is a British-Indian who lives as much on his wits and casino turns of gambling as from the salary of a nine-to-five job so surely he cannot be wholly innocent.

His driver, Mel, who I have befriended, has more of a problem. We sit all together in their cell – against the rules, as prisoners in Belmarsh are not meant to be in each other's cells even during Association – and I look at the police case against him.

Mel did regular taxi work for a local man. This man asked him to go to Liverpool and pick up a package. It was heroin. Mel insists he did not know he was a drugs courier but accepts he will have to plead guilty. By bringing another of his clients, Ran, into the story, the police can produce a charge of conspiracy or joint venture which carries a far higher penalty.

So I ask Mel who the man was who asked him to go to Liverpool and pick up the heroin. Has he given the name of this man to the police?

'No, not yet. I've got to talk to my brief.'

'But, Mel, the case turns on this guy. If you don't give his name to the cops, you're sunk.'

'I'm worried what could happen to the wife, my kids,' Mel mutters. He tries to change the subject by showing me all the cards sent in for his 54th birthday today. (I wonder what has happened to all my mail sent before Christmas, as I have not received a single Christmas card, just a few welcome emails. And nothing at all since the middle of last week.)

'Look, you have to give his name,' I insist. 'Even if you are trying to protect him the judge can force you to give his name in court. There's always bluster and threats. But they evaporate. Anyone who touches your family in a revenge attack will get into real trouble.'

'I dunno. I'll talk it over with the solicitors.'

Was this the age-old rule of not grassing and giving nothing to the police, who were not liked or trusted? Or a real fear of harm to his family?

I can live anywhere in Europe, even the world, and feel at home. England formed me, made me, gave me the beauty of the English language to use and the magnificent history of England to learn. But there is not a drop of English blood in me. I was born near Glasgow, grew up in London, worked in Birmingham, lived for fifteen years in Switzerland and France, and then half in South Yorkshire and on planes and trains to the continent. As an MP I specialised in foreign affairs and was constantly in and out of other countries. Living outside England presents no problems, so I can live anywhere.

Mel, however, is Romford. He is an East Ender. He is Essex. He would stick out like a horse's head transplanted onto a cow anywere else. So to give the name of someone he knows well, has drunk with, chauffeured around, done 'a bit of business' with, may mean he has to uproot his family and live somewhere else.

I suggest he turns Queen's Evidence (could I have done that against expenses-plundering MPs?) in exchange for a low sentence and then realise I don't know what I'm talking about, so shut up and leave him to his worries and fears.

I go downstairs, where Ali comes up to me in a fluster.

'I have been trying to call my solicitor ahead of the court hearing tomorrow. But when I call the number of the letter he sent me, it's the police station that answers.'

So tomorrow he is expected to appear in court to answer accusations from the police and he will be represented by a solicitor who uses the same police station as his out-of-office answering service. What chance justice when the prosecution and the defence are in each other's pockets?

He badly needs the documents he has as exhibits to sustain his story. Without these, an Arab being processed by the white British justice system has little chance.

Another Levantine-looking man wants to talk to me about his case. He says I can use his real name as it has been in the papers.

Robert Ekaireb is in fact a Jew whose family came from Iraq. He is a murderer. Rather he has been found guilty by a jury of a murder. But it's a murder that no one would dare put on screen.

He sits opposite me, head bowed to fold his long body into the bottom half of a cell bunk bed. He was born here and sounds as English as I do. He went into the north-west London rental business just as it took off when London, and especially areas like Hampstead and Swiss Cottage, became home to the many high-paid foreigners who swarmed to London's booming banking and financial sector.

In addition, the British government does not want to see any homeless on the streets. In consequence, it will provide capped rents to give the poor – asylum seekers, immigrants and others without sufficient income – accommodation in flats and houses. Moreover, foreign investors buy London properties and keep them empty so that they can sell them at a big profit a few years or even months later as property prices in London go up and up. Forty per cent of all the flats and houses in Belgravia are empty, never occupied, and this puts more upward pressure on rents elsewhere in London.

The Robert Ekairebs of the world who know how the rental market works have done very well and he is worth a reported £68 million.

For skilful hard-working landlords and property managers, the last twenty-five years have been a bonanza. Wealth requires permanent management and being a landlord is a full-time job even if money flows in. There is little time for relationship building. The nouveau-riche landlord may have a Rolls-Royce, a swish penthouse apartment behind gated security and concierge in elite Frognall, with gold taps in the bathroom, but a relationship is different. In 2006, Robert Ekaireb, just in his thirties, married in haste a Chinese-Irish lap dancer.

The marriage lasted three weeks. His wife kept running away back to her old life. There were rows. One day, he tells me, he came home to his plush flat and found his wife had gone for good. Disappeared. No message. Nothing. There were no children and the brief marriage had been tempestuous as the husband realised that his wife had been active in the sexual entertainment business to a considerable degree. There were few memories except of strenuous sex. He forgot about her and threw himself into getting richer and richer by renting out property.

Then, in his words, he had a row with a woman tenant who welched on the high-end rent to such an extent that he went to court and she was declared bankrupt. She went to the police and said she and Robert were friends and he had boasted to her about killing his wife. He denies any such conversation happened and there is no proof, evidence or witness to support the woman's allegation that he confessed killing his wife to her.

The police had an unexplained missing woman to account for. And now an accusation of murder from someone close to the husband. They opened an inquiry. Robert tells me he cooperated fully. No body was ever found. No blood. No weapon. No DNA. No explanation of how, if he killed his wife, he got her out of an apartment block with gates and doors to open and sixty-four security cameras recording all movements in and out. There was no proof the woman was even dead. The police closed the inquiry.

The CPS knew better. The circumstances surrounding the wife's disappearance were suspicious. An accusation had been made. Let the matter be decided in open court. Let the jury decide.

The CPS QC admitted there was no evidence. He told the jury that it was the constellation of circumstances that surrounded the case that should make them find Robert guilty. He could not prove he had not killed his wife of three weeks. He was fabulously rich. He made his fortune as a landlord, a profession probably on a par with Members of Parliament in terms of public low esteem and jury prejudice. The jury was told in detail about the gold-plated Hampstead penthouse. About his ostentatious wealth and how he flaunted it. About his bad temper and rows. And he was not a full-blooded Englishman.

And Robert could not prove beyond a shadow of doubt he had not murdered his wife. No one knows what happens in the minds of a jury. The CPS QC took two and half days in painting the blackest possible picture of the man as he had no direct evidence of the crime. Robert's QC spent only three hours painting the opposite picture. Robert's QC had earlier called for the jury to be dismissed and replaced by a new one. The judge refused the request. So each juror now had a grudge against the defendant's QC.

The jury had to decide on whether they liked the man in the dock and believed he might be capable of killing a woman. Jurors have grown up on modern sensationalist media with its exaggeration, simplification and endless denunciations. Just 70,000 print copies of the *Financial Times*, Britain's only calm, balanced, objective paper are sold in Britain. Instead, millions of Facebookers, YouTubers and tweeters get and exchange information without any need to be truthful. Judges lecture jurors not to read the internet. They might as well tell them not to go to the loo.

So, from his story, Robert Ekaireb was judged for what he was, not for what he did. Perhaps he is a murderer. He was certainly sent to Belmarsh as one. He was put in a cell with two other sensible prisoners who were told to keep an eye on him in case of suicide. I have never seen such a broken man, though, as with everyone I meet in prison, I hear only his side of the story.

Surely, I asked myself, a state prosecutor must have some evidence, not dislike, of a rich Iraqi Jewish landlord? The CPS needs convictions like

Ryanair needs passengers. It will do anything to obtain them and fill our overcrowded prisons with ever more people.

OK. Time for the usual correction. Maybe Robert Ekaireb's story is BS. I'll check in the papers, in the court record, with his QC when I get out. But if he really is in Belmarsh for a murder which he says he didn't commit, and for which there is no evidence, no DNA, no body, nothing, that is truly frightening.

Is it because journalists have now stopped investigating miscarriages of justice? Court reporting, in the sense of reporters being there day after day, seeing the story of a trial in the round, has all but disappeared. Reporters roll up for the stentorian denunciation that judges issue as press releases via the court's news service, in acknowledgment that a short-hand note has disappeared from the toolbox of modern journalism.

Perhaps in the old days when judges sentenced innocent people to hang there was more willingness by a Ludovic Kennedy or a Paul Foot to challenge the dreadful wrongs done in the name of justice. Judges have become like today's journalists, preferring comment to fact and unable ever to admit they might be wrong.

I tell Robert to write to his MP, Glenda Jackson. She is retiring from the Commons and perhaps this is one last drama in which she should perform, if indeed a man against whom there is no proof is in prison for murder.

1112H Sunday lunch. I had ordered jacket potato and tuna. But there is no tuna. Instead, the revolting chicken lump concoction on offer yesterday. I ask the food counter guard if I can swap the chicken muck for cheap baked beans and, blow me down, he says yes. I had found some salt that I saw in another prisoner's cell – he said I could have some in exchange for some sugar. I poured a large teaspoonful into a piece of loo paper and took it down to my cell. A guard who allows me to swap one 'main dish' for baked beans and a little salt. Things are looking up.

As my cell door is locked, I hear a guard tell a prisoner he has to take his meal inside. 'No, Matthews. You cannot exchange your dinner for a burn. That's your food. You have to eat. Go inside.'

I worry about Chris Grayling's proposed cigarette ban. Even though I consider myself a hard-liner on smoking, I am not sure that taking away this small pleasure from prisoners is worth it. Cigarettes are a tiny relief from the boredom and anomie of Belmarsh. Their smell and smoke does not pervade the block so I have no sense of passive smoking, especially if the smoker blows out of the window or towards the fan that circulates air in the cell.

Darren was cynical. 'The screws will just bring in cigarettes and sell them for money anyway. You can get anything in prison from the screws if the price is right. They will also enjoy having a go at any prisoner desperate for a smoke.'

We'll see what happens but since there is no political or journalist interest about what happens inside prisons, no one will notice until there is an explosion.

I keep pushing stale, dry bread out of the window railing for the pleasure of seeing the birds come and sit on the ledge. Now I see the outline of a guard with a two-way radio outside my window.

'I think I can see crumbs,' he says into his radio. Will I be sanctioned? Even Nelson Mandela was allowed to feed birds on Robben Island. Is Governor Wragg the Birdhater of Belmarsh? But they know they will soon be rid of me. I hope.

1526H Exercise. A good brisk walk with Darren. Another victim of the obsession of judges with sending men to prison for short, pointless, but expensive and family-destroying sentences.

My old symposium comrades are from a different block and there seems to be a new policy of separating the exercise times of different blocks. I am first out as my cell is closest to the block gate. A quick pat-down search. The guard asks if I have anything on me. It's an odd question. Of course I don't. The young man who comes out with me falls in beside as I walk as briskly as I can. Exercise in the afternoon means no shower after and I don't want to get too sweaty.

'It's a shithole here, isn't it? The screws just take the piss, don't they? You don't need any qualifications to be a screw. They just take anyone.'

This dislike of prison officers is so prevalent it is worrying. But it is justified, alas. The petty throwing around of weight just because one can is the worst trait of anyone in uniform and bestowed with authority. There is no trust, no relationship between guards and prisoners. Perhaps it is different in prisons with permanent populations. But Belmarsh is there to bring people down, not build them up.

My new friend is Greg. He is in for an odd length of time – five months. He was picked up by the police on suspicion of being involved in a town centre punch-up.

'I didn't mind being arrested. But the way the cops put on handcuffs so it was agony and then twisted my lower arm so bad I thought it was going to break, I just kept wriggling and pulling and pushing to stop the pain. That just made the cops tighten the handcuffs still further and made me more nervous and frightened, and when you're frightened and in pain, you struggle more.'

So the end result was a charge not related to whatever reason the police had for picking up Greg in the first place, but one of resisting arrest. The Lord Chief Justice's admonition that sentencing someone to spend less than six months in prison is pointless was ignored. Greg is in Belmarsh on a five-month sentence.

He is miserable. Coming from a poor, single-parent working class background, he was just getting back on his feet and earning money to look after a new wife and thirteen-week-old baby girl, Winnie, when the police with a casual teach-you-a-lesson twist of the handcuff ratchet turned his life upside down.

'I was a personal trainer working with clients from Canary Wharf. I charged £60–£100 an hour and gave £25 to the gym, so I was making decent money. I also worked in the gym if they needed shifts and I was available.'

Above all he wants to establish a home for his new family. 'But it's impossible. My wife and Winnie are living with her parents and I live with my Dad in a one-bedroom flat. Of course there's cheaper property further out in the country but it costs a fortune to commute and my customer base is in London.

'The government do nothing. There's no jobs at decent pay. There's no homes for us. I don't blame the kids who see no help of any sort and go out and start buying and selling drugs. They don't have any work. What else can they do?'

His moan about the government was not tinged with any party politics. Labour, as well as the present coalition, have not had any real solution to the crisis of Britain's uneducated, broken-society working class. The swathes of jobs once associated with east London – the print industry, the docks, Dagenham – have gone. Canary Wharf is one of the world's taller redevelopment schemes but it provides few steady working class jobs. The police officers who patrol east London live far away in comfortable suburbs. Very few officials of the state apparatus who administer to the east London poor live amongst them. The last Conservative politician who regularly came to east London was John Profumo, who did charity work in Toynbee Hall after the Profumo affair. Most senior journalists know Tuscany or the Luberon better than east London.

Greg is without a lifeline, save his own determination. He promises me he will get his reflexes under control and try and rebuild a life.

'Well, if the judge gave you five months that's only five weeks you have to do here and then it's a tag,' I say.

'Nah. I'll do the whole fucking time here. I don't want no tag.'

As our exercise period ended my heart sank. Belmarsh was better than the life he led outside. Here at least he was fed, had all the television a human can take, and did not have to worry about his wife and daughter. That was someone else's responsibility. I think he may be back.

1557H Dinner, where the usual cubed swede is replaced by my favourite, Brussels sprouts. There is even a piece of cake – a Sunday treat – as well as one orange half the size of those sold as Sainsbury's Basics. Where do they find such miniature fruit? The cell door is locked and it will be seventeen hours before it opens again.

MONDAY 6 JANUARY 2014

Prisons, cachots, lieux bénis où le mal est impossible, puisqu'ils sont le carrefour de toute la malédiction du monde. On ne peut pas commettre le mal dans le mal. Prisons, dungeons, blessed places where evil is impossible because they are the crossroads of all that's accursed in the world. One cannot commit evil in what is evil.

– Jean Genet

0825H Up doing my exercises. Yesterday, Darren told me I might be moved today. 'There's a bus transferring prisoners so you may be on it. No one understands why they have kept you here so long. Sometimes they give you no notice, just a screw telling you have ten minutes to get ready to leave.'

No luck. The cell door does indeed open, with a shout of 'Exercise'. I hurry into trainers and sweatshirt but when I leave my cell, the barred gate is shut. I see prisoners out in the exercise yard but they are called in. There is a fine drizzle, Scotch mist, which soon dries out leaving puddles on the cracked concrete of the exercise yard. But the screws like any excuse to cancel the exercise half-hour. I go back to the cell as the door clangs behind me. I open the window, which brings in a rush of cold, and breathe the fresh air to try and stop my lungs clogging with the stale prison atmosphere.

On television I am amused at George Osborne announcing £25 billion in further cuts this year, targeted it seems at young, poor, working class families like that of Greg's, with whom I walked and talked yesterday. Then Osborne pops up again to say he will find extra money for the UK's space programme.

We can go to the stars but we cannot lessen the poverty and inequality that sends so many to prison. The BBC says the UK's main space effort is linked to the Galileo satellite programme but somehow cannot mention the European Union, which funds Galileo – a programme strongly attacked by Tory Eurosceptics like William Hague and Iain Duncan Smith when it was launched.

0930H There has been some kind of riot in a private prison near Wolverhampton. G4S, which makes a fortune for its directors from private prisons, says it will not reveal what took place or how serious it was. The BBC morning news presenter announces this incuriously. It seems astonishing that a major disturbance can take place inside a public institution and there is no journalist curiosity. I hope an MP raises it when the Commons is back. But I doubt it. MPs like having prisons in their constituencies, especially in former industrial areas. The prisons provide jobs for those without any skills to find work in what are, in any event, high unemployment areas.

Three envelopes of emails are shoved under my cell door. There is a lovely card from Irène, the children's favourite aunt. It is written in German and sent from Switzerland more than a week ago. Normally, letters sent from the excellent Swiss postal service arrive in a day or two. This letter was sent by expensive express service but took eight days to get here. *Vielleicht hatte der Gouverneur Wragg Schwierigkeiten einen Übersetzer zu finden?* Who knows? The letter Vicky sent with stamps in it has not arrived. I am down to two envelopes with second-class stamps and have £3 to use on the phone. The Belmarsh dehumanising process continues.

I put two old used tea bags in my blue plastic cup and hope there's enough strength to give me a cup of tea.

1019H The cell door opens. I look up with hope. But it is the screw who likes to tell me to 'get used to prison' whenever I ask him a polite question. He rattles the window, looks under my pillow and then grins when he examines the shelf where I keep my plastic plate, bowl and cutlery. The first plate I had was so stained I asked for a second one when I got one of my meals.

Plates, bowls, cups and plastic forks and spoons are handed out freely. But for this screw it's a pleasure to find a prisoner in possession of two plastic plates. He grabs one and, with an ugly smile, throws it out of the cell onto the floor of the cell block and walks out triumphantly, slamming the heavy metal cell door shut with an extra bang as he noisily turns the lock.

1108H Cell door unlocked for lunch. I am out of my cell for less than three minutes to be given a tiny tuna roll, a packet of chemical cheese puffs, but hooray, a packet of noodles. I will use half to allay the constant hunger which I hope is a sign of weight coming down. I use my second last stamp to write to my brother, Martin. He is high in public administration and featured big in a weekend newspaper interview. He spells his name slightly differently from mine (don't tell Judge Sweeney), but writes that sometimes people come up to him and ask, 'You're not by any chance related to that MP in prison, are you?' When Martin replies, 'Yup. He's my brother,' the reaction is 'like you get when a turd is dropped in a swimming pool'.

There are dreadful snowstorms disrupting North America and Canada. I hope Laura got back OK. The frustration of not knowing how your children are adds to the Belmarsh dehumanisation policy.

1245H My stomach pangs are too much. I crack. I pour boiling water over half the noodles. I watch *Daily Politics* on BBC2. Once again it is just a platform for Nigel Farage. Outside the sun shines. I notice palm trees behind the faraway grill fence. Within this giant prison complex there must be a microclimate – warmth from the buildings, protection from the wind and traffic fumes or industrial effluent. *Gardeners' Question Time* should come here.

No exercise. No fresh air. No shower. Where is my solicitor? The last time I saw him was two weeks ago. Surely I should have a legal visit by now? I watch the BBC1 news at 1 p.m. Not a single story outside the UK. Provincialism rules.

1457H The cell door is unlocked. Two warders come in. Do they bring news? Have I been re-categorised? Will I move?

'We're here to do a cell search and strip search. Get your clothes off.'

I take off my sweatshirt, T-shirt, socks, tracksuit trousers and prison underpants as a man half my age peers at my genitals as if I had a secret weapon hidden there.

It is a foul, humiliating process without the slightest reason or justification given my age and obedient, docile behaviour here. But Sir Nigel Sweeney knew what he was doing and I can hear all the politician-hating judges as well as the BNP and Paul Staines (Guido Fawkes) cackling with pleasure as they read this.

I ask if I am to be locked up all day in my cell. I have asked to use the gym and go to education classes and am quite happy to work. The younger guard, who seems better spoken with a second stripe on his epaulette, asks if I have a gym card. I point at it. He asks if I was told where to go this morning when let out.

'I wasn't let out this morning,' I tell him.

I hang around outside until they are finishing searching the cell. The younger one beckons me in.

'Did you make those marks?' he asks, pointing at the old bits of solidified toothpaste on the wall.

'Of course not. I didn't leave those disgusting stains on the mattress, nor the blood on the door, nor that disgusting waste bin,' I reply.

He leaves, slamming the cell door shut. I suppose there is some odd pleasure for the screws to peer at my genitals but I cannot fathom it. I would like to record that I welcomed the brief human contact. It's true they weren't wearing a red gown or a white wig but this need to humiliate and demean is beyond my comprehension. I just have to close my eyes and think of all the people out there who know the truth, know me, and I can feel their love and solidarity coming to the cell to form a force field that protects me from the guards' attempts to break my spirit and turn me into a Belmarsh Prison number without his real name.

1620H It is getting dark. There has been no rain for eight hours. The exercise yard is dry but still I am locked in my cell. What does Governor Wragg have against fresh air and stretching your legs? I hear prisoners talking to each other across the yard from window to window, from locked cell to locked cell. The human need to communicate cannot be crushed.

1745H Still locked up. I have been out of my cell for just seven minutes so far today. I might as well be in solitary confinement. I wonder if the next four weeks will be like this.

1755H Dinner. White rice, corn and a tiny piece of boned pork with a spoonful of MSG sweet and sour sauce over it. I grab a cold shower as the food service is so slow.

Ali tells me he went back to court and his solicitor didn't even bother to turn up. He showed the judge my letter in which I pointed out that it was Ali with his smashed face who was arrested, as an Arab, not his Romanian white assailant. The judge read it and said he would release Ali on bail if he could find someone reliable to vouch for him and presumably stand some bail. But what kind of police and judges do we have, when at significant cost to the taxpayer this poor man is sent to prison because no one stops to think.

I find myself talking in French to an Algerian, Tahrir, who has been in the UK since 1991. He is an opponent of Algeria's military regime, with its generals controlling substantial sections of the economy in this oil-rich but deeply sad, corrupt, oppressed nation. If he has been here for twenty years, it is unlikely he has been involved in actual terrorist activity.

The conversation grew tiresome as he sought to claim that the 1995 Paris terrorist attack was carried out by Algerian state security. I have listened to this garbage for too long. Terror attacks on women and children have been in the toolbox of Islamism for three decades. There is always a justification, like the IRA killers who thought they were justified in killing children with bombs to put pressure on the British state.

The strength of democracy, however, is that it does not give up on democracy and rule of law and decide to use just executive action. Yet too many of the arrests, detentions and deportations have not passed through the sieve of law. I don't have Tahrir's full story but, unless it can be proven beyond doubt that he took part in terrorist activity, I would not be happy to see this father of young children, born here amongst us, handed over to the un-tender mercies of Algerian torture cellars. Stupid, reactionary, homophobe, misogynist Islamist chatter is not reason enough to Belmarsh someone and try to deport him to a regime none of us would live under.

I had hoped to get in a phone call but the queue was so long for the one properly working phone.

1838H Bang-up. That's more than twenty-two and a half hours locked in my Belmarsh cell at the start of my third week of prison.

2230H There is an endless chitchat as prisoners shout news and gossip to each other from cell windows. It's like a noisy pub bar, voices rising to be heard.

TUESDAY 7 JANUARY 2014

Oh who is that young sinner with the handcuffs on his wrist?
And what has he been after that they groan and shake their fists?
And wherefore is he wearing such a conscience-stricken air?
Oh they're taking him to prison for the colour of his hair.
– A. E. Houseman

0720H Belmarsh wakes up around 6.30. A light goes on and gleams through the cell door. Warders clanking their keys, though they sound a bit like chains, go out and wake up prisoners destined for a day in court.

It's also early in the morning that prisoners get transferred to another block or to another prison. Now in my third week here, I have been given no categorisation and no news of a transfer to a prison where I might be able to read my own books, study a new language, or spend fewer than twenty-two hours in a small cell.

Two weeks without a newspaper. Or a drink. I feel no withdrawal symptoms. I remember the excitement of the BBC newsrooms I once worked in. News and booze. Stories and Scotch. My first years made a bond between uncorking a story and uncorking a bottle. The man who fused the grain and the keyboard to perfection was Christopher Hitchens. We stayed together in France, in Portugal, in Italy, in Cyprus, above all in Washington, where each evening fell out of a bottle, wine to begin with and then the inevitable quart bottle of Teachers.

I can't really take the drink and as the years went by I couldn't keep up with Christopher. He made a marvellous roast chicken lunch for my son and myself on a visit to Washington but with Scotch as his drink at table.

Yet, as I was handling a hangover, Christopher was busy at his type-writer, an Olivetti 22 to begin with, a MacBook Air at the end, producing one, two, even three thousand words. He was a writer, above all a journal-ist, who threw words up in the air that came down in perfect patterns. The news–booze axis was reinforced by the fact that most of the meals and drinks were covered by 'exes' – expenses.

During the hot summer months of the MPs scandal in 2009, it was hilarious that BBC journalists were working themselves into a fit of denunciatory morality over MP perks and exes when so many of them had been the most creative fillers in of expense forms. One day perhaps there will be Freedom of Information on newspapers (and judges) and we shall be surprised at what is claimed as exes. My BBC friends say it is all cleaned up now. But in the days when Hitch and I began our trade, exes were part of pay and, sadly, MPs are often the last to realise the world has moved on.

So today, I have had no newspapers to read and no drinks for more than two weeks. But I miss neither. I have become like most voters – getting my news and views as I channel hop by day and evening. Prisoners are

not allowed access to the internet. There may be newspapers or the week-
lies in the library at Belmarsh but I haven't been allowed there yet. Treat
'em mean and keep 'em keen. Keep 'em dumb and sheep they'll become.
The first stage of turning the criminal back into the citizen is to let him
take an interest in his country. Belmarsh's newspaper-free environment
treats the convict as permanently stupid, a useless idiot fit for nothing.

0810H I have carefully divided my muesli ration in two and eat a
slightly healthier breakfast than the dreaded chemical cornflakes. I have
yet to see the toaster used and I wonder if it's there to remind prisoners of
how wicked we are, as a slice of warm buttered toast – let alone a decent
cooked breakfast – fades into memory.

0825H The cell door is opened. Exercise. I do a little jogging and then
rejoin my symposium comrades. Mumble, Cliff Hobbs – he said I could
indeed use his real name – fleshes out his story.

'I know I'm a criminal. I was given a safari outfit as a kid and swag-
gered around the estate in it, pointing my rifle and saying, "Bang!" But
I never, ever used violence. We did the big BBC payroll robbery in 1984
– £800,000, which was a lot of money in those days – you didn't do
bank transfers or credit cards. It was an inside job but we never did any
violence. I scarpered from a court after another trial. But again, I never
raised my hand to anyone. They tracked me down in Europe and arrested
me. The judge brought up the 1984 conviction and the fact I absconded
and decided it was life. My barrister couldn't believe it. Life when every
day you read of rape or muggings and people get off with community
service or a suspended sentence. Yeah, we're going to appeal but the judges
all look after each other. I admit I'm a habitual criminal. But I have never
harmed anyone in my life.'

It seems strange that the taxpayer would now pay scores of thousands
of pounds a year to look after Cliff Hobbs until he is nearly eighty. Is
it really impossible to invent some other system of control, surveillance

and supervision that, after an appropriate sentence, would release him? If life is right for non-violent crime what is appropriate for harming or killing someone?

To cheer me up, Cliff told a terrible joke about two Irishmen, which, dear reader, even with my Irish heritage I think is too politically incorrect for publication, but I'll tell you when I see you.

0910H After yesterday's twenty-two and a half hours locked in my cell the screws are being generous, as I am allowed out for another Catholic service. That's four times in a church in under three weeks. Mother Helena, headmistress of St Joseph's state primary school in Wealdstone, would surely have approved.

In the holding room I learn that Robert, the man convicted of killing his wife without any evidence of any sort at all, has gone for sentence today. A cellmate of his tells me he was shaking with terror last night and called a guard to say he had chest pains.

'Nah. It's just anxiety,' said the guard. Maybe, but on the eve of execution are you not allowed a little leeway – maybe an aspirin or valium to try and calm down?

Church is a wonderful two hours – the longest I have been out of my cell since Judge Sweeney sent me here. Father Edwards reminds us it is the Orthodox Church Christmas Day. I say we should all pray for Vladimir Putin, which gets a big guffaw from the Russian and East European prisoners and from the Polish Father Edward himself.

I read a lesson from St Paul who, of course, himself experienced the probity, independence and integrity of Roman judges. I wonder if at any time in the 2,000 years since Roman jurisprudence was first shaped, judges have ever questioned what they do or, as a collective, stood back and reflected on whether their sentencing politics makes for a more just, more civilised world?

These thoughts are promoted by a talk with a prisoner who sits down beside me in the chapel. Hugh is fifty-two, a neat, slight Canadian who has lived in England all his adult life. He has been in Belmarsh since last summer and will stay here at a cost of £50,000 until June, when his trial takes place. He told me he had been on constant medication in recent years. He has a girlfriend a decade older and one day, having taken a huge mixture of drugs, he was on the way to her house when he 'just blacked out'.

'I woke up in a police cell. They said I have been found in a flat with a knife. The charge is aggravated burglary. No one was in the flat. No one was hurt. I cannot remember being there, where or why I got a knife.

'At my trial the expert pharmacologist said it was an enormous cocktail of drugs. He was asked if there was any possibility I could have known what I was doing. He said there is always a slight possibility. That was enough for the judge who sent me here for a year to await my trial. I have no passport so cannot leave Britain. My girlfriend will vouch for me. In Canada you cannot deny someone bail for as long as the British judge has,' he said.

The usual disclaimer. Hugh could have been spinning a tale. But again and again I keep meeting people sent by our judges to Belmarsh because they do not have the imagination or leadership to behave otherwise. Newspapers occasionally complain about the continental system, which allows lengthy detention before a case is concluded. Are we any better?

Yesterday on the news, I saw barristers protesting cuts in legal aid. A QC with a Johnny Depp beard was saying the cuts in legal aid for crimi-nal defence would stop young lawyers going to the criminal bar as there were much richer pickings in other fields of law – commercial, divorce, working for Russian oligarchs. That may well be true. But might there be another factor? If criminal defence barrister after criminal defence barris-ter are utterly unable to help their clients because judges see everyone as guilty and send them to prison without any evidence, or impose a custodial sentence when a non-custodial one would be the norm in most democracies, why should any smart young lawyer go into criminal law, when judges obey no rules except their own prejudices or stretch the rules on sentencing to placate the tabloid press?

Labour's Michael Foot got into terrible trouble in the '70s when he made the commonplace – and true – statement: 'If it had been left to the judges, there would be precious few freedoms in England.'

To paraphrase the old saying, '*Fiat justitia ruat caelum.*' The heavens did indeed fall in on poor Michael Foot, who was excoriated by the Conservatives and every judge for telling a historical truth. It was about this time that a succession of High Court and Appeal judges were condemning to life imprisonment some utterly innocent Irishmen, for bomb attacks they knew nothing about. It was an MP, Chris Mullin, not a QC, who put right that evil injustice. No judge was put on trial for stealing fifteen years of liberty from innocent men. They didn't even forfeit a gong.

Since then, judges have been immune from examination or criticism, except from editors denouncing them for being too soft. There is no Lord Chief Justice with the intellect or courage to call time on the offshore-owned press, and do a judicial equivalent of Stanley Baldwin's famous speech in 1931, when he described newspaper owners as being like 'the harlot throughout the ages'. Today our judges cower before the rich and powerful and do editors' bidding by filling our prisons pointlessly.

1120H My second cup of Nescafé – a reward for going to a church service. Father Edward gives us a fascinating history of the Carmelites – the order that has given its name to Whitefriars streets up and down the country. And at last I see a newspaper. It is *Hürriyet*, the biggest Turkish paper. It is brought in by Asil Nadir. Sadly, Turkish isn't one of my languages.

Asil translates the front page, which has pictures of all the generals sent to prison by the Turkish leader, Erdogan. Now he has ordered retrials to be held very fast. Erdogan's authority is crumbling rapidly. It is unclear how loyal the security and police apparatus is to his highly personalised – though democratically elected – rule. Perhaps if he throws a bone to the military by getting some of their generals out of prison, he can win some support from the military to stay in power. Asil is convinced the shadowy, but hugely influential, Gülen movement, with its strings pulled from Pennsylvania, has turned against Erdogan and his time is up.

I wish I knew more about Asil's case. I worked abroad in the 1980s: in Poland with Solidarity, in Brazil with Lula's trade unions, in South Africa with independent black unions and in South Korea with unions that staged a six-week general strike and occupation that ushered in democracy.

So many of the dominant stories and developments of Thatcher's Britain, including Asil Nadir and Polly Peck, passed me by. I don't think he killed anyone. And he could not have done anything like the fraudulent financial harm of RBS and other banking executives that led us over the financial precipice in 2008. He seemed to have the loyalty of top Tories. So why, a quarter of a century later, is he banged up in Hellmarsh?

As we drink our coffee, he tells me there is an agreement between the Turkish and British governments, based on standard prisoner exchange agreements. This means he should be released on 17 January. But the British authorities, including judges, are trying to keep him inside. He says judges talk openly of concern over press reporting if he were out. It is difficult in prison, without files, papers, access to the internet, to sieve what is chatter and chaff and what is real and true. I really don't want to leave Belmarsh carrying in my mind individual cases where justice and judgments have been less than desirable. I have done my service helping others. I want to act for and be myself.

And yet. And yet. There is something rotten in this state of British justice and prisons. I take down Asil's prison number and will stay in touch.

1127H This is the oddest cheese I have ever come across. I ordered a cheese baguette. Again the soft bread is unpleasant. But the half-grated, half-crumbled light yellow filling is what? It is no cheese I have ever come across. Not Cheddar, nor Cheshire, not Wensleydale, and certainly not Stilton or any cheese with taste. I ordered it to have a change, perhaps remembering happy meals of raclette or fondue or tartiflette in my beloved Alps. But this crumbly white-yellow stuff is as tasty as powdered chalk.

1415H As if to make up for the long bang-up yesterday, today is all action. Vicky's letter, sent before Christmas, still hasn't arrived. When I asked Father Edward if he had received in the internal mail the note I sent him on Sunday apologising for missing mass, he said no. I assume Governor Wragg is obeying some directive from Chris Grayling to double-check mail and sit on anything suspicious.

On the noon BBC2 politics show, in addition to the BBC's charter obligation to show a daily interview with Nigel Farage, there was a bizarre row over an anodyne European Court of Human Rights ruling. This said judges should be able to review compulsory life sentences if they wanted to. The ECHR did not call for lifers to be freed and judges can keep bad criminals behind bars until they sink into terminal Alzheimer's, Parkinson's and cancer and rot to death in prison. The power will still reside with our wonderful judges.

But for some reason all our senior Conservatives are having fits. The ECHR stepped in to stop torture in Northern Ireland, prevent paedophile sadists from thrashing little boys in schools and uphold gay rights. British practice and some laws have been massively improved by ECHR rulings. This is the most minor of decisions, saying British judges can if they want review lifelong imprisonment. I am baffled as to why it is causing such caterwauling.

The cell door opens. 'Gym,' barks a screw. At last. Some proper exercise.

I take a towel and soap and plod off. Again the twists and turns of the maze-like corridors of Belmarsh finally take me into a large well-equipped gym with an indoor sports hall next to it where an game of indoor cricket is under way. The gym is crammed with machines – mainly weight focused. But it's a joy to try them all. A prison gym instructor looks at the mainly Afro-Caribbean men lifting huge weights. They have bursting biceps already.

The gym instructor says he calls them 'genies'. They do indeed have huge wide shoulders and big chests and arms and tiny, unhealthy-looking legs, like a genie coming out of the bottle. Before I went to the gym, an Asian stopped and asked me to pass on a message to say he wasn't coming along for the indoor cricket. He said he had played for Essex. The indoor sports hall has room for a full basketball or half-pitch-size indoor soccer match. A wicket is set up and there are some wicked bowlers amongst the prisoners. At least they can't be worse than the England side who have just been comprehensively humiliated in a 5–0 defeat by Australia in the Ashes.

The gym leader says he wanted to get out of prison service. 'When I joined I was promised that a key part of the package was a non-contributory pension. They are now taking that away. I have had no pay rise in four years. I can take that because we all have to pull in our belts in the public services. But taking away my pension is not right.'

He told me he would take redundancy and train to be a London cabbie. 'I'll be my own boss and work as often or as little as I want.' He was clear I was in Belmarsh because I was a politician. 'The public put you MPs on a par with bankers.'

I asked him if he had ever seen a banker in Belmarsh.

'No. They are protected, aren't they? No one is ever going to prosecute a banker, are they?'

The gym session was far too long. I enjoy a workout and the equipment was as good as that in the Bannatyne gym at Westminster. But two hours was just too much. I talked to other prisoners, including one on a very long remand charged with a counterfeiting conspiracy.

'In the sixteen months I've been here there have been six, maybe seven suicides. Two with med overdoses, the others through asphyxiation, hanging themselves or by putting a plastic bag over their heads. I bet you haven't read about that in the press.'

Too right I hadn't, but I can imagine how a young, confused, mixed-up kid coming here and confronting, perhaps for the first time in his life, the casual, bullying, authoritarian style of some guards, might be driven over the edge. I said I would try and get parliamentary questions tabbed in the Commons. You go to prison to lose liberty, not life.

There is a large open shower at the gym but all the men were wearing underpants as they showered. Prudishness? Muslim shyness about nudity? There are nearly 200 Muslims in Belmarsh with many converting to become part of a distinct community. It would be very easy to put up small partition walls that would mean either privacy or respect for culture but

I suppose any concession is just that – a concession and, for our tabloids, prisoners washing themselves proves how soft prisons have become.

1650H Back in the cell, locked up. But today has gone by quickly so far. If I can make a phone call to my daughter and Vicky I will be satisfied, through I don't understand why I have not yet had a legal visit and why my books and clothes remain confiscated. Had I known, I needn't have bothered bringing my suitcase to the Old Bailey.

1802H Doors open. Again I try to get in a phone call but the screw shouts that if I want any food I can't talk to someone whose voice is a lifeline. I cut off the call and eat the horrid dark-brown slush – some kind of mince stew with carrots and overcooked potatoes.

I learn I will finally be allowed a legal visit tomorrow after more than two weeks. Belmarsh says they haven't recategorised me. So I am still here on Judge Sweeney's status as a Category A prisoner – along with murderers, terrorist killers and major drug dealers. I suppose I should wear the badge with pride. Sarah has to go to Rio on Thursday so I won't see her for some time yet. I am so proud of my daughter. Family solidarity will triumph.

Robert comes back from the Old Bailey with a 22-year minimum sentence for a murder where there is not, he insists, a single shred of evidence. I go and hug him and promise I will look into this case. How can a British judge send a man to prison for more than two decades without a body, fingerprints, witness, a trace of a crime, a criminal record, any proof at all? Answer: He is an English High Court judge.

I watch *Channel 4 News* – far better than any other television news. Over the last three days I have seen three young women shadow ministers whom I like and admire. But they just don't come over as saying anything interesting or leaving a trace as politicians with passion, wit or conviction. I wish my beloved Labour could say something and start to make an impact.

Interesting that the courts have found guilty two tweeters facing sentencing after sending abusive tweets to a woman who campaigned for a woman's face on a banknote. The hate tweets against me over the years were foul, defamatory and very upsetting, even with my tough skin. Any chance the cops will act?

WEDNESDAY 8 JANUARY 2014

It is said that no one truly knows a nation until one has been inside its jails. A nation should not be judged by how it treats its highest citizens, but its lowest ones.

– Nelson Mandela

0825H Dozing in bed after the 6 a.m. chain rattling and key turning – but not for me. Apparently Belmarsh doesn't want to let me go. Cup of tea and the cereal. Floods on TV news. I cannot find out exactly how many homes have been evacuated or utterly destroyed or people left permanently homeless with businesses ruined. Actually, come to think of it, there are no reports of homes or businesses being so flooded out they are now destroyed. I wonder if this is one of those great news stories we work ourselves into a lather about but a few days of warmer, drier weather will quickly solve the problem?

0843H Exercise, and I find our symposium members back with me – Mumble slips me some first class stamps so I think, in theory, as I have now been in here for more than two weeks, I should be allowed access to my own books and notepads, even clothes.

But Chris Grayling clearly doesn't like me and I don't like him. Now I have some stamps, though, I can write more letters. I know people have written to me but Governor Wragg seems to be sitting on my mail. A common complaint from all prisoners in Belmarsh is the gap between mail arriving in the prison and it coming to prisoners. This is poor, lazy management and there's no excuse.

I had had no time for a cup of tea as I leapt, well, got out of bed and slipped into my tracksuit to get some blessed fresh air. Cliff keeps asking if I need anything – toiletries, food. He is so insistent and I will never forget the sheer human spirit of kindness shown to me by the inmates here and what a contrast that is to the ugly approach by the state prison apparatus.

I say some shaving foam would be great and he says he can get a can delivered into my cell. There are networks within networks, money changes hands, the screws and the prisoners come from the same poorly educated working-class background.

'I just don't know why you're still here, Denis,' he says. 'You ought to be out in an open prison by now, or even out on a tag. What's the point of keeping you here?'

He warns me to be careful about who I talk to or confide in. 'Look, it's the lowest of the low in here, some of the worst people in society. Even in open prison you'll meet people at the end of a long sentence who are still dodgy. Don't trust no one.'

He gives me the name of a friend in one open prison I might be sent to. 'Tell him Cliff says to look after you and make sure nothing happens.'

I leave Cliff talking to his pals as I fall into step with my Algerian friend Tahrir, with whom I speak French, though after twenty-three years in England his English is excellent.

He has to see his lawyer today as he was out on a tag and Serco, the company that defrauded the government of £69 million together with G4S over tagging cost claims, said he tried to tamper with his tag.

Tahrir says he has faithfully worn his tag around his ankle and reported every day to the police station. He does not face public charges but his father was mayor of a town in Algeria who was not in favour with the military regime. I can see an earlier myself in Tahrir: bolshy, articulate, opposed to any existing order. But I had free journalism, trade unions and the Labour Party through which I could channel my desire to see change.

Algeria has no such outlets and, as the pressure cooker heats up, the only outlet is the fake radicalism of Islamist politics. He says he knows a journalist on *The Guardian* well-known as a *sympathisante* of radical Palestinian militants. Yeah, we all know her. I suspect he's appeared on too many email and mobile lists and even if I think (though do not know) that he wasn't directly involved in any violence, after 9/11 and especially after 7/7, the security agencies (MI6, GCHQ, MI5, Special Branch) are under too much pressure, and round up anyone they have on any list they make up themselves or get given.

And if I have to choose between the Jew-haters of Islamism and the right of the British people to be safe on their own streets, I know as a boring old liberal-leftie where I stand. A free people over a conservative ideology any day.

0912H We go back into the spur as there is now an Assocation period. I desperately try to convey to him that he is in, or close to being in, utterly dead-end politics.

'The British state is hundreds of years old. It isn't opposed to justice but it believes in order more,' I explain to him. 'If the British state feels under threat it can be brutal and cruel. The state acted harshly against communists. It was against Irish republicans. Now it sees a threat it cannot understand from Islamism. Britain could deal with IRA terrorism. That was rooted in a specific context. It doesn't know how to handle Islamist violence, which is seen as global and validated by religion. The English protestant state was born out of religious revolution and needed decades if not centuries of torture and repression against its religious enemies before it learnt to live with them. Islamism is the new threat. The state is frightened and ready to do ugly things.'

'But Islam is a religion of peace,' protests Tahrir.

'*Soyez pas idiot!*' I tell him flatly. 'All religions have provoked war and violence,' I continue. 'Christianity throughout the ages sanctioned conquest, massacres, the Inquisition and the most evil violence, to promote the Christian faith and turn state power into an instrument of faith expansion.

'In 1066, the year of the Norman Conquest, the Muslim rulers of Granada took out all the Jews and massacred them. We all know 1066 in England but how many have heard of the anti-Jewish massacre in Granada done by *soi-disant* peaceful Muslims?'

Tahrir protests that Jews lived peacefully under Islamic rule in Medieval Spain.

'Sometimes, sometimes not,' I reply. 'All religions announce they are religions of peace and there is powerful teaching in the Bible and the Koran to that end. But the moment religion sniffs power it will crush, kill or convert the unfaithful.'

I wish he was in our symposium group. But I think it is better to talk about crime and prisons with them and leave Islamism and Muslims outside of that circle.

He is a smart, likeable man, gentle and polite. He could be a powerful proselytiser for a peaceful Islam, ready to shed anti-Semitism, domination of women and hostility to gays. I tell him to make contact with the Quilliam Foundation and Maajid Nawaz.

'Is that Ed Hussain's group?' he asks.

'Maajid and Ed went through a process of Islamic radicalisation and came out the other side much clearer about the dangers Islamism poses. Work with Quilliam and challenge any hint of violence in the name of Islam,' I urge him.

Tahrir goes into his cell and brings out the so-called expert's report on the twisted tag which is being used as a reason to keep him in Belmarsh. It is full of elaborate language but in the end the 'expert' who put a tag around a cylinder of wood to simulate an ankle – as if oak was the same as the flesh and bone of a leg – cannot say what broke it.

The picture in the report looks to me like it is the same plastic used in the kind of wristlet key rings you get in a swimming pool. They sometimes crack or bend over time. If Tahrir wanted to do a runner and leave his wife and eight-year-old daughter alone in Manchester, then one minute's work with a Stanley knife would have done the trick.

He has been wearing the tag for eighteen months since the secret courts in Britain that deal with Islamist militants last saw him. Perhaps he tried to bend the tag but if he wanted to remove it completely it would have been child's play. And where would he run to? Algeria?

Straight into a torture chamber. France? His life has been in England since 1991.

I listen to his story and protests but give no quarter on the evil menace I think Islamism represents. But this is a political creature not a criminal one and Belmarsh is not where he should be. The theory of permanent bang-up that is Chris Grayling's philosophy of making life as hard for prisoners as possible, in the belief that they will leave prisons model citizens, gives me no time.

Perhaps if I talked politics with Tahrir, sympathised with his desire to see justice and democracy in his native Algeria but tried to explain that Islamist violence would never achieve this, I might have been able to make him see the world differently.

But here in Belmarsh, although we have all the time in the world inside our cells, there is no time in prison to work with, work on if you like, political prisoners to get them to see the world differently.

1030H Hooray, I have a legal visit. My first in seventeen days. It is not my solicitor who handled the case but another prominent solicitor with whom I have campaigned on big issues, especially to do with media freedom over the years. I talked to him all during the saga of the BNP complaint and the twists and turns of the CPS and parliamentary handing of it, so it is a legitimate Rule 39 visit.

He is giving me legal advice on a few things I plan to do once out. He says I made a big mistake in not fighting my case much more politically from day one. 'The fact that you were never interviewed by the Parliamentary Investigator is such an obvious denial of natural justice, for a start. Then you had all the Tories on the committee gunning for you. The Conservatives are much better at looking after their own than Labour.'

I am tired of this old ground. I trusted the system and it had its own rules and reasons, which I failed to read. Small print often catches you out but unspoken small print is fatal.

He tells me that one Labour MP friend has had a word with the Prisons Minister, who said he would see what he could do provided it was all kept quiet. But Grayling's regime means that, unlike other MP prisoners, I am now well into my third week in Belmarsh. I don't even know who the Prisons Minister is. I don't trust Christ Grayling and if the Prisons Minister is a Lib, trusting one of them doesn't come naturally after all their broken promises and lies.

We keep our meeting going for ninety minutes just for my pleasure of seeing an old, dear friend and having again an intelligent, structured talk. He says Keir Starmer QC is said to want to succeed Frank Dobson as MP for Camden. Given Starmer's terrible record as Director of Public Prosecutions, all smooth talk and no delivery on rape or violence against women, I suppose the House of Commons would be a natural next step. Luckily, I do not live in that part of London as I certainly could not vote Labour if a man like that is the candidate after my experience at the hands of the CPS when he was in charge.

I ask my lawyer friend if he could leave me his green felt-tip pen so I can write. But as I walk from the legal interview cubicle to go back to my cell I can hear a guard calling out, 'MacShane's got a pen, he's got a pen, take it off him.' I protest to the guard and the pen is clearly visible on top of my legal papers.

He takes it off me. 'They'll give you a pen in your houseblock.' Another day, another prison officer lie.

In the waiting room I meet a man I have seen in the Catholic services. He has waited ninety minutes and neither solicitor nor barrister has turned up. Indeed, his solicitor has sent him a letter saying she thinks the appointed legal aid barrister is 'uninformed and uninterested in the case'.

To be sure, he is a criminal who has been out on a tag and then committed a crime. Against stupidity, as Schiller wrote, the Gods themselves contend in vain. But he has been remanded for several months. His first court appearance was at the Harrow County Court, yet here he is in Belmarsh. He has sent the letter from the solicitor with her negative assessment of the defence barrister to the judge. But he is not even sure if the judge who first heard the case will be the judge who will finally deal with it.

His main worry, though, is his nephew, aged thirty and seriously mentally ill. The nephew is also in Belmarsh and is constantly being given the wrong mix of complex and subtly calibrated and balanced drugs necessary to keep him from going completely insane.

'My sister is going out of her mind with worry. Her son should be in a mental health facility, in secure conditions but getting proper treatment. Instead he's dumped in here.'

1117H Back to my cell and jacket potato and baked beans to eat while watching Prime Minister's Questions. Not a single question on a foreign affairs issue such as I usually tried to ask. PMQs sound more and more like a county council meeting. I learn that my friend, Paul Goggins, the MP for Wythenshawe, has died aged sixty after collapsing while out running. Time to worry. My uncle, who was the main GP in Wythenshawe from 1960 until retirement, was Paul's family doctor.

I remember going to Wythenshawe Labour Party dinners with Uncle Joe. Paul and I became great friends and he kept sending Christmas cards even after I was ousted from the Commons. One in 2012 had the line: 'I just do not understand why you were forced out given what so many other MPs did but I – we – miss you.' Bless you, Paul. RIP.

Labour MPs lead with their chin. The rent-a-quote John Mann asks Cameron why policing has been reduced in Worksop. Cameron replies saying crime has gone down 27 per cent in Mann's constituency. The Tories roar and cheer and Mann looks silly.

Another Labour MP asks about some Conservative councillor of Pakistani background who is said to have committed a crime. The PM says that at the time the gentleman is alleged to have committed the crime he was a Labour councillor and Labour have done nothing about the allegations.

Again I am puzzled. The iron rule in the Commons is to never ask a question unless you know the answer and have thought through all the possible replies which can undermine your point. Labour MPs seem to have eaten too much plum pudding over Christmas and forgotten that elementary rule.

Watching PMQs, I have not the slightest desire to be there. Our nation needs reform. Our slow decline must be reversed. But there is nothing in current politics that suggests anyone can make the arguments and take the decisions that can stop Britain's ineluctable slide.

On the news, I cannot believe my ears. Sadiq Khan, an immensely likeable solicitor from Tooting, now Chris Grayling's shadow, is ranting about the need to send more people to prison. He should spend two weeks here. Our judges, CPS and police funnel more people to prison than ever before. What is Sadiq up to? Does he want a prison in every constituency? Has the Labour Treasury team calculated the cost of sending many more people to prison? Which other part of the public sector will take cuts to satisfy Sadiq's demand that prison numbers should go up?

I always thought Sadiq was a nice, Tiggerish, sensible man. Any shadow Justice Minister at any stage of any political cycle can dredge up statistics to show that many court or police processes end up without custodial sentences. Crime is falling all over the developed world. It is going non-violent into computer, cash-point, VAT, gambling and other frauds. Bank robberies have all but vanished – now banks steal from us.

So why is Sadiq setting Labour in the American direction of sending everyone and anyone to prison? Labour should be the party of reform, reform, reform. Intelligent modernisation based on best practice and outcomes from elsewhere. And, as much as Labour may dislike the Lib Dems, if Labour scalpels out any fibre of reform, it will not increase its voter base. At any stage, Chris Grayling can trump a Labour demand for more people to be flung into prison. Bad politics, Sadiq. You are worth much more than send-more-to-prison clichés.

1520H Banged up in the cell since 11.20. My long excursion to the gym yesterday appears not to have broken the general rule that I should spend as much time in solitary confinement as possible. The window slit in my cell door opens and it is the wonderful Father Edward, checking up on me. I assure him that the system hasn't broken me yet.

Then Benny on houseblock cleaning duties also opens the cell door window slit on the pretence he is cleaning it. He had a meeting with a probation officer today who will make a report on his mercy life-ending of his terminally ill mother in agony with her cancer. I suppose by Sadiq Khan's rule he should spend yet more time serving a sentence in addition to the months he has spent in Belmarsh on remand. Benny is in tears through the thick window glass as he says he had to relive his mother's last moments. I oppose euthanasia but the idea this man should spend years in prison makes no sense.

I wonder if I will ever be allowed to see inside the Belmarsh library, a workshop or education class?

1605H The cell door opens and a wodge of emails and letters are handed. The first one I open is from the prison. It contains the Visitors' Order forms I sent out more than a week ago. A tiny, handwritten note says I cannot see my children until 20 January, a fortnight away. This is truly cruel, inhumane. I was supposed to get what's called a reception family visit within a day or two of arriving here.

I have seen two of my four children so far. This news takes the shine off all my other letters full of warmth, love and solidarity. I read them all carefully. They come from France, Denmark, Switzerland, with emails from America, Canada and Australia. I savour them. I read every word. Why does my generation have such tiny, crabby handwriting? Except dear old Roger A, who promises a ski trip when out. I smile at Laura's French mistakes. I want to reply to them all, to hug all the friends who write. Jane has sent an email daily from Sydney. She has lived there for twenty years. But all the happy times together come back.

Poor Simon Hoggart has died of pancreatic cancer. He kept it at bay for three years. A wonderful writer, amongst the best of craftsman journalists of his generation. Vicky says the press coverage of his death was on a brief affair a decade ago. Journalists can be utter shits.

1650H Cell door opens. 'MacShane, you're transferring to Brixton tomorrow at nine.' Brixton! Is that an open prison? Is that where there is fresh air? The guard says, 'At least it's a step up from Belmarsh.'

Who is it that has it in for me? Every other politician prisoner has done his time in an open prison. I go to one of the sink-holes in the European network of prisons. I am utterly dismayed and now quite depressed.

Cliff told me to file my nails using the small green torn piece of pan scourer. I try but it makes hardly any impact and turns the tips of my finger nails bright green. I understand why the famous file is banned. But can an emery board file through the thick bars on my cell windows?

1705H Out of cell. Usually we get ninety minutes or two hours of association. Now it is barely an hour in which to eat dinner, shower and use the phone. I talk briefly to Vicky who was with Gisela Stuart in the Commons. I adore Gisela and do not understand why Blair and Brown did not find a use for her manifest talents. Don't be silly. Of course I know. Gisela is her own woman, beholden to no one, clear of thought and confident in her views. In her native Germany, politicians like that get on. Look at Angela Merkel. In Britain, she, like many able Conservative women, have to wait obediently until the chaps notice their ability. Vicky is always positive and practical on the phone. She would make a marvellous field commander in a war. So she sees Brixton as better for visits and close to home. But will I get any more visits?

I ask prisoners and screws about Brixton. Ray has spent time there. 'Food's better. You're out all day. It's better than here but anywhere would be.'

I eat my last Belmarsh dinner. Meat sludge pie, mash, peas and the nice prisoner who hands out fruit or bananas gave me two bananas – a special treat.

I eat and shower and go out to call Sarah who is going to Rio tomorrow for work. The first call doesn't go through as it's the broken phone. I lose my place in the queue and go back to wait again. Just before bang-up I get through for ninety seconds to talk to Sarah and Emilie. I wonder when I will see them. I say goodbye to friends on my floor.

Paul, who is waiting for his trial after attempting to kill his wife, shows me a letter from the Pension Office saying he will lose his pension. He is angry. 'I've paid taxes all my life. This £100 a week is for my wife. Do they have the right to take it off me?'

I have to confess I don't know. Does going to prison mean you lose your pension, your savings, your house? I can only hope that one day some brave MP can take up these issues.

There is a younger prison officer on duty, who locks me up. He has been polite. The older Scottish officer who is also a human being says that the broken phone has been the curse of this block. 'So why not fix it?' I ask. After all you can buy a phone for a tenner anywhere. He shrugs his shoulders sadly. I wonder what Governor Wragg looks like and if he ever visits his prison.

I pompously tell the young officer, 'You can take away liberty but prison does not exist to take away humanity. If you stay in the service and move up in the ranks please remember that.'

He smiles and says, 'I'm getting out.'

1750H Bang-up in Belmarsh for the last night. I have given up on the Elizabeth George novel as the last forty pages had been torn out but I don't really care who did it. I wonder if I will be able to see my own books again when in Brixton and be allowed to use my own toothbrush or even an emery board to file my nails. Like the Abbot in the French Revolution, I have survived.

My heart sinks as I reflect on all the people who do not need to be here and who will never have a voice to convey the utter futility of sending the old, the lame, the weak, the half-mad, the idiots who briefly lost control, as well as those who have not, and will never, commit an act of violence, to this incarceration unit. I feel sorry for the prison guards who have far too many people to control so that all they can do is bark orders and often be crudely unpleasant because there is no room or space or money for helping prisoners become full humans again.

Of course the Soho nail bomb killer must be locked away. But for fifty years? Do we allow no room for repentence or for rebirth as a full citizen? Must our prisons be waiting rooms for death as our judges become ever more reactionary and our prosecutors just want to meet quotas? And why, oh why, did I not invest an iota of my political life in prison reform? If I was such a coward, why should I expect higher behaviour from the police and legal apparatus, who would lose pay and perks if we emptied our prisons and kept inside only those who truly need to be in Hellmarsh?

THURSDAY 9 JANUARY 2014

A prison wall was round us both,
Two outcast men we were:
The world had thrust us from its heart,
And God from out His care:
And the iron gin that waits for Sin
Had caught us in its snare.

– Oscar Wilde

0650H Woken up an hour ago by the rattling metal noise of a guard's long key chain swinging by. BBC News reports the same story from last night about how the police shot dead Mark Duggan, the black Tottenham man. When he came out of the people carrier he was holding up his hands in surrender. He was gunned down in cold blood. Every time I take the Stockwell tube I see the plaque to Jean Charles de Menezes. He too was executed in cold blood as he lay on the floor of a Victoria Line tube I have taken hundreds of times. We have abolished the death penalty but instead execute dark-skinned persons the police are suspicious of.

When the police surrounded the two Islamist psychos who axed to death the poor off-duty soldier, Lee Rigby, in Greenwich last summer, they shot at the legs of the killers to bring them down. Duggan was surrounded by cars of armed policemen so why was he shot in the heart without a by your leave? The cop made a dreadful mistake. But the justice system should have some mechanism for holding the police responsible and giving some closure to the dead man's family.

I have my last shave in Belmarsh using the TV screen as a mirror. I am reading a John Grisham crime novel Mike gave me. In it, the death row cells, 10 by 6, seem bigger than my Belmarsh home. And they have a metal mirror on the wall.

0835H Last symposium with Mumble and Mole. I ask them if they have any money waiting for them on the outside.

Mumble smiles. 'I am often asked that question and my answer is invariably the same. Yeah, I've got £2 million waiting for me outside but Securicor don't know it. You going to get a job outside?' he asks.

I explain my plans to start earning again as a writer and helping people with EU networking.

'Fuck. That doesn't sound much. Tell you – go and get a job with Securicor and wait for us to get out.'

I try to get the symposium members to focus on why and how they became criminals. Both Mumble and Mole have done long stretches. So why did they keep at it?

'It's family, innit? You just grow up and that's what you do. You belong to a firm and if you hear of a piece of work that makes sense, you do it,' says Mumble.

'I am in east London and Mole is south London and we know each other but our firms operate differently.'

Their wives were friendly, though Mumble is now divorced. He escaped while en route from prison to court. 'Some stupid cunt had a gun and shot a driver in the leg. I didn't know that was going to happen. When I was recaptured in Europe the judge dredged everything, even the

BBC job twenty years before. He kept adding the possible punishments together so he gave me eighteen years, basically for escaping.'

I look at this middle-aged Londoner wrapped in his thick woollen cardigan and can't quite fathom why he chose the life he has enjoyed so far. Is it that desire to be in the literal sense an outlaw, beyond the laws and rules and conventions that bind the rest of us? An Ayn Rand or Manchester Liberal belief that no one should pay taxes, the state should be small and unconstraining? Or just a rejection of the limited offer that the London working class has unless you are lucky enough to get one of the rare elite jobs that provide a decent income?

Mumble gave a clue, 'You get up of a morning, maybe at midday you go down to the (boxing) gym. You meet one or two people, have a drink, see what business is around. You might go racing or watch telly. In the evening you can go out to the pub or take the wife out to a nice restaurant.'

It's a lazy life, much as enjoyed by aristocrats throughout the ages. No real work, a little outdoor recreation and lots to drink, as the money rolls in unseen from the exploitation of land, tenants and a lumpen labouring class who work for pittance pay so the rich can live an easy life.

As they watch *Downton Abbey*, or read *Hello!* with its rich celebs, why shouldn't some of the working class think they can lead similar lives? Because the government refuses to treat drugs like the biggest killer drug of them all, alcohol, they become bootleggers to supply the demand for cocaine or marijuana or khat. All the front-benchers and journalists who have snorted a line of cocaine or puffed a joint are the demand side of a global industry that needs supplying. Some of my Belmarsh friends are just like bootleggers in Prohibition America, as they provided what Old Etonians and Bullingdon Club boys saw and see as just a necessary component in an enjoyable Notting Hill evening or a Tuscan villa party or a Mediterranean yachting holiday.

The old saw runs: 'If you want to steal a little money, rob a bank. If you want to steal a lot of money, run a bank.' My thieving symposium comrades are at a loss as to why Keir Starmer's CPS has not charged a single banker with anything connected to the false prospectuses, insolvent trading, dishonest insurance selling and other examples of false accounting.

The taxpayer and British citizen has had to transfer ten per cent of national wealth to the banksters because of their criminal incompetence. Great hardship has been imposed on the poor and on public services as a result of the way bankers abused our trust and our money. (The great Conservative lie is that all the hardship due to cuts is the result of Labour profligacy. It isn't. It is the 2008 financial crisis that has required a massive re-organisation of public money. The great Labour lie is that it is a wicked Tory policy that has caused the cuts. It isn't. Had Labour won or formed a coalition government in 2010, pretty much the same cuts in public budgets would have been needed as they have been in most comparable EU member states.)

Talking to another prisoner in jail for carousel fraud he complained that only a small tweak in the way VAT transfers between countries was organised would have prevented the racket. This has now been done and VAT carousel fraud is now a thing of the past. The trials with the batteries of QCs, weeks of jury service, and endless court time ran into millions of public expenditure the taxpayer has to cover.

'Why didn't HMRC close the loophole years ago? It's almost as if they preferred to pay twice – losing the VAT and paying for expensive court cases which never caught the big boys – rather than admit their system wasn't foolproof,' was the reasonable argument he advanced.

I left my last Belmarsh symposium with regret. These were men I had never encountered before and would never mix with again. A very old dear friend, the *Guardian* journalist, Duncan Campbell, has written about Britain's criminal class and got to know serious criminals. He is a journalistic rarity. I cannot think of any other recent journalist who has explored modern crime and the professionals and craftsmen for whom crime is a way of life. *Tout comprendre c'est tout pardonner*, so perhaps it is better not to understand criminals too well or too much. Better to stay with our stereotypes and clichés.

Yet what is the difference between the public schoolboy who snorts coke or the journalist who produces a joint with coffees at a dinner party and the man who supplies it? What is the difference between the VAT cheat and the city lawyer who fixes up contracts in tax havens so as to avoid paying tax? A policeman can shoot dead at point black range an unarmed black man holding up his hands in surrender and there is no sanction. The line between crime and excusable behaviour is gossamer thin.

I shake hands with symposium members, with others accused of murder and financing terrorism and say Goodbye. Belmarsh has been one of the most intense three weeks of my life. I wouldn't have missed it for the world.

0940H I throw my bits and pieces into a thick transparent plastic bag and walk back along bleak corridors, with their white and green tiled walls, to the reception. Again, an unnecessary and humiliating strip search. If I really, really wanted to smuggle something out of Belmarsh I would shove it up my deaf and dumb, a new bit of rhyming slang I have picked up here. I have some other prison argot I must check with my friend, the lexicographer of slang, Jonathon Green. But my bottom is un-probed and I put back my Belmarsh trackies, T-shirt and sweatshirt.

I am not sure why I am not going to an open prison but instead to Brixton, which got a terrible prison inspector's report late last year. Was it a mistake for MP friends to raise my case with the Prisons Minister? Having a Labour politician at his mercy must be a treat. Can they stop me getting out on tag in early February?

Six of us, including a heroin addict in a desperate state of withdrawal, wait to go. He fidgets and jumps up and down shouting pointlessly at the guards, peppering them with questions they are not interested in. He is thirty-two with a Belsen-thin, emaciated body. He pulls up the sweatshirt sleeve of his left arm. The inside of the arm is marked with red slashes where he has cut himself.

'It's the only way I could get out of Hellmarsh,' he says through his mouth, where half of his teeth are missing. This is a sad, sick wreck of a half-man. A younger black man wearing a mentoring T-shirt tries to talk to him.

'Look, bruv, you're not doing yourself any good. If you keep on shouting they'll put you in the block and you'll get nothing.'

The badly ill drug addict just twitches, desperate for anything – a cigarette, a tobacco patch, something sweet – to ease the state of cold turkey he is going through. If he gets some burn – tobacco – he can trade it for heroin when he gets to Brixton.

Two other prisoners are also sick. Jimmy has a colostomy bag under his shirt. He had bad diverticulosis – a word he cannot pronounce – and had an operation, which means he has to carry the bag until his intestines are ready to be reconnected again.

'I'm very frightened. To open the bag you have to snip very carefully with small surgical scissors. The Belmarsh nurse was a brute. She took big scissors and just hacked away. She made two bags useless. I don't know what's going to happen in Brixton.'

This fear of Brixton is worrying. I still have no piece of paper saying what category I am but it doesn't sound as if Brixton will be that big an improvement.

Another very thin man pulls two long green sheathes out of his pocket. They are catheters, which have to be inserted into his penis for whatever illness or malfunction he suffers.

We wait endlessly in a glass-walled holding room in Belmarsh reception. Lenny is there and hopes he can get a needed eye operation in Brixton, which was denied in Belmarsh.

There is talk about categorisation I have no notification of what category I am in. Perhaps as Ian McShane they don't know.

So here I am with the seriously disabled, sick and detoxing insane. I am sure they all have done something wrong. The penile catheter man says he managed security at some rave club and he was taking a knuckle duster to the office to hand it in when he was stopped and charged with possession of a dangerous weapon. I think of all the people leaving John Lewis or a Jamie Oliver kitchen shop with the latest super sharp kitchen knife and think of the bonanza the police could have outside Peter Jones in Sloane Square if they stopped, searched and charged every *grande dame* of Chelsea who'd bought a blade.

At any rate, surely tagging and daily reporting to the police would be more sensible than Belmarsh and Brixton.

The transfer coach is an odd vehicle. You sit in a tiny cubicle with less leg stretch room than an Easyjet seat. You can stand up but the hard metal plastic seat offers no comfort. I can see for some terrorist murderer such an iron cage might be appropriate. Another prisoner told me it costs £1,500 on a prison budget to have one of these vehicles, so prisoners are kept rotting in the wrong jail until there are enough of them to justify a transfer. I would have been happy to take the bus.

The attendant looks at me and says: 'Are you a Muslim?' I say no. 'Good, I've only got a ham sandwich left,' he replies.

I think this is the first racist crack I've heard from someone in uniform since arriving in custody. He allows himself his low-grade racism because he is an employee of Serco, so not a public servant.

The sky is blue and through the darkened reinforced Perspex slit of my tiny cubicle I can see the Thames. I watch Woolwich merge into Greenwich and then more familiar sights – Brixton market, TK Maxx, Poundland, Iceland, the Ritzy cinema as we go down the Brixton Road.

The journey is punctuated by banter between the Guv – as anyone in a uniform is called – and the Bruvs, the term prisoners use when addressing each other or calling to a fellow inmate.

It is sexist and homophobic. 'Look, look, there's a ladyboy crossing the street. Ain't she gorgeous? Fucking poofs.' The word nonce always pops up. The Bruvs shout jokey insults to each other while the Guv tells a complicated story about a prisoner who tried to smuggle in a mobile phone charger by inserting it in his anus. There is a technical discussion as to whether it is more difficult thus to smuggle in a two or a three-pin charger.

I doze intermittently as, from early days in the Scouts or Cadet force, I have learnt to half-sleep sitting up – a small talent of great use in the House of Commons. We go up Brixton Hill and I dream of getting out and taking the number 37 bus home. The press, John Lyon CB, the judge, Kevin Barron and Keir Starmer QC, the BNP and my political opponents in the Commons have had their fun and left me on the cross long enough. Why should the taxpayer's money continue to be wasted on feeding, clothing, washing and bedding me?

We go up Brixton Hill and turn right into a small road I had not noticed before. There is a small sign with 'Brixton' on and the 'HMP' and 'Prison' broken off. The transfer vehicle has to manoeuvre carefully to get through the narrow archway, built when prisoners arrived by horse and cart. There is barely six inches either side and a large notice warning that any damage to vehicles is NOT the responsibility of HMP Brixton.

We wait a further hour in the vehicle until we are let out, one after the other. The heroin addict is screaming and banging the side of his cubicle like something out of a Rowlandson cartoon of Bedlam. The colostomy man is desperate for food as he needs something to go into his stomach.

I assume they unload by age so I am last out. A prison guard with a very slight foreign accent I cannot place but I reckon is Hungarian takes the details. Then a strip search, my fourth in less than three weeks. Fingerprinted again. When first I was fingerprinted after being arrested on trade union picket lines in the '70s, it was a messy affair with inky fingers rolled back and forth over ink and paper. Now, like arriving in the United States, there is a little fingerprint reader. My right forefinger doesn't read well – 'You've been rubbing out too much,' jokes the guard but my index finger on my right hand is fine. There is something symbolic that my first action in HMP Brixton is giving it the finger.

I get a natty little identity card. It says 'Ian McShane'. I smile. Clearly the prison service has not read Judge Sweeney's belief that to spell my name wrong was an imprisonable offence. I was no longer *Denis MacShane* but *Ian McShane* – both names spelt incorrectly – and I will carry the card in my wallet as a reminder for the rest of my life.

More waiting. It takes six hours to move from Belmarsh to Brixton – a distance of thirteen miles. Our heroin man is now very sick, ranting and raving, and finally a medical orderly arrives to lead him away. Jimmy is clutching his stomach and colostomy bag and also is uncomfortable.

I ring the bell and a screw opens the door. I pompously use my PhD title. 'I'm Dr MacShane and this man is not well with his colostomy bag. Please can you stop starving him as it will make him very ill.'

The door opens soon after and we are ushered in to collect our Belmarsh bags. I briefly see again my suitcase but not my anorak, scarf, suit or shirt. Nor my wallet, still less the £340 I arrived with. I wonder where they are?

I am allowed to take a few of my own T-shirts and a pair of jeans but not my casual shoes or my washbag with the precious dental floss. The guard with the slight foreign accent does allow me to take four books. 'Make them long ones,' he advises. I go for Alexandra Richie's 740 pages on the Warsaw Uprising, the Houllebecq and a couple of thrillers. He clicks suspiciously on a biro and rifles through a brand new A4 pad but allows them through.

I had been told that, once a D Category prisoner, you could have your own clothes, books, toiletries, pens and paper, and money to make phone calls. Obviously I was misinformed, or Chris Grayling has changed the rules. I suspect the latter.

1513H Finally I enter C block of Brixton Prison. It is a shock. Brixton was built just after the Napoleonic wars. It was a mid-nineteenth-century women's prison and, at the end of Victoria's reign, became the main remand and trial prison for London. It has some delightful Victorian architecture with a very handsome church and a wonderful octagon tower. C Wing sadly has no charm. It is just a dull four-floor, long rectangular block, with twenty-four cells on each side of the floor, built sometime in the middle of the last century as more and more buildings were crammed onto the Brixton site. There is a warders' office on each landing but they are rarely occupied.

The top ceiling consists of iron bars with a high-vaulted metal roof. There are metal grids stretched out between the narrow corridors either side of the landings. There are two phone booths on each landing but I quickly find out that the one on my top-floor landing has been broken for months. The prison governor, Ed Tullett, is too poor a manager to get the phone repaired.

The ground floor is long with ground floor offices, a large display cabinet full of different prison forms, a food delivery counter, a prison staff room, a clinic and store rooms. There is a reception desk behind a counter, where a guard usually sits. One stylish screw, with tattoos covering his arms and an earring, gently plays his banjo. I ask him if he can do any George Formby songs and he looks at me in disgust.

'I'd rather kill myself than play George Formby,' he said.

The two-prisoner cell is 3 metres by 2 metres. It has a double metal bunk bed, two noticeboards, one chair and one stool, some low cupboards to store things, a table, a TV set with eight of the Freeview channels, and a high window, impossible to look out of unless you stand on the chair.

There is a bathroom with a lavatory and sink and a door that doesn't shut properly, but prison, as well as taking away liberty, takes away privacy – just a small added humiliation to help build up resentment and ensure prisoners leave prison with an added sense of injustice and dislike for a system that seems designed to break the human spirit.

I am to share a cell on the fourth floor at the end of the landing. Outside is a pool table and the click-clack of balls carries on all day. There are three dust-bins. In Belmarsh and Brixton everyone loads up their plates for fear of hunger but a few mouthfuls is more than enough. I will boil a kettle to wash away into the loo the greasy film of sludge that rests on the plastic plate. So in the dustbins outside there is endless swill from dumped food.

I am to share with a young fifty-year-old good-looking Scot, a successful businessman, who found himself edged into VAT fraud by a more dynamic partner. The partner has gone off to Pakistan where there is no extradition treaty but Douggie is in Brixton. His former cellmate, an Irishman, has covered the pin-boards – in Brixton at least there are drawing pins – with rosaries, pictures of the current and previous Popes, palm crosses, and most poignant of all, a London Underground map. I have been using the tube for six decades, and look at all my favourite stations and the ones I have never got on or off at.

Douggie and his previous cellmate have quietly stocked up the cell with all I couldn't have in Belmarsh. There is salt, pepper, chilli flakes, soy sauce, tomato ketchup, Sarson's vinegar, Heinz hot chilli sauce and muesli. Douggie is exceptionally friendly. I am not quite sure why he is still in prison. His sentence was forty-four months and he has spent the last six months in an open prison in Kirkham, not far from Blackpool. He was brought back to court in London for a confiscation order. The judge ruled he should pay just £1. He was a junior cog in the VAT fraud swindle. Now he has to spend the rest of his time in Brixton where the Victorian architecture clashes with twentieth-century additions in a hideous architectural mess, which sends any aesthetic sensibility into a spiral of despair.

I leave all my belongings outside the cell door and go down three flights to ask a guard to open the door. On the whole the screws here, in what is meant to be a D Category prison, are not as aggressive and domineering as in Belmarsh. But they are more incompetent. The officer pants as he climbs the four flights of stairs to let me in.

'Never forget everyone here is a liar,' he warns me. I am tempted to ask if that includes the screws but bite my tongue. I have to ask for bedding and the non-smoking bag with another box of tea bags to add to the one I got at Belmarsh. They are cheerfully enough brought to me as I settle into my Brixton time.

1712H A shout of some sort. I see prisoners leaving their cells. It is roll-call, which never happened in Belmarsh. An officer walks along the two narrow corridors, either side of the meshed opening in the middle of the landing, which look 30 or 40 feet down to the floor. He has a list and checks names against it.

1735H The menu system is the same as at Belmarsh and as I have arrived midweek I have to wait until next Monday before getting food of my choice. So it's rice, chickpeas and diced carrot. But there is chilli waiting for me as I take my plate upstairs to be locked in – again. I had been told that after Belmarsh a move to a Category D prison would be utterly different with the chance of moving freely around the prison to the library, or a common sitting room and some chance of association. But no, it's a bang-up at 5:30 to be locked away for the next fourteen hours.

FRIDAY 10 JANUARY 2014

The delinquent is to be distinguished from the offender by the fact that it is not so much his act as his life that is relevant to characterising him. The penitentiary operation, if it is to be a genuine re-education, must become the sum total existence of the delinquent, making of the prison a sort of artificial and coercive theatre in which his life will be examined from top to bottom. The legal punishment bears upon an act; the punitive technique on a life.

– Michael Foucault

0750H Up by eight as Douggie has to go off to work in the Bad Boys' Bakery – a bakery inside Brixton Prison. It was set up by Gordon Ramsay and provides some rolls and muffins for local Brixton cafés and lemon tart for some London Café Neros. The staff are prisoners. The next idea is to open a restaurant called Clink, again with waiters from the prison. Two Clink restaurants operate already in Cardiff and Sutton prisons. I can see one close to fashionable bourgeois Clapham taking off. How very chic to come dine with convicts as waiters.

I am left alone for the day until an induction meeting in the evening. But the old problems remain. I have very little credit to call anyone. I fill in forms for a visit. So far I have only seen two of my children. Colostomy Bag Jimmy says his father is coming for a three-hour visit. I am still waiting to see my oldest and youngest daughters.

I send out the forms but a guard comes to me later to say I have not filled in someone's precise age. The rule book, the rule book. John Lyon CB would understand. So it looks as if I will be well into my third week before I see my two daughters. This seems mean, even by Chris Grayling's standards.

As in Belmarsh, other prisoners come up to say hello as my name has gone before me. But as in Belmarsh everyone is friendly. 'No one wants you to be under any pressure,' says a very big Afro-Caribbean. 'We'll make sure nothing happens to you.' I get to know Bill better soon. He was involved in the professional boxing business at heavyweight level and looks the part. But this is a gentle giant and he keeps an avuncular eye on me even though I am twenty years older.

I get a letter from my friend, Simon Heffer, dated yesterday, so some mail does get through.

> I am sorry not to have written sooner. I had foolishly believed you'd be in Belmarsh for about forty-eight hours before being moved to some rural idyll. AND THEN Colin told me last night you were being moved to Brixton. I've emailed Mark Field (the Conservative MP for Westminster and thus my MP) to protest against this insanity. I rang him but he is off the map. I await his response. Your treatment has been vindictive from the start, and this is no different.

The letter cheers me up. I had dreams of six weeks of calm writing time. But prison does not allow solitude. As a former journalist I have worked in noisy, busy newsrooms and can write in almost any surroundings. But it is hard to concentrate with the television on, visitors to the cell, going up and down four flights of stairs to check a notice or ask a question from the duty guards or just get out of my cell. Other than my cell, with its odd seat-tablet cemented into the wall with a folded blanket to sit on, there is nowhere to write.

1130H Lunch is a soft 'baguette' with lettuce, a tomato and one or two slivers of cucumber shoved into it. No dressing or mayonnaise or a hint of onion to give some taste as bland, tasteless salads blend into bland, tasteless bread. Again, as in Belmarsh, we are locked away after lunch.

1415H The cell is unlocked. A knock on the door and Brian comes. He is older than me, a slight man with floppy grey hair and spectacles. He brings me a copy of last weekend's *Sunday Telegraph*; a thoughtful paper with good reporters once you get past the boring, in-your-face Tory propaganda lines. But I am in post-newspaper mode. Prisoners are de-citizenised. Politicians are obsessed with insisting prisoners should forsake politics, losing their right to vote, and without a vote why should anyone take interest in the nation's direction of travel?

I had watched Andrew Neil bravely trying to inject interest into the minutiae of Commons activity. His noon BBC2 programme is as good as it can get and I always enjoyed going on it – usually to act as a whipping boy for anti-European MPs and MEPs from the UKIP wing of the Conservative Party and to parry the barbed comments from Neil and his dripping contempt for anything European.

Politics just doesn't exist in prison and after decades of talking, reading, doing politics, I am glad to be out of it. Soon the big question of Europe will have to be settled one way or another. I would like to play my part in taking on the isolationist ideology shaped by William Hague as Conservative leader, 1997–2001, and strengthened by all his predecessors with the help of the populist xenophobic right-winger Nigel Farage and the proprietors of our offshore-owned press. But for the time being politics is not a turn-on.

Still, it's kind of Brian to give me his paper. He is about seventy and serving a sentence for some white-collar crime presumably connected to his profession of accountancy. No individual lost money. But Brian is here. As with Douggie I cannot see the point of the taxpayer keeping Brian endlessly in Brixton.

There is a complicated sequence of getting prisoners back into normal life. A set of hoops to jump though has been created. First, short visits, then a two-day overnight stay, followed by a longer home visit. All this assumes that a prisoner has a home. But judges pointlessly sending non-violent men, and especially women, to prison set in chain events that destroy homes and split families.

Prisoners, ahead of their release date, are encouraged and helped to find jobs with charities or firms willing to take on a prisoner. Many decent employers reject the prejudice against anyone in prison that editors enjoy promoting, and give a prisoner a chance. But this only really works if the prisoner has the basic skills – reading and writing, numeracy, computer, tablet, modern mobiles and emailing abilities.

In Brixton, these simply don't exist. You can use a clunky wall phone but mobiles are banned, though there are plenty around. So prisons keep feeding and providing housing, laundry, gym sessions, television and medical care free of charge to men and women who could easily be set free to make and pay their way in the outside world.

Instead, the main lesson of prison is how to do crime better. Brian explains, 'You get these cocky youngsters coming in here. They're spotted by older men and told how to make serious money when outside, not the chicken-shit small scale stuff that's landed them here. There's no rehabilitation. Just a patient wait to get out. But the longer you rot in here, the more rotten you become.'

I do not know how to balance punishment and re-entry into a productive crime-free life. But C Wing of Brixton is not how you do it.

I am allowed out, as in Belmarsh, for a short twenty-five minutes' exercise – walking round and round a small basketball yard. There are huge rolls of razor barbed wire on the top of every wall, fence or railing. Above the yard is dense netting, whether to stop something thrown in or out is not clear. All around are the grubby, shabby buildings with nothing green or pleasant to be seen.

1736H Dinner is whatever is left over after other prisoners have been served. I had been told Category D prisoners were properly fed but that is another deceit, an unpunishable fraud which, unless you are a prisoner, you do not know is being perpetrated.

1815H An induction session for the new prisoners. It is done by a more experienced prisoner, again here from a renowned and respected public institution. He mutters about being a scapegoat for an in-house scandal in which more senior officials covered their backs. He is, of course, black. And the police, CPS and judge were all white.

Whatever.

There is no self-pity, just a matter-of-fact explanation of how to survive in C Wing and the various bureaucratic formalities of getting out on the various release schemes.

'It's a shit-hole. Everything is shut down as the screws say there's a staff shortage.' Yet, as in Belmarsh, I always see the prison guards in clumps of two, three or four not doing very much. This is about better management, giving prison officers a worthwhile job and a sense of purpose. Other than locking away violent men, sexual predators and depriving men and women of periods of liberty because at a given moment society judges certain behaviour a crime – to be in debt was considered a crime in the nineteenth century – it is difficult to divine a sense of purpose in prisons.

I go and get my second Hep B injection in the medical room. It is more painful than the first. I ask for some aspirin because I have a dull, slight head-ache and because I have been told to take one each evening as a prophylactic against heart and stroke problems. The nurse says no unless I come back and get a prison doctor to prescribe it. Prescribe? Asprin? Ah well. I check my weight, which is down a bit, and my blood pressure, which is stable at 141/83.

1920H Back in my cell and lock-up. Douggie is keen on *Coronation Street* and *EastEnders* and otherwise we just look for the best films or action dramas on TV. I have forgotten current affairs programmes existed.

SATURDAY 11 JANUARY 2014

A prison taint was on everything there. The imprisoned air, the imprisoned light, the imprisoned damps, the imprisoned men, were all deteriorated by confinement. As the captive men were faded and haggard, so the iron was rusty, the stone was slimy, the wood was rotten, the air was faint, the light was dim. Like a well, like a vault, like a tomb, the prison had no knowledge of the brightness outside.

– Charles Dickens

0830H Late get-up as there is no work or education for prisoners today. I wonder if I will ever do any? Breakfast is some muesli – at last! – which my cellmate has and shares generously. He also has supplies of fruit, which again he is happy for me to plunder.

Douggie takes *The Sun* on Saturday for the TV supplement so as to spot what to watch over the next seven days. Prisoners say there was some talk last year, when Chris Grayling was playing to the tabloid gallery, of removing televisions from the cells of all but the few prisoners who had 'earned' the most privileges. Luckily someone with a modicum of common sense stayed Grayling's hand. There is so much tension in prisons as it is.

A number of prisoners order a Saturday paper, mainly to get the TV supplement for the week ahead. A sensible prison would print off the day's TV programmes so that prisoners can see what to watch in the long hours of being sealed in a cell. But common sense is not a prison practice, so prisoners who have a little cash to spend can buy a paper. This Saturday none of the papers arrive. There is no explanation. Just a simple rise in tension.

Pat, a 62-year-old Irishman, tells me his story and again something stinks. He is a professional pub manager and had never been in a police station, let alone a prison cell, before a drunken Englishman set in train a sequence of events that brings Pat to Brixton.

His pub in west London is in the interstice of super-posh Notting Hill and Afro-Caribbean Ladbroke Grove. There was one customer, a former solider, who had served in Northern Ireland and let everyone know about his service. His nickname was 'Shell-shocked' and he made little secret of his dependence on drugs to stave off depression. He liked to buy cheap beer at nearby off-licences and drink the cans on chairs outside the pub. According to Pat he was obnoxious, drunk and on serious medication. Over time he had behaved so badly he was permanently barred.

In August 2011, London rioted and burned for three days and the Metropolitan Police chiefs as well as the Home Secretary, the Prime Minister and the Mayor were all on summer holidays. They lost all grip and control. Riots, arson and looting and attacks on food and drink locations erupted all over London, with the Ladbroke Grove area targeted as much as anywhere else. Pat was away on holiday with his wife. The replacement manager got a pick-axe handle to keep handy, like the Turkish delicatessen owners with their machetes, to defend the pub in the absence of an adequate police presence or leadership in the weekend London burned.

The next year, Pat found the wooden handle useful. He had one encounter with the police who came to the pub and asked him to act as a police spy on any drug dealers in a part of London where cocaine-sniffing bankers and members of the political–city–media elite like to live, close to the source of their favourite drugs. Pat refused to become a Metropolitan police drug squad auxiliary. Instead Pat simply banned drug dealers from the pub. He said he also had a problem with a barmaid from Brazil.

As Minister for Latin America a decade ago, I received an angry phone call from Home Secretary David Blunkett. He had a planeload of illegal immigrants in a government-chartered plane at RAF Brize Norton that Blunkett wanted to ship home to Brazil with maximum publicity, in order to discourage other economic migrants from Latin America's biggest country.

However, the Brazilian government was refusing landing permission to this plane with its mass expulsion cargo of Brazilian citizens. Brazil said this modern-day equivalent of convict transportation breached the human rights and dignity of the Brazilians.

David wanted me to persuade Brazil to change its mind. The plane was loaded and ready to take off. I called the Brazilian Foreign Minister but to no avail. They would take their citizens, who had sought to work *chez nous*, back one by one on a regular flight but not the showpiece mass transportation.

Brazil since the late '90s has been one of the most dynamic countries in the world, getting steadily richer year by year, as a giant new middle class came into being. One of the paradoxes of economic take-off is that the richer a country becomes and the better paid its citizens are, the more they seek to spread their wings and try to work elsewhere, legally or illegally. British citizens work all over Europe, just as hundreds of thousands of French, German and American citizens work in Britain.

Pat just hired the pretty young Brazilian woman with her charming accent to work on bar shifts, without checking too closely on her status.

'I asked her for her NI number and she kept saying she'd forgotten it at home and I just let it drift,' he explains. Before long, however, he noticed she was helping herself to £20 or £30 from the till and he fired her. It was a fatal mistake.

The ex-solider turned up again and drank steadily from 2 p.m. onwards. When Pat turned up for the evening's business he spotted the barred drunk and threw him out. The ex-solider tried to come back again and Pat evicted him. When he closed for the day with a taxi waiting to take him home he found the drunk, drugged, angry solider waiting for him. He headbutted Pat and, according to the soft-spoken Irish publican, came into the bar and the CCTV shows him lunging at Pat, who picked up the wooden handle from behind the bar and whacked him on the shoulder.

A general mêlée broke out and, as different people grabbed the wooden instrument, someone – not Pat – grazed the drunken soldier's temple, where the slightest cut causes copious bleeding. An ambulance was called and the drunk was taken to hospital, where he discharged himself before a doctor had seen him.

The next day the police arrested Pat and he was charged with aggravated grievous bodily harm. Between the army veteran and the Irishman who had refused to work for the drug squad, it was an easy choice for the police. To make matters worse, the dismissed Brazilian bargirl, seeking her revenge, gave a damning statement to the police in exchange for not being deported as an illegal immigrant.

The police had a box ticked; the usual half-hearted defence and a judge wanting to fill prisons did the rest. Pat was sentenced to forty-two months. 'My son is a solicitor in Ireland. He said, "Dad, you're Irish. The man was a soldier. The police and the judge are English. What do you expect?"'

Unlike me, who had been detained by the police while working for trade union rights in England in the '70s and in South Africa a decade later, as well as seeing the inside of cells in Warsaw's notorious Mokotow prison, where both wartime Nazis and post-war communists held political opponents, Pat, who came with me to mass the next day, had had no contact with police and prison before.

His sense of injustice was strong but he was helpless to get redress. My sense of concern was that there was no point in wasting much more British taxpayers' money on him. As ever, I only have his side of the story. Perhaps he is a terribly violent man who savagely attacked a harmless, sober, ex-squaddie. But somehow I doubt it. What I don't doubt is that it is a pointless waste to keep him in Brixton.

1130H Lunch is called. I go down to wait until all the prisoners who have submitted menu choice have been served. I go in and there are two 'pork' sausages and a tray full of halal sausages, whatever they are made from. I offer to take the halal sausage and leave the greasy, fatty porkers for one of the other recently arrived inmates.

'You can't have halal,' says a prisoner-server. So I take the last pork sausages as there is nothing else. The halal sausages will simply be thrown away.

1400H The cell is unlocked and I go down to get my second visit to a gym in three weeks. Apparently there is a new and well-equipped gym somewhere on the Brixton site. The one we go to is sweaty, scruffy, with equipment dangerously close together. It is good to lift weights, pedal, row, push and try some abdominal exercises.

As at Belmarsh, the prisoners are obsessed with upper body work. Great arms and torsos emerge from smaller lower bodies. Steroids are in widespread use. So are drugs. A report by the Independent Monitoring Board – a prison watchdog – found that 10 per cent of all Brixton Prisoners out on temporary release tested positively for drugs, or were found in possession of them, in 2013. Like producing a disgusting alcohol by leaving fruit and sugar to ferment in a plastic bottle, if you want drugs and alcohol in prison, it's there.

I like exercise gyms. It might nevertheless be better to invest in strengthening inmates' minds rather than their biceps. My Ian McShane Brixton ID card is stamped 'gym' so with luck I'll leave here slimmer and fitter.

1451H Back in C Wing I pick up the laundry I left to be washed in the morning. Again, I am delighted that Her Majesty's servants are so keen to get my laundry done free of charge. In the laundry room, the prisoner in charge shows me some fetching HMP Brixton Prison shirts in chic Kings Road blue prison stripes. I find a well-fitted pair of prison jeans and am annoyed that I bought new ones at Gap in Chelsea at a half-price sale just before Christmas. Again, I am surprised at the generosity of Her Majesty's Prison tailors in providing me with a new set of distinctive clothes that perhaps – once I am out – will make me at long last someone who dresses fashionably.

1730H Dinner of rice, something described as a Cornish pasty, and green beans. At least Chelsea have won and are top of the premiership.

SUNDAY 12 JANUARY 2014

I was naked, and ye clothed me: I was sick, and ye visited me: I was in prison, and ye came unto me.

– Matthew, 25:36

0830H No need to get up early. I am now finally enjoying breakfast, as Douggie has a supply of muesli and fruit. He even has some strong instant coffee, not quite the real thing but better than Nescafé.

0907H There are vague shouts from the wing's central command – the reception desk beside the single entrance door on the ground floor. But they are impossible to understand. Instead you need to assume when an outing – to the gym or this morning to mass – will take place. A small group assembles. The screw leads us outside through one gate and then a hundred yards or so to a steep outside metal staircase that leads to another barred gate and, behind that, the door of a side entrance into the church.

It is a handsome confident mid-nineteenth-century Victorian gothic-style building with arched windows and big carved wooden beams. It was the high moment of Anglican self-confidence before other faiths started demanding space and respect and before the Empire, which Anglicanism so faithfully meshed with, began its decline.

Now the chapel, as it is called, has to serve all faiths. The floor is carpeted to allow Muslims to kneel in prayer. The main wall has a giant crucifix and Catholic stations of the cross behind a small altar and well polished brass lectern. On the east-facing wide wall further back an outline of a minbar, a mosque equivalent of a pulpit, has been painted, and screens are ready to cover up the Christian end of the chapel for Friday prayers.

The different wings come in including those from the VP – Vulnerable Prisoners – wing, where sex offenders or those who might be attacked by other – what? more manly? – prisoners are housed. One elderly white-haired man, bent over his stick, comes in from G Wing, where the 'nonces', to use the hateful prison term of contempt, live. I wonder who he is. A monk from my old school? A soap opera star from the '60s?

After the arrests of famous names from the '60s and '70s for having sex with teenagers, I am surprised that none of the young teenagers who as groupies serviced the voracious sexual appetite of our famous, now pensioner, rock stars have come forward to claim £100,000 from one of our tabloids, with allegations against the big names of rock 'n' roll. The bent, sad old man at mass looks too frail to be a threat to anyone. But if released, he will be chased by newspapers wherever he lives.

I remember the odious campaign launched by the *News of the World* – or was it *The Sun*? – to have released paedophiles publicly humiliated by listing their addresses. The first woman to be attacked in consequence was a paediatrician in Southampton.

Paedophile, paediatricians – for Murdoch's minions, what's the difference? At least the old monster has been humiliated globally as a pathetic cuckold by his Chinese wife, Wendy – or at least so Rupert believes. *The Sun* seems to be the paper of choice for criminals, to judge by the old, stale copies I see lying around. Read by criminals, employing criminals, and edited by – ah well, let's see what the future reveals.

Mass is celebrated by a Jamaican priest with the help of an Italian nun and the hymns are sung to Afro-Caribbean threnodies, though there is a good sprinkling of Irishmen, Poles or those brought up Catholic like myself. I prefer Father Edward's Polish warmth. A Pole knows what prison is like. They lived in a giant Soviet prison until 1989.

Unlike Belmarsh, there is not much chance to mix with Catholics from other wings as the prison officers march us off smartly back to our own wings. At least there is some music, and some very decent prison-visiting Catholics come in and help lead hymn singing.

1036H Back in my cell I go through my 'canteen' double-sided sheet in tiny print to order some extra goodies. I know I have £39.84 to spend. I cannot account for this sudden swelling in my spending cash. I have not worked nor done any education classes. Still, don't look a gift horse in the mouth. I still don't know what happened to the £340 in notes I brought into Belmarsh. I spend all my money on phone credits so I can talk to my children and close friends. I would like a can of shaving foam, which is in my still-confiscated toiletries bag, but none is on offer. The list is a paradise for fatties, with endless sweets, chocolate, biscuits and sweet drinks. One thing Chris Grayling isn't doing is joining the fight against obesity. Anything ordered cannot arrive until next Saturday.

Douggie kindly lets me order anything I want on his canteen so I can keep all my money for phone calls. I'll have to start calling abroad now to set up work once I'm out and that will be more expensive. I don't understand the need for such centralisation, with every 'canteen' sheet sent to the East Midlands to be processed with orders placed in plastic bags, even if for a single bar of chocolate. Then DHL, on a lucrative contract paid by the taxpayer, ships the orders all over England and Wales.

Surely it would make more sense to have a small shop in each prison to stock fresh fruit, stamps and toiletries? I remember running the school tuck-shop, and if I could do this at sixteen it can't be that difficult to do it at sixty. It would allow goodies to be bought as and when needed and keep perishable products like fruit, which I can now order a lot fresher. And why not newspapers and magazines? Perhaps the *New Statesman* and *Spectator* could send in last week's copies for free, as few can afford the cover price these days?

1135H We drop the canteen sheets when getting lunch – jacket potato and beans. I hope I get my phone credit soon. Until the phone credit I have ordered on my canteen sheet arrives, I am down to just over £1 of phone credit, so calls to Vicky and to my daughter, still putting off her university course in Spain because she has not been allowed a visit, are far too brief, abrupt and unsatisfying.

1420H Maybe it's because it's Sunday, but the cell doors are left open. I shower in a shower room with six shower heads separated by small, chest-high partitions. There are three black guys who are full of chatter about my case. 'Why aren't all those other MPs who made real money on expenses in here?' they ask.

I tell them the expenses system with its abuses had been put in place by Margaret Thatcher and extended by all her successors until it blew up. 'If every minister or MP who made a profit at the expense of the taxpayer was sent to prison you'd have to build a new prison,' I tell them.

In fact there was no *mens rea* – a deliberate sense of obtaining money they were not entitled to. There was none in my case but the newly knighted Sir Kevin and Sir Keir decided otherwise. I just hope it ends with me. I know my fellow MPs and how hard they work and how badly they were treated by their leaders over pay and transparent expenses. There is a poor woman Tory minister, Maria Miller, waiting for judgement on helping herself to mortgage interest payments on a London home she and her husband bought twenty years ago and which has been sold at a profit. But that is exactly what the newly knighted Sir Kevin Barron did. As he chairs the committee that sanctions erring MPs over expenses, he cannot sanction her without calling into question his own profit-taking.

One of the prisoners in the shower offers to cut my hair. A previous occupant of my cell left a do-it-yourself haircutter razor. I try it out but with odd stripy results, so if I can find a prisoner who knows what he's doing, I'll be happy.

1715H On the way down to dinner – rice, a chicken patty so hard my plastic knife won't cut it, and some welcome cabbage – I go to the medical room. I have to bend in half to speak through an opening in a barred gate with a sheet of plastic Perspex. The nurse is a young Spanish man. I have a headache and start of a cold. He gives me a Disprin in a tiny plastic shot glass.

I cannot make sense of who is in charge or how to get anything done. All so inefficient. A notice says to go and see landing officer if you have a problem. But the landing office never has anyone in it.

A guard comes up to find me to say that he did not write a number on a Visitors' form. He even manages to do so apologetically. This will mean more delay. Will I ever be allowed to see my children? I try to call Vicky but the call is cut off after ten seconds. Douggie's fellow bakery worker, Ian, told me to call after six as BT has its usual tariff racket in prisons. But we are banged up before six and cannot make calls in the evening, the time when you most want to hear a voice you know and care about. I now have a definite head cold! Belmarsh had one temperature. My cell is warm, but go down to the ground floor and it is freezing.

Before bang-up I go down to ask the reception desk screw about how I find out when I may be leaving on tag. He tells me to write an 'App' – an Application form which prisoners are meant to use for all requests for information, for a transfer, for anything – and put it through a slit in a yellow box marked 'Complaints and Applications'. A guards calls out, 'That's the wrong box', even if it's marked 'Applications'. I do another one. The guard has to sign it before it is deposited. 'It'll go to the Governor but he won't do anything,' he says reassuringly.

1728H Bang-up. The lock-up time is not as bad as Belmarsh but there is now seventeen hours before the cell door opens. We watch Sunday-night TV. I sit at the small table and Douggie lies on the bottom bunk. I write for a couple of hours and have no idea what's on television. When I look up from my pages Douggie is snoring gently.

MONDAY 13 JANUARY 2014

The degree of civilisation in a society can be judged by entering its prisons.
– Fyodor Dostoevsky

0825H Cell door unlocked. Douggie had ordered some bananas which arrived in his canteen plastic bag on Saturday. The skins were already turning black. I don't mind squishy bananas so I share one with him for breakfast.

On Friday the Belmarsh and other new transferees were told we would have a full induction course today. I was looking forward to seeing what education course or prison work I might usefully undertake. In my dreams I was hoping – as a regular guest lecturer at universities around the world – I might be allowed to do some teaching or even help with literacy classes for prisoners whose schooling under the control of local education authorities and teacher unions had left them unable to read or write. But there is to be no induction class, apparently. I don't mind, as I can write, but it seems unfair on other prisoners anxious to get on education courses or start doing some work, both to have something to do and to make a little extra money.

After tea and muesli I go downstairs and see some prisoners with towels and sports drinks bottles assembling to go to the gym. I ask the guard but am told I am not on the list. She is a young Spanish woman. Whatever happened to Gordon Brown's promise of 'British prison guard jobs for British workers'? As a proud European internationalist I have no problems with employing foreigners in public services. Perhaps it is a fair exchange. We send all our criminals to live on the Costa del Crime in Spain, so why shouldn't Spanish citizens work in our prisons?

To be sure, since the introduction of the European Arrest Warrant, the old tag of Costa del Crime has been meaningless – any criminal wanted in Britain has to be instantly extradited. Luckily for criminals, there are lots of MPs and some ministers who want Britain to pull out of EU justice and anti-crime cooperation and abolish the European Arrest Warrant. Phew! My friends in prison have Conservative Eurosceptic friends in the Commons who realise how irritating it is for criminals to face arrest and extradition without fuss and bother.

0855H Back in my cell with the door locked by a screw. I hope this week to get to the Brixton Prison library where prison rules and orders are kept. So-called Category D status is a bit of a joke. I wonder why other politician prisoners were treated differently?

I am halfway through my six weeks in prison. I have no release date yet and have seen more of the inside of two of the worst prisons in England than I expected to. I wonder if my stay will be extended.

1100H The cell door is opened and I can chat to other prisoners. Men who thought they were going to the gym have been sent back as it was closed. 'It's a shambles here. They just scramble your head and then expect you to go out and lead a useful life,' said a well-muscled black man.

Pat, my publican friend, who has been in Wormwood Scrubs, says that mobile phones were common, and there is plenty of weed. The going rate for a prison employee to bring in a mobile phone is £500. I can't blame the prisoners. Only one phone works on my landing. The other has been broken for months and the prison management too useless to get it repaired. It is expensive to call. As in Belmarsh, you have to wait ten minutes for another call if you cannot get through. There is a queue. It is noisy. Why can't I have a mobile? We now know GCHQ listens in to all our conversations. Any prisoner using a mobile phone to make contact with criminals is giving away their numbers and can be listened to.

I am sure that, in the past, prisoners were not allowed to send and receive letters as they might enable communication for nefarious purposes. I can see Home Office civil servants writing out their tedious memos in past decades, explaining why it would be dangerous and create a terrible precedent to allow prisoners to receive and send letters, and then to make phone calls via BT. The same argument applies to letting them use mobile phones. Instead Chris Grayling and his officials encourage illegal smuggling of mobile phones into prison by trying to enforce an unworkable ban.

1230II Lunch is an ice-cream cup of egg mayonnaise where I can't find any egg. I hear a shout which sounds like my name. But it's 'Rashid', not 'MacShane'. Guards bellow out from four floors down. They echo and re-echo through the bars and grills and are quite impossible to make out. The poor women guards have no training in parade-ground shouting and their cries become unintelligible shrieks. It just adds to the confusion and uncertainty and lack of sense of purpose and reason that pervades the English prison network.

I am meant to have my first visit from the solicitor who handled my case tomorrow. But where, or when? I have no idea. My cellmate, Douggie, had an order to go to a food safety course in the education wing. It was written down on a tiny slip of paper placed under the door late last night. Yet when he got back he was told he had a 'red' mark on his file because he had not turned up for his shift in the bakery. The prison system that told him to report for a training session was incapable of telling itself that he could not turn up for work.

How prisoners are to adjust to a world of work where strict order is the norm, when they experience the chaos and disorder of prison, is hard to judge.

I talk to a 78-year-old man whose son-in-law asked to borrow an unused garage to store some stuff. The stuff turned out to be cocaine and a gun. The man refused to snitch on his daughter's husband. The judge sent him to prison for ten years.

Clearly, the garage-lender should have cooperated with the authorities. His son-in-law is locked up. Is it still necessary to keep this stubborn old man, unwilling to inform on his nefarious son-in-law, in prison until he is eighty-eight? In a number of democracies, old men of eighty and over cannot be sent to prison and are kept under control and scrutiny by other means. Our judges are not ageist. They will send anyone of any age to prison. How long before the red dressing gowns send their first centenarian to Belmarsh or Brixton?

It is lovely and sunny today. Would it be so impossible to go out for a walk around nearby Clapham Common?

I promise I won't run away.

A stack of emails arrive. Jane in Sydney sends me a list of Old Brixtonians – George Lansbury, Oswald Mosley, Mick Jagger, Bertrand Russell amongst others. She says I should come over to Oz to see a fellow convict friend, Howard Marks, who has also done time. I'd love to. The vistas of warmth in the winter open up.

My brother says there are brown patches at Avoriaz, one of the high modern French alpine stations, where I did a lot of serious skiing in the '80s. Benjamin is back from Val Thorens having gone with his university chums to find excellent snow. Vicky says Emilie came for dinner and cooked a perfect fish pie. I can't avoid the endless TV cookery programmes and dream of food that tastes of something. So my son skies faster than I can and my daughter cooks better than me.

1405H I walk up and down my landing reading a Michel Houellebecq novel out loud to hear French again. For a French novelist who keeps winning literary prizes, he writes surprisingly uncluttered French.

I go downstairs to check on my legal visit tomorrow. Two prisoners due out on tag this week are anxiously enquiring if there is definitive news, so the reception desk guard checks on his computer but can find nothing.

'It's not the fault of the screw,' says Matt, the calm, easy-going white-haired man who is in charge of the laundry. 'They are never told anything by the back office and are as much in the dark as we are. They get fed up and that frustration gets taken out on us sometimes.'

The two prisoners keep calling the guard 'Guv', an archaic term of subordination you don't much hear any longer except from older cabbies in London. They don't (quite) knuckle their foreheads but this sense that these men are the lowest of the low, held in check by some black uniforms who have to be addressed so obsequiously, further degrades and reduces the prisoners to low self-esteem.

The laundry man jokes about a man – 'a big black guy' to be precise – who he met in Belmarsh. 'He was puzzled. He had simply cut off his tag 'cos it was itchy and wasn't sure why he was back in prison.' His younger comrade has another tag story. 'This guy was on tag. He realised he had missed getting home in time so he just got the train to Wandsworth and said he'd do the rest of his bird inside.' Thus British prisons equip their inmates for one thing – to come back inside again.

1530H Gym. Again the ageing, crowded gym and again the obsessive biceps training is depressing. How many jobs require great fat arm muscles? A good forty minutes on different training machines. I speak to Vicky very, very fast as my phone credit is down to under £1. She says there is a visit for Emilie and Sarah listed for Saturday, so after four weeks in prison I get to see my four daughters. I am deeply grateful for Chris Grayling's compassion.

A prisoner asks me for some sheets of A4 paper which come off my precious pads. He seems to think because I was an MP I am a mini Rymans – it's odd that paper to write on is a commodity in such short supply. I wonder when Bertrand Russell was here if he was allowed to write. When the Italian Fascists sent the Marxist Antonio Gramsci to prison, Mussolini's prosecutor said, 'We must stop his mind working for twenty years.'

England is not pre-war Italy and Signor Grayling may be very right-wing but is fully democratic. Yet I can see how easy it is for the mind to slowly disengage and stop working, as independence of thought and paper to write it all down is actually discouraged by the prison regime.

1740H After roll call, Brian the Librarian says he hopes to see me in the library tomorrow. I hope so too. His release date for being tagged was in December. But, so incompetent and capricious is prison management, he is still here, costing taxpayers ever more money for no reason.

1753H I join the queue for dinner. Unlike Belmarsh when the flow to the server was strictly controlled so that only a single line was formed, here in Brixton there is a crowded two or three abreast queue. Two prisoner orderlies give you a tiny slip of paper on which they write your choice indicated by a letter or number. The server prisoners at the counter look at the slip of paper and dish out what you have ordered from the hot trays. I see trays with the nicer food being taken away with some chicken legs or whatever still on them. A perk of the job.

Dinner is a huge mound of mashed potato – dry without a hint of butter and milk, a slice of not bad chicken pie and peas and carrots. Smothered in hot chilli sauce it is eatable and fills the stomach.

A quick call to Sarah just back from Rio and my phone credit runs out. I fill in a form for emergency phone credit. Now starts a pirouette between one guard and his line manager, a woman new to the wing. They have an earnest debate about whether the £38 I put on my phone via the canteen system at the weekend will appear tomorrow. But they don't know. The prison system has changed and its custodians and applicants don't know how it works. Then there is a debate on how quickly the office staff can do the transactions. Finally, whether it is an emergency or not.

The slight bespectacled officer says I raised it with him two days ago. The youngish, pretty woman officer with three stripes on her epaulette also wants to be helpful. I wind up the charm and try and get them to understand that talking to family is a good thing. Like being before one of Labour's innumerable lady chief whips trying to get permission to be absent for a vote to see a child in a school play. Prison, Parliament, warder, whip. The same rules apply. I'll find out tomorrow if it works.

1835H Going upstairs I see my friend Brian the Librarian having his hair cut. The barber is using a barber's electric razor. He invites me to sit down and gives me a very professional one and a half. I feel a new man with my hair neat and tidy. A crowd gathers. They find it hilarious that an MP is having his head shaved in Brixton. Their remarks on the Prime Minister and his Justice Minister are unprintable.

'When you get out, Denis, tell your MP mates about how rotten Brixton is and how useless the Governor is.' I have yet to encounter one unpleasant, sarcastic, aggressive or unkind remark directed against me from a prisoner in Brixton. I wish I could say the same about every one of my old comrades in the Labour Party.

1920H Bang-up. I settle down to write up the day. Douggie lies on his bottom-floor bunk. It's the only way the two of us can fit in. Thank God there is no dispute on what to watch. Douggie sweetly falls asleep midway through whatever is on. He snores softly, irregularly. I write and write. I wonder if it will be worthwhile. Brian told me there were no copies of Jeffrey Archer's prison diaries in Brixton. Apparently a previous Lambeth Council librarian had banned them. I will read them when out and see how my experience a decade after the noble Lord Jeff compares.

TUESDAY 14 JANUARY 2014

You say 'society must exact vengeance, and society must punish'. Wrong on both counts. Vengeance comes from the individual and punishment from God.

– Victor Hugo

0800H Breakfast. Thanks to Douggie's canteen mini food store I can now have muesli with a bit of fruit chopped in. I would die for a bacon sarney. Again I am not on any list to do anything. I talk to Steve who has been waiting fifteen months in Brixton with his Category D status for a transfer to an open prison. 'I'm here for non-violent theft. This shithole isn't a Cat D prison. They just dump us in here to fill the cells.'

I shower, shave, write a letter. Daytime television is mind-rotting. Around ten there is a muffled cry for exercise. By the time Douggie and I get down, the door allowing us out of C Wing is locked. We troop sadly upstairs to our cell.

I get the low-down on prison violence from Douggie. 'You have all these lifers who love nothing but letting rip at some screw who's humiliating and bullying them. I was in A Wing here when a bunch of guys jumped a real bully of a guard. They waited around a pool table and used a pool table ball to hit the man. All the sirens went off with guards running like mad to break up the fight. The guard was in hospital. The guys who took their revenge on him were all sent to different prisons. They might have got an extra few months but they don't care, especially if they're doing a long sentence.'

The obsession of David Cameron with 'life means life' and his advocacy of 100-year sentences will only feed a sense of despair and hopelessness in prisoners with a horizon of years locked up. What is needed is a much clearer set of incentives, with the promise that good behaviour would bring an earlier release on tag. Sadly, filling not emptying prisons is today's *maladie Anglaise*.

1105H Hooray, at last I get to see the library. In a normal Category D prison, the library would be open and available to all prisoners who wanted to study there or make notes on material that cannot be taken out – for some reason there is just one copy of Prison Regulations, which is kept only in the library, like pornography in bygone days. I can borrow three books.

The trip to Brixton Prison's library involves four gates or doors being locked and unlocked. Once you get to the library you find a small room full of books but no readers. A library without readers could only be created under Chris Grayling's vision of prisons as centres for retribution and punishment. The Brixton Library is a bit bigger than a mobile library that visits remote areas.

There is a fair selection of books, with thrillers and airport book stall choices. I am vaguely trying to learn Greek; there is one book in Greek for any Greek prisoners but no dictionary or guide to learn the language. Instead, I take one of the wonderful Teach Yourself books – Italian – first published in 1943. On the first page one prisoner has kindly written, 'From the bottom of my arse I hate Italy.' Presumably a UKIP voter.

I am allowed to stay ten minutes, which is the shortest time I have ever spent in a tiny bookshop let alone a library. The warder accompanies me back to C Wing and the door slams shut. But at least I have been inside a prison library. I wonder what the library in Belmarsh is like.

1226H Lunch is two small sausages in a soft white bread roll and some half-cold chips. I am dying for a salad. Anything green, please.

1300H My first legal visit from my Bindman's solicitor, the able Martin Rackstraw. You are meant to see your lawyers very early in the prison stay. I am more than halfway through my incarceration term so this is a bit late. But a fresh face, and a face from outside, is always welcome. I have been half-pondering an appeal against Judge Sweeney sending me to Belmarsh and now Brixton. By any standards it was cruel for a 65-year-old's first ever offence when no money was obtained and the police and CPS full inquiry had cleared me. He ignored context, comparison to other MPs' expenses abuses and compassion in his quivering desire to imprison me.

Now all I want is to be kept inside not a day longer than necessary. I was sentenced on 23 December. Sir Nigel said I should spend three months of the six-month sentence under a prison regime. So that's 23 March when it all ends. Half of that is spent tagged. There are ninety days between 23 December and 23 March. So I should spend forty-five days inside. This means 7 February is my release day. According to prison regulations, a prisoner should have a supervising officer assigned to him and a release date scheduled within fourteen days of arriving in prison. I have not received a single piece of paper with any information on who is my supervising officer, nor a release date.

Martin, my solicitor, says some lawyer friends are shocked at the casual way the judge swept to one side the mitigation arguments or the decision of the CPS to prosecute without any fresh evidence. He tells me about the latest case of Metropolitan Police dishonesty. During the school and student demonstrations late in 2010, against Nick Clegg's dishonesty in endorsing a Tory proposal to increase student university fees to £9,000 despite his solemn promise to vote against any such measure, two youngsters were arrested.

My own son, Benjamin, a sixth former, took part. His mother and I were called to the London Oratory to hear a rebuke from the head teacher, an excellent, good man, about Ben's involvement in leading out his schoolmates in defiance of a teacher's instruction. It was a clear breach of rules. The head teacher was more intelligent. He listened as we accepted his rebuke and promised Ben would keep on the straight and narrow until his A levels.

Inwardly, I have to confess I was dead proud of the boy. I didn't lead a demo or defy authority until my twenties. Here he was doing just that, taking on authority and the Lib Dem liars, at seventeen. His grandfather, whom he never knew, had gone into battle at a young age to defend what he believed to be right when the Nazis attacked Poland.

Whitehall, with its rule-obeying CBs, had appeased fascism and the parliamentary bureaucrats had tried to remove Churchill as an MP in 1938 to shut up his lonely voice against Tory isolationism. I don't wish my life on any of my children but a life of faithfully following rules and waiting for a knighthood or a gong is never the full life men should live.

My solicitor and I agree there is no point in appealing the sentence. He says we have the most reactionary, prison-happy bench in years. Periodically, a Lord Chief Justice says prison sentences of six months or less are pointless. But the LCJ doesn't mean it, and appointments of die-hard reactionaries to the Appeal Court show the gap between the LCJ's words and actions also. But he is angry, and rightly so, at the CPS briefing the press that I had skulked behind parliamentary privileges as there was material not given to the police. This was simply a lie used to blacken my name as there was no fresh evidence to justify a prosecution.

He will write to Keir Starmer's successor. I tell him not to hold his breath. I am still disappointed at some *Guardian* journalist called Rajiv who told me he had to print these lies because other papers were doing so. 'The *Telegraph* and the *Indie* are running this line. I have to go with them,' Rajiv whined to me on the phone. I know I probably was guilty of similar herd mentality and distortions of the truth when I was a journalist but it is shocking that Alan Rusbridger, who likes to portray himself as the shining knight of ethical honest journalism, allows such Murdoch-style reporting on *The Guardian*.

My solicitor gives me a sweet note from Tam Dalyell who writes, 'You were an ass but asses are not villains. If the PM (Blair) asked you to do a job, why were your expenses not promptly met? "No good deed goes unpunished."' Dear Tam. Old Etonian. Ex-Scots Dragoon Guards or some ancient elite regiment. European. The most independent, fearless MP ever. He lives in 'The House of the Binns' near Edinburgh – surely one of the great addresses?

I have digressed from the latest Met story of dodgy CPS and police behaviour. Two students on the demo against Lib Dem lies were arrested, charged and convicted. But clear video footage shows the police were lying and the students have been paid £100,000 of taxpayers' money by the Metropolitan Police as compensation. I assume Sir Bernard Hogan-Howe has been on television expressing his total confidence in his officers.

In the library I picked up the last two issues of *Converse*, a monthly paper for prisoners. The November 2013 front-page headline reads 'CORRUPT FIT-UP COP JAILED He Accepted £19,000 to Plant Guns and Drugs'. The December front-page headline is 'COP JAILED FOR RAPE LIE'. An inside headline reads 'Top Cops Must Repay £100,000' in false expenses. Naturally, as they are not MPs, the CPS is not interested in this massive expense robbery of taxpayers' money.

Good for dear old Sir Keir Starmer not prosecuting these reprobate cops! The paper has page after page of questionable police and CPS practice. I don't recall any newspaper giving these stories much prominence, editorials calling for action, or columnists saying that far from one or two rotten apples, the whole barrel is contaminated.

My solicitor says he was shocked at the distorted reporting of my sentencing. 'I expected that in the tabloids but the so-called quality papers were completely biased and one-sided,' he said. Luckily I didn't see these stories but I am not surprised.

On the way out of the prisoner visitors' centre network, a tall screw addresses me as 'Guv'. Wait a minute, that's how prisoners address screws. Are tables turning?

Back in my cell, Douggie says he has loads of money on his account and do I want to order some papers? I choose the *Sunday Times*, *The Economist* and *Le Monde*. I suppose I might as well get back into what's happening and I shall be amused to see if the prison censors allow a European paper printed in a foreign language into Brixton!

1600H I wander along the landing and everyone says hello and wishes me well. But in every brief exchange the bitterness surfaces. 'There's no rehabilitation here. The education is a joke. No one helps with housing. You leave with £46 and a phone number if you're homeless. Of course everyone has to live. And if you don't have a job or anywhere to stay you go straight back to what you know how to do – nicking or dealing,' says Lester, a gangly Afro-Caribbean.

Earlier today, a prisoner came to my cell with a form to fill in for my housing needs. That's not a problem for me but the questions were cursory. I wonder what real help can be given, especially in London. There is such a chronic housing shortage. Between 1997 and 2009 Labour sold nearly 500,000 council homes. In Yorkshire and the Humber region in the same period just twenty-four council houses were built.

Prison is one of the biggest family-destroyers we have. Even a short sentence can sink a precarious family set-up. Judges don't care. They have no problems with rent or mortgage repayments. Several excellent charities try and help, and their selfless work deserves praise. But the prisoner released without a home or job to go to is standing on a turntable where the exit is a return to prison.

'They all tell you to get yourself educated. But there's none in Brixton. You need to have someone talk to you about your crime, why you did it. That way they can get you thinking about staying straight outside. But no one does. They just leave you here. They don't care.'

This was an intelligent, articulate man. Not, I think, a habitual or professional criminal. 'I just did a bit of thieving to buy a van, have some cash in my pocket, take my girlfriend on a holiday', he says. 'I'd like to learn a trade, bricklayer or plumber. I'm not useless. But no one helps,' he said bitterly.

1630H My phone credit runs out as I am talking to Vicky. I want to talk to Sarah as well but the money has gone. Yesterday afternoon, two of the better screws said they would get some extra phone credit for me. Another day. Another lie.

I go to the laundry room to try and get a sweatshirt that fits. Matt also gives me some comfortable slippers. I cannot complain about prison clothing. It's like what good Marks & Spencer clothes were like before M&S descended to Primark quality.

WEDNESDAY 15 JANUARY

> Sometimes it seems like we're living in some kind of prison and the crime
> is how much we hate ourselves.
>
> *– My So-Called Life*

0745H Up and breakfast of some muesli and a half-rotten banana. I
go downstairs and post some letters. The stamped envelopes Vicky sent
before Christmas have finally arrived. Mary Creagh, the Wakefield MP,
a dear friend, wants to visit, as does David Blunkett. I go down and get a
Visitors' form. It demands the date of birth of each visitor. How on earth
do I know when David or Mary were born? I just guess and write a date
roughly approximating to their ages. Once again I am breaking the rules,
which will upset John Lyon CB. But how else can I organise a visit? Is
there a Prisons Commissioner who will investigate my rule-breaking and,
eh, send me to prison?

0845H I am again locked in the cell. The prison rules stipulate that each
prisoner must go on an induction course before he can go to an education
class or to do some work. The Governor of Brixton prefers to lock me away.

1000H Door unlocked. I was told there would be a chance of going for
an hour's gym today. When I go downstairs I am told no gym. Apparently
the woman guard who locked us all away could have let us go to the
gym but decided to keep us in our cells. It is the petty arbitrariness of
power. I am reading an account of the German occupation of Warsaw
in the war. What are striking are the instances of sheer casualness in the
decisions of low-rank Wehrmacht soldiers. Put a person in uniform and
give them power of people without rights and, sometimes, the power of
the uniform turns a normally humane human being into a thoughtless,
unkind – or worse – person.

We chat disconsolately as the lack of exercise and fresh air is demoralising. One prisoner has come from Spring Hill, the open prison near Aylesbury. All the prisoners there are Category D and, if they want, they can walk out. 'But it gets to you. One guy just after Christmas was in the Chapel. He couldn't take it any more. He climbed up to the gallery, tied a bed-sheet around his neck, tied the other end to a railing and jumped.'

I suppose suicide is the ultimate way of leaving prison behind. Like the other open prison close to London, Ford, where prisoners burned down buildings in their despair, the fact of not having stone walls and iron bars is no guarantee of becoming a better, fuller citizen in the English prison system.

I return to my cell. There is nothing else to do, nowhere else to be.

1120H Emails, but not good news. Governor Edmond Tullett is still refusing a visit by my children. Benjamin has had to go back to Edinburgh University. The stamped envelopes which I assumed were those sent by Vicky before Christmas are actually from the children. I wonder where those sent by her three weeks ago are or if someone has stolen them.

Nathalie reports on François Hollande's press conference, which she followed live. George Parker, the usually level-headed *FT* political editor, was on this morning saying the French press were losing so many sales they did not want to attack their country's president.

Last year, *Closer*, the French scandal celebrity rag that revealed Hollande's new love, published banal pictures of an attractive thirty-year-old woman sunbathing with her husband in France. Like millions of British holidaymakers in France she wasn't wearing her bikini top. Her husband will soon be one of the most powerful men in Britain as our putative head of state.

The English press exploded in an orgy of anger and condemnation at this invasion of privacy. But when a French president falls in love with a woman, he is not entitled to navigate through the *Sturm und Drang* of a relationship break-up without it being a matter of rabid panting pubescent excitement for the British press. What humbug!

1155H I send out Visitors' Orders for Mary Creagh, David Blunkett and Tom Harris, three MP friends who want to visit. It has been curious to see how a whole twenty years' worth of political friendship evaporates once I am in legal trouble. Still I can understand. If you're an MP who helped himself to taxpayers' money to do up your house, or speculate, or pay a handsome salary to a daughter or wife, or have a guilty conscience about all the petty cash or food claims, without a single receipt of course, you don't want to be reminded of a former colleague and friend who has got into trouble over much smaller amounts.

Before I get too censorious, let me place on record the fact that I did not go and see David Chaytor, Eric Illsley, or Elliot Morley when they were sent to prison. None were close friends, though I like them all. But did I at the time seek to avoid guilt by association, just as former MP friends are doing now?

1230H Lunch. A soft baguette roll with, for once, some cheese spread with onion chopped into it. Taste at last.

Strange bellows from four floors down. I don't know what they mean. They might as well be shouting in Arabic. I am fed, can watch TV, shower and now and then do a little gym work. Otherwise I don't exist. I remember that rugged sense of being suspended from reality, no longer master of my own fate, when imprisoned in Warsaw thirty years ago. My only visitor was a diplomat from the British embassy. He brought a Harrods bag with two apples, a packet of Ryvita and an old copy of *Country Life*. Little did I think then that Tony Blair would ask me – I still wonder if by accident? – to take over his chair at the European Council meeting which admitted Poland to full membership of the European Union.

1982: I was frightened in a communist cell locked up somewhere in Warsaw.

2002: I represented Britain as Poland signed fully and finally for European democracy and human rights which had been denied to the Poles over so many centuries. I thought of my father, also nervous as a young second lieutenant, leading his men into battle against young Germans in the grip of a right-wing xenophobic ideology. He took a bullet that went through his shoulder into the neck of his corporal behind him. Polish officers of his time never shouted 'Forward!' at their men. The command was 'Follow me.' He died when I was ten, in part as a result of the damage caused by a Nazi bullet. The pre-war Poland he grew up in had twenty years of independent existence.

Now, I sat in the Prime Minister's seat at a European Council and lifted my hand to agree that Poland, whole and free, could join Britain, Ireland and France – the three other countries that made me what I am – in the community of European Union nations.

I don't want to do any more politics, I tell my fellow prisoners who think a spell inside is good training to be an MP. But I won't stand idly by as the political descendants of the isolationists and appeasers again try to weaken the natural affinity between the two great peoples at the western and eastern ends of the European Union. That duty, at least, I owe my father's memory.

1600H I don't believe it. This morning I asked a screw when the gym was. He took me over to a timetable. There, quite clearly, for C Wing was a gym session at 15.45. After lunch I went down to post a letter. Twelve stamps have by now arrived so at last I can write letters. I see some gym regulars I had been with at two previous sessions. I asked them what time the gym session was.

'Half past three,' they chorused authoritatively. So at 15.20 I came downstairs. No gym crowd. 'What's happened to the gym?' I ask the guard with tattoos, an earring and a banjo.

'They've gone.'

'What?! I was told quarter to four by an officer and that's on your timetable. Then I was told half past three. What's going on?'

'I shouted gym. You should have heard.'

'Come off it. Up on the fourth floor you can't hear a word. Every cell has music or the TV on. It's impossible.'

'I called for gym,' repeated the screw, strumming the banjo on his ample paunch.

'OK. So no gym for me today. But can I go out into the yard for some fresh air?'

'Exercise was at 12.30.'

'What! Where is that listed? Who announced that?'

'I called exercise at 12.30,' said the banjo man with that satisfaction that pervades every guard's face and body at the realisation that another prisoner has lost a precious moment of being outside his cell.

So no fresh air today. I filled my lungs more at Belmarsh than at Brixton. I start running up and down the metal stairs. 'And you thought this was a Category D prison,' grinned a couple of prisoners, amused at my annoyed discomfiture.

I run up and down the stairs and the length of the bottom floor and do exercises on the floor outside my cell.

'One more, two more,' says a kindly prisoner as I pant past him. 'When it hurts, you know it's doing some good.'

1750H 'MacShane, get your shirt on. You have to see the senior officer.' I have changed into easy clothes for the rest of the day – Primark's finest – after a bracing cold shower. The hot water seems to be off.

Ever obedient, I pull on a T-shirt to meet the slight, serious youngish woman who runs C Wing.

'I have something serious to say to you so sit down, please.'

She tells me that the Belmarsh screws have sent over a note claiming I had been given two 'red' or negative entries, which were put on my official prison file by warders over there.

This is Kafkaesque. The big ugly bully of a woman warder who screamed at me to stop trying to talk to my daughter had come back later in the evening to tell me with pleasure in her voice that I was to be given a red or negative note.

But a second one? Absolutely not. This journal has tried faithfully to note down all I saw, heard, said or was told. No one came to me in Belmarsh to tell me I was to be given a second negative note.

'Can officers give a prisoner a red note in secrecy without informing the prisoner?' I asked.

Ms Greer looked embarrassed and said, 'No, that shouldn't happen.' The other warder in the office smiled to himself. Later, Brian, the pensioner accountant who works in the library, told me that here in C Wing in Brixton he had been given a negative report without being told about it. This, he thinks, may have led to delays in his release date.

Ms Greer tells me, 'Look. We've no problems with you. You're affable and cooperative. Maybe you had issues in Belmarsh.'

I tell her, no, other than the bully, I tried to get on with everyone. 'Does your note indicate if there was a witness to the first allegation? And who is the liar who said he gave me a negative report without telling me?'

She looks away embarrassed and tells me I can complain to some Independent Board or to the Governor. Yeah. I'm sure that works.

I think she will be helpful but I am dismayed at the clear dishonesty from Belmarsh. I can look after myself. But what if I were some poor black kid that the warden in Belmarsh decided to damage as he worked his way through the system? There is something rotten here.

On a better note, Ms Greer accepts my idea of holding a talk for prisoners on 'Politics and Parliament'. Brian agrees to copy Jenni Russell's excellent article in *The Times* which flays John Lyon CB and Judge Sweeney. At last I am talking, answering questions, debating.

And then I learn that Sarah and Emilie will visit me tomorrow. Hip hip hooray. Another visit from my brother and Vicky on Saturday. At last I can hug my two daughters, whom I haven't seen since Sir Nigel did his business. I cannot wait.

THURSDAY 16 JANUARY 2014

The mood and temper of the public in regard to the treatment of crime and criminals is one of the most unfailing tests of the civilisation of any country. A calm and dispassionate recognition of the rights of the accused against the state and even of convicted criminals against the state, a constant heart-searching by all charged with the duty of punishment, a desire and eagerness to reha- bilitate in the world of industry all those who have paid their dues in the hard coinage of punishment, tireless efforts towards the discovery of curative and regenerating processes and an unfaltering faith that there is a treasure, if only you can find it in the heart of every person – these are the symbols which in the treatment of crime and criminals mark and measure the stored up strength of a nation, and are the sign and proof of the living virtue in it.

– Winston Churchill

0900H The noise of lousy music is everywhere. C Wing empties at 0830 as men go off to education or work. I was told by a screw last night that there would be a gym this morning but no one knows anything about it. I desperately need exercise. Last night Ms Greer said to me: 'You should do gym. We need people to stay healthy.' *Mens sana in corpore sano*. But, as ever, even a senior screw's words quickly become inoperative.

I write another letter for a prisoner. Del lives in Romford. I keep meeting men from Romford whose narratives, with some credibility, all involve a degree of casual stitching up by the police. When the cops decide to put someone in their sights, then the more charges they can bring the better.

My Brixton comrade is here for drug possession. His mother had been convicted of animal cruelty – keeping too many dogs in her kennels. He was also charged but his passport showed he was out of Essex, in Thailand, for the period of the alleged crisis. So his case was dismissed.

End of story? Not quite. Somehow the accusation of animal cruelty has ended up on his prison file. This matters because his parole date (release on temporary licence, ROTL or 'rottle' in prison jargon) has gone by and a reason given for the delay is the prison file accusation of a conviction for animal cruelty.

He is frustrated. He cannot find out who placed the wrong infor- mation on his prison file. A judge should sign any document stating someone has been convicted. Surely our honest judges could not casually sign a false condemnatory statement?

I can only suggest he write to his MP and ask Chris Grayling to investigate fully. I draft a letter for him. But, knowing Grayling, I doubt if much will happen, and my friend will stay much longer in Brixton Prison then he needs to.

0945H A talk with Ms Greer. 'Aren't you at the gym?' she asks kindly. I told her the gym session she promised me yesterday never materialised. She shrugged. I tried to find out more about her. She's nearly fifty, though looks much younger. She won't tell me where she lives. Information on where prison officers live must be a valuable commodity in some circumstances.

Why did she become a prison officer? 'I began as a secretary and I worked for a small company. In those days women couldn't get on so I decided to try this. It's been very interesting. I like working with people.'

There are different entry levels into prison work. It's not like the police service, where everyone has to start as a constable. Graduates can enter the prison service and move faster up the ranks. So far I haven't met anyone – nice or nasty – who appears to have had a university education.

A workman equipped with his key chain comes into Ms Greer's tiny office, smaller than a cell. She wants to hang a picture painted by an inmate. It is six panels: a still life of fruits and vegetables. A splash of colours, not art. It weighs about six ounces. The workman makes a huge hole, smashes in a large rawl plug, and inserts a large screw. A tiny pin and hook would have sufficed. He picks up the painting and cannot get it to balance horizontally so hangs it vertically. It doesn't much matter. It's just a little break in the institutional dull cream paint on the walls. 'Council workmen,' sighs Ms Greer as the man leaves.

I am getting worried about my release date. Serco, or whichever private firm now operates tag systems, have to go and inspect my house and make sure it is safe for me to be curfewed in. Ms Greer is surprised I haven't yet been given a supervising officer, I think that's what she called it, to oversee tagging on supervised release. She arranges for me to see some-one tomorrow so at least, at last, I get a whiff of professionalism from a prison officer.

I go up to my cell. On the landing a young man, Grant, is smoking a roll-up. I ask him how he will react to the announced ban on smoking.

'Dunno. I don't really smoke outside, maybe a cig with a beer. I just started inside out of boredom. There's nothing else to do.' He worked for American Express, where he was in charge of devising security firewalls for their computer systems. 'I was the only guy who knew how the bank was protected but also the only guy who knew how to get inside the security firewalls. I took £48,000, which my mum paid back. I didn't take it from any client.'

The sum of £48,000 wouldn't even register on the scale of the bonuses bankers pay themselves, especially if the bonus money is coming from the taxpayers who now own some of our key banks. The case took three years from arrest to conviction. He was sentenced to two years and four months so the cost of keeping him in prison is around £100,000.

'You can't blame the judge. They have huge investments from their QC days in the banking and financial systems. So any damage done to a bank is taken very personally by a judge,' I tell him.

He has been a model prisoner, faithfully working or following education classes. He puffs on his thin roll-up. 'I've lost two stone. I'll never come back. I was just stupid. I just want to be home with my family.'

He was worried about the new regime imposed by Justice Secretary Grayling.

'Suddenly prisoners have had their status changed and they don't know why. They can get their release date put back without any reason. I think I'll be okay. I've never gotten into trouble and just do what the screws say. But I worry about other guys who are very bitter at the new regime. Just losing their canteen of burn can be very demoralising.'

I explain that Grayling is desperate to make his mark in the graveyard job of a Justice Minister: 'He keeps announcing that he is getting tough with prisoners and making prisons into places of punishment, and that goes down well with right-wingers in politics and the press.'

Del gives me a T-shirt as a thank you for writing a letter for him. I have a good stack of T-shirts but the thought is kind. At his cell door is a Jehovah's Witness pastor. Are missionaries allowed into prison? Any friendly face from outside is welcome but I have politely declined to be converted when the converters from Salt Lake City have knocked on my door in the past, so I make my excuses and go back to the 1944 Warsaw Uprising. I wonder if preachers of atheism like Richard Dawkins and the excellent National Secular Society would be allowed into prison, or do the Abrahamic and Asian faiths have the exclusive franchise?

1225H Lunch of chips and some very odd chicken wings which taste off. But it's food. When will I see a salad again?

I am keeping an eye on the exercise half-hour. But four floors up, you might as well be in another wing in terms of internal communication. I go downstairs and find exercise started ten minutes ago. I run around the little playground yard as fast as I can. The sun is out and I slow down to take in the vitamin D. I wonder if those who devise prison policy know that the vitamin D you get from the sun is important for health. By the time I went to bed last night I had a dull headache, due, I think, to twenty-four hours without a breath of fresh air.

I feel better and go and shower and wash my hair to get ready to hug the two girls who will see their father for the first time since Sir Nigel hung out his Christmas stocking and popped me in it. Back in my cell I shave using a prison razor. Up to now I have been relying on the twin-blade throwaway razor Mike gave me in Belmarsh. It's getting blunt. But so cheap is the official HMP razor I immediately cut my chin. I dab and dab but the blood dribbles out. Oh well, the girls have seen their dad's face in more bloodied states.

1500H A hug from Sarah, Emilie and their mother, Nathalie. The visiting room is horrible. There is one seat for the prisoner and three classroom chairs packed closely together. There is no family intimacy and every conversation can be overheard. At Belmarsh there is a clear separation between the clusters of visitors. At Holloway, you sit around tables with discreet spaces between visitors. At East Sutton Park Category D prison the visitors' room have sofas, easy chairs, a tea counter, and an open door to the garden with its bench and glassy slopes to lie on in the sun. Brixton is the waiting room for a sanatorium in a communist bloc county.

But no matter. I haven't seen my two daughters since a last lingering look at them watching, with dislike and contempt, Judge Sweeney's selective and inaccurate choice of words to justify sending me to Belmarsh.

'Laura's so upset at the judge and all the other people who did you down, she doesn't want to live in England when she comes back from Canada,' says Sarah. 'She wants to live in Sweden, where the conservative government is closing prisons, not filling them up and building more and more for judges to fill like here.'

I worry about mail coming into my house. Sarah says she opened one letter from my bank, Lloyds, about closing my current and savings accounts. That doesn't make sense. Banks don't close accounts just because you are in prison. It just becomes a worry.

Inside prison, the convict doesn't have to think about anything. But the outside is still there. The bills come in. Direct debits and standing orders have to be paid. The prisoner has no help on how to sustain his outside life and the home he needs to come back to.

Nathalie says I look ten years younger and fat has fallen off my face. How sweet. If anything, my new-found healthy, less jowly looks will be due to the fact that the five years of the BNP shadow over me, the parliamentary process, the police inquiry, the CPS dishonesty and the unpleasant distortions on the BBC or in *The Guardian* are now locked in a file titled 'The Past'.

We discuss what meal I will eat when I get out. I tell them rather I am thinking what bottle I'll open. Emilie wants to me to go skiing with her in the Sierra Nevada, not far from where she is studying at Córdoba University. Laura wants to see me in Canada. And next Christmas somewhere hot.

The ninety minutes pass so quickly. Breaking the rules, I slip a bit of paper over with a list of friends whose address and mobile numbers I would like to have. I ask if I can take some chocolate back from the visitors' centre to friends in C Wing. 'No' is the bleak reply. Will a bar of Cadbury's really bring the prison system crashing down?

In two days' time I will see Emilie again and my brother, as well as Vicky, if she gets back in time from a conference in Paris.

Next to us is Lee, who is in the cell opposite mine on the fours in C Wing. No one turns up. Later I learn that his wife, a senior schoolteacher who had booked leave for the afternoon, had been asked to stay at work to cover for a sick colleague. He sits disconsolately for thirty-five minutes before realising that no one will come.

I feel for him and almost invite him to my family group, except that we are speaking French and a screw would have objected. Back in C Wing he tells me the story. He is philosophical. I think his wife's headteacher should have more sensitivity to how important a nearest-and-dearest visit is to a prisoner.

Few have any knowledge of the loneliness of the prisoner. Surrounded, crowded by others, without a private moment, you can feel lonelier than ever. You share a bedroom. You cannot share yourself as you do with spouses, partners, friends. That only happens in a visit and if it doesn't happen, it's a small tragedy.

1820H There is a knock on the cell door, which opens. It is a burly man, a headteacher perhaps, in an anorak, key chain, and a loose shoelace on his brown shoe. He is puffing slightly from the walk up to the fourth floor. He says he is the Governor and shakes my hand. I never met the Governor in Belmarsh and feel flattered that the Brixton Governor, Ed Tullett, has climbed up the stairs to say hello.

'Everything OK?' he asks as I stand up, since there is nowhere for both of us to sit unless he wants to get onto the bottom bunk.

I mutter yes. Never tell the truth until you know what is wanted.

He comes quickly to the point of his visit.

'You are eligible to go to an open prison you know, but perhaps Brixton is better for visits and release.'

I make the point that I don't have a release date yet but show him on a calendar that Monday 3 February is exactly six weeks – half the allotted three months – since Monday 23 December – Sweeney Day.

Clearly he has heard my protests to Ms Greer and in all my letters (which can be read by the Governor as I am not allowed to seal them) that I have been treated differently from other politician prisoners sent quickly to open prisons. He has clearly been sent to give me the message that a transfer to an open prison is possible for me too.

I am not sure how to react. The lack of fresh air and exercise and lock-ups are depressing, as is the shockingly poor food. I vaguely want to see what an open prison is like, though most prison writing by Jeffrey Archer and others is based on rural open prisons of green fields where you can seal your envelopes, go to the gym when you want and get decent food.

Mr Tullett tells me cheerfully, 'This is a Category D open prison set in Brixton.'

I say nothing but inwardly reel back in shock. Brixton locks you up; I have no access to fresh air; phones don't work; and the library is locked behind four or five gates and doors. What is he burbling about?

I keep these thoughts to myself. He has shown willing either because he was told to make me an offer of a transfer to an open prison or, after hearing my moans to his subordinates, has decided to take the initiative. And, to be fair, his demeanour is that of a decent headteacher in an average comprehensive school.

Suddenly, instead of being cocooned in a decision-free world, I have to make a choice. Ford Open Prison near Littlehampton will be full of people like me. Middle-class, middle-aged professionals. That's a two-hour journey from London. Ditto Ley Hill in Gloucestershire. So far, family and friends and the increasing number of MPs who want to visit Brixton only have two stops on the Victoria line from my house in Pimlico.

I tell the Governor that a lot depends on my release date and I haven't been given that yet. There is a meeting with my Offender Supervisor tomorrow, two weeks later than the regulations stipulate. I'll let him know afterwards and after some more consultation and advice.

He hasn't made a precise offer, naming the open prison I might go. It is an odd, unsettling discussion, leaving everything in the air.

I go first to Brian, the assistant librarian, who believes he should have been given a release date weeks ago.

'The Governor shouldn't come and see you. He should treat everyone equally, not give you special treatment.' He is really quite angry and the last thing I need is for news to circulate that I have been given privileged access. Yet I am here because of who I am, not what I did.

I change the subject and tell Brian to write to his MP if he is being denied a fair deal.

'Where do you live?' I ask.

'Orpington. My MP is Jo Johnson.'

'He's a good guy. I've played tennis with him. His wife is a great leftie *Guardian* journalist. He'll help. Mention my name.'

'I'll contact Jo Johnson when I'm out. If you write to your MP about a problem with the prison system, they just make life worse for you.'

I expect Brian is right, though it's depressing to hear that an MP's support and help can make matters worse. What else are they (once me) good for? However, all power lies with the screws and the prison system. Once convicted, the citizen loses all rights and is at the mercy of the system.

Douggie isn't sure what to recommend. He is really fed up with the incompetence of Brixton.

'At least in an open prison they've got proper systems and they know how to get you out on day release and then tagged as soon as possible. It is such a shambles here. I reckon you can go past your tag dates by weeks because they are just too messed up to process things properly.'

I'll sleep on the decision, talk to more people tomorrow.

1930H Bang-up for thirteen hours. How on earth can Governor Tullett claim I am in a Category D open prison?

FRIDAY 17 JANUARY 2014

I kissed my boy in the prison, before he went out to die.
'They dared me to do it,' he said, and he never has told me a lie.
I whipped him for robbing an orchard once when he was but a child –
'The farmer dared me to do it,' he said; he was always so wild –
And idle – and couldn't be idle – my Willy – he never could rest.
The King should have made him a soldier, he would have been one of his best.

But he lived with a lot of wild mates, and they never would let him be good;
They swore that he dare not rob the mail, and he swore that he would;
And he took no life, but he took one purse, and when all was done
He flung it among his fellows – 'I'll none of it,' said my son.
– 'Rizpah', Alfred, Lord Tennyson

0900H Do I stay in Brixton or continue my guided tour of HM Prisons? Still not sure. I am, however, sure about the first meal I want when out. A proper breakfast. The full monty. A giant fry-up. Bacon, sausage, black pudding; eggs, mushrooms, beans, fried bread, brown sauce, freshly ground pepper and a good strong pot of tea made to George Orwell's instructions, which I can almost recall word for word and which somehow convey mid-twentieth-century England, which I grew up in as a boy and which now is as remote as Victorian England was to me.

No other country knows the glory of the great British breakfast. The bacon tastes different in America or South Africa or Australia. Winston Churchill complained about the fruit heaped on his breakfast platter when in New York in the 1930s. American links and US bacon have nothing to do with the great British porker and proper back bacon.

Years ago I made my own sausages but, as political activism took over, there was less and less time to do some useful activity like making sausages. With leaflets to deliver and dull ephemeral pamphlets to write, how can be time be 'wasted' fussing over food?

My first ever pamphlet was written for the National Union of Journalists in the '70s. It was called *Black and White: Race Reporting Today*. It examined the extraordinary casual racism prevalent in British journalism. People were routinely described as 'coloured'. The managing editor of the *Daily Telegraph* wrote to me justifying his paper's continual reference to a man as 'Asian' in an ugly story about benefits that he was claiming. The *Daily Telegraph* editor insisted that if the paper did not identify the object of their attack as Asian, 'readers would assume he was Irish'. Quite.

I argued in my pamphlet that newspapers and broadcasters should employ more journalists from ethnic backgrounds. I urged more journalism exposing the xenophobia, racism and hatred of Europe of the neo-Nazi National Front party. Little could I have foreseen that its successor would be the BNP, whose complaint John Lyon CB would prosecute with such zeal, to take me all the way from the Privy Council to Belmarsh. In *The Times*, Bernard Levin, now forgotten, but at the time the foremost opinionated columnist of the day, devoted an entire column to trashing the pamphlet. I was never so proud.

Bit by bit the arguments in that first pamphlet entered decent journalist practice. Men and women, other than of white Anglo-Saxon stock, became journalists, some quite outstanding. Overt racism died away on the whole. It has been replaced by xenophobia about Poles and other Europeans the tabloid writers and politicians in UKIP and the UKIP wing of the Conservative Party do not like.

Again, we have been here before. George Orwell described anti-Polish feeling generated by post-1945 xenophobes, objecting to the presence of 250,000 Polish solders and their families who stayed here after the war, as 'the new anti-Semitism'.

Decades later, the ugly xenophobia that always surfaces at times of economic dislocation had entered daily political discourse, with Poles – more recently Romanian and Bulgarian citizens – again in the firing line. England, dear England, never changes.

0930H I go down to get brushes and mops and give the cell a good clean. As I walk along my landing floor I hear a plaintive cry. A prisoner looks miserably through the glass slit in the door. He hasn't been unlocked. The screw opening the cell doors an hour ago simply forgot him.

There is a small room with two microwave ovens and it is permanently dirty. I try to wipe some surfaces clean but it is hopeless. C Wing's squalor is shameful. Food falls off plates on stairs going up to landings and stays rotting on the floor. Little wonder there is always a queue outside the bars of the medical room. Deny men fresh air, offer them stodgy food and don't worry too much about cleanliness, and a perfect culture for illness flourishes.

1005H Yesterday, Ms Greer told me to wait at 10 a.m. today for my offender management supervisor. That's the officer who will supervise my release, contact Serco for a tag, inform Belgravia police station that a terrible criminal is coming to live in SW1 and check my house so I can go into every room with my tag. Having seen the slow incompetence of prison management systems, I want to get this process under way.

So, obedient to Ms Greer, I wait outside the offender management office. No one comes. I wait. A screw asks me about the ugly red gash under my chin. 'I used a prison razor for the first time,' I say.

'They're shit, aren't they?' he replies.

I wonder if there is any other public service which deals with people – schools, hospitals, even the police – where the staff are openly contemptuous of the quality of the *matériel* they work with or so scornful about the institution they work for? If prison officers don't believe prison works, why should the public?

1035H I give up on Ms Greer's promise. I go to the gym. It is a good fifty minutes of spinning, cross training, ab exercises and a few weights. I can hoist myself up on a parallel bar so, whatever else is happening, I am getting a little stronger in my body.

1135H Back in the wing I wait for lunch and chat to Jim, who arrived from Belmarsh with me. He is desperate to see a doctor and replumb his bowel system so he can throw away the colostomy bag in place following his diverticulosis operation. He has already had to have a five-hour operation after an abscess developed in his digestive area as a result of the first operation. Routine digestive tract operations like appendicitis, or diverticulosis, often leave scar tissue and other internal disruption that can cause unpleasant complications.

In an earlier prison, the doctor sent Jim away with some paracetamol and failed to spot something serious was going wrong. By the time the extent of the problem was realised, the abscess had become an internally destructive monster. A ten-minute intervention turned into a five-hour operation because of the default casualness of a prison system that holds prisoners' health cheap.

Not just health. C Wing is agog with the story of the 84-year-old Canadian suffering from Alzheimers, who was handcuffed by deportation officers as he was held at Heathrow when arrested en route to see his daughter in Canada. Thus manacled, the octogenarian Canuck had a heart attack and was not able to hold his chest to get any relief as he died in agony. The handcuffs were removed once he was dead. The officers, of course, were obeying Chris Grayling's orders to treat anyone they don't like in a suitable manner. Deportees, Canadian or otherwise, have no MPs, so Grayling will not be held to account for this sordid brutality.

Jim now is frightened. 'The surgeon who did the operation is a real specialist. She should do the reconnection job so I can get rid of this,' he says, patting the plastic medical bag sticking out from under his polo shirt. 'But if I don't turn up for the operation on the day I'm listed, I lose my place. It happened to me once already. I can't get through to the screws that I need this operation at a specific time on a specific day.'

Paddy, an elderly Irishman, hobbling on a stick, also looks worried as he listens to this conversation.

'I've got a hernia this big,' he says, making a vague shape of a small cabbage with his hands and holding them over his lower belly. 'I badly need an operation to put it right. It's agony walking around.'

He grimaces in discomfort. Since, luckily, I've never had such a condition, I can't tell if he is swinging some lead or if it is genuinely urgent. All I know is that no one should come into prison with a medical condition, especially one that needs treatment by outside specialists. Prison is for punishment, not for cures or rehabilitation of malfunctioning human organs and bodies.

At noon there is meant to be a 'surgery' for prisoners wanting to see their offender manager I ask a woman warden, a Ms Blake, if she has any messages from Ms Greer on my case. 'I'm not your offender supervisor,' she snaps, after checking on her clipboard.

1215H Wow! Lunch is a plastic box of lettuce, tomato, some beans and a hint of tuna. No dressing but at last, for the first time, a passable imitation of a salad. I eat it with pleasure, dreaming of the moment when once again I can dribble some oil and vinegar over a pepper, mustard and garlic base and make a salad come to life.

After lunch, I go out for the allotted fresh-air period. The yard has a huge pool of water covering one end, so the circular walk is over. No matter, up and down, up and down, with a watery sun providing a little vitamin D.

I walk and talk to Matt, the 67-year-old laundry man. He has always been cheerful, positive, encouraging, in short, a model prisoner. But it's not all sunshine and rainbows.

'Look, I'm in here for nine months. White-collar crime. No one hurt. No one robbed. Stupid. I just don't get the point of keeping me in all this time at public expense. Why can't they do people like me with a week or two in prison and then tag us, take away our passports and make us pay from our income to the prison. It's potty keeping me here. I've got a home, a family, I won't do it again but I just don't see the point of spending all this money on me. I'd pay anything not to be here.'

He agrees that, while he might be able to pay some monthly contribution in lieu of imprisonment, many prisoners could not. The poor and inarticulate are far more likely to be arrested and imprisoned than the educated middle classes. Even in today's unequal England you should not be kept in prison simply because you are without income.

Matt's real point is the sheer pointlessness of locking up for such lengths men who are punished by arrest and conviction, not by months or years in prison. That seems such a self-evident fact, yet it appears impossible to translate into policy, given the poor quality of judges on the criminal bench and the cowardice of politicians.

1405H The door opens and a guard hands me a dozen letters, emails and Christmas cards forwarded from Belmarsh. I was certain when in Belmarsh that mail was being deliberately withheld as an extra punishment for prisoners. Now I am getting my Christmas cards three weeks too late but I put them up on my cell ledges and walls anyway. You cannot write too often to a prisoner.

The delivery screw jokes, 'All we do now is deliver your letters.' I take his friendly remark as a chance to send back into the system my worry about not knowing how long I'll be here and whether I should move to an open prison. I explain my talks with Governor Tullett and Ms Greer and add, 'Do I stay here? – but if so, why can I never find anyone to tell me what's going on? Governor Tullett said this was like an open prison, but you never get enough fresh air and for the first time in my life I am getting regular headaches. Prison takes away freedom. It's not meant to make you ill.'

He smiles gently at the conceit that Brixton is a Category D or open prison. He tells me he will go downstairs and take up my concerns. 'Look, I'm not telling you what to do. But every time you move prisons all the procedures have to start all over again. Probation have to check on your house. That takes time. It will take longer if you move.'

It sounds good advice but here I am – in theory seventeen days away from my release date – and I know nothing. Lack of information is further punishment.

I read my letters. Sadly there are some where the handwriting or signatures are just illegible. Old friends I haven't seen in years are moved to write, having seen or read the news of my incarceration. It is so kind. But even if your handwriting isn't great (mine isn't), please, oh please, spell out your name!

I get a Season's Greetings card from Tony Blair and Cherie. 'Thinking of you,' writes Tony, and I know his hand so it's for real. Bless. Whatever the hate poured over him, he is still the best centre-left politician of my lifetime. The Rotherham in which I became an MP in 1994 was full of unemployment, schools with window frames that let in water, long waiting lists for operations, social housing with plumbing dating back decades; a wrecked community at the end of the Thatcher–Major experiment. After a decade of Blair it was vastly improved and, even after the years of the post-crash cuts, Rotherham is still in much better shape than in 1994.

To be sure, I wish all the northern nations, from Russia to the United States, had stayed out of majority Muslim countries in the last three decades. I think Cameron's and Sarkozy's adventure with Libya has also turned out a disaster. To blame Blair for Iraq or to blame Gordon Brown and David Cameron for the hundreds of lives pointlessly sacrificed in Afghanistan is as pointless as blaming Asquith, Grey, Balfour and Kitchener for going to war in 1914.

Blair did not take Britain to war in Iraq. Four hundred and seventeen MPs did, including most members of the present Cabinet. In the debate on the so-called dodgy dossier, William Hague told the Commons that Saddam Hussein had 400 nuclear arms installations hidden away in farms and schools. He is now Foreign Secretary but I do not doubt his sincerity when making his claim late in 2002.

Yes, Blair has gone off to make zillions but most of it is poured back into his charitable and faith foundations and I have witnessed their good inter-faith work in the Balkans. Margaret Thatcher and John Major were also remunerated beyond the dreams of avarice after they stopped being Prime Minister.

I know it is fashionable to hate Blair but if in my lifetime the British and European left finds another leader able to win election after election and wield power to such good purpose in Britain, I will be content.

Of course there are 101 reforms I wish Blair had not initiated – not least, the rotten, corrupting, self-inflicted destruction of parliamentary pay and expenses, and now, I would add, the prison system. Yet, although I guess the last thing Tony needs is an endorsement from a convict, I still think Blair's premiership (leaving Iraq to one side, though at the time I and 416 other MPs voted to use military force to uphold UN sanctions) was hugely impressive. He did not have to send a card. I wish Belmarsh had let me have it while there to show Father Edward. But that he did, says more about Tony Blair than all his denigrators put together.

Look at Obama, our great hope of 2008. I campaigned for him, staffing a phone bank in Virginia, wondering if my English accent would produce a single extra vote. Now we know that Obama has presided over the biggest example of state espionage of its own citizens in world history. Or take *mon copain* François Hollande, who is revealed now as someone who has been lying to his partner for two years or more. Is a man who lies in private ever to be trusted to tell the truth in public? Yet, as I prefer Obama and Hollande to their ugly right-wing opponents, so I prefer Blair to any Tory and now, alas, I have to add Lib Dem, as Nick Clegg has broken so many pledges and betrayed trust in a way Blair never would have dared to.

1100H Still reading the letters and emails. Gosh I didn't know I had so many friends. So many want to visit but, despite this being a different prison from Belmarsh, the visit regime seems harsher. I'll try MP friends, as I think they can come in on their own status. *Le Monde's* former London and Washington correspondent, Patrice de Beer, reminds me of the old saw, 'the dogs bark, the caravan moves on'. He tells me to avoid newspapers. Certainly, the *Economist* I ordered earlier in the week hasn't arrived. James sends me *The Spectator*, two weeks old. Its boring Europhobia is not my *tasse de thé* but the book reviews are good. He also sends some first class stamps. I now have more stamps than envelopes and do not know where I will find the time to reply to everyone.

1155H Another tasteless salad baguette for lunch but at least there is a little Carson's vinegar, and salt and pepper to put on it back in my cell.

1605H A prisoner comes in and asks if I will give a talk on politics tonight. I tell him I have suggested this to Ms Greer and asked her to put up a notice so that anyone who wants to can come. I'd better wait and see if she takes up the idea or whether, like so much in Brixton, it disappears into thin air.

1755H Roll call and another unpleasant mince stew with rice.

2200H Douggie and I reel back at the news that a former soldier was sentenced to just six years for smashing his little baby about so senselessly that she died of her injuries. The judge said the man, a former soldier from the elite Guards brigade, had been involved in fearful fighting in Afghanistan. The resulting stress, said the judge, had to be taken into account in sentencing. Indeed so. But why does the terrible stress by survival of men I've met, doing as long or longer sentences for non-violent crimes not get taken into account in sentencing? I don't question the judge's decision, just the extraordinary double standards and highly personalised judicial sentencing which today's judges are capable of. *Quis custodiet ipsos custodes?*

SATURDAY 18 JANUARY 2014

British ministers said after 1937, anyone volunteering to fight in Spain would be 'liable on conviction to imprisonment of up to two years'.

0900H We remain locked in the cell for an hour longer on Saturday. Normally one might imagine a weekend to be easier, more relaxed. Not in Brixton, where keeping prisoners cooped up in cages is a priority. I am sure Chris Grayling will award bonuses all round to prison executives who can show they keep grown men isolated as long as possible each day.

The gentle giant of C Wing, Bill, a former professional boxer, asks solicitously after my well-being. 'It's different from what you hear on the outside, isn't it?'

I think of all the tweets from Paul Staines (Guido Fawkes), the BNP and UKIP hate merchants, promising I'd be bullied and buggered and beaten by all the serious criminals I'd meet. The opposite is true. I have only encountered kindness, gentleness and warm solidarity.

Bill is the gym orderly and encourages all ages, shapes and sizes to use the gym and, from his two-metre height, makes sure the gym is run fairly, with no one hogging a training machine.

Why is he here? Another sad, bad, story. Emotion running over, converted into a prison sentence. Bill lives in Walthamstow with his small children. Their mother and he do not get on. After one blazing row she stormed out and called the police, saying he had beaten her up. There were no marks, but the police have a duty to investigate any accusation of domestic violence. Bill was alone. His children in bed. Suddenly the front door was smashed open and police came running in.

'On the floor, quick,' they screamed at the unarmed but black man.

'No. This is my house. My kids are upstairs. Why are you here?'

The response of the police was to taser Bill four times. He was dragged away, his body wasted by the taser attack.

The charge, of course, was resisting arrest and, without paying attention to Bill's story, the judge flung him in prison. One less black man on the streets of London.

Panic in the cell. A screw clambers up to the fourth floor to tell Douggie he has a visitor.

'What! Who?! I'm not expecting a visitor.'

He rushes out of gym clothes into jeans and splashes water on his face. A prisoner wants to look his best. Douggie is a neat man and is angry he has to rush off unwashed with a two-day prison beard.

He comes back angry and dishevelled. He did indeed have a visitor – his ex-wife and her sister from Edinburgh. He had sent a Visitor's Order some time ago. Like most modern women, Douggie's ex-wife lives on her mobile phone and hardly any other means of communication. A phone, however, is no good for communication into prison. Normally, prisoners are given a slip of paper announcing a visit. In Belmarsh, a whiteboard listed all the prisoner legal and social visits for each day. Brixton is so badly run, it seems a prisoner doesn't know about his visits until the last moment.

Yes, his ex-wife and he should have established better communication. She had come all the way from Edinburgh for a short, mean hour in the crowded, unrelaxing Brixton visiting room. In some countries, male prisoners and female visitors are allowed real, intimate time together.

At the East Sutton Park women's prison – a Category D open prison, the same category of prison which Douggie and I are meant to be in – the visitors' room has generous sofas where couples can hug each other, armchairs, a garden and a tea counter, and exudes warmth, with the guards politely keeping their distance. Brixton treats its Category D prisoners with open contempt. The high security Category A Belmarsh visitors' centre is more welcoming, better for morale.

Morale, though, is not a Brixton priority. All the other politician prisoners were allowed to have their own clothes, toiletries, books and writing material. A week ago I wrote an 'app' – prison jargon for an application or polite request to the prison management. I asked to be reunited with my personal possessions: some warm clothes; a razor that doesn't scar my face; books and notepads. I have had no reply. It is a two-minute walk to the reception area where personal possessions are stored and a two-minute task to get what all my other MP colleagues were allowed.

I am warned about a blonde woman warder who seems under pressure to use the word 'fuck' or 'fucking' in every sentence. Bad language doesn't faze me. 'Fuck' and 'fucking' are the first words any newly arrived foreigner learns in England. Yet rehabilitation begins with language. If, in prison, all you hear is the brutalism of the English language at its coarse, dull worst, why behave differently when outside? This warder is a 'right bitch' according to other prisoners. She is the only one on duty, so I have to deal with her.

I ask her about the 'app' and if there is any chance of getting my clothes and, more importantly, my books.

'Have you had a reply?'

'No.'

'Well, put in another app.'

'I have to put in an app to ask for a reply to an app? When do I get an answer?'

'In a week's time.'

'So I am in prison for five weeks without access to all my books. Why am I being treated differently to all other MP prisoners?'

'I don't make the rules. I just apply them,' she replies.

The Bitch (excuse me, all feminist friends and daughters, but that is what she is known as) just purses her mouth. The pleasure of doing down and demoralising a prisoner shines through.

'You're part of a team. Can I politely suggest you pass upwards that not replying to a polite, reasonable request to be treated as other prisoners is just not right?'

She doesn't bother to look up or say a word. I am a fly that's been swatted away.

Douggie has ordered *The Sun* for today but again, as last week, it doesn't arrive. Prisoners are banned from using Amazon to buy cheaper books and DVDs. Instead, in a squalid little racket, the Justice Ministry has given an exclusive contract to a firm that will supply DVDs at twice the price of Amazon.

I get my canteen sheet, which allows me to order extra food, toiletries, and other bits and pieces you would find in a poorly stocked corner shop selling only the cheapest products. When I came in four weeks ago I brought with me £340 in notes, which I then handed over in Belmarsh. Where is it? The canteen sheet says I have £16.87, which can disappear in three days on phone calls alone at the rip-off tariff BT charges.

I look out of the window on my landing. Just across a car park I can see a neat Lambeth council estate. In the summer, prisoners' friends come and throw socks full of drugs over the wall. With better catching ability than the English cricket team, prisoners dash out and catch the carefully weighted and precisely thrown drug balls. Sometimes the aim is poor and the sock hangs forlornly on the barbed wire. In the end, the prison officers will smuggle in what's required. This is cynical and wrong. But it's the prison system we have.

When do I get out? Poor Brian, the gentle grey-haired accountant, was given a release date of 2 January. Here we are more than two weeks later and the taxpayer is still paying for him to be kept in Brixton.

What can I do? There is no one who seems to know what is going on. The screws hide behind probation officers, who are meant to do checks. But they have known about my release date almost since I arrived in prison. I have been a model prisoner. It was a white-collar offence. I keep writing to the Governor, to anyone. But there is no reply. They just treat you as if you didn't exist. I have made arrangements back home but everything is up in the air.

This is psychological torture of the worst sort. You sit nervously in the dock waiting on the mood or caprice of the red dressing gown man. Another prisoner, Eamonn, is an Irishman and lawyer, and is in for four years. He stole £130,000 from his tax law firm to pay for cocaine. (I had assumed tax lawyers, like bankers, got cocaine on expenses.)

'A week later, a judge on the same bench had an accountant in front of him for stealing £1.6 million. He got just two years. I was guilty. I accept I did wrong. I accept my punishment. But why am I serving 50 per cent longer than the criminal who stole ten times as much as me?'

Again, the problem of erratic, inconsistent, incoherent judges. If surgeons produced such variable outcomes in their professional work there would be a national outcry.

But once sentence is handed down and you begin the walk from the dock to captivity, a calm that it is all over descends. However unfair the judge was, that's that. At the end of a sentence, however, there is a sense of life lost that can now begin anew. To delay or play with a prisoner's freedom date is penitential cat and mouse. It is torture to keep a man in prison a minute longer than necessary. When the reason for thus torturing somebody is managerial incompetence or bureaucratic buck-passing, it is shameful.

1135H I go downstairs to check when the Saturday gym will happen. I have a visit from my brother, Emilie who is going back to Spain tomorrow, and Vicky. If I can squeeze in a gym, so much the better. But as usual no one knows when the gym will happen. It says 1 p.m. on the timetable. But we are often banged up between lunch and 2 p.m. The reception desk screw doesn't know. I notice the door from C Wing is open and put my nose out to see the exercise yard gate is unlocked.

'When did exercise begin?' I ask the unpleasant woman warder.

'Ten o'clock.'

'But no one told us,' I protest.

She doesn't look up. She doesn't reply. I don't exist. And she doesn't have to tell anyone if they can get their daily ration of fresh air.

I go out and run as fast as I can round and round and round the exercise yard. After six minutes the nasty woman orders me inside. Six minutes of fresh south London air is today's ration. I suppose I should be grateful.

Lunch is a matted, dark brown circle of some bizarre matter. The prison service thinks it is a hamburger. Douggie arrives spluttering with anger. On his plate there is some rice and two hard-boiled eggs. The servers have given the food he ordered to their chums. There have been some nasty shouting exchanges when prisoners are cheated by this favouritism of the food they expect to get. The guards just let this happen. One day there will be a real explosion.

1220H Locked up again. Saturday seems the day the screws turn the key and lock you in the tiny world of your own cell for more hours than any other.

I have decided to contact my own MP, Mark Field, to ask why I am getting such utterly different treatment to other MP prisoners. I write out an email to Mark, copied to other MPs, and fold it small to go into my sock to get past the body search.

At 3 p.m. I go down for my visit. There is a young Romanian who is showing everyone a beautiful carved balsa or plywood bi-plane, only a few inches in wingspan, that he has made as a present for his daughter. It looks as fragile as a butterfly and as pretty. The screw taking us to the visitors' centre says he can't take the present for his child. Other prisoners say: 'Yes, you can. You can't bring anything in but you can give someone a gift you've made to take out.'

The Romanian produces his trump card.

'Look, I've got an app to say I can take it out. It's been signed and approved by Ms Greer and she runs C Wing.'

The guard shrugs. 'Ms Greer. Ms Greer,' he repeats her name with a sigh that merges into a sneer. 'She couldn't run a fucking bath. I don't care what she says.'

I cannot believe I am hearing a public service official so openly trashing his superior in front of prisoners. It would be like a junior surgeon telling patients the registrar was useless. What kind of a world is this?

My third family visit in four weeks. It lifts morale. My poor doctor brother is now one of the NHS's most senior managers, reporting directly to the Health Secretary, Jeremy Hunt. He says one of his responsibilities is the health of long-term offenders in prison. He looks concerned when I tell him about how little fresh air prisoners are permitted to breathe and about the carb-heavy nature of the diet. I'll discuss this further when outside.

Being a prisoner is easier than running the NHS. Its founder, the great Labour politician Aneurin Bevan, said the Secretary of State for Health would be responsible for the state of every bedpan in every hospital. His successor right down to the current Secretary of State for Health must feel the same responsibility.

Alas, I doubt if there has ever been a Home Secretary or, today, Justice Secretary, who feels any sense of responsibility for prisoners or the state of prisons. I was always impressed by Douglas Hurd, the former senior Tory minister and an ex-Home Secretary, who is an exception to this rule. In an occasional article in the *Financial Times* he would plead for a more humane, modern, rational policy on sentencing and prisoners. Sadly these were gestures, not effective politics.

I slip my letter into Emilie's hands to smuggle out and tell someone to ask Chris Grayling why I am being treated so differently from the other MP prisoners. I dislike doing this but what choice has Governor Tullett left me? His officers refuse to treat me honestly or fulfill their obligations under prison rules and regulations.

Vicky is very tough when I tell her that I have no release date, no meeting with probation officials, no news or notification of any sort. She insists that I must ask for a transfer now. She insists that open prisons have better management and are used to what needs to be done to release prisoners on their due date. My brother says, 'You must have more fresh air,' a commodity no one in Brixton Prison believes in.

Yet when I report these comments to experienced friends in C Wing they are not sure. 'You've only got a short time left. If you transfer to another prison to get out of this shithole, it will take longer to sort out your release,' sums up the argument of most. I wish I knew what to do.

1700H Dinner: pie, mashed potato, and a wedge of tasteless cake. No fruit, no fresh vegetables.

1715H We are locked up for the next sixteen hours.

SUNDAY 19 JANUARY 2014

The most anxious man in a prison is the governor.

– George Bernard Shaw

0857H Unlocked. I had my breakfast – what wouldn't I give for some bacon and eggs and, dream of dreams, black pudding – some time ago and have been writing since, waiting to be let out like a battery animal allowed a tiny bit of time out of the cage. The weekend is when you want to call everyone. So it's the two days the Brixton establishment ensures Category D – the safest, most respectable of prisoners – are locked up the longest.

Eamonn, the Irish tax lawyer, comes upstairs in a sulk to say those going to mass are leaving. I pull on pants and a grey Brixton sweat-shirt – Sunday best – and troop off. The Jamaican priest is not well and the service lacks fizz. A Catholic mass is a show. If the actors are poor, the reading bad, the production lifeless, the audience–congregation gets bored.

1043H Eamonn is due to leave in nine days. He is fed up, as the money he earns in his enhanced status as a fully approved prisoner has been reduced. What he has will hardly be enough to buy good-quality instant coffee instead of the undesirable Nescafé.

He is uncertain about leaving. His house was repossessed last year. For enthusiasts of prison-as-punishment, a prisoner losing his home is part of the price of white-collar, victimless crime. Eamonn shared a cell for three and a half months with a man he considers a friend. 'He promised me a room in his mother's house and a job. But as soon as he left, nothing. I wrote three times to the address he gave me for his mum, but I got no reply.'

If you want friendship in prison, read a book. Men of all ages are forced into close confined space-sharing and mutual living together. Being cheerful and friendly is a sensible survival technique. But it should not be confused with friendship.

Poor Eamonn has been waiting fourteen extra weeks to get his release date on tag confirmed. 'They went to the wrong address. They spelt my name wrong. I was never told anything.' Eamonn has been a model prisoner. He says he was glad he was caught and convicted and can start life afresh. But there was no help or advice on keeping his house by renting it out on a long-lease or for holiday lets or indeed to MPs under the fatuously expensive new bureaucratic MPs expenses system, which costs the taxpayer three times as much as the old, rotten but much cheaper system.

An old friend, the former England rugby international and witty Labour MP, Derek Wyatt, wants to visit. I write to tell him I am not allowed any. Never mind. He lives just round the corner and there will be six weeks of tagged evenings when I can cook dinner for friends.

Goody. The door is open to the exercise yard. The *Sunday Times* I have ordered on Kenny's canteen sheet has arrived. I thought I would be reading it word for word, as it's the first paper I've seen in four weeks, but no, I skim the news section in five minutes.

The brilliant Rod Liddle confirms that the BBC's Nick Robinson is a Conservative, though having observed Nick's barely disguised Euroscepticism over the years I would have thought Nick is cheating UKIP of a membership fee. Nothing new on François Hollande. The main point of a weekend newspaper in prison is the TV programmes pages. At last we can work out what we want to see. After four weeks, I don't want to watch any more British television for four years.

1113H On my way out I ask the woman guard on duty on the reception desk if she knows who my 'Offender Supervisor' is. In theory every prisoner is on NOMIS, the prison computer system. This was the system that passed on to Brixton the fact that I had had a secret red entry on my file placed by a screw in Belmarsh. The guard on duty is the blonde who was very abrupt to the point of being unpleasant yesterday. Today, she is helpful. I explain I know nothing about my future, that prison regulations have been broken, or that I do not know whether to apply for a transfer to get out on my release date. Nothing can happen without this mysterious creature, the 'Offender Supervisor'.

She cannot find anything on her computer but phones a number of someone who should know. There is no reply. She sends an email and promises she'll come and find me as soon as she knows the name of the 'Offender Supervisor'. Will it happen? Too many other prisoners have stories about requests to guards that go unanswered. I'll see.

I walk briskly around the exercise yard. Fifteen minutes of fresh air is a tonic.

1149H The exercise gives me some appetite, though I have noticed a kind of tuning out of normal needs and emotions. Why let yourself be hungry or angry if you are powerless to alter your state? Lunch is cheap chicken leg with roast potatoes and cabbage. There is a nice-looking if fatty sauce in the trays holding chicken legs. I ask for some. 'Sorry, we haven't got a spoon,' says the prisoner-server holding up his serving tongs. No spoon for gravy. My dream of a better Sunday lunch evaporates.

1245H Locked in the cell again. I was hoping to make some phone calls to the children. But being locked in my cell with Douggie is the Brixton priority.

1430H Hallelujah, my lovely blonde guard (scrub description from yesterday) looks me up on her computer and says my tag date is 7 February. That's a Friday and I will have done my Sweeney six weeks by Monday 3 Feb. Just a little extra to remind me who's boss. She gives me the name of the Offending Supervisor screw – a Mr Calman, Kama? I can't work out the name. She tells me to write to him. The tunnel end has light. I go into the exercise yard and pound round and round for fifty minutes.

1525H On the first-floor landing there is a Governor's message printed on a yellow sheet to stand out. It informs prisoners that following a riot in Brixton Prison there will be changes to the distribution of prisoners' tobacco allocation. It is signed by Governor Amy Rees. It is dated 2 March 2010.

1726H Dinner is a pie or pasty. Not nice. Still, there are some early James Bond movies on obscure channels I never watch at home. But since I haven't watched television other than brief glimpses at news and a bit of sport for twenty-odd years, all this is new to me.

MONDAY 20 JANUARY 2014

The confinement … of any man in the sloth and darkness of a prison, is a loss to the nation.

– Samuel Johnson

0750H Bless Douggie. I start the day with half an orange and a week-old apple. Douggie bought some oranges on his canteen allowance and he is sharing them with me.

0805H The cell door is opened. 'MacShane. Induction.' That happened on Day 2 in Belmarsh. I have been twiddling my thumbs in Brixton for more than a week.

0830H Induction. Endless barred gates open and bang shut. Brixton reminds me of nothing so much as a South Yorkshire scrap metal yard. Iron and steel and wire and skips everywhere, with grimy, dirty buildings and shabby-looking men walking about. Like scrap metal, prisoners are thrown into a melting pot and recycled. Like scrap metal there can be a good end product but plenty ends up unfit for much use. Amongst younger prisoners, seven out of ten emerge from the prison system and go straight back to crime. So much for Chris Grayling and other Prison Ministers' warm words on rehabilitation.

Finally, I arrive in the induction room. It is run, unbelievably, by A4E, the firm that has caused uproar over multi-million-pound fraud cases involving public sector contracts. I wonder what A4E fraudsters will get by way of prison sentences and why A4E are running education in Brixton. There are twenty-five prisoners. Five are white British or European. I don't notice colour but if I chose to count the number of non-white prisoners they would be a far greater number than their share of the population.

Our first talk is from a vicar, Phil, dressed in a grey fleece over his dog collar. Then comes a ramrod stiff ex-army officer who says there is a good charity to help ex-servicemen. No one takes up his offer. I have read somewhere that 10 per cent of all prisoners are ex-military personnel, the sad detritus from our failed wars in Iraq and Afghanistan. If so, I have yet to meet any prisoner who who has told me of military service.

Another charity representative, this one for housing, announces the bleak news: 'There is no council housing of any sort available. Don't even dream about it. You might get a bed in a hotel. Otherwise it's couch surfing. Sorry.'

A pretty blonde woman, looking as if she had stepped out of *Call the Midwife*, announces that she is from another charity which helps prisoners' families. She says she has a team of charity workers ready to call wives, parents and children, and help them with their difficulties. The best way to keep prisoners in touch with their children, wives, husbands or parents is to let them stay in touch with visits, phone calls, Skype. But, according to Chris Grayling, punishment means limiting such communication and contact, thus speeding up family disintegration. All the worthwhile charity work in the world cannot replace the smile of a child, the touch of a father, the hug of a partner.

In the healthcare talk, protests rise up. One prisoner says he has been waiting for a shoulder operation for twenty months. His tendons were torn and are now, he says, fusing with bicep muscles. In different prisons he had been trying to see the prison GPs, without success. The chief nurse at Brixton lists all the healthcare on offer. A GP. Dentist. Optician. Podiatry.

Stress. Blood pressure advice as well as guidance for alcohol and drug abuse. It looks good on a PowerPoint presentation. But, like Potemkin Villages, it exists more on paper than in reality. Prisoners do get medical treatment but late and inadequate, if at all.

Earlier, Colostomy Bag Jim, who is also in the induction session, as he was transferred from Belmarsh to Brixton the same day I was, came up to tell me he had been rushed to hospital after collapsing with pain. The hospital told him he had a hernia resulting from the delayed treatment over his diverticulosis and the colostomy bag.

He begged the guards to let him move to a lower floor, as walking up the steep metal stairs to the third floor was agony. There was an empty cell on the bottom floor. The screws wouldn't let him move there. In fact, he is due to leave on tag in two months. No doubt a Prison Minister could explain why the taxpayer should pay a few thousand extra pounds to keep Joe doubled up in pain for a few more weeks inside. I cannot.

I cannot turn off decades of asking questions when I feel something is unjust. I ask the nurse in a crisp, clear voice, 'Who actually in this prison takes responsibility for medical care? Who decides?'

The room falls silent. Prisoners are not meant to ask such questions. We must be meek and keep our heads bowed. The chief nurse stutters, 'Eh, eh, my boss, you know, the chief medical officer. And the people he works with.' I remember asking civil servants simple questions to which they had no answer. It is not comfortable. And I am sure the nurse means well. But she works in a rotten system. Erwin James rightly says 'good health' is vital for 'coping with a prison sentence'. That, presumably, is why the prison system keeps us as unwell as possible.

1120H On my way out of the morning induction session we go through the healthcare waiting room. On the wing I see Brian, the septuagenarian prisoner who should have been released two weeks ago. Such is Brixton's managerial incompetence, he is still waiting. He suffers from depression and other stress-induced illnesses and is on permanent medication. He asked to see the GP. He tells me that he has been waiting since 0830. When I saw him later, he reported that his consultation had lasted all of two minutes.

1127H Back in C Wing and before lunch I race up and down stairs and do cell exercises. As I am on an induction course the gym is denied to me.

As I go up and down the metal stairs, Bill, the former pro boxer, salutes approvingly. I tell him I hope to use the big gym in Brixton before I leave, as the tiny boxer's gym, with its focus on weight-lifting, isn't for me.

'Yeah, you've gotta keep fit,' he says. I tell him I try to do a serious run every other day and I have run a couple of marathons.

'What time did you do?

'Four and a half. Old man's time.'

'Christ, I'd be happy to do a four. I've done a couple of half-marathons but never the big one.'

He balls his hand into a giant fist and touches it to mine. It is a gesture of fellowship which makes me feel oddly content.

1202H Lunch is a salad baguette. I throw away the slimy soft bread and just eat the salad with a little Sarson's vinegar on it but no oil.

1350H I tuck a book under under my sweatshirt to read in the pauses in the afternoon induction session. During breaks, one prisoner goes off to sneak a smoke in the loo. The head of education, Sheila, has warned that CCTV – which you can see every few inches in the ceiling – and smoke detectors would catch anyone smoking and it is a capital offence. The prisoner can't help himself and lights up a very thin roll-up, taking two quick drags before snuffing the fag out. He puffs out the smoke evenly, turning around as he does so, so no alert is sounded.

1647H Back on the wing, a nasty scene. Ms Greer calls me into the office with Mr Blackman, another officer. There are two Mr Blackmans on Wing C, one white, one Afro-Caribbean. They are known inevitably as Mr White Blackman and Mr Black Blackman, a differentiation they accept with good humour. This is Mr Black Blackman, who seems a decent guy.

Ms Greer says she has to do a painful duty. I now have my third red mark. I will be on the basic regime for seven days. Prisoners have three levels of status – basic, standard and enhanced. Mainly the status level determines how much money you get each week. In theory, enhanced prisoners can stay out for half an hour longer than lower-grade prisoners, but Douggie, who is on enhanced status, always get banged up at the same time as me.

Since my only spend is on phone credits and I have enough for calls over the next few days, I am not worried about dropping down to basic, but I am cross that this has happened for offences I did not know I was committing and was not told about.

What?! When?! Who?! I protest.

Apparently last Wednesday a woman officer had judged me to be lacking respect. The C Wing exercise period last week had been twenty-five to thirty minutes of fresh air in the exercise yard. I had been working in my cell and at 1135 had gone down to see if, indeed, the exercise yard was open. It was. I asked why no announcement had been made. The woman warder said she had called out exercise at 10 a.m.

I hurried into trainers to run round the yard, as I knew it would be the only chance for fresh air that day. After barely ten minutes, the guard announced that exercise was over. As I went in I muttered sotto voce, 'Is that all the fresh air and exercise I am to get today?'

Unbeknown to me, the warder decided this remark was an assault on her authority. Unbeknown to me she had made some negative entry in my file. She had not said one word to me about this.

And now six days later I am to be sanctioned. I protested at this Kafkaesque practice of entering secret marks against a prisoner without telling him. I insisted I had been cooperative throughout my stay in Brixton. In two weeks' time – assuming I had the same treatment as other politician prisoners and would be tagged having done half the custodial sentence – I would be out of their hair.

Governor Tullett, I say, has offered me a transfer to an open prison but I am content to stay at Brixton as long as I am treated fairly.

Mr Black Blackman tells me it was not true that C Wing has been allowed only thirty minutes' exercise on some days the previous week. 'The doors are always open,' he says.

I stare at him in disbelief, keeping my eyes on his big black boots, summoning up every reserve of humble submission I can muster.

'Honestly, Mr Blackman. Just go out and ask any prisoner. We were told that exercise was at 1230 for half an hour max.'

He isn't sure and I can sense Ms Greer isn't happy at the idea of one of her subordinates placing a red mark against a prisoner without informing him.

I also protest that I have been told I can't have any visits for fourteen days. Mr Black Blackman seemed perplexed. 'Who told you that?' Of course, I can't remember which of a dozen screws gave me back a VO for my brother and daughter, telling me to resubmit in two weeks' time.

Mr Black Blackman tells me to resubmit the VO but, when I go back to get one from the distributor for all the forms next to the screws' office, there are none left. By the time I've blagged one off a friend, Mr Black Blackman has disappeared.

I seem to be spending all this afternoon with prison managers. A senior prison officer, a Mr Cama – that's how you spell his name – comes to see me about release. He tells me what I knew. That a probation officer has to inspect my house. A report has to come in. A board has to meet.

I gently replied that I knew all this. I was due to spend six weeks in prison from Monday 23 December. That deadline expires two weeks from today, Monday 3 February.

'What the judge says has nothing to do with us. We'll decide when you're released, once all the formalities have been gone through. You'll be treated no differently from any other prisoner in Brixton.'

My heart sinks to the soles of my feet. If there is one common complaint at Brixton, it is the inability of the management to honour prison sentence release dates.

'I appreciate that,' I grovel. 'All I want is the same treatment as other politician prisoners. I am sure you will do your best. After all, you can't really want to keep me here at cost to the taxpayer for a minute longer than necessary.'

We part on polite terms – I hope.

1752H But my dinner, even with my favourite vegetables, sprouts – overcooked and watery but sprouts nonetheless – tastes bitter in my mouth and sits heavily in my stomach with the stress of these encounters.

They are so small, piddling, and in the greater scheme of things, utterly irrelevant. Yet for a prisoner, even one in for the shortest of times, they cause the trip between normality and a worried uncertainty.

I try and call my daughter to discuss these worries but a screw shouts at me for using a phone next to their office. All the other phones are occupied. I retreat upstairs and there is bang-up at 7 p.m., half an hour earlier than usual. Douggie is on the way to a shower when the screw tells him to go back to our cell. 'I've been working all day. This morning there was no time before I went to the bakery where I have been at it all day.' Tough. Better a dirty prisoner than the screws keep the doors unlocked till the official 7.30 p.m. lock-up.

TUESDAY 21 JANUARY 2014

Soon be over.

[Message from former TUC General Secretary, (Lord) John Monks.]

0750H I hear John Humphrys on the radio burbling about an anti-Jewish gesture by a West Brom footballer. In bewilderment, he asks if anti-Semitism is common in English soccer compared to the Continent, where all sorts of dark forces pullulate. In my 2008 book *Globalising Hatred: The New Anti-Semitism*, I devote pages to anti-Jewish chants and slogans. 'I'd rather be a Paki than a Jew' is a favourite West Ham chant when playing Spurs. John and his interviewees agree that this is a first and English football is free of anti-Jewish behaviour. Do *Today* researchers do any research?

0802H Half a banana shared with Douggie. He puts a carton of milk in the jug kettle to heat up to make his porridge. He has been more than generous in sharing his bought-in fruit with me.

I dash off a letter to the Channel 4 News political correspondent Michael Crick, who has sent me a two-page email. We first met in Warsaw in 1980 when he was a gofer for Nik Gowing, one of the best foreign affairs correspondents of our generation. Serious, balanced, reflective. I suppose John Simpson has captured the kudos for foreign reporting but there is something so conventional, conservative and in tune with the line of the *Daily Telegraph* of the day in his reporting.

I prefer the foreign corrs who like the politics of what they are doing, who ask the whys, rather than list the whats and whos. Patrick Cockburn, Peter Beaumont, Jason Burke, Lyse Doucet, and, in his glory days as *The Guardian*'s star foreign corr, the incomparable Martin Walker.

0815H Over to Induction. I pass five or six guards huddled against the cold. I call a breezy, cheerful 'good morning' in my thin sweatshirt. In his email, Michael Crick says he sometimes accompanies Chris Grayling to Old Trafford, as both are keen Man Utd fans. I wonder why Grayling won't let me wear my anorak. None of the guards returns my 'Good morning'. When you treat men with scant courtesy, why should the prisoner believe that good manners and courtesy are worth an investment?

Most of the computers are down in the education centre. ICT pupils are turned away. I sit and do English and Maths proficiency tests. I stumble over whether 'wonderful' is spelt with one or two 'l's. It is fifty years since I did a Maths O level and then dropped, shamefully, all study of numbers and science to concentrate on History, English and languages ancient and modern to go to Oxford. I have to drag out of the bottom of my memory a little algebra. I stumble over group numbers – what are they? – and find a scrap of paper in a bin to do some multiplication and decimals.

0950 I finish all the tests and sit quietly waiting for evaluation and allocation to a course. Going for a pee, I notice the tell-tale flecks of burnt tobacco in the loo. It seems mad to risk a sanction by so stupidly breaking the rules. But who am I to talk? It's why I'm here.

Having finished my tests and had a chat with the nurse, I am now twiddling my thumbs. I am meant to have a one-to-one interview with the head of education, a kindly woman. But working with some of the less literate prisoners takes all her time. She asks me to help with a Somali. He can barely manage English and I have to help him fill in every detail. The one date he does know is 19 April, when he is due to be released. He is in prison for being caught with khat – which every Somali consumes, as we consume another herbal leaf stimulant called tea. In Saudi Arabia you are sent to prison for possessing beer. In England, for possessing khat.

1015H Waiting quietly to be interviewed, I listen to other prisoners chatting about their release. 'Listen man, they never let you out on your tag date. You can wait weeks, never less than two weeks.' The others nod. They are all due to be released and some are past their tag date. It's with a depressed resignation that they accept that tag dates are a prison fiction. My ex-ministerial blood boils inwardly at the scandalous waste of public money. But I say nothing.

1110 Damn. I have been waiting, letting other guys go first to talk to Sheila. A mistake. I am at the back of the queue. Everyone else goes back to the wing for a coffee while I am stuck here. The minutiae of prison life dominate our lives.

1235H A bit of a walk in the exercise yard. It is open for exactly twenty-eight minutes, which gives the lie to Mr Blackman's assertion yesterday evening that it is open all day long. I don't doubt he probably believed the nonsense he was spouting yesterday. But this is the problem. The guards just do not know what is going on and are as much in the dark from each other, from reality, as they are inept at handling prisoners and preparing them for the outside world.

Douggie joins me in despair. He had come back to the wing for lunch today so he could meet his offending supervisor, the god-like screws who decide when a prisoner can go out on leave, and finally on tag. But the screw dismissed him out of hand with no information on any tag date, even though Douggie has done near half of his 44-month sentence. This is cruel and demoralising. I wonder why Governor Tullett allows this to happen. Perhaps he doesn't know. Or he does, and doesn't care.

1315H A little plastic box of salad with chips for lunch. No dressing, but I throw the chips into the landing dustbin. I am now dieting on the prison regime, as I am enjoying my trimmer profile. I hear a great shout of 'MacShane!' which arrives to the fourth floor. Down I go for the over-50s gym. A friendly Spanish gym warder, who was obliged to listen to my Spanish, has written me down as a participant. In fact, I am the only C Wing inmate over fifty. The half-dozen others are gym addicts with bulging biceps.

We troop off through the various gates that have to be unlocked and relocked. This time it is to the new and very well-equipped gym. A couple of spacious, airy rooms in a new building full of running tracks, cross trainers, rowing machines and muscle machines. We have it to ourselves and it is forty minutes swiftly passed.

I spend the rest of the day on the wing writing letters and, as the wing is relatively empty, calling friends. Although I am now back on basic I still have all my money put into phone credits and that has not been removed. A stack of emails arrives, including an invitation to go on television when I get out. We'll see.

A screw knocks on the door. 'You're wanted downstairs.' It is Mr Cama, holding a form which has my release tag date of 7 February. This is four days later than the six-week anniversary of Sweeney's finest hour but I don't care. I quickly write out the address of my London home, hoping I have got the BT landline correct. I say to Mr Cama that I hope 7 February is guaranteed. He gives a half-assent. 'If probation do their job, it will happen.'

In my emails there is one from the Commons, intimating that my case has been raised with David Cameron. I always got on well with Dave. Person-to-person, he is, or can be, charming, friendly and very witty. In June 2005, standing naked in the Commons dressing room after a shower – him from biking in from Notting Hill, me from playing tennis with MPs – I urged him to run for the leadership of the Conservative Party.

'You're the nearest you lot have to Tony Blair. Even if you don't win – and I think you stand a good chance – the very act of running for leader of a party propels you to the top ranks and guarantees a major shadow Cabinet job. But if you do get it, you'll have to change the way the party is seen. And you can start by dropping its increasing Europhobia.'

'Thanks, Denis. But I don't think you realise I am much more Eurosceptic than you imagine,' Cameron replied.

I know MPs have been told about the fact I have been given such poor treatment compared to the other MP prisoners. Frankly, I will pull every string in England and use every contact to de-Sweeney myself as soon as I can. I am putting on a calm, brave face and have learnt loads. But this has been a foul, demoralising Christmas and New Year. I have so little time left and so many better things to do with it than provide satisfaction to the BNP.

So if Mr Cama's half-smile is right, I just have to keep my head down for sixteen interminable days. As I settle down, another knock on the door. A screw says I am wanted downstairs. There I am shown three Freedom of Information requests from people wanting to know if I am indeed being held in Brixton. Apparently, before confirming my presence here, my authorisation is needed to release the information. Two of the requests are from a Labour MP and a Labour peer. The third is from a woman whose name I don't recall, though it looks vaguely familiar. I scribble an assent signature. I hope the parliamentarians can visit me outside the Visitors' Orders scheme.

The Lib Dem scandal, over their ghastly peer who debased politics with by-election campaigns that mixed lies with homophobic or racist attacks, rumbles on and on. His behaviour towards women is disgusting, as were the smears and dishonest literature the Lib Dems put through the letter-boxes to win seats, using every deceitful technique imaginable.

The rest of politics is corny and predictable. As in almost every political cycle since 1951, the Tories ingested tough medicine in the first years and are now giving out election bribes in the last eighteen months or so before the elections. It's a proven election-winning tactic but a dreadful way to rebuild, renew and reform Britain's economy and broken society.

1700H There is a curious pre-dinner convention, rather like *fare la vasca* in some smaller Italian towns. Prisoners stroll up and down the landing, pausing to chat and exchange news and views. The favourite posture is a casual lean on the railings of each landing. We look down the forty or so feet through the three sets of netting strung between the top landing and the ground floor.

'Wanna jump?' says Derek. 'I don't. I'm out tomorrow.'

Prisons have a curious architecture. Like monks' cells going off a collonaded quadrangle, the idea is to have maximum visibility of the prison block dwellers at all times. So men retreat to their cells to sit on the hard bench tablet sticking out from the wall. I am not a devotee of sofas or armchairs but I long for something to sit on other than a hard piece of wood.

1830H After a dinner of liver stew with rice (actually better than it sounds) I catch Michael Portillo on one of his excellent Bradshaw railway tours. He is at Broadmoor, which in Victorian days was a prison with a library and a gym. He shows a nineteenth-century print of Broadmoor, in which can be seen inmates playing croquet on a sunny lawn. It looks like paradise compared to Brixton Prison in 2014.

TUESDAY 22 JANUARY 2014

Hope you are OK. Bit of a grim Christmas. Just been reading about getting money to Solidarity in Poland. Very brave stuff about which you have been very modest. Take care and see you soon.

– Greg Rosen

0740H Fruit and muesli breakfast. When I go downstairs, I find that the second day induction is scheduled for this afternoon. Am I now well and truly inducted into prison life? It doesn't look as if I will get to go on any courses or do any work. I get a mop and pail and some cleaning liquid and brush and clean out my cell.

1200H Lunch is a small meal of tuna paste with some sweetcorn and a Brixton baguette. I suppose I should go and try and flatten it into the toaster to crisp it up a bit but I can't be bothered.

After lunch, a walk around the exercise yard with Alan, a former Royal Marine Commando. Alan is the first ex-serviceman I have met. He served in the Gulf War, Northern Ireland, Sierra Leone and Iraq.

We agree that Sierra Leone was a 'good' military intervention. In and out quickly. Suppression of a ghastly rebel army which tried to impose its will by lopping off the arms of children. Order was restored. The greedy kleptocrats who ran, and still run, the country were soon back in business, dealing with the diamond smugglers and commodity multinationals who are the new colonial masters of Africa. But the worst of the violence was put down by British troops acting in effect as tough policemen.

'I left the Marines after twelve years without any training, not really fit for any civilian job. I fell in with a bad lot and ended up delivering cocaine from London to Dorset.' Ah, Charlie again. The county set's favourite drug. What would the hunters, shooters, fishers, City boys, second-home lawyers, bankers, and children of judges in Dorset do without their cocaine? They never got nabbed, of course.

Instead it's Alan, who risked his life for his country, who is dumped by his officers into the strange world of Blair's Britain and starts doing something stupid. His punishment was twelve years for acting as a purveyor of thrills to the Dorset bourgeoisie. That's six inside and he has done five.

He opted to return from Spring Hill open prison to Brixton. He is allowed to go out to work, and his brother who works in the building trade has got him a job as a scaffolder. His Spanish wife has stuck by him. Many young men when they get a long stretch just tell their wives, partners or fiancées to leave, cut loose and start a new life.

'I made a mistake. I'll never do it again. Every day has been hell. I hate it. But I won't come back.' I think he means it. You, dear reader taxpayer, will pay a further £50,000 to keep Alan in prison for another year. Pointlessly.

No induction this afternoon, so I can write letters. I said to the induction lady that, as I hoped to be leaving in a fortnight, it might be wrong to give me a place on a course that could be more usefully given to a prisoner who needs it more.

I go downstairs to get some prison envelopes. Three guys are arguing with a senior officer about having their enhanced status reduced. A tall, thin black guy is incensed. 'I have been on enhanced for two years. I did everything to earn it. I helped prisoners. I cleaned the landing. I did every work, I did every course I could. I have no red marks. But as soon as I get here, it's removed.'

The poor senior officer can only repeat that it is a government policy change and they have to implement it.

To my surprise I find myself defending the screws. I flick into Commons or *Newsnight* voice of controlled authority.

'Look guys, it's not his fault, or Governor Tullett's. They are just following orders from the Minister of Justice, Grayling. He wanted to show he could make life worse for prisoners because that's how you would get on in politics. Stripping you of enhanced status is a way of enhancing his status.'

'So what do we do then, Mr MP?'

'Write to your MP. Ms Greer is holding a wing consultative meeting on Friday. Ask her what steps you can take to win green points on your record and get up to enhanced status again.'

'You mean write to my MP?' said the main protestor as if I suggested writing to President Obama or the Pope.

'Yes. Set it down calmly and factually. He or she will have to send it to Grayling and maybe he'll realise how dumb his policy is, though I wouldn't hold my breath.'

The reduced-status men ponder a moment and then start complaining that it wasn't fair, they had earned their enhanced status and had done nothing to justify it being stripped from them.

'Guys, guys, that's like me saying because the cops cleared me a judge shouldn't send me here. It's not right, but stripping you of such status as you've earned is what Grayling needs to walk tall with other MPs and the press.' I almost said, 'Prison's unfair, get used to it,' but that's screws' language so I shut up and moved upstairs.

I told Joe on the first-floor landing about the chat. He laughed. 'Unfair! I shared a cell with an ambulance driver who got seven years. Why? He was driving an old lady with a heart attack to hospital as fast as he could – lights flashing, sirens, the lot. A woman went on to a zebra crossing ignoring the sirens and lights and he touched her and knocked her down. The judge decided it was worth a seven-year stretch.'

1530H Gym again. Rowing, spinning, cross-trainer, weights. A prisoner comes up. 'You're the fittest guy on our wing. We watch you belting around the yard, going up and down the stairs.' If only. But my weight and waist size are coming down, and my liver is having a good rest. On the pool table outside my cell, a prisoner called Mohammed has left two certificates which state he has passed a drugs and alcohol awareness course. I wonder how many of my MP and journalist friends need to go on the latter.

1630H I am talking to Brussels, fixing up work for after I'm out. Then a quick shower. There are half-partitions for some modesty but all the black and Asian men still shower in their underpants.

As I am towelling dry, I get a shout from a landing mate. 'They want you downstairs.' I hurry down and find an elderly Irish officer who this morning has signed my application asking for access to my clothes in the suitcase. I applied for this eight days ago and finally, in my fifth week of incarceration, I can get all my books, my writing pads and an anorak against rain and cold.

The guard tells me he is off to winter sun in Sharm el Sheikh on the Red Sea and owns a holiday home in Turkey. I am hearing stories of prison officers arranging their shifts to have good chunks of time off so they can have businesses on the side or a second job. This moonlighting culture in public services – fire and police officers are notorious – is understandable given the huge pressure on the cost of living after the public sector wage freeze imposed since 2010. But it always seems wrong for one person to have two jobs when so many have none.

I ask if I can take my razor. Yes. My shaving foam? No. Dental floss? Yes. My electric toothbrush? No. My hotel mini shampoo? Hmm, OK. But I am now reunited with my books and little else matters. The guard gives me a tip: 'A few days before you leave, ask to get your suit out of the case, hang it up or iron it to get the creases out. There will be all the press out there so you need to look your best.'

1700H Douggie is really fed up and is having a board meeting in our cell on what to do next. Try as he might, he cannot get a straight answer from anyone in Brixton about his future. When his rottle time arrives shortly, will he be allowed to go back to Edinburgh for home leave? He'd like to go and work as a chef in the Clink, the posh restaurant due to open within the Brixton walls next month. But no one can confirm this will happen. It is this lack of a future, of permanently being in limbo, that most demoralises prisoners. Tell Douggie what he has to do and he will cheerfully do it. But although prison is full of petty authoritarianism and petty authoritarians, it is a system without order and structure. It's a snafu world.

1800H Dinner is an emaciated chicken leg. The budget for each prisoner is £1.68. A piece of fruit costs 10p. The budget for pudding is 13p. An individual tub of ice cream costs 18p. So that's out. Tonight, a slab of shortbread biscuit. OK if you like dry biscuit and cake. I don't.

2350H There is a huge racket. Shouts and screams inside and outside the wing. Doors bang and there are other unidentifiable noises. It sounds riotous.

THURSDAY 23 JANUARY 2014

Often, and often afterwards, the beloved Aunt would ask me why I had never told any one how I was being treated. Children tell little more than animals, for what comes to them they accept as eternally established. Also, badly treated children have a clear notion of what they are likely to get if they betray the secrets of the prison-house before they are clear of it.

– Rudyard Kipling

0815 Up for an hour, writing. The free-flow bell, signalling when you are meant to go to work or education, has rung. Despite this, the cell door remains locked. There is a very poor *Today* report on the riot at Oakwood prison near Wolverhampton earlier in the month. A BBC reporter has got hold of a prison guard who helped put down the riot, which, anonymously, he describes in detail.

The men took over a wing in this giant, 1,600-prisoner private prison. It is run by G4S, the private security outfit, whose inefficiency and public money grabbing was exposed during the scandal of its failure to provide security at the 2012 London Olympics. The army had to be called in as panic developed amongst Conservative ministers, as they realised that their pet private security firm could ruin the Olympics. These giant prisons remove prisoners from local contact with their families. They have far fewer staff, as that's the only way they can be profitable and deliver the bloated pay for G4S executives.

Prisoners enter and leave prisons every day and visits continue. So I cannot understand why the BBC has failed to find a recently released Oakwood prisoner to interview. Chris Grayling's policy of stripping the hard-won enhanced status from thousands of prisoners has caused real tension.

To judge by the anger and despair of men who have reached the date when they could be released on tag but are still in prison, I can understand that at some stage, somewhere, prisoners would revolt. And if Oakwood has the same culture as some screws in Belmarsh, of treating prisoners as sub-humans and putting secret negative reports which damage future status on prisoner files, then, again, someone would crack. If I were here and twenty again, I would be a natural shop steward and organiser of prisoners for a fair deal and humane treatment. But that kind of person doesn't exist. Instead the anger boils up until it explodes.

I listen in dismay as the *Today* presenter interviews a G4S prison boss waffling away. Sadly, Justin or Evan – twenty minutes after the interview I've forgotten who it was – just doesn't know or hasn't been briefed on the right questions to ask, so the G4S man leaves unscathed. I hope other journalists dig into the story.

0840H Twenty minutes after the bell rings for education or work, the door opens. I get up to leave with Douggie and go downstairs to post some letters. 'Not you, MacShane,' says the woman warden, holding up her arm to bar me leaving the cell. 'You're not on the list today,' she says as she turns the key in my door and again I am locked in my cell. I feel like shouting, protesting that I am a Category D prisoner who is allowed to spend all day out of a cell, but keep mum.

An interesting report follows on *Today* about a British firm making drugs from cannabis extracts. These are for export to the United States where, step by step, states are moving away from criminalisation of recreational drugs.

I wish we had British politicians, not just rent-a-quote clown MPs, who would get into this. Until the '60s and '70s, abortion was illegal in big European countries, just as herbal or chemical intoxicants are today. In France in 1976, three hundred prominent women signed an open letter in the *Nouvel Observateur* stating they had had an abortion. It was like an electric shock. There was a younger, more liberal president in Giscard d'Estaing, and France faced down its conservative instincts and gave women the freedom to choose.

Is there any chance of that happening on drugs in Britain? Can the George Osborne generation of MPs, lawyers, bankers and editors admit they have smoked pot or snorted cocaine? Is there a David Steel with a private member's bill willing to push for recreational drugs de-criminalisation? More tax for the Treasury. Fewer people in prison.

No education today so I go back to the cell, which is then locked. I really don't understand these hour-long bang-ups, which Category D prisoners are meant not to endure. But since I cannot go out to get any fresh air maybe it doesn't matter.

1200H So why does the thirty minutes of exercise and fresh air coincide precisely with lunch! Tomorrow there is a meeting convened by the Wing manager, Ms Greer, to discuss eleven agenda items covering every aspect of Brixton Prison life. Each agenda item could easily take the hour. And I am meant to give an inspiring talk on Parliament and politics!

I talk to my young Romanian friend who is a genius at making model aeroplanes and pyramids from matchsticks. He has lived in Britain for eight years, working as a carpenter for a British building firm on big government contracts, including a big MoD job at a nuclear arms facility. His boss would love to have him back but he faces deportation. His crime? He produced fake weekly London Tube and train tickets. His computer skills were so developed he could decode the ticket-reading system and then replicate it in such a way that the police could not work out how he did it. He got four years. It might have been smarter of London Underground to hire him as a security consultant.

When I worked in the BBC Radio newsroom in Broadcasting House the top brass there, like the Director General, had use of a private underground car park. The entrance pass in those far-off days was based on a metal pattern hidden in a plastic card. It was child's play to sprinkle iron filings on a paper over the pass, hold a magnet underneath and the metal pattern emerged. Seal it, and bingo – we had our own pass to the bosses' car park, handy for all-night and weekend shifts. Like the copious amount of marijuana smoked in newsreader studios to while away the tedium of night newsroom work or over Christmas (news rarely happens at night or over Christmas), the minor criminality and expense padding of BBC journalists – some of whom became and are still household names – was part of life. Today it puts someone in prison.

Once again, the BBC midday politics show, presented by the Eurosceptic Andrew Neil, has Nigel Farage on it for a full hour. A woman Tory MP and an Olympic medallist who is a Tory MEP candidate giggles and agrees with Farage's anti-Europe remarks. No wonder most of Europe thinks the UK will exit the union.

1415H Over to the big gym. Del stands beside me on a cross-trainer and gives me a lesson on how to get the best out of the machine. I am learning so much and the taxpayer is paying for it.

Sarah and Vicky have got a visitors' slot for 9 a.m. on Saturday. My brother, who lives on the Isle of Wight, is also listed. But can he make a 9 a.m. visit slot in Brixton? We have the visit number but neither Sarah nor Vicky has received the actual order, which is necessary to get in. It has been floating around the prison mail system since the weekend. It could all happen by email. But that is so twentieth century.

1530H Another stack of mail. I have received more than 150 emails, letters and cards so far. A lovely one from Tony Blair in his distinctive hand:

> Dear Denis,
> I have been trying to track down how to contact you.
> I just wanted to say how sorry I am about the situation you find yourself in. You were always a good supporter of mine and a thoroughly sympathetic colleague, who contributed a huge amount to the government.
> I can only imagine how ghastly this is. But please come and see me after you emerge and I will do whatever I can to help.
> You still have a lot to give and you should know you have a friend in me.
> Yours ever,
> Tony

For Blair-haters, a letter like this will prove that Starmer and Sweeney were 100 per cent right to speed my passage to Belmarsh.

I just think of a man who sends a message of compassion and solidarity to a former colleague (and, I hope, friend) not seen in years. Passing by on the other side of the road is the norm amongst political leaders when they see a colleague in trouble. The reason Blair was a different kind of politician is that he never conformed to the norms of political caution – or, if you prefer a more accurate word, cowardice.

I have always admired at the way the Conservative Party turn their leaders into heroes to worship. Failures like Anthony Eden or Edward Heath are discovered to have great qualities of leadership even if their premierships were a disaster. The hapless, hopeless John Major, still best remembered for his Dominique Strauss-Kahn-style affair with

Edwina Currie, is now revered with glowing profiles in the sycophantic Conservative press.

By contrast, Labour treats its Prime Ministers and leaders with a destructive contempt that vitiates the party's achievements and service to the nation. The one exception is Attlee, but even his elevation to iconic status is recent. As a young Labour activist all I read were left-intellectual attacks on Attlee as a US puppet, an anti-communist, a PM who left unreformed the City, the House of Lords or public schools. His successors – Harold Wilson, Jim Callaghan, Blair and Brown – are still in a file marked 'Failure. Liar. Twister. Two-faced. Pro-American.' Or – Labour's favourite insult – someone who betrayed socialism and the working class.

Every political leader has feet of clay and is rarely a hero to all. But Labour's negativity about its leaders, especially Tony Blair, who won three handsome majorities in a row, does the party and the democratic left great harm. The Tories are smarter.

Jimmy Burns, stellar *Financial Times* journalist and chronicler of Spanish football, sends me a copy of Gerard Manley Hopkins's poems. Not a favourite, but the magic poets perform with words most of us can barely place in order has always entranced me. It is a very thin volume, so presumably slipped by Grayling's ban on sending books to prisoners inside.

I drop everything else and start softly reading aloud *The Wreck of the Deutschland*. Hopkins, a Jesuit priest, wrote a warm poem called *The Bugler's First Communion*. He always felt uneasy about how his passionate poetry co-existed with the rationality and blind obedience demanded by the Society of Jesus. On his poem he wrote to his friend Robert Bridges, the Poet Laureate, 'I am half inclined to hope the hero of it may be killed in Afghanistan.' Hopkins would have to wait 130 years for British Prime Ministers to grant his wish.

There is a knock on the door and it opens to reveal a man in black and a clerical collar. He announces himself as Robert, a lay deacon in the Catholic Church. I hear traces of French in his accent. He turns out to come from Quebec.

I find myself slipping into French with Robert. Like Father Edward in Belmarsh he has been contacted by my Parish priest, Canon Pat Browne, who is also the Commons Catholic Chaplain and a family friend. There seems to be a worry that, given my MP status, I will suffer at the hands of inmates. I tell Robert to tell Pat the opposite is the case. Here in Brixton, as in Belmarsh, I am douched in kindness, talk to interesting people and am learning so much about fellow citizens and our flawed justice and prison system.

I repeat to Robert that it has been an enriching and simultaneously humbling experience. He says he is worried about the young prisoners who have nothing to go back to when released. 'There is one young man. His mother has disowned him. His father disowned him long ago. He was sleeping in the garage of a friend. He committed some stupid crime. When he reaches the end of his sentence he has nothing to go to, so he will soon come back to prison.'

I have no answer. Since the '80s, the labour market has been tilted away from skills, training and apprenticeships. Unions have disappeared and, with them, fair wages and the struggle to make work fit for human existence, instead of making humans conform to the needs of maximum profit extraction. The housing for poor people, like ex-prisoners, has never been bleaker. 'Sorry, Robert,' I tell him. I don't know what can be done, given the way our politics is structured.

A start would be to empty the prisons of all the people who don't need to be here. But that means taking on the media and editors' obsession with swelling the prison population. It means a major rethink by our prison-junkie judges. That won't happen. It means decriminalising drugs on a par with alcohol.

'But you can say or write all this when you're out, launch a campaign.'

'Sorry,' I say. 'I will give some first-hand witness but no one will listen to me. It will have to get far, far worse before a prison reform movement worthy of the name emerges,' I tell him.

Robert is a campaigner against the arms trade. 'I know the real criminals and they live near me in Walton-on-Thames. But they are never held to account for what they do in corrupting politicians and spreading death around the world.'

I remain impressed by the quality and time the faiths give to work in prison. Priests, ministers, imams, rabbis and others tending to world faiths are like Florence Nightingale with her lamp at Scutari. They bring normality and hope, which is in such short supply. The prison service allows these carers of the soul to wander pretty freely in prisons, and go and see prisoners in their cells rather than in a more formal interview setting.

Might it be possible to create a secular, humanist group, not in opposition to the faith representatives, but just another outfit, a kind of Prison Authority International, with the same right to go freely and organise weekly get-togethers for prisoners? There are wonderful volunteers who do prison visiting. Over to Chris Grayling's successors to see if a more humane approach to augment the valuable work of the faiths can be developed.

FRIDAY 24 JANUARY 2014

The prisoner's worst enemy is boredom, depression, the slow death of thought.

– Arthur Koestler

0600H I wake early, have a piss and go back to sleep. A December *Sun* has been left lying around. A headline refers to 'Pervs Delight' or '108 Sickos Left to Prey'. This because 108 people had won a case to have their names removed from the sex offenders' register. Good to see the spirit of Rebekah still rules at *The Sun*. The only really ugly language I have heard from prisoners is about 'nonces' or the men in prison because of sexual offences. No, I don't like them either. Some of the monks who were at the school I went to, St Benedict's in west London, are in prison, and one is still on the run in Italy, protected by the Order of St Benedict. Weak, bad men.

When I was in the fourth form, Year 7 in modern school parlance, the Head Boy was Chris Patten, Captain of Cricket, a place at Balliol, Under

Officer in the CCF and so forth. Patten looked remarkably like Boris Johnson, with unruly blond hair and a commanding voice that always had a twinkle in it. He was clearly destined for great things.

After Oxford he worked in the Campaign Office of a long forgotten Mayor of New York. Nobody knew if he was Conservative or Labour and his liberal Europeanism has never endeared him to today's Europhobe Tories. Indeed it was Tony Blair who made him a European Commissioner and, in their tolerant, internationalist, liberal, pro-market outlook as well as their Catholic faith, the two men have much in common.

Our school made it to the front page of *The Times* a few years ago. Some sad monk had been sent to prison for his sins of the flesh with pupils. That evening I attended a black tie dinner at the Banqueting House in Whitehall as a member of the council of the Royal Institute of International Affairs, better known as Chatham House.

The Queen was bestowing its annual statesman of the year award on the president of Brazil or Turkey. I sat on the top table opposite the, by now, Lord Patten. At these grandiose dos – Guildhall, Lancaster House, Windsor Castle – you pray for interesting companions to your left or right. The chance of talking to the person across the table is rare given the clatter, clinking and chatter that gets louder and louder.

Chris was sat opposite me when suddenly there was a lull in the noise. He asked me if I had seen the front page of *The Times* about the naughty monks at our old school.

I nodded and, as the break in noise continued, asked:

'Were you buggered at school, Chris?'

He paused and thought for a moment. 'Not as I remember.'

Neither of us realised the whole table of the great and the good was hanging on every word. The polite chatter resumed as the decorated president got up to make his speech.

I've checked with other school friends about the monks and none can remember the slightest hint of impropriety. We guessed we didn't give signals of vulnerability, so were left alone.

The Rebekah hate campaign, still continued by today's *Sun* editors with language about 'sickos' and 'pervs', reinforces the denigration of people who commit crimes. It plays into the prisoner's sense that the 'nonces' – the men convicted of sexual crimes – are sub-human. Substitute the word 'Paki' or 'nigger' for 'nonce' and you would think prison is full of racists.

Prison is full of notices warning inmates against racism, bullying or homophobia. But we are allowed to express hate against the sickness of paedophilia. All violent or hate crime against children and women or, for that matter, men, is odious.

The hate generated by tabloids against one set of criminals just generates more hate in prison and slows down rehabilitation.

1000H Going back upstairs after posting some letters, Pat asks me to go into a cell. He leads me walking stiffly with his stick to ease the discomfort of his hernia. Del and two other men are there.

'You know it's Friday today. How come when the Muslims go to the chapel all the Christian signs are covered? Why can't they respect our Christian faith?'

'It's a multifaith room,' I explain. 'The Muslim images up on the wall are there at the back of what used to be a church. I guess if any Catholics or Anglicans protested they'd be covered up,' I tell them, speaking in best multicultural fashion.

'Yeah, but it's not right. Why should they cover up the cross in our church?'

'Look,' I say, 'All over the country defunct chapels and churches have been turned into mosques because the Christians have stopped going to worship and it still matters to Muslims. It's actually rather a good thing that all the faiths can use the same place!'

I don't think this is what they want to hear but if you don't stamp hard and stamp early on disrespect for a religion – provided the faith stays in its zone and does not dictate behaviour to others – then unnecessary problems emerge.

Del beckons me to go into the cell lavatory. He points at the grubby mat in front of the loo seat. It has an image of one of the big mosques from Mecca, Damascus or Constantinople on it.

'Do I get into trouble for putting my feet on that when I sit on the bog?'

'No, Del. Muslims would think it's a prayer mat and you're about to convert.'

My reassurance is not quite the answer he wants and we leave it at that.

Del was in Oakwood, the 1,600-strong private prison in the West Midlands where there was a riot two weeks ago. It has all been hushed up.

'There were riots when I was there. Some of the screws were selling drugs and that's a guarantee for trouble. I don't know what caused the recent one but, as long as prison officers can make money by bringing in stuff, it causes tension and violence.'

1030H Gym. My fifth this week. How kind of the taxpayer. A gym regular turns left into the exercise yard with a dog. It's a cross between a bulldog and a staffie. Her name is Minnie and she is quite delightful. She belongs to the Governor who, for some reason, has let C Wing look after the pooch, to the evident pleasure of everyone.

As we go off to the gym, Minnie is released into the exercise area with her temporary keeper, Grant. The dog takes one look at the miserable little yard, squats and drops a giant turd. We all cheer as Grant looks around for a poop scoop but there is none to be found. It is not approved prison equipment.

Grant is the computer nerd who stole £48,000, about the same amount David Laws gave his partner in rent, in absolute breach of Commons rules. Grant stole the money to pay for a drink and drugs obsession. He accepts his stupidity but is upset he shared a cell with another computer fraudster who stole £1.2 million. Grant got two years and four months. The much bigger thief got sixteen months. Grant had been told that with his full repayment, contrition, cooperation with the police and proof he had given up on drugs and alcohol dependency, the judge would give him a suspended sentence. Oops! Judges today are in love with prison and the wildly oscillating sentences for identical crimes reflect their mood and temper and have little to do with justice.

Grant was also banned from using computer or the internet for three years after his release. 'But the first prison I went to was one of those new private ones that had a computer terminal in every cell. I can go onto the education centre computers here and, with what I know, get on to the net in a couple of minutes. I don't, of course, because I don't want any hassle but these guys haven't the faintest idea about what you can do with computers.'

Grant gave me an example worth passing on. 'Take Facebook. Everyone who uses Facebook has to access their account using their email. The same email is used to access their bank account. It is the easiest thing in the world to go back from Facebook to the email and then into the bank account. Everyone should create a new account to use only for accessing Facebook.'

I asked Grant how on earth he could be banned from using the internet for three years after release. He shrugged as if it was the best example of computer-illiterate judge nonsense.

There is a new guy in the gym who is on D Wing. There the cell doors are open until 10.30 at night. They are not even locked from the outside. I don't understand why the same D Category prisoners are treated so differently on C Wing.

'This prison is a permanent fire hazard,' he says. 'All those men crowded into narrow corridors waiting for doors and gates to be locked and unlocked. Look at this gym. It's completely overcrowded. The walls and roof are made of thin wood.'

Suddenly, I feel I'm in a fire-trap. I'm sure all precautions are taken but the plain fact is that Brixton needs a giant overhaul. But where would the judges send all the prisoners in London they take such delight in incarcerating?

1135H Back in my cell and Daniel, the young Romanian, comes in with a perfect, tiny matchstick model of a bi-plane. He is miserable about being deported. He has been in London since he was seventeen. His wife and three small children who were born here are at home here. He was a good worker and his boss wants him back. But return to Romania he must.

Eamonn pops in and hands me a sheaf of poems. Will I choose the four best he can submit for the Koestler award. Arthur Koestler's masterpiece, *Darkness at Noon*, was a transformatory novel about Stalinism, published at a time when worship of communism was at its height. I read loads of Koestler as a teenager, including a copy of *The Yogi and the Commissar*, which my father must have bought. He wandered off into more obscure fields of research and writing in later life but, in the middle of the last century, Koestler was one of the those Jewish Mitteleuropa intellectuals who understood what was happening in Europe and, more important, what was going to happen, and tried to dun some understanding of evil totalitarian ideology into the complacent English establishment, with its tolerance of both Hitler's Germany and Stalin's Russia.

Koestler spent time in different prisons and wrote about his time interned in a French prison camp in his book *Scum of the Earth*. In 1962 he set up the Koestler Trust to promote art and writing in prison and it continues its fine work today, encouraging prisoners to write, paint and engage with art.

Eamonn's poems are all strong and well constructed – the kind of poem you might read in the *London Review of Books* or *The Spectator*. I make my selection, discarding the overly religious ones, inspired by his Catholic upbringing in Galway, and wish him luck. Since he'll be out the same time as me, I'm not sure if the award will go a released prisoner. But I can see the patient work, thought and draftsmanship that has gone into each poem and, as a way of doing time, writing a poem can hardly be bettered.

1820H Dinner is the thinnest pork steak I have ever seen. At least the cooks have sprinkled it with rosemary and oregano and it vaguely tastes of something. After dinner there is a 'consultative' meeting for all the prisoners. The new wing manager, Ms Greer, seems intent on a new, more open style of management. She has asked me to talk on 'Parliament and Politics' in this session. My original proposal, after requests from a couple of politically conscious inmates, was for a more ordered seminar. But am happy to oblige with a short talk.

First though, the meeting tackles a long agenda of eleven quite distinct items – early release to work, tag dates, food, education courses, gym access, staff-prisoner relationships and so on. Each could easily take up the entire allotted thirty-five minutes.

About a quarter of the inmates attend. It's a poorly organised meeting, on the ground floor where the echoing acoustics make hearing hard.

The three officers present deal clearly with the questions. The basic problem remains Grayling's new regime. As a veteran screw there puts it: 'We are just following orders. If you don't like what's happening you have to ask Mr Christopher Grayling' – his voice makes the Justice Secretary's name sound like a nasty disease – 'and those people in Parliament who decide what is done inside prisons.'

Cue me. I have two minutes to speak and easily switch into Commons mode. Stand up, a clear voice that carries, a couple of jokes.

'I have only been in prison, Belmarsh and Brixton, for five weeks and I have already collected three red entries, two of which they didn't tell me about!'

Poor Ms Greer goes bright red. The prisoners all laugh and cheer or perhaps it is a jeer as their VIP prisoner has been caught by the secret red entry device.

'So I am far worse than anyone here. I am the lowest of the low. But believe me, you would have to hunt through all the MPs before you find someone as low and disliked as Mr Christopher Grayling.'

The mention of the hated minister brings a huge cheer of laughter.

'There isn't a single minister, a single MP, a single judge, a single journalist who knows what it's like to be in prison or even be a prison officer.'

Both inmates and screws applaud loudly.

Oh dear. For a minute I am back in the old, old business of bringing a meeting – a party meeting, a union conference, a protest demonstration, the Chamber of the Commons itself – under my sway with a mix of argument, insult and, above all, humour. I don't know how to explain it. I just know I know how to do it, or perhaps knew how to do it. Once again I am on my feet explaining, cajoling, leading. But where to? Soon I will be out of this and my energies elsewhere.

Two Twitter trolls are sent to jail. When will Paul Staines' collar be felt? Since he's a right-winger, probably never.

SATURDAY 25 JANUARY 2014

It is better that ten guilty persons escape than that one innocent suffer.

– Sir William Blackstone

0855H The door is opened and I have to belt out in my own jeans and British Heart Foundation T-shirt for a visit. I carefully carry the matchstick aeroplane with the app form signed by two screws allowing me to take it out.

Some men are going out for home visits or to work. A prisoner going to the visitors' centre asks a comrade leaving on a day visit to bring back some 'burn' – tobacco.

'Sorry, I've already promised two guys.'

The disappointed man accepts he isn't going to get extra smokes this weekend.

Sarah, Vicky and my brother Ed turn up. Poor Sarah has taken over the task of managing my emails, while starting a new and challenging job herself. She is fed up with the inability of friends to master the www. emailaprisoner.com system to send emails.

The Guardian apparently wants to do a story based on the news circulating about me. A Radio 5 producer wants me to do fifteen minutes with Victoria Derbyshire – for my canteen money, one of the best news or current affairs interviewers in the business. Like Kirsty Wark, Emily Maitlis, Cathy Newman or Martha Kearney, the women who interview politicians knock spots of their ageing male rivals. Derbyshire's BBC executive husband or partner got into some trouble over expenses, so maybe she won't be so censorious and judgemental as her colleagues.

The BBC man promises me a fair and balanced piece – yeah, just like the distorted dishonest, one-sided news report by every BBC hack who has covered me so far.

I'll look to the future and deal with the past in a book where I control what appears, not some *Spectator*-guided *Daily Mail*-reading Eurosceptic BBC cynic.

The talk turns to getting-out-of-prison parties, though both Sarah and Vicky say I need to keep my new fitter body and look. Ed's jaw drops as I tell him a couple of prison stories. He asks if I will do campaigning to try and put right the dreadful things I have seen, and learnt.

'No, I want to report it like in my early 1980s books on Polish Solidarnosc, and the black independent unions in South Africa. Information the public and policy makers simply don't know because it hasn't been reported. But I don't want to become a rent-a-quote prison expert. I need to tell the truth about the dirty politics in Parliament and the dishonesty of the CPS but that's just for the record. I need to move on!'

Loads of journalist and political friends have asked about visits. I guess coming to Brixton for a chat is very good dinner party conversation and I would love to see them but how many visits do I have left? One, at best, if I'm lucky.

1029H Back in the wing. It is a day for mandatory drug tests. Or piss test as it's known. I had two cups of machine coffee during the visit so my bladder is full. It's fairly simple. A clinical bathroom with a bath for handicapped people and you pee over a urinal into a plastic beaker. Of course I'm OK, though the two officers say there is a real drugs problem on the wing.

They also tell me all the funding for the programme comes from the NHS as part of a wider programme to tackle drug dependency. 'So the NHS pays for this test and if it's negative you get punished. Thanks NHS,' I say. The officers laugh. They grin even more when I ask if there is any type of retrospective drugs test that politicians and lawyers would have to pass to stay in their chosen profession.

'Sadly not,' one says.

In Belmarsh, I'm told, you have to do your piss test naked. They really are obsessed with male genitalia there.

It's the day to fill in menus for the following week. I agree to order two sausages next Saturday and Douggie orders two eggs so we can each have a sausage and egg lunch. The egg is hard-boiled not fried but the idea is nice. I suddenly realise this is the last Saturday menu I will have to decide on. In a fortnight's time I can at last have a proper salad with a vinaigrette dressing. Can't wait.

Mr Brown, a nice officer, calls by for a general chat with me and Douggie. He advises Douggie on property still missing and circulating somewhere in the inter-prison transport system. He says I shouldn't expect to be strip-searched when I leave.

The news of my two-minute speechette has gone round and prisoners stop me to shake my hand. One brings in pictures of his beautiful Italian wife and her Dolomites home and says I'll always be welcome there for skiing or mountain walking and climbing. Gradually, as the last fortnight is here, the mood is changing. Could I get to like prison, as inmates – whether convicts or warders – become more and more friendly?

1245H Midday meal. Horrible sausages made just palatable by some mustard that Douggie bought on his canteen. Over-fried potatoes and baked beans in a red sludge make up the meal. Just down the road is Brixton Village with its terrific covered avenues of restaurants and cafés. Could we not be manacled together and go down under armed guard to have one decent meal?

1345H My benign view on prison life evaporates. On the previous two Saturdays there have been Saturday afternoon gyms so I go down with other men. Then, suddenly, we are told it is reserved for men with the top rank of 'enhanced' status. I am reduced to 'basic' status because a screw gave me a secret red mark. It didn't matter last week because the gym was open irrespective of your prison status.

There is an explosion of anger.

'Why could I use it last Saturday, but not today?' exclaims a gym regular.

'I work every day. This is my only chance to get to the gym,' says another angry prisoner.

'I'm sorry,' says the woman guard escorting the prisoners through the endless locked gates to get there.

'What do you mean, "sorry"?! Who decided this?' shouts a furious prisoner.

'Charlie said it's for enhanced only.'

'Who's Charlie? Where is he?' the men demand. Charlie is the senior prison gym teacher who runs the two gyms in Brixton.

The woman and another guard who has come out to see what the row is about look at each other miserably. The second guard was the friendly one who had come up for an agreeable chat ninety minutes ago.

'We are just doing what we're told. There's nothing we can do. You'll have to take it up with Charlie.'

I can feel the tension. These men have been able to follow Gerard Manley Hopkins's advice: 'Not, I'll not, carrion comfort, despair, not feast on thee!'

They have worked hard, followed all the courses, got to Category D, achieved 'enhanced' status only to have it taken away at a stroke of Chris Grayling's pen. Now they bottle up their despair as their only weekend pleasure – there is no gym on Sunday – is removed from them without reason or explanation.

'They keep saying we are in prison to be rehabilitated but then they treat us like shit,' says a bitter man.

I try and make up for the gym by running round and round the basketball yard. I lie down on the damp surface to do leg and abs exercises. Looking up, I see a hole in the netting high above the yard. Through the metre square hole I see the grey clouds scudding along, bringing bad weather. A bird flies over the gap in the netting. It is a little sign of freedom beyond bars and walls and nets.

The atmosphere is morose, heavy. You are locked up for much longer at weekends. There isn't the staff.

I shower and listen to two black guys in the showering stalls.

'I ain't coming back ever. You make sure you don't either.'

'No way. I did the crime, I've nearly done the time and never again.'

'I've learnt stuff man, so much stuff. I want to be a good father, a good son, a good brother. We've got to change.'

They have been in the shower for ten minutes, still wearing their underpants. I am naked but in and out in ninety seconds. I hope the exchange I am eavesdropping is for real and that after whatever they did, these men will never return. Do they have jobs, a good income, homes, loving families to return to? I don't know. I hope so. If not, I fear the worst, despite their good intentions.

1715H Dinner. Meat pie, mashed potato, carrots and swedes. Heavy. Filling. Too early to eat all this. The cell door is locked until tomorrow morning. The guard says 'Goodnight'.

SUNDAY 26 JANUARY 2014

> I count the dismal time by months and years
> Since last I felt the green sward under foot,
> And the great breath of all things summer –
> Met mine upon my lips. Now earth appears
> As strange to me as dreams of distant spheres
> Or thoughts of Heaven we weep at. Nature's lute
> Sounds on, behind this door so closely shut
>   – 'The Prisoner', Elizabeth Barrett Browning

0850H Sunday, Bloody Sunday. It's Brixton's longest day. No visits. No gym. No work. No classes. Unlock late. Lock-up early.

I go to Mass and challenge Father Howard on a psalm about girding for war or some such militaristic exaltation so common to both the Bible and Koran. Why do we drivel on about Islam or other faiths being religions of peace? Only once they're tamed and booted out of power and politics. Otherwise the men of faith are booted and spurred for the faith militant. Onward Christian soldiers, forward jihad's suicide bombers en route to paradise. It is time for Christians to say sorry and for Muslims to wake up to the monster of violence lurking in Islamism and validated by some Muslim preachers.

Father Howard neatly parries my point by saying the psalm is old testament and along came Jesus to transform militaristic messages into those of love. I'm not sure. The history of '*Gott mit uns*' European Christian imperialism, even if from the eleventh century onwards the great spur to Christian military violence, was the tide of Muslim military violence sweeping out from the Arabian peninsula to conquer and colonise.

Later I bump into Father Howard in C Wing and he comes up beaming. 'Thank you, thank you. You brought the Mass to life. I want the prisoners to ask questions.'

On television there is an interview with a brave German woman who lives in England and was raped eight years ago. She has now met her aggressor in prison under a restorative justice scheme. She has forgiven her rapist and he has expressed remorse for what he did to the woman. But why have the CPS and the judges been so poor at tackling rape? They are prosecuting Nigel Evans for rape, but if he is a rapist I am Vladimir Putin. Why has Keir Starmer put so much energy and public money into trying to take down Nigel? His parliamentary career as Deputy Speaker has been destroyed, whatever the verdict. The CPS has plenty of time and resources for non-violent crimes, but when it comes to protecting women, our legal officers and judges are dreadful. I wonder if I will ever meet Judge Sir N. Sweeney and take him through the errors of his sentencing statement and get him to express remorse for the crime of pointlessly sending a 65-year-old father of four to Britain's toughest jail over Christmas. It's Sunday, so I can dream.

Thanks to other prisoners, I get to see *The Observer*, *Sunday Times* and *Sunday Telegraph*. The *Economist* I ordered has not arrived and I get a sad little chit to tell me *Le Monde* cannot be delivered to Brixton

Prison. *Quelle surprise!* I read the TV programmes for the coming week first. That's far more important in prison – and, I suspect, many households – than the news and review pages. One report catches my eye. It's by Toby Helm, the *Observer*'s fine political editor. It's an analysis of why Parliament no longer works. One reason is that there has been acceptance by MPs of the pre-2010 intake that some, too many, used the expenses scheme to make personal profit or gain and the way they filled in the different forms was clearly motivated by a greed for gain paid for by the taxpayer. To be sure, five Labour MPs of that generation were sent to prison, including me. It was easy to go for Labour MPs, as the Conservatives and Liberal Democrats took power. Those in office always protect their own. Those on the way out of power cannot, as hapless Tory MPs discovered in 1997.

I have on in the background the Sunday political coverage. The chubby, beaming face of Andrew Neil appears. He introduces Nigel Farage, who is allowed a two-minute party political broadcast on what the UKIP boss says are the criminals or Nazi sympathisers in the Liberal Democrat, Conservative or Labour Parties.

As a BBC news trainee fresh out of Oxford, I had to spend time in the BBC Midlands newsroom with a stopwatch, clocking the precise number of seconds given to reports, ahead of the 1970 election, which mentioned the Labour and Conservative parties. (We had binary politics then.) If at the end of a week my list showed a minute more for Labour visits and speeches, I would swiftly write a news bulletin with the required mentions of Conservative policies or candidates, to even the balance.

I wonder if anyone in the BBC logs the never-ending Nigel Farage appearances, especially on the 24/7 politics programmes presented by the Eurosceptic, if ever enjoyable, Andrew Neil? Watching far more television than ever (or any politician or journalist does) I have seen how the BBC provides a permanent platform for the xenophobic populism of UKIP and its main spokesman.

My Royal Marine Commando friend, who has already served five and a half years for delivering cocaine to the wealthy homes in Dorset, comes up in a state.

He was out on a day visit yesterday as part of the sequence that allows prisoners out to work and then out completely on tag. He simply forgot the piss test and now is worried that it can go down as a negative report and delay his return to normality.

'I didn't hear any announcement. There was no notice up anywhere. When I came back I didn't see anyone waiting. I've passed every drugs test in five and a half years. Ditto twelve years in the army. In other prisons, a guard would come and tell you to go down for a piss test.'

Lordy, Lordy, Brixton incompetence again. I offer to write a clear letter of apology and explanation for him. I just set out the facts. Any reasonable person would accept his explanation and get him to do the test later.

But in prison, the word 'reasonable' is hard to construe.

1209H Lunch is a chicken leg, cabbage and potatoes. OK, but made special by some lemon tart smuggled out of the Bad Boys' Bakery. Smuggled is too strong a word for a small slice about three inches by half an inch. It is shared with my cellmate so it's about a bite each. But delicious. Prisoners can buy all sorts of horrible, industrially produced cake products on their canteen sheets.

Why can't families bring in home-made cakes, or maybe a salami, or a treat like roast chicken or ham, smoked salmon and lemon, or some pâté? Prisoners would share this with cellmates and friends. It would relieve the dreary monotony of the standard menu and the sugary, chemically enriched industrial food that is allowed.

1240H Bang-up. The cell door is opened an hour later. Sunday, fucking Sunday. I go out and pound around the exercise yard. The one day the gym should be open all day, it is closed. That's Brixton.

C Wing is strangely quiet. There is a sense of lethargy everywhere. Normally you see men playing monopoly or poker or pool. There are always a few chess games going on. Not today. Sunday is a non-day in prison.

I take advantage of the quietness to go down to the ground floor to get my final Hep B jab. A slip is put under my door. Tomorrow I have a GP's appointment. I must attend. If not, 'You will get a red entry.' Ah. The dreaded red. I will do as I am told.

1700H Dinner is a beefburger (made from what?!), chips and mushy peas. I am back in my beloved Rotherham again. For anyone of my Labour generation, any mention of mushy peas brings up the fable of Peter Mandelson confusing mushy peas with guacamole when first he inherited his safe Labour seat in north England. I wish today's Labour Party had a Peter Mandelson. I remember Labour's open-mouth MPs, like Paul Flynn as shop steward of the Mandelson haters in the Parliamentary Labour Party and the press.

There is always an element in all left politics, and especially Labour, that thinks politics is about anything and everything except power. Mandelson roped himself to the unelectable Labour Party of the 1980s and, working eighteen hours a day, helped haul it back, not just to electability but to re-electability, something Labour had never before known. For the decade up to the US initiated banking crash of 2007/08, Paul Flynn saw more improvement in the quality of life of his not-rich South Wales constituents than he had ever seen before in his political life. Mandelson delivered for South Wales in a way no Welsh politician had in generations. But in politics no good deed goes unpunished. I have never seen Peter eat either mushy peas or guacamole but the story sticks.

I read in *The Observer* about a man held in an Egyptian prison. He writes about an exercise session – 'four glorious hours in the grass yard behind our block'. Four hours! Grass! Don't tell Chris Grayling.

I read something Richard Branson once wrote: 'If I want to do something worthwhile or even just for fun, I won't let silly rules stop me.' That was my approach but I reckoned without John Lyon CB. What a perfect prison warder he would make, dashing around awarding red marks for some infringement of the prison rules.

There is a sweet smell of dope on the landing. Maybe that explains the lethargy of the men. It strikes me as insane that a Cat D prisoner, just a little distance from freedom, should risk it all for a few puffs of weed. But in prison humans don't stop being humans. Evelyn Waugh's brother, Alec, was a German prisoner in the 1914–18 war. He wrote that 'whole days were drenched in incurable melancholia'. A joint allows some escape.

MONDAY 27 JANUARY 2014

I came across Jean again in Brussels, a worker and a trade-union organiser, still a fighter for liberty after ten years in jail. For my part, I have undergone a little over ten years of various forms of captivity, agitated in seven countries, and written twenty books. I own nothing. On several occasions a Press with a vast circulation has hurled filth at me because I spoke the truth.

– Victor Serge

0810H Unlock. I now enter my sixth week in prison.

Last night a slip was put under the door ordering me to see the GP today. I go out the door as fast as possible to avoid too long a wait. Some of my gym friends are there, complaining of shoulder problems.

The doctor is in a tiny surgery. A young man wearing his Manchester University hockey club jacket, he seems puzzled to see me. I too am puzzled why I am here. We agree I have no health problems other than lack of fresh air. He takes my blood pressure, 124/76, which he says is just fine.

Later on, in the wing, I bump into Jim, my colostomy bag pal from Belmarsh. Yesterday he was in great pain and taken to hospital. This involved handcuffing both his wrists in front of him. He held out his hands to show me. Then he was chained to an officer and a third came as an extra escort. The previous week Jim had gone to the hospital escorted by just one guard, without the humiliation of handcuffs. Jim moves slowly and carefully as his diverticulosis operation, complicated by a hernia, causes serious pain. He is only a few months from his release. The chances of escaping while on a hospital visit are not high.

'I was on gas and then morphine in the hospital, so that was okay. It's agony to walk up to the third floor. It leaves me really weak, moving up and down the stairs.'

Jim has asked to move to a bottom-floor cell. There is one empty. Another friend, Lee, has moved to D Wing where cell doors are not locked. He says there are four or five empty cells there.

'Next time I go to the hospital, I'll ask them to write to the Governor. If my tag date wasn't so close and I didn't need to see my daughter I'd lie down and refuse to return up to the threes (third floor landing in prison jargon). But all they'll do is knock back my HDC' (Home Detention Curfew, or tag in common parlance).

I feel such a coward. In every previous part of my life I would have stepped forward to be Jim's advocate, his shop steward. But in prison so much power lies in the hands of the screws that they can get away with handcuffing a prisoner in pain and too weak to abscond and forcing him to limp up and up landings in pain, and no one dares to make a protest.

Every man is waiting to get out. As we are told again and again, being tagged is not a right. We merely become eligible for it halfway through the custodial element of the sentence. The decision to say yes or no to being released on tag is the divine right of the Governor. A no, or a let's wait a bit, from him can destroy all hopes and plunge a prisoner back into despair.

0950H Back from the GP, I am called in by the senior officer to say I have been restored to the standard level. But she warns me there is a negative comment on me from an officer. Apparently, I have not been sufficiently energetic in getting to the front of the queue for meals.

My jaw drops. Sometimes I am first, if hungry. Usually the queue forms as food arrives on trolleys from the kitchen to be kept on hot plates in the server. There is no announcement or bell and on the fourth-floor landing we are rather far away. But I am certain I have never been late or even last to arrive for a meal. For me it doesn't matter, but these computer entries will be in a prisoner's file forever. A screw who takes a dislike to someone can sneak in a snide comment that, years later, and in a very different prison, can be held against a prisoner.

I clean out my cell, brushing and mopping vigorously. I would love to throw sheets, clothes, even the plastic mattress halfway out the window. But there are bars, bars, bars everywhere and the cleansing effect of fresh air is unknown in prison.

1145H Lunch. A prison soggy baguette with a tub of tuna paste and sweetcorn. I add a hard-boiled egg, though Douggie, who has passed all the food safety exams, tells me later I should have thrown it away. 'It's only two days old,' I say. But with a broken shell, apparently eggs become bacteria breeding grounds. Does salmonella await?

The skin on the banana handed out at lunch is split too. I look for one with a whole yellow skin – no luck. I must look disappointed.

'It's prison, man. What do you expect?' smiles the server.

'Yep, it's prison.'

1400H A visitor to the cell. It's the residential manager. He says everyone has been reading my letters to Mark Field, the Conservative MP in whose constituency I live. Good, I think inwardly. The message is getting over. All prison staff are 'officers' but some are officer class. We have a long, friendly conversation standing up in my cell, as there is only one chair to sit on. He is more than aware of the pointlessness and the cost of keeping so many men locked up. But he doesn't know what to do.

'We're given policy by the politicians. Our job is to try and make it work.'

I give him a few instant suggestions based on my five weeks' depth of knowledge. He smiles. A major problem is that prison officer pay is very low. Absolutely no qualifications are needed to become a prison officer.

Pay starts under £20,000 p.a. and it can take a decade or more's service to get up to £30k plus. That's not much of a salary in London.

Governor Tullett is on a more generous £95,000, about the same as the Minister for Prisons. Unlike other public services – hospitals, schools, police, councils – prison professionals have not benefitted from the bonanza of public sector pay hikes that Gordon Brown authorised under the Labour government. I wonder whether, if prison staff at all levels were better qualified, better paid, more professional, prisons would be less training centres for future criminals and incarceration centres for men and women who don't need to be here.

1530H A good gym workout. Rowing, spinning, running and some weights. Can I get my weight to under 80kg? That is worth a prison sentence. Sort of.

1700H Phone calls. Bit by bit, my post-prison life is coming into shape. I wonder if there will be a blip turned into stories to entertain friends. Have I changed? Or should I try to use what I've experienced to help push for reform of our semi-functional, counterproductive judicial prison sector?

TUESDAY 28 JANUARY 2014

What heart shall touch thy heart? what hand thy hand?--
And I am sometimes proud and sometimes meek,
And sometimes I remember days of old
When fellowship seemed not so far to seek
And all the world and I seemed much less cold,
And at the rainbow's foot lay surely gold,
And hope felt strong and life itself not weak.
Thus am I mine own prison.

– 'Aloof', Christina Rossetti

0810H Douggie had kindly bought five oranges on his canteen sheet at my request. For decades I have begun the morning by eating an orange. As I went to get one this morning, I found they had all gone. I asked Douggie if he had scoffed them. No. So where had they gone? And then I remembered I was in a house of thieves. Sad, as on the whole I have had no sense of nicking here. Cell doors are open much of the day. I walk past empty cells with heaped bowls of fruit and other goodies. It's back to the uneatable Chinese pears for a morning fruit.

Since yesterday afternoon, there has been a heap of brushed-up dirt just outside my cell door by the pool table. Cigarette butts, an old biro, used tea bags, bits of paper and other dirt swept up by a big brush, presumably by a landing cleaner. So what has he got against using a dustpan? On the second-floor landing I see my friend, Del, who exudes knowing everything there is to be known about life in prison. Of course he has a dustpan. I borrow it and clean away the dirt. I hope it inspires the delegated landing cleaner to finish the job next time.

I am not listed to do anything today. Reading time. Good.

0900H Breakfast TV has a report of East European workers being exploited and paid sub-minimum-wage pay in Tottenham and Cricklewood. Well, that's a surprise. Still the economy is growing. That's also not much of a surprise. Given the amount of money that's been pumped into it via quantitive easing (aka printing money) it would be a weird economy that didn't respond to such a pure Keynesian shoot-up.

Like injecting heroin, injecting loads of money always creates a high. We've had bust, 2010–13. Now we have an anaemic boom. It's little different from classical Tory economic management since 1950. Get the pain in first, then ease off the tourniquet to get economic blood flowing again in time for the next election. It's worked in the past. It may work in May 2015. But surely soon we will realise the economy is too London-centred.

1025H I go down to post a letter to Spain. I'm glad I did. Earlier I had asked about the chances of a gym today. Two-thirty, I was told. Brixton time is different. The gym is at 10.30. Beforehand, I wander over to a group of gym regulars. One of our group is vigorously cleaning the servery trays. Most of the bicep boys in the gym are black. In contrast, he is a young, white, spotty, heavily tattooed man. He does weights obsessively. Lifting, lifting, lifting, so his arms become massive attachments to a rather weedy body.

He is upset because, although a Cat D prisoner with thirty-five weeks left before his release date, he is not being allowed to work.

'The probation officer said I was not ready to go out and be with the public.'

He is here for a burglary with aggravated violence. No weapon, but I can see his pinched mouth contorted in rage and his fists lashing out. For all that, he has obviously been a model prisoner to be on this wing. The probation officer, however, saw something menacing in his report or perhaps the insufficiently docile demeanour.

'The probation officer said I was still a danger to the public.'

I grunt a commiseration. 'But, you know, everyone is terrified of violence. Any hint of it, any threat, and people get frightened and want it dealt with quick and hard. In my constituency of Rotherham, I sometimes wanted to build a wall 50 feet high and put everyone over sixty on one side and every young person on the other. Older people are terrified of just a group of youngsters hanging around on the street. Even if they are quite peaceful, the old expect nothing but violence. You've got to prove, show, demonstrate any violence or aggression has completely left you,' I say, realising I am sounding like a moralising prat.

But his other friends nod agreement. They know him and like him but can sense the coiled-up aggression that can spring out for no special reason.

'I don't give a fuck. I've only thirty-five weeks left. I'll just do my time,' he says.

'Shit, bruv, you don't want to do more than you need to do. Try again,' says his servery pal.

'No. Fuck the probation officer. In two days it's February and soon it will be November and the probation officer can go fuck himself.'

We stop the talk to go to the gym, where I see his tattooed arms lifting weight after weight. As we queue to leave the gym I see Bill, the undisputed master of the gym with his pro-boxing background, telling the young man to go easy.

'It's gotta change up here,' he says, pointing to the head. The man flexes his biceps and stares ahead. I fear he'll be back.

1130H After the gym I see a miserable Alan, the ex-commando who had missed the piss test on Saturday. He was not allowed out to work today on account of his mistake. His boss was waiting for him to work on a scaffolding job. Alan's no-show without any explanation may be very damaging. He has sent in his explanation I drafted for him to the Governor.

Putting an app, or letter, or explanation or complaint in the box is an act of hope without any guarantee it will be read, let alone actioned. Alan waits patiently to try and talk to a senior screw. My instincts are to speak up for him. But already, after just a few weeks, I have learnt the prison cringe. On every prison street you learn quickly to walk by on the other side.

1215H Lunch is horrid chips and horrid beefburger. Ugh! Do I have to wait to be out to see a tomato, a pepper, a slice of onion? Why can't a kilo of salad vegetables come in with visitors?

I have been listening to National Prison Radio and heard Eamonn's Irish lilt as he read poems written by prisoners. He has a good radio voice. I felt, though, the presentation has to be more *Good Morning Vietnam* than Radio 4.

'Good morning, Brixton,' he smiles. He knows as I do that any expression of personality that isn't couched in tones of obedience and acceptance of the prison status quo will not be well received.

Lively radio is cheeky, questioning, irreverent. These qualities are not welcome in prison. Eamonn has a copy of the 2013 edition of poems written by prisoners. This stems from an initiative of the writer, Rachel Billington, part of the extraordinary Holland Park tribe of Pakenhams. Her father, Lord Longford, took time to visit the loneliest and most hated of prisoners like Myra Hindley. Her sister, Antonia Fraser, works with a friend and neighbour, Victoria Gray, on a project to send books to prisoners and encourage reading.

Like the Koestler Award initiative, these are excellent meritorious schemes like the myriad of charitable initiations and outfits that help prisoners. But they touch only a minority. A spark is encouraged to flame into talent and throughout history there is no better way to pass time in prison than by reading and writing. But our prisons do not need charity or do-gooding. They need reform and justice.

The middle-class energy that goes into prison charities would be better expended on changing a regime that spews out so many to return to crime, destroys the families and future of others, and seems to believe that the more prisoners judges send to prison, the better justice is served.

I am reading Erwin James's marvellous vignettes of prison life in his *A Life Inside*. He is a real prisoner who did twenty years, whereas I will have done little more than twice eighteen days. In 2001 he writes that 'almost 63,000 people were living behind bars in prison, equivalent to the population of Guildford'. In 2014, in just England and Wales, that figure is 89,000 – equivalent to the population of Hemel Hempstead.

James reports on the 600-page inquiry of Lord Justice Woolf, published just before Michael Howard became Home Secretary. 'I can still vividly remember his dark, pinstripe suit, so skilfully tailored that it retained its immaculate shape even when he sat down,' notes James.

James was amongst suitable prisoners allowed to meet the Lord Chief Justice. In his report, Woolf deplored the rise in prison numbers and said politicians should stop 'playing the jail card'. In fact, it is judges as much as, if not more than, politicians who play the jail card but these powerful (mainly) men are never held to account. The prison population increased by 20,000 between 1990 and 2000 and then by a further 20,000 between 2000 and today. In twenty years the prison population in England and Wales simply doubled, so that today we have more prisoners than the planned number of soldiers in the British Army.

Blaming politicians and ministers is easy. They live in subservience to the mass circulation papers. The one group supposed to be immune to press influence is judges. There are strict rules on reporting criminal cases so as to ensure juries are not influenced. But the media can write what they like, true or untrue, on anyone editors don't like, outside the narrow confines of a trial period because, so the theory goes, judges live in a rarefied world, above being influenced by negative press comments. I am sure Judge Sweeney had not read any of the extravagant media denunciations of me, including downright lies, before he sent me to Belmarsh.

Yet judges pride themselves on being apolitical and unswayed by politicians and their demands. So why do judges so cravenly do the bidding of politicians and the offshore proprietors who own the papers, clamouring for more people in prison? Why, when today's President of the Supreme Court says it is pointless sending people to prison for under six months, have I met so many men on short sentences soaking up public money to satisfy the appetite of judges to see who can send the most to prison?

Is it time for judges to stop 'playing the jail card'? Or are our judges even more subservient than the politicians?

1600H I chat to my Romanian friend, Daniel, and ask him to make a little 50th birthday card out of matchsticks. He also offers to make me a perfect box in a kind of Russian style of inlayed wood. It will be a great souvenir and a memory of one of the gentlest guys I've met here.

Norman comes in for a chat on business ideas. Prison has been redemptive for him, at least. A tall, slender 44-year-old Afro-Caribbean, he is in prison after a fight with a man he found in bed with his wife. In France, that would be a *crime passionnel* and although French law has been thoroughly modernised, there is some understanding of the loss of control in moments of fury and rage.

In England, adultery is an approved sport for the legal profession, MPs, police officers and editors, so irate husbands have to be kept under control. Norman got four years, but under an IPP – Indeterminate Public Protection – order. This means his sentence can be extended without any new trial or sentence, so he is now in his fifth year of prison.

But he is philosophical. 'I've changed. I decided to rid the anger from my system. I was regularly beaten by my father, who said I wasn't his son. I left school at sixteen and just fell in with a bad lot. A criminal record from that time didn't help my sentence or IPP. I did four years in a therapeutic prison. I think I've changed now.'

Norman has nearly finished his Open University degree in business. He is frustrated in Brixton. 'I had a Samsung in my cell in my last prison. Here I can use a computer just one afternoon a week.'

When out, he'll move away from his home area of Hackney, where his old friends, including some bad boys, still hang out. He'll live in Hammersmith. He wants to start a business. I rattle off all the unmet needs in London that maybe could be filled by someone ready to work long hours and for little revenue to begin with. I wouldn't pass even the preliminary tests for *Dragons' Den* but ideas have never been something I'm short of.

It's a pleasure to meet another person for whom prison has been a transformatory moment, when a good person emerges from a bad moment of space and time. Norman doesn't complain or say he shouldn't have come here. I only hope he makes it when he returns to today's world, where honest work is not well rewarded.

It's one thing to read Tom Peters and other business gurus in prison. The railway and airport bookstalls can't sell enough of books promising business success if only their advice is followed. Life is more complicated. I think Norman knows that, and a prison system that produces too much failure can take pride in this success.

I write letters to journalist friends who want to write about me. Not yet. Maybe not at all, unless the journalist discusses the five- and six-figure profiteers of the MP expenses scheme who are not just still at large without paying a penny back but in some cases are senior members of the government or chairs of key Select Committees. Or is that me becoming bitter again? Unlike Norman, do I still have anger in my system that has yet to be expunged?

1913H The post arrives. Sometimes it comes in the morning. Sometimes in the afternoon. And now an evening delivery. But always welcome. Thanks, friends.

WEDNESDAY 29 JANUARY 2014

The things people say of a man do not alter a man. He is what he is. Public opinion is of no value whatsoever. Even if people employ actual violence, they are not to be violent in turn. That would be to fall to the same low level. After all, even in prison, a man can be quite free. His soul can be free. His personality can be untroubled. He can be at peace. And, above all things, they are not to interfere with other people or judge them in any way. Personality is a very mysterious thing. A man cannot always be estimated by what he does. He may keep the law, and yet be worthless. He may break the law, and yet be fine. He may be bad, without ever doing anything bad. He may commit a sin against society, and yet realise through that sin his true perfection.

– Oscar Wilde

0710H Up a bit earlier than usual. Douggie sets up a smart audio set so I can listen to the radio. Music beckons. I write out a proposal for him to send to Gordon Ramsay, who oversees the Bad Boy Bakery in Brixton where he works. He is bubbling with enthusiasm and ideas of work he can do when he is out. I have suggested that all the prison food production operations in prison could be brought into a single network linked to local restaurants with a specific prison brand.

I suggest the invention of a new pudding – 'Prison Pudding' – as a contribution to the world repertoire of desserts and the first new pudding in British cuisine since the invention of the Christmas and summer puddings.

I have no idea if it will work but if Gordon Ramsay's energy and enthusiasm and proved entrepreneurial skills can be harnessed, who knows? It might help people see prisoners in a different light. I tell Douggie to rewrite my few pages as his own idea and offer himself as unpaid or low-paid labour to do a scoping exercise for Ramsay while he is doing resettlement work outside Brixton.

0835H The cell door opens. A thirteen-hour bang-up. I get up to leave to go downstairs to post a letter. 'Not you,' says the guard, and slams the cell door in my face. So much for Category D!

I don't care but I cannot believe this obsessive locking up men in tiny cells helps them become better people. Some prisoners rise above this kind of petty humiliation – after all, they have lost their liberty – and remake themselves. Many don't and the pent-up resentment against petty authoritarianism is palpable. They will keep docile with heads down as that subservient lowering of the eyes allows early release on tag or to work outside. But many will think they can be smarter next time and not get caught. It is not quite 'Abandon Hope All Ye Who Enter Here', but not far off. 'Abandon Belief That Prison Will Make You Better.'

1015H The cell door is opened and I go out to post letters. The male prison officer is sitting disconsolately in front of his computer screen.

'I've been waiting seventy-one minutes to log on. The prison computer system is down and I can't start work,' he moans. He has worked in prisons for six years and is very frustrated. 'I'd like to get to know prisoners and find those that need help and are willing to let me help them. But you are moved from wing to wing, from job to job, with changes every day, so you can't build up long-term relationships.

'There are some officers here who are happy to sit around not doing much but there are lots of us who want to make the best of things and help the prisoners, but management never listen.'

We chat a bit about Parliament. He thinks all MPs can retire after two terms on a full pension and that all the restaurants and bars are massively subsidised. I disabuse him of those two beliefs. But when I tell him of how the expenses system was used as a substitute for pay by successive Prime Ministers from Margaret Thatcher onwards, his jaw drops. I wonder if the MPs who made the real profits from the expenses system by taking out huge interest-only mortgages to spend as they wished will ever get exposed. Minor misdemeanours in terms of money improperly claimed have been heavily sanctioned, but the big-money profiteers have so far got away with it.

There is no prison officers' canteen in Brixton. When there was, they ate the same low-grade food served to prisoners. But it was more expensive for the screws. 'A chicken leg lunch and a soft drink cost £4,' says the guard. They can use the gym but only in their own time and when it is not used by prisoners. As before, as I listen to the life of a warder, I wonder who the prisoners of the prison system really are.

1112H Go downstairs to post a letter. The senior officer grabs me and asks me to advise a prisoner with a problem. He's a 49-year-old British-Jamaican man deported from the United States after being arrested for drug dealing. It is a complicated story of buying houses in his wife's name, but she now lives with another man. She arrived from Jamaica to marry him without declaring she had a drugs conviction from America and three children from previous relationships. It's pretty clear that properties were put in her name to launder money from crime.

Like the Russian oligarchs who buy flats in Belgravia, property is where much dodgy cash is recycled into 'legitimate' investments. He wants to know if the Home Office would deport his wife if officials are informed of how she entered Britain without disclosing all her personal data.

Together they had a son, now ten years old and well settled in London. I tell him that a mother married legally for a decade to a British citizen with a British-born son might well have grounds to stay here to bring up her son. I also warn against writing letters of denunciation to the authorities, as that might raise questions of the provenance of all the money used to buy properties. All I can do is suggest a quickie divorce with an agreed sharing-out of assets. But I warn that lawyers and divorce can be horribly costly.

1215H Lunch is a thin slice of industrially processed ham in a soft baguette. Only nine days and I'll see a tomato. Eamonn is overjoyed. He's heard he's going out on tag, maybe as early as tomorrow.

'You get so many knock-backs and then something good happens. I am not sure I'm ready.'

He has a job in Pinner in the commercial property market, which seems to be on a roll in booming London. No more Charlie. He won't be back. These prison acquaintanceships border on friendship. Then separation. The intensity of experience of being locked up throws people together, like in the Commons tea room, where it's better to be friendly with everyone, even though you would rarely be friends in the outside world.

It's raining but I go out for a brisk walk to breathe other than wing air. On the way back up to my cell I pass a group playing cards.

'Good afternoon, Mr Blair,' one says with a smile.

1445H I go down to check what time the gym is. Eamonn is on his landing looking worried. He was told to report at 2 p.m. to get the definitive news on his tag and his release, which could happen tomorrow. But he has been told nothing. Until the very end, the prison regime tortures men with no news, with uncertainty and lack of standing on firm ground. It is a subtle way of demoralising someone, right up to the last hours in jail.

1530H A good gym. My thoughts, though, keep drifting to all this coming to an end. I don't understand why prisoners cannot be informed about anything. When I get back Ms Caan tells me my request for a Visitors' Order won't work. I've had my quota of January visits. I point out it's February on Saturday and thereafter. Then she tells me that an earlier Visitors' Order has gone out. But no one at home has received it. Maybe it will happen. But I just don't know.

Eamonn knows his release has been approved at a ROTL board meeting chaired by the Governor today. But he has no idea of the date. Why not?

1745H Dinner is a chicken vindaloo. It bears little relation to the food or the curry. No matter. I sprinkle chilli flakes over everything. Today is Douggie's 50th birthday. We have a little party, eating a chocolate Yule log left over from Christmas. At least he gets a chorus of 'Happy Birthday to You'. Come to think of it, a wing sing-song would cheer us all up.

1840H The mail arrives. There is one letter from my solicitor franked last Monday, 20 January. Nine days for a solicitor's letter to do WC1 to SW2. That's not acceptable. I get a letter posted three days ago in Geneva. Solicitors' letters are the most important correspondence a prisoner can receive. To delay delivery for a week is an attack on justice.

1935H Bang-up. There is a poor fluorescent light in the ceiling. I have noticed my reading sight deteriorate in prison. I have asked to see the prison optician as well as a dentist, but doubt if anything will happen. Douggie tells me of a mate in one of his earlier prisons who had testicular cancer. Despite repeated requests, he wasn't properly examined. He didn't want to moan, so bore the increasing pain by just putting in requests for proper expert medical examination. In the end, the cancer was so bad even the prison authorities had to acknowledge it. Instead of one, both his testicles had to be removed. Don't be ill in prison.

THURSDAY 30 JANUARY 2014

I was kind of excited to go to jail for the first time and I learnt some great dialogue.

– Quentin Tarantino

0330H I wake up for a pee. Climbing back to the top bunk, I slip on the steel and wooden chair and fall heavily, twisting my back and bumping my head. The cell is a death trap, with sharp metal corners everywhere and slippery surfaces. The loo door doesn't shut, so there is little privacy. Douggie wakes up at my cry but, other than a bit of back pain and a bumped head, I'm fine. Can I sue the prison under Health and Safety?

0813H Cell door opens and Douggie goes to work. I have nothing to do, so I write letters to friends in Australia and America. I am a little perplexed that some of my oldest, bestest friends haven't written. Is it because we don't write any more? We text instead. Or have I become an invisible man for six weeks? A few MPs have written and I am grateful. Those who haven't tend to be those who made big profits from the expenses scheme, so perhaps they just don't want to be reminded of how they got away with helping themselves while I am in prison for not helping myself.

I go down to post letters and cross Mr Brown. I tell him my solicitor wrote to me on 20 January but the letter arrived on the 29 January. 'That's not right, especially for a solicitor's letter.'

'Nine days. That's fast by Brixton standards,' came the cheerful reply.

1150H Roll call. You stand outside your cell and a warder counts you and checks against a list. It's Ms Greer. She beams and asks if I have seen the minutes of the wing meeting last Friday. 'No,' I reply. I go downstairs and see four pages of yellow paper pinned to a board to join all the other notices up on walls and boards on the ground-floor couloir. It's how I imagine the Democracy Wall in Beijing in the early days of the experiment fusing communism and capitalism in China. Large sheets in variable typeface cover much of the walls. There is a narrative of a Christian Christmas and Jewish Hanukkah. Closely typed instructions on how to become eligible for ROTL. The account of the wing meeting is not bad as minute-taking, though my reference to 'Parliament' has become 'the House of Lords'. Maybe that's what the prison world associates with Parliament.

1215H Lunch, and at last half a tomato and four thick cucumber slices and, as I hunt down through the lettuce in my pasta and sweetcorn salad, I come across a smidgeon of onion.

On the BBC2 politics programme, one of my nemeses, 'Sir' Keir Starmer QC, is asked if he wants to be an MP. I don't see why not. He would make an excellent Liberal Democrat MP, slippery, changing his line, not to be trusted.

A prisoner comes up and asks me to check an appeal letter he has written after he failed Saturday's piss test and lost his Category D status as a result.

'I took a little puff,' he says, 'but they say I drank too much water to dilute my piss. Since when has it been a crime to drink water?'

Everyone on the wing knows he is one of the biggest pot smokers here and, since drugs and alcohol are a big no-no, he was taking a huge gamble. In fact, the prison drug-testing policy encourages the use of hard drugs like crack or heroin. They only stay in your body for a short while. On the other hand, if you smoke a joint it still shows up days later. So for the drug-dependent prisoner there is every incentive to leave behind a soft drug like dope and head for the highs of heroin, as he stands more chance of passing a piss test. I read his letter and it is couched in suitable respectful tones so I tell him to send it off. I doubt it will have any impact.

1415H Luckily I went down to post a letter. I found an over-50s gym group assembling ready to go off. We were told it would be 2.30. The prisoners here are weeks or at the most months off being released into communities controlled by clocks and time. Instead of teaching the men the value of orderly time-keeping, C Wing screws hold time in disdain. They decide what time means and when something will happen as it pleases them. It is a disastrous example to set.

Back after the gym, I am told Ms Greer wants to see me. I'd like to call her Julia, her first name. But prison protocol insists that men only have surnames and officers cannot have first names. It's like the formalities of an army depot seventy years ago.

She says she has a favour to ask. Will I go to a Queensland meeting in the Governor's office tomorrow and take the minutes? I can choose two other prisoners to represent C Wing. I ask Ms Greer what a 'Queensland' meeting is. She doesn't know where the name comes from but it's a kind of senior managers and prisoners meeting. I joke that I have been taking minutes all my life, though in fact it's a chore I prefer to shunt off onto someone else.

'OK,' I say. 'I'll do it and find two sensible wing representatives. But in exchange I need some help.'

'Ha! The politician speaks,' snorts Mr Asari, who is in her office, but he says it in a kindly manner.

I tell them I need to have confirmation that I will indeed be released next Friday on my tag or HDC day.

'I just want the same treatment as all the other politician prisoners who were out having served half their sentence,' I insist.

Mr Asari gives me the same old story about the probation service needing to check my house. I say my house isn't the problem, it's the slowness of the prison and probation bureaucracy. Not just slow but costly, as the quicker eligible prisoners are shipped out of jail the less the taxpayer has to fork out to feed and lodge them.

I tell them that all prisoners fretting over their tag release days believe 'there's a legendary woman called Charlie, with goddess-like powers over when prisoners can leave. She sends out and receives in all the reports of external agencies deemed necessary to allow a prisoner release on tag or parole.' Mr Asari kindly calls her extension at 3.55. She's gone home.

'She's on flex-time,' he explains.

Nice for Charlie. But it's flex-despair for prisoners who don't know when they will leave, despite having done their time.

Mr Asari talks to the mythical but absent Charlie's assistant. He learns the appropriate form has been sent to the sprawling probation service in London. A very good South Yorkshire friend, a young miner sacrificed on the twin altars of Margaret Thatcher's pathological hatred of miners and Arthur Scargill's Messianic desire for government-topping strike action, went on to university and joined NAPO, the trade union for probation officers. He reported regularly on the anger and fed-upness of probation officers, who were targeted for cuts as soon as David Cameron and Nick Clegg took office.

I see a stretched probation service for whom checking the status of a politician's house will not be a priority. But I am determined not to stay in prison a day longer than I am obliged to.

Ms Greer points out that at least tomorrow I will see Governor Tullett so can make this point. I have already worked this out. I think I will cause a stink by going on a hunger strike if the Grayling system keeps me in prison for its own pleasure and incompetence.

I tell that to Martin, my Birdman's solicitor, who gulps. He agrees to fire off letters to Tullett, Grayling and Mark Field, my MP, who has not exactly over-exerted himself on behalf of this constituent, but, as a Labour guy, I don't blame him.

If there is one common moan I hear from prisoners it is that their tag days are not respected by the Brixton Prison bureaucracy. It comes up again and again as we chat on landings or in meal queues. It is a dreadful management error. The prisoners here on Cat D have worked so hard to get to this stage of tagged release. They have done everything the prison system asks of them.

Now, as they should be planning the key stage of reinsertion into the economy and society, they are left dangling in the air waiting for a date that is never given to them on the day it is due. They end their prison term, not on a sense of achievement at rescuing themselves from the bad life they led before, but twitchy, depressed, moody and incapable of focusing on life outside, as they wait in limbo for Charlie to turn up for work and do the business. This is the last revenge of a system on men it despises. A public service serving itself, not the public.

For the first time in six weeks I am quite depressed. I could take the 23-hour Belmarsh bang-ups in my stride and didn't over-worry about not being sent to an open prison with unlocked cells, open air walks, a proper library, eating at a table, not with a plate on your lap in a cell. But if I can't see my children and all my friends next weekend, I will break down.

1918H Poor Douggie comes rushing in dripping wet from the shower. The bang-up screw has already been round asking where he was. He doesn't have time to towel himself dry. Yesterday we were banged up at 7.40 p.m. In normal Cat D prisons and on D Wing here, prisoners have keys for their cell doors and can move around until ten. Why the difference for us? And why can't they at least have the same time each night?

FRIDAY 31 JANUARY 2014

I was most happy when pen and paper were taken from me and I was forbidden from doing anything. I had no anxiety about doing nothing by my own fault, my conscience was clear, and I was happy. This was when I was in prison.

– Daniil Kharms

0730H A morning busier than an early breakfast in the Commons tea room. There, MPs with no home to have a family breakfast in crawl into the Commons to enjoy the best breakfast in London – my favourite of kippers, or the full Monty English breakfast, a terrific juice, fruit and muesli bar, all varieties of tea and coffee – served by the loveliest, kindest women of all ages at wholesale cost prices. A few elderly Labour peers, nice ex-MPs usually from Scotland, come in from their nursing home end of Parliament to enjoy the gossip. It's a welcome escape from *Today* or Sky Morning News. MPs are usually in transit in the early morning hours, so the BBC's John Humphrys and his team dictate the political agenda of the day to everyone in Britain except politicians themselves.

But the Commons tea room at breakfast tends to be a silent place, as MPs help themselves to piles of newspapers and speed-read them, looking for newsy political stories, especially any that hold up to exposure or ridicule fellow MPs, preferably from their own party. *Schadenfreude* is stronger in an MP's character than any other emotion.

The slim foreign pages are skipped over in favour of the parliamentary sketches and columnists. No one bothers with editorials, often the most elegantly written words in a paper. I still treasure a *Sun* leader denouncing my pro-Europe views under the single-word headline 'MacShame'. Later that day I met Germany's Foreign Minister, Joschka Fischer. '*Guten Tag*, Denis, or should I say Herr MacShame?' It was cheering to know that *The Sun* was *the* English newspaper of choice for German diplomacy.

MPs butter their toast and bury themselves in the papers. Later, the hum of chatter fills the far end of the tea room, where Tories and Lib Dems sit, and the half with the counter, which is Labour's end. Unlike switching sides of the Chamber when a new government comes in, the two halves of the tea room remain either ConDem or Labour.

The morning begins with Douggie and me dozing. There's so little of any use to do in prison that staying in bed or lying on it during the day becomes a norm. No nocturnal falls overnight but I wake up and lie in bed worrying whether this time next week I will be packing to leave or plunged into despair at being kept inside beyond my tag release date.

Suddenly the door is unlocked. An officer comes in and snaps, 'Mackie.' Douggie struggles up. 'Aibheen wants to see you. Now!' Aibheen is the Irish woman who runs the Gordon Ramsay-sponsored Bad Boys' Bakery in Brixton Prison.

Douggie has nine months to go (in my judgement he could be released tomorrow as he will never be so stupid again. He has lost weight, been weaned off booze, and can easily pick up his business life again) and hopes to extend his chefing and catering skills by working in one of Ramsay's outfits on day release from prison.

I drafted a set of ideas for him to look at and rewrite with his own thoughts on how he could help Ramsay. He gave this to Aibheen on Monday and she has talked to Ramsay's office. Now a 7.30 morning meeting an hour before the bakery begins operations. Douggie leaps out of bed and has a quick shave. He goes out and the door is re-locked.

Twenty minutes later it is again opened and a youngish man in a shiny grey suit is standing there. It's quite hard to wear neat business clothes in prison, with the great mass of keys and chains officers and staff have to carry around all the time in fetching little pouches like small Prada or posh Smythson accessories. They would fetch a good price if sold in Sloane Street.

The man in his grey suit announces himself as Governor something or other. It's the third Governor-rank prison officer I've had in my cell. I think his title is Director of Operations. He asks if I have sent out a Visitor's Order for 'Mary Cree-ack'. He struggles to pronounce the Irish name of my friend, Mary Creagh, the Wakefield MP and Shadow Transport Secretary.

Bless you, Mary. The diary of a shadow Cabinet minister is crowded beyond imagination. And transport is one of the most intractable of briefs.

The Governor – do I call him 'Guv?' – says the visits office thinks an MP coming to see a prisoner is a social visit. I tell him that, no, in my experience MPs make parliamentary visits to prisoners and they should not count against the meagre allocation of visits for children, spouses, parents, partners and friends Chris Grayling allows the incarcerated 89,000 in English and Welsh prisons.

Mary has asked to see me at 1.45 today or perhaps that's the time the useless visits office has told her to turn up. I tell the Operations Governor that I am required to be at the Governor's prison consultative meeting at 2 p.m. I tell the suit to contact Mary and try and find a different time. It's a real buggeration moment. Last night I was miserable at being denied a visit from my daughter and now I get a visit chance from one of the cheeriest, smartest MPs I know, whose political intelligence is only matched by the prettiest smile in politics, and it won't work. *So ist das Leben.*

Ten minutes later the clatter and clink of the door opening operation happens again. The officer says 'Mackie?' 'No, MacShane,' I reply. I am not on his list for education or work so he shuts the door in my face again. I settle down to write and listen to Ben Ainslie on *Desert Island Discs* enclosed in my concrete and steel cocoon. He has spent more time in a tiny enclosed space as a world champion sailor than I ever will and he sounds utterly composed, and without any side, unlike so many 'great' men I have had to meet or spend time with.

0945H Again, noise at the door. Two letters are pushed through. One is addressed to a prisoner in Cell 9 – three cells away. Then the door opens. Not to let me out but to retrieve the misdelivered letter. The other letter is a reply to a complaint I submitted in Belmarsh more than a month ago asking why I had been denied a family reception, which every prisoner is entitled to in the first days of arriving in prison. It is full of waffle. It is utterly pointless to send it to me now. I must not be paranoid but I wonder if there is a secret BNP or UKIP or *Daily Telegraph* cell somewhere in Grayling's ministry or the prison service? What else can explain the utterly different treatment I have received compared to all other MPs in recent time? That's bonkers, of course, but what other explanation is there?

Roger Alton sends a card with a bottle of claret on the front to remind me of what I'm missing. He says dear Georgina Henry of *The Guardian* is in bad shape.

1015H Grant rattles my slit window and says there is a gym at 10.30. I point out I am still banged up. He goes downstairs and a woman warder, a Ms Delaware or Delaway, opens the door. No word of apology for keeping me locked away well beyond Cat D norms. 'Sorry' is not in the prison service vocabulary.

1130H My fifth gym this week. It's the high point of otherwise empty days. Body building is the only thing that seems to interest the men. There are twenty-two in a tiny gym and the men mill around sharing weights in a crowded space. I retreat to a small landing where there are dilapidated spinning bikes and a rusty rowing machine. Del is my companion. He is in his fifties. Downstairs the bicep boys bash on. But what real use are huge biceps apart from not getting sand kicked in your face, or being an Austrian Governor of California?

1400H Over to the Governor's office. Like so much in Brixton, it appears to be a brick-cladded Portakabin. Narrow stairs, like on a ferry boat, lead up to a low conference room filled with a table around which twenty-two people sit, half senior prison staff and half prisoner representatives from A, B, C, D and G wings. There is no E or F wing.

I am there to take the minutes. It's a bit difficult, as I don't know any of the names or what they do. Still, I've been doing notes of meetings all my life so it shouldn't be too hard.

For an earlier visit today, Governor Tullett has brought out the Governor's record book, a kind of log, from earlier years. It is written in a clear longhand in ink, in a handsome big book with leather-bound covers and thick, lined cream paper inside. I see an entry for September 1961 which states 'Earl Russell was discharged by the back gate to avoid the press.'

There were 743 prisoners then, with sixty or seventy entering and leaving each day. There are about a hundred more prisoners today compared to the Brixton Bertrand Russell was detained in by a Conservative government anxious to crush the anti-nuclear war sit-down demonstrations the nonagenarian world-renowned philosopher was leading.

I can imagine the self-publicist philospher's fury at being shuffled out of the back gate at Brixton instead of walking out the main entrance to face the flash of cameras and make one of the global threat pontifications in his thin Bloomsbury voice.

Brixton Prison's income in 1961 was recorded as £52,000, and expenditure as £41,000 all recorded in a neat copper-plate hand. The prison regulations book is a printed volume of 500 pages, with the saddest paragraphs detailing how a prisoner condemned to death should be treated.

There is a 1940 letter from the Home Secretary, Sir John Anderson, written in perfect Home Office turgid officialese. When Churchill became Prime Minister in May 1940 he ordered the detention of all the anti-Semitic Nazi sympathisers and leaders of the British Union of Fascists. As today, xenophobic feeling in the '30s against immigrants and (mainly Jewish) asylum seekers fused with a lick-spittle approach to dictatorship.

In the '30s the tyrannies were European. Today they are in the oil-rich Arab world, Putin's Russia, and above all China. The City and the ruling elites of England have always turned a blind eye to dictatorship and torture if there is money to be made. Before the war, the Duke of Wellington presided in 1939 over the Right Club, set up to 'oppose and expose the activities of Organised Jewry', which had the charming initials PJ – 'Perish Judah' – on its letterhead.

Churchill dared not imprison the descendant of England's greatest general but he had no hesitation in ordering the detention of Sir Oswald Mosley and his lieutenants like the former Labour MP turned English fascist, John Beckett. They were kept in Brixton. But, wrote the Home Secretary to the Governor, they were not convicts but detainees and thus should be treated differently. They were also former colleagues in the House of Commons. The status of an MP in that era was not as low as it is today. The Brixton Governor is not given specific instructions by the Home Secretary, just the best kind of Whitehall hint that a different regime would be appropriate. The problem was solved by moving Mosley to Holloway to join his wife, Diana. In Holloway Prison, the fascist couple took over a house on the prison grounds and hired prisoners to act as servants, cooks and valets. The English ruling class always looks after its own.

I have spent so many happy hours in archives here, in America and Europe. To turn the pages of original letters or minutes is quite thrilling in that perpetual voyage of discovery called history. At the Foreign Office I sometimes asked to see original documents like the Treaty of Utrecht of 1713. It was like a small paperback of one hundred pages written in Latin, French and Spanish. After scores of pages in which various French princes renounced any claim to the Spanish throne, there is a short page and a half giving the rock of Gibraltar to England. The said rock was given 'in perpetuity' to Queen Anne on the condition that all Jews and Muslims were to be expelled. There was to be no commerce with mainland Spain 'save in times of tempest'. There should be no seaborne trade from the rock, which would only be a naval harbour and fort. Of course England being Perfidious Albion quickly ignored all three conditions, and has done over three centuries.

I made a point of writing little ministerial comments on the 'Blues', the minutes on thick blue paper submitted by officials to the Foreign Secretary and ministers. Some of them were full of brilliance and insight. Some mind-bogglingly poor in judgement. Over the years I have often used a red pen to highlight. I began my ministerial life by writing in red on a blue FCO minute. My private secretary ran in utterly panicked. Only the Foreign Secretary was allowed to use a red pen in the FCO. That way all the other officials could see what the great man was thinking. So I switched to black and wrote a couple of lines as neatly as possible, so thirty years later, when the minutes are published, those interested in the meanderings of foreign policy at the beginning of the twenty-first century can have the benefit of my probably utterly wrong observations.

Torn away from Governor's record books I settle down to take minutes. Governor Tullett moves the business along at a brisk pace over the two hours. The complaints come in thick and fast. Showers are scalding or freezing. Why can't men doing ten education sessions a week get to the gym? Why are there such delays in delivering mail? Why are the education classes so limited in what they offer?

A woman explains she is going to put up boxes everywhere surrounded by posters in many languages. Last year, she said, there were twenty-five 'Dirfs' (Diversity Incident Report Forms) submitted. Gosh, two complaints a month. I haven't seen any hint of racism. Halal food is served, even though it is more expensive to buy than non-halal food, and non-Muslims are not allowed to choose halal meat, which seems unfair. But Brixton Prison now has a full-time Equalities Officer to deal with a fortnightly complaint.

Then the deluge begins. The one thing that is a disaster in Brixton, something that demoralises prisoners and makes them turn their face to the wall and give up, is the utter incoherence of the ROTL – rottle in prison parlance. It is the final part of a prison sentence. A prisoner can begin to leave the prison, first for day visits and then for home leave. He can also start to work outside in a normal job, returning just to sleep in prison. Finally comes the all-important HDC day, when the prisoner does the final few months of his sentence under Home Detention Curfew.

This entails wearing a waterproof plastic anklet placed around the ankle and which cannot be taken off without sending a panic signal to the monitoring authority. There's a monitor at home to check you obey the hours you are allowed out and when you have to be at home. It's made clear throughout a sentence that being allowed out of prison before the formal end of the custodial element of the sentence is not a legal right but depends on good behaviour, obedience to what screws say, doing courses or cleaning wings and kitchens with cheerful enthusiasm.

Yet in Brixton I haven't met a single prisoner who has got his ROTL on the due date and many whose tag date has come and gone are still inside.

From all the wings the complaints come in. The Governor tries to defend himself. But unconvincingly. Thirty to forty prisoners are rottled each month. But it is meant to be a D Cat prison, one that knows how to get prisoners into the community. The ROTL system requires the Probation Service to submit a report. Yet probation officers tell prisoners' wives they have emailed Brixton with an approval and it isn't actioned.

People have been exerting pressure to make sure my tag date is respected. I hate doing this but I simply don't trust the integrity of a system that sends so many men spinning into despair. The reader may wonder what's the difference with an extra few weeks or a month or two in prison. You've done the crime, don't moan about doing the time, is the sneer. Perhaps. But one-crime non-violent men (one man in Brixton is doing three years for signing the housing benefit claim form of his bed-ridden mother, struck down by Alzheimer's) shape their life and prison comportment around the idea of getting home to their children and home in the belief that the ROTL system will be respected.

The main problem in Brixton is that a part-time clerk works just three days a week on rottles and tags and, given the bureaucratic hoops and the interface agencies, it is clearly a full-time job.

I note down the defensiveness and obfuscations of the Governor. They will appear in neutral language in the minutes but for the first time I am really angry. I expected little humanity in Belmarsh where many officers were just boring bullies who took pleasure in being as unhelpful and as unkind as possible. But this is Brixton, with its large contingent of good behaviour non-violent prisoners easily able to reintegrate into the community. Why on earth are they locked up a second longer than necessary?

The Governor got the prison bakery to bake two dozen scones with whipped cream and raspberries in a gooseberry sauce for the official delegation who came in this morning. If the prisoners can make such efforts to give him and his visitors a delicious treat with their morning coffee, why cannot he reciprocate by reorganising the inefficient ROTL and HDC system and stop wasting taxpayers' money?

There is another revelation which surprises. Only 75 per cent of short (hour-long) visits are actually taken up and only 25 per cent of longer two-hour visits. I have a grumpy exchange with the head of visits, a curt Scot in rimless glasses. I ask him why I have had only four visits in seven weeks, in comparison with the normal weekly visit to which Cat D visitors are entitled. He says I am being treated like other prisoners. I politely point out that, from personal experience of Cat D prison visits, this simply isn't true. He clearly isn't used to, or perhaps doesn't like, any prisoner trying to extract an answer to a question.

'If that's your attitude I am not replying,' he said.

I instantly shut up as I can see another red entry on the horizon, even if we are all sitting comfortably around the Governor's table. Never, ever have or show 'attitude' in prison.

I also keep my eyes down and scribble notes, having heard that there is so much space in the visitors' rota.

Keeping in touch with children, hearth and home is essential to help turn the convict into a citizen. To limit visits, or not to arrange things so that all visit slots are filled up, is just another example of the dysfunctional prison system. I stay silent.

The Governor also complains that up to 20 per cent of Brixton inmates use drugs, mainly marijuana. He is under pressure to cut down on drug taking. If it continues, all Brixton ROTLs or HDCs may be withdrawn. Not before next week, I hope.

Trying to staunch the modest use of marijuana is as likely to happen as stopping the drinking of whiskey in the Prohibition era in America.

Sensible countries or states in America are decriminalising it. Here, the Governor appeals to the prisoner representatives to tell him which prisoners are using drugs. Snitching or grassing is a no-no for prisoners. The way they survive is to construct a world inside their cells or inside their heads which no screw or prison manager ever enters. Informing on another prisoner destroys the inner existence that allows prisoners to survive. The comparison may be unacceptable to some but to inform on another prisoner is like telling the Germans in Colditz that a prisoner has a secret radio. It just isn't done.

The smell of dope is easy to detect. But that would mean prison guards up on the landings at times when dope is smoked. Costly in work-hours, to be sure, but as long as drugs are so easily brought into prison, often traded by screws themselves, and as long as the professional elites light up a puff themselves, it won't stop in prisons.

1736H Dinner is a bean salad with no dressing. I borrow one of Douggie's cans of tuna to make it palatable. Governor Tullett is there at the serving area. Prisoners crowd around him to complain. I see he is holding a House of Commons letter. Finally he escapes and comes to me.

'Why are you wearing prison clothes?' I am wearing baggy tracksuit bottoms and T-shirt.

'Because they are comfortable,' I answer.

He shows me a letter from David Blunkett. He has kindly written asking why I have not been transferred to an open prison, why I am banged up for so many hours and why I have no access to books or paper. I tell the Governor the letter reflects my situation of three weeks ago. Would he like me to check his letter?

'I can write my own letter.'

1900H *Channel 4 News* has a report on Amanda Knox and the awful murder of her fellow student in Perugia. Will Knox be extradited from Seattle to Italy? Matt Frei, the great *Channel 4 News* presenter, says the question of her extradition is about 'justice being polluted by public opinion'. *Lieber Mathias!* Our judges are influenced or polluted by public opinion, as is the CPS. So many of the high-profile trials in recent years are about public or political opinion.

Channel 4 News or *Panorama* or *File on Four* or any of the better TV or radio current affairs programmes never investigate how public opinion shapes and guides decisions of juries and sentences of judges. Like the *Daily Telegraph* journalist, Christopher Hope, who asks the French head of state about an affair he is having, but would never have dared or dreamt of putting the same question to our future head of state when he was openly adulterous with a woman not his wife, the British journalist thinks everything is improper or worse in other countries and never applies the same criteria here in perfect England.

FEBRUARY 2014

SATURDAY 1 FEBRUARY 2014

'He was a very private person, and sometimes it seemed to me that he was no longer interested in the world or in other people ... I got the feeling that Julián was living in the past, locked in his memories. Julián lived within himself, for his books and inside them – a comfortable prison of his own design.'

'You say this as if you envied him.'

'There are worse prisons than words.'

– Carlos Ruiz Zafón

0830H Unlock. It's February. Will I wake up next Saturday in my own bed? Yesterday Nathalie said she was seeing the probation officer on Monday to let her into my house. Sounds good. Then I talk to Sarah. She has taken a call from the probation officer who has called my mobile! Do these idiots decide to call a prisoner's mobile phone to check on his tag? Luckily, Sarah has it switched on to check emails, texts and calls, and makes sense of the probation officer's call.

Saturday is a dead day in Brixton. Just a few men are allowed to the gym. You need enhanced status to go on Saturday, the one day when prisoners are free to go. Del is pissed off.

'In my last nick I made a video about how everyone benefits by working hard to get onto enhanced status. You do as the screws say. You do all the tick-box courses. That's the way to get enhanced. They used the video in induction courses. Then I come to this shithole and they take enhanced off me. I've asked for the video back.'

His cellmate, Vinnie, gets out his electric hair razor, covers my shoulders in a plastic bag and expertly reduces my hair to a neater proportion. He has given up on the ROTL system.

'My wife works for the Home Office and phones up the woman in charge here and gets such a mouthful of abuse for daring to ask what was going on, she just gave up. I can't be bothered,' says Vinnie. 'It's just rotting on Rottle.'

I wonder if the Taxpayers' Alliance knows how much it costs to keep prisoners fed and lodged far beyond their release date? I'll have dinner with my old friend Margaret Hodge MP, the wonderful if fearsome chair of the Public Accounts Committee, and see if she can get the National Audit office to look into this spectacular waste of public money.

It's laundry and change sheets day. A laundry orderly brings my clean sheets up to the cell. Gosh, this service could grow on me.

Sadly, there are some prisoners for whom Brixton is just a revolving door. One man, drug dependent, incapable of holding down a job, without any real home, is said to have been here thirty times. An urban prison myth, and I have neither time nor desire to knock on every cell door and look for social rejects who need help, not punishment. Channel 4 has just spent a year and loads of money on a programme called *Benefits Street*. Could they do one called *C Wing Landing* and dig into why all these men are here and, more importantly, whether each one should be here?

1202H Sausages, beans and fried potatoes for lunch. Comfort food from childhood. Ian brings his Saturday treat, a slice of lemon tart. It's the best food I eat. I save it to be eaten half tonight, half tomorrow.

Eamonn, who had his HDC approval on Wednesday, but for some reason is still in prison, is furious. He had a Saturday out today and his girlfriend made the two-hour journey from Harlow to see him. Each prisoner going outside prison to work or for a social visit has a pass-book, like an old fashioned passport. When Eamonn presented himself to leave, the woman screw said his passbook hadn't been counter-signed authorising the visit, so he couldn't go out to his waiting friend. 'She just dismissed me. It didn't matter to her. She's a real bitch and doesn't give a damn about any of us.'

Eamonn is a mild-mannered man not given to violent language. He said that a more senior officer arrived, who checked on the computer and, indeed, Eamonn was on the list to go out. So he had his visit minus half an hour. But the casual willingness of the woman warder to stop him going out has shaken him. Days away from his release he will say nothing to the system but the bitterness burns acid into a man who should be composed and at ease before re-entering the orbit of the normal world.

1510H Denied the gym, I run round and round the exercise yard and do some press-ups and other exercises on the ground. It's better than nothing.

1715H Dinner and lock-up. Governor Tullett told me last night that he would tell David Blunkett that prisoners in Brixton were out between 8 a.m. and 7.30 p.m. Today the door was unlocked at 8.30, locked again between 12.30 and 1.45, and now we are locked up again until 9.00 tomorrow morning. I hope Tullett tells David Blunkett the truth. With everybody in the wing, the queue for phones was heavy. I could only have one brief chat with my daughter.

SUNDAY 2 FEBRUARY 2014

'X claimed me as his property and I didn't dispute it. I became obedi-ent, telling myself at least I was surviving ... He publicly humiliated and degraded me, making sure all the inmates and gaurds [*sic*] knew that I was a queen and his property. Within a week he was pimping me out to other inmates at $3 a man. This state of existence continued for two months until he sold me for $25 to another black male who purchased me to be his wife.' This is one of the more printable first-hand accounts from the 'Slavery' section of a Human Rights Watch report entitled 'No Escape: Male Rape in US Prisons.' And, as a description of the state of affairs in many jails, the term 'slavery' is no exaggeration. An inmate who has been 'turned out', as the saying goes, may become the wholly owned subsidiary of an individual, or even a gang. Not only is he a slave in the appalling sexual sense of that term, but he is compelled to turn over all his property, any gifts or money from 'outside,' and then be rented or hired out for tasks that might be described as demeaning: from cleaning toilet bowls to doing laundry before being subjected to recreational beating or coercive intercourse.

— Christopher Hitchens, writing about American prisons, 2005

0730H Up and reading in the loo with the light on so as not to disturb Douggie. At nine, down for mass. There is a wonderful notice up on the whiteboard by the door. 'ALL COMPUTER BASED ENQUIRIES NEED TO BE PUT ON A GENERAL APPLICATION FORM. THANK YOU. WING C MANAGEMENT.'

I love this. Brixton Prison staff must have shares in the paper industry. Several times I have asked prison staff something that with two computer touches comes up and an answer given. Now I have to write out my request in longhand. I have to find an officer – if I can tear him away from looking at the BBC sport pages on his screen – and ask him to sign the app form, put it in a postbox, and then wait a week or two for a reply. It is beyond parody.

All the Catholics assemble for mass. No screw turns up to take us there. We are all Cat D prisoners but cannot be trusted to leave C Wing and walk thirty yards to the old Victorian church, which is surrounded by high walls, razor wire and other buildings.

It gives me a chance to meet a delightful woman, Patricia Moberly, a prison visitor who has come to see me. She was head of the sixth form at Pimlico School and a good friend of a fellow head of sixth form at the nearby comprehensive girls' school Grey Coats who, in turn, is one of my oldest friends. Hence her hunt for me. We have a brief intense chat on the utter absence of any political pressure for prison reform. 'How I wish we could have a real reforming minister like Roy Jenkins. The prisons need real reform. Ken Clarke was sympathetic or seemed to be but no one else.'

I explain that in my two decades in the Commons there were few MPs who took an interest in treatment of prisoners or reducing the numbers incarcerated. 'As long as the *Daily Mail* and *Daily Telegraph* tells us prisons are holiday camps,' she raises her eyes at the thought, 'you'll never get a big movement to reform prisons.' She blinks as I suspect the *Daily Mail* may be a paper of reference, as it is for our mutual friend, who gets all her news and views from Lord Rothermere's organ.

She has to dash off, and we promise a three-way dinner before long. Anyone who controlled the pupils at Pimlico is perfect as a prison visitor. She spends more time on A and B Wings, where harder, more disturbed prisoners, some with serious mental issues, are housed. 'There's good in everyone,' she says without pretension or piety. This is generous indeed from a lifelong teacher! I like her very much. The goodness of prison visitors gets little acknowledgement. Take the CBs off the seat-polishing Whitehall hacks, Prime Minister, and give them to prison visitors!

At 0920 we are still waiting to go to mass. Two women warders huff and puff, waiting for someone else to come and escort us a few yards. I suggest we form ourselves into the Martyrs of C Wing, with our faith stamped on and denied by Chris Grayling's minions. We should sit down and sing 'Faith of our Fathers' in the face of Brixton Prison's denial of our right to go to mass. My tongue is firmly in cheek, as regular mass-goer I'm not, though I have always respected the devotion and faith of devout believers and devout atheists. It's just another prison snafu and eventually one of the women warders, who is particularly foul-mouthed and fond of the c word, cracks and takes us over to mass.

Back in my cell, the top headline of the *Sunday Times* reads, 'How corrupt detectives shielded crime lord.' *Quelle surprise!*

A jury has failed to believe the Metropolitan Police and CPS case and convict the black woman barrister, Constance Briscoe, after she was charged with talking to a *Daily Mail* journalist. That's stupid but not criminal. Instead of dropping the case, the judge decides there will be a second trial at serious public cost. A second trial will allow the CPS QC to re-order his arguments to try and get a conviction. Like a footballer able to take a penalty a second time if he doesn't score the first time, a second trial is massively advantageous to the prosecution and hugely detrimental to the accused. But the CPS must always have its way.

1210H Last Sunday lunch. I thought I had ordered the usual Sunday chicken leg but a slab of meat is dumped on my plate. I give the blonde woman warder a smile as I leave the server. She blanks me totally. What price being friendly on Sunday? As I go upstairs, a prisoner asks who is the MP covering Brixton. It's Chuka Umunna, I tell him. He takes the news back to his cellmate. Everyone likes Chuka. He has a bright future. I hope he can find time to take an interest in prisons. But why should he? I didn't. On the final flight of stairs, I see the strawberry jam sachet and dirty tissue paper that were there three weeks ago. I'll go out after lunch and remove them.

1235H Cell door locked up again. What is this obsession with keeping us in cells on Saturday and Sunday?

1345H Unlocked. I read the *Sunday Times* bought mainly for the week's TV guide. It's a huge mass read of pages and pages but, like the proverbial Chinese meal, it fills you up and leaves you empty simultaneously. I cheekily asked for *Le Monde* as, other than President Hollande's un-uxorious life, I have been cut off from all foreign news for weeks. In the *Sunday Times*'s excellent book pages, Dominic Lawson trashes a book by Alain de Botton that advances the unexceptional argument that British newspaper coverage of abroad is lamentable. Lawson mentions a couple of foreign correspondents including the incomparable Marie Colvin, killed in Syria.

This misses the point. There are terrific British foreign correspondents. But they are never allowed space. British newspapers will go bonkers on the sex lives of French or Italian political leaders but don't tell readers, including British policy-makers, what is happening in France or Italy, or, more worryingly, Europe's key political economy, Germany. As a result, MPs can go off into fantasy land about, say, the German Chancellor supporting the isolationist anti-EU cravings of the modern Tory–UKIP desire for a loosening or repudiation of British links with Europe. But the non-existent coverage of Europe (or Latin America, Asia or rising powers) in our papers and on our TVs means that policy positions or political decisions are taken without any reference to external reality.

I go out for a walk before the Ireland–Scotland rugby game. I circulate the exercise yard endlessly with Paul. He's a chartered accountant. His story is that he was in a partnership with fellow accountants that went sour. Partnerships of high-earning professionals – lawyers, accountants, architects – are tricky when it comes to sharing out the earnings, as different partners can earn different amounts, in different ways, at different times.

According to Paul, he moved onto a form of regular payment at a daily rate. His other partners objected and told the police he was stealing from them. A year-long process started. The judge confessed he couldn't see where the crime lay. I report what Paul told me. Once the CPS has preferred charges it is hard to let go. Paul offered to settle with his partners and they were content with the proposal. The judge was baffled, but deferred to the CPS, whose officials have to fill their quotas of convictions.

Paul's lawyers assured him that if he pleaded guilty to close the hassle, he would get a suspended sentence. Bad advice. If anyone reading this is getting advice from lawyers on the basis of hints from the CPS, or the nature of the charge, that a reasonable judge is bound to impose a suspended sentence, don't believe a word. Judges love prison, and filling prisons with white-collar professions fills them with satisfaction.

So Paul is here for a few months. In Wandsworth he was offered a mobile phone and saw one prisoner with an iPad. Maybe Apple can sponsor prisons. He was swamped by the sale of drugs. Wrong, dumb, but for real. Until prisoners are more carefully supervised, and perhaps segregated by crime or mental illness, the herding of hundreds of men – Chris Grayling wants prisons with thousands of inmates – will never control the smuggling of drugs or mobile phones. Trying to appeal to prisoners' common sense, or better nature, or threatening them with harsher treatment will not work. Until intelligent reform takes place, matters will only get worse.

MONDAY 3 FEBRUARY 2014

It is more dangerous that even a guilty person should be punished without the forms of law than that he should escape.

– Thomas Jefferson

0700H Wake up and read until I make my muesli. Monday is prison's worst day. The start of another week to be got through. When I ran my first marathon I asked Peter Elliott, the Rotherham Olympic middle-distance medal-winner, how on earth you even began running twenty-six miles. 'You put one foot in front of the other,' was his laconic but perfectly accurate reply. So it's one day in front of another in prison, then one week in front of another, and so on. The first day of the week is always the longest even if, I trust, it will be the last Monday I spend in prison.

I have to write up my minutes from the meeting between the Governor and the wing representatives. The reception desk officer lets me use a computer in a side office. It's an old-fashioned PC not connected to the outside world or even the prison intranet. It's good to be back at a keyboard and in front of a screen. I don't think I've written so much longhand since school days. The cheap prison ballpoints must be the nastiest writing instruments in the world.

I type out eight pages of single-spaced minutes on last Friday's meeting. It's pretty accurate, though I varnish the paragraphs on Brixton's problem and demoralising delays in releasing prisoners on the due day of their tag. Of course, it matters to me. Today it is six weeks – half of my three-month custodial sentence. For some reason my tag day is not today but five days later, on Friday. If I don't get out I will be utterly depressed.

As I am typing up the minutes, the door opens and two women, one about sixty and one in her twenties, come in. They say they are from the IMB. This is the Independent Monitoring Board, the internal prison complaints system. I had forgotten I had put a complaint in their box when I was furious on being told I had two secret red entries – negative comments by screws – put on my prison file. I don't think it can affect me but I was and am outraged at such sneaky secrecy in condemning someone without telling him.

The older lady is one of those wonderful middle-class, middle-of-the-road professional do-gooders who give of their time to make our country a bit better to live in. She agrees with me that secret entries in a disciplinary record are not fair. But without being demob-happy, I am past caring, on the assumption I will soon be out.

We have a good general discussion about politics and MPs expenses and why so few of the MPs who helped themselves to the taxpayers' millions have been sanctioned. I rattle through my tale of being investigated and cleared by the police and the CPS, and then how the decision not to prosecute was reversed and here I am.

'But I worked with Keir Starmer. I am a trainee barrister,' says the younger woman. 'He's a really nice guy.' I give her an alternative truth about Sir Keir. She looks uncomfortable, but charm and nice manners can co-exist with other less attractive qualities and Sir Keir is one reason I was put in prison. He is, consequently, a pin-up for UKIP and the extreme Europhobe right, as the man who prosecuted one of politics' unashamed pro-Europeans. Of course he was just doing his CPS duty. I am sure that is what he believes. The opposite is too hard to think about.

1430H Twenty-four letters and emails arrive. And that's the first delivery. How will I return to normality when hardly any personal letters come in, except by email?

A lovely letter from Michael Gove, who is much in the news, which is exactly where he loves to be. His note is flattering and he sweetly asks if I would like a visit: 'I've always enjoyed our conversations and my respect for you as a friend and brave fighter in many good causes remains undiminished.'

When I later tell my elder daughter, she is appalled Gove and I are friends. The problem is that Michael is an original. I am not sure I believe his schools policy but when I see how Labour education secretaries allowed our schools to keep spewing out adolescents who couldn't read or write properly I don't think all the wrong is with Gove and all the right with his opponents. To paraphrase Admiral Beattie at the Battle of Jutland, 'There's something wrong with our bloody schools.'

Anyway I can't give, and never have given, a flying intimacy about the politics of people who are fun and dare to be Daniels, dare to be alone, dare to have a purpose and dare to make it known. Gove is the closest the Tories have to a Tony Benn, a true original, mad, sometimes bad but always delightful to know and talk to. Michael wrote a brave book attacking Islamism and its ideology at a time when it was deeply unfashionable. He told the truth on the menace, to every decent value, Jew-hating Islamist Ideology represents at a time when the Westminster and Whitehall elites were pretending it was just about adjusting the multicultural volume and, of course, trousering votes, as well as hoping for the bankrollers of Islamism in the Gulf to keep putting money into London. If for nothing else, Gove's principled stand, well ahead of the 7/7 wake-up call, has my respect and friendship.

I remain incorrigibly Labour, despite the behaviour of the inexperienced Labour leadership that failed to ensure I was treated on a par with say, David Laws and MPs who, unlike me, massively profited from the expenses system. A number of senior Labour people sent in warm testimonials, which Judge Sweeney dismissed out of hand. I have received letters and emails from Labour MPs and peers but only one from a shadow Cabinet minister. Tony Blair and Michael Gove are made of braver stuff.

1530H A gym and the old magic of sweating the body and stretching muscles works its charms. I talk to a woman officer from Santander on the Atlantic coast of Spain who is a gym officer.

'I came to England to study English and just loved it here. Not the weather but everything else about England.'

Her eyes light with genuine enthusiasm for my country.

'I wanted to be a police officer but at the time you had to be a British citizen. So I decided to be a prison officer as it's sort of like the police service and then maybe move on to join the police. The police stopped recruiting and, although I became a British citizen, I decided to stay here.'

I ask if there are any Brits working in Spanish prisons.

'I don't think so. The British don't like foreign languages do they?'

That was my cue to try out my feeble Spanish but she wouldn't use her native Castilian.

'We're not allowed to speak a foreign language to prisoners. It's not giving the impression I am saying something in Spanish that can be quoted. Better to speak English all the time.'

1646H I call Nathalie, who let two probation officers into my house to inspect it for suitability for a tagged prisoner. She says the probation officers were positive they would inform the Governor tomorrow and so there really appears no reason to stop my release on Friday.

Then I bump into Eamonn, who reminds me that his tag release was approved last Wednesday and he's still here. Then I chat to Brian, whose tag date was 2 January but he's still here. Come on, come on. They are unlucky victims of Brixton's notorious inefficiency. I'm different. They can't keep me here much longer. Can they?

2210H I just want out. I forget what was for dinner tonight, what was on television earlier. I don't belong here any more. I am writing and watching Darren Aronofsky's uneven film on ballet, *Black Swan*, when suddenly a slip is pushed under the door. It announces a visit at 8.30 a.m. for Douggie.

He is furious. He had indeed sent out a Visitor's Order to a London friend. But the friend cannot call in and did not write, so Kenny didn't know it had been approved. The Brixton visitor's system must have known about the visit earlier in the day. Why couldn't Kenny have been informed? He'll have no time for a shower and will miss part of an important workday tomorrow morning. It's the Brixton system at its most contemptuous of its charges.

TUESDAY 4 JANUARY 2014

This is the real objection to that torrent of modern talk about treating crime as disease, about making prison merely a hygienic environment like a hospital, of healing sin by slow scientific methods. The fallacy of the whole thing is that evil is a matter of active choice whereas disease is not.

– G. K. Chesterton

0900H I had the pleasure the explaining the meaning of 'snafu' to a pleasant, helpful screw this morning.

When the cell door was unlocked the guard barked, 'MacShane, free flow.' I looked at my movement slip and it definitely stated I should report for a computer class in the afternoon.

'Excuse me, sir,' I said. Try as I might, I cannot manage the archaic 'Guv' address, not out of rudeness but it just doesn't come off my lips. I doubt if even Downing Street cops address the Chief Whip as 'Guv' when he leaves 12 Downing Street to go to the Commons. Instead I 'sir' everyone as much as possible. It's always been my policy to upgrade forms of address. All academics are professors, all army officers colonels, all policemen inspectors, all diplomats and ministers Excellencies. It usually smoothes openings.

'Excuse me, sir, but my slip says I should go over to education in the afternoon.'

'You're down on my list for free flow this morning. You'd better be on it.'

I feel a dreaded red entry looming so I hurry to brush my teeth, put on trainers and go downstairs.

I see the wing bossette called Ms Delaware or some such – everyone calls her Ms Tupperware – and show her the form which states clearly I should be doing 'PM' – afternoon – IT classes this week, starting today.

I explain that I told the education officer I would shortly be leaving and, while I value and enjoy any training course, it might be better to hold the popular IT courses for a prisoner who could really benefit from it.

Ms Tupperware looks at her list. 'No, you're in education. You'd better go over. If they don't want you, they'll send you back.'

Ever obedient, I enjoy the fresh air and hint of sun as I stroll through the unlocked gates, which, for a brief fifteen minutes, four times a day, are open so you can walk more than twenty yards without waiting for gates and doors to be locked and unlocked.

In the education building I find my way back to the IT suite, where a kindly if harassed tutor tries to find me on his list.

'There you are, for the afternoon,' he says.

'But I am listed for the morning and I just obey orders.' I explain it's a bit pointless anyway. I'm out on Friday.

'I've got fifteen students and only ten computers that actually work. Look. I'll take you off the list. That'll be one less to worry about.'

I go downstairs to return to C Wing to find, like Cinderella after midnight, that all has changed. Every gate and door is locked and all I can see is bars.

The warder looks puzzled. I explain my predicament that I have been sent over on a false basis. The education bit of the system run by A4E had me down for the afternoon. The prison bureaucracy said I should be educated in the morning.

'You'd better wait here until free flow for lunch,' I'm told.

'I'd love to, sir. I can sit and read and make notes anywhere. But I know the Governor is waiting for the minutes from last Friday's Queensland meeting.'

This, of course, is a fib. (For foreign readers, fib is a word used by the English bourgeoisie and is both a transitive verb and noun for to lie, or a lie. If you fib, you are playing games with truth and this is perfectly accepted and merits a mild rebuke at the most. If you lie, you lose your job and might go to prison. The lower classes and ethnic minorities never tell fibs. They are always liars. MPs never tell fibs or lies. They are incapable of speaking anything but truth, as are judges, Sir Keir Starmer and offshore newspaper proprietors.)

So my half-fib about Governor Tullett wanting a finished set of minutes has the desired effect. The nice screw goes off to make a call. He comes back. 'I'm taking you back to C Wing. Ms Delaware said she told you not to go to education but you insisted on it.'

That's a flat lie or fib but inside Brixton and Belmarsh, prison officers never tell fibs or lies. Like MPs they believe as total truth what they utter at the time of utterance.

As we begin my escorted journey back through the endless gates and heavy metal door to be unlocked and locked, I say to my screw, 'Just another Brixton snafu.'

He clearly doesn't know the acronym. I explain that snafu is an American army term – Situation Normal: All Fucked Up. Snafu is the normal state of affairs in much of the military and, as far as I can see, it applies to prison life as well. The left hand not knowing what the right hand is doing. Orders and counter-orders. Opaque bureaucracy. The PBI (Poor Bloody Infantry) have to come to terms with it.

My escorting screw is cheered by the snafu concept. It helps to explain Brixton.

0940H I was told by three of the gym regulars that there would be a session at 10.30. As I wander down an hour earlier to ask about getting some civilian clothes out of my suitcase ahead of my presumed release, I spot a crowd of the gym regulars. I dash back upstairs to get my 'Ian McShane' gym card and, when I come down, catch the end of a crew leaving for the gym. Nine-forty, not ten-thirty. No one in Brixton respects timetables, I mourn half-heartedly to a fellow gym prisoner. 'That's Brixton, mate.' A typical snafu.

1211H Chips and a quietly disgusting thick brick pasty pie with some odd things in it. I think it is a Cornish pasty but unlike one I have ever seen before. Don't the Cornish have name protection for their delicacy?

I read a letter from the MP Hugh Bayley. His neighbour Anne McIntosh has been de-selected as MP for the safe Tory seat that surrounds the Labour city of York. She is very hardworking, respected, not yet sixty, utterly loyal to every Tory leader since 1997 and, I would say, an MP other MPs like and work well with. Tim Yeo, the much longer serving Tory MP, has also been de-selected.

I remember Chris Mullin standing outside the Labour Party conferences of the early 1980s selling his pamphlet *How to De-Select Your MP*. At the time, such Bennite or Militant Tendency (a Trotskyite sect which infiltrated the Labour Party in the '70s and 1980s) behaviour (Chris was of the former faith, never the latter) was denounced by all the press and by Labour MPs, and held up as proof by Tories of how looney and unelectable Labour was.

Now the English Taliban or Tea-Party Tories are caballing in tiny unrepresentative party grouplets to deselect loyal, hard-working Conservative MPs, and the media and other Tory MPs treat it as an absolutely normal process. Laura Sandys is another first-rate conservative MP who is quitting the Commons. What do Anne McIntosh, Tim Yeo and Laura Sandys have in common? They have spent most of their political life supporting Britain's place in Europe.

Even if they have kept their views well hidden in recent years, a Tory Europhobe militant can sniff out an erstwhile pro-European and try and engineer a de-selection or create an atmosphere of such discouragement that the MP simply gives up.

Hugh Bayley sends a wonderful letter saying he has been trying to track me down. He wrote first to Wandsworth Prison which was the first port of call of most MP prisoners. Hugh got a reply: 'Dear Sir, there is no one by the name of Denis MacShane in the prison system nationally. Regards, HMP Wandsworth.'

So I haven't really been here. Don't tell Sir Nigel Sweeney or Nick Griffin!

A constant companion here has been *The Smoking Diaries* by Simon Gray. His younger brother, Piers, was one of my brightest, most amusing friends who taught at Hong Kong University and drank himself to death while still under fifty. Christopher Hitchens, another comrade and fellow traveller in my life, also drank too much, to the worry and fear of his *copains*.

Piers cold-bloodedly closed himself down, so the gay, creative critic and writer of his thirties was so riddled with alcohol dependency a decade later, he was barely functional for more than a few hours a day. The week of his death, he came to the Commons Terrace on a brief excursion from the Cromwell Road clinic where he checked in for his final moments. We all begged and begged him to stay with us but the friendship of whiskey and its fatal embrace proved more powerful.

Simon Gray, one of the great playwrights of his time, lived longer because he gave up drink but not three packets of cigarettes a day, which eventually took him away. His *Smoking Diaries* remain a joy, even on a re-read. I had forgotten that Simon was a proper little thief while at Westminster School. He was arrested and appeared in front of a juvenile court that let him off with a suspended sentence. Like Nick Clegg, who was convicted of arson when a schoolboy in Germany, Gray benefitted from the forgiveness of his judges. To err is human, to forgive is divine and to send to prison is Sir Nigel Sweeney. I have met so many in prison who did less than Gray or Clegg. But Simon and Nick went to Westminster. My prison friends did a few desultory years in what Alastair Campbell charmingly called 'bog-standard comprehensives'.

1500H No fresh air today. The wing door to the exercise yard remains shut. I look at the blue sky with longing. The door opens to let in a new prisoner. Behind comes a screw pushing a trolley and then a second one, both loaded down with thick plastic bags full of his possessions from other prisons. I count nine, enough to fill a small flat. Lord knows how he is going to get all that stuff into a tiny two-man cell.

1722H Dinner. As I queue, some Afro-Caribbean guys push in. Three screws are checking people off a list but remain indifferent to the tension gently building up amongst irritated and hungry men of all backgrounds. My annoyance boils over. 'Hey man, give the rest of us a break, stop pushing in.'

'Look, bruvs, he's saying we're pushing in,' shouts the man I addressed. They all flex huge biceps and just smile at me condescendingly. The screws look on with indifference, copping a def 'un. Not my problem. Someone will push back at the pushers in. Turning a blind eye may be the proverbial recipe for a confrontation and worse.

1835H The phone is less and less reliable. The buttons stick and two calls don't go through. Suddenly the bell for bang-up rings, an hour earlier than usual. Men clutching soap and towels for a shower, or with sheets of paper with their phone and PIN numbers ready to call children or spouses, look at each other in frustration. When the woman warder comes to turn the key in our cell, I ask her with exquisite non-irritated politeness, 'Why the early bang-up, miss?'

'We've got to take someone to hospital and there's no staff left.' I hope it's not Colostomy Bag Jim. But I am not sure why Category D prisoners have to lose the chance to wash and clean themselves, or make longed-for and awaited calls, just because an ill prisoner trying to survive on prison medical treatment has to go to hospital.

WEDNESDAY 5 JANUARY 2014

Often a man endures for several years, submits and suffers the cruellest punishments, and then suddenly breaks out over some minute trifle, almost nothing at all.

– Fyodor Dostoevsky

0845H Unlock is very late. Everyone has to hang around at the bottom as no doors are opened and no one knows what is going on. Is it the stupid London tube strike rather crudely provoked by Boris Johnson? Dear old Boris has been milking the media for maximum exposure.

The right-wing press are trying to big up Bob Crowe, the train union leader. But this isn't Maggie versus Scargill. Disruption to London transport happens all the time – snow, a royal event, the London Olympics, weekend maintenance. Boris is desperate to become leader of the Conservatives and Prime Minister. Last night on *Newsnight*, Simon Heffer, cleverly brought in as an outside contributor by the programme, outlined the shocking decline of Conservative Party activists. Those left are very right wing, obsessively anti-European and longing for a re-run of Mrs Thatcher biffing the unions. Boris needs only a handful of activist votes to take over. Thus, Londoners have to suffer an unnecessary tube strike as he refuses to talk to employees unless they capitulate to his demands and sacrifice their jobs and family hopes.

As a result, HMP Brixton, like every other outfit in London, is facing staff shortages today, as employees struggle to arrive on time. The strike has been announced for some time, so some contingency planning might have been put in place – a day off, like a Saturday, for example.

But no. That would require imagination. The first training session for the 'Clink', the flagship new restaurant project, is due today. Prisoners have competed to get selected. If it works it could be a useful, real-time introduction to proper professing catering business. But no one turns up to do the training. The men mill around helplessly in the biting cold wind before being sent back to the wing.

I check and find I am on the free flow list for a computer training course. I speed over to the education block. As I go up to the top floor, I pause on the landing. There is a wonderful vista of a large green field with a handsome windmill, a real touch of *rus in urbe*. In Brixton? No time to imagine the freedom of seeing green again after the concrete and steel landscape of Belmarsh and Brixton.

Like yesterday, a harassed A4E tutor tells me I shouldn't be on his list. I sign the attendance sheet to prove goodwill and scurry back to my cell. I'd love to brush up on my computer skills, which are limited to basic word processing. But as I've told everyone from the Governor downwards, there is little point in my taking up a valuable and popular computer course place for only a few days.

For the screws, however, I am down to go to education this morning so off I go to come back. I am not sure why my suggestions in both Belmarsh and Brixton, that I teach or at least do some talks on politics or Europe or at least help with literacy training, or English language training for all the foreign inmates, have not been taken up.

Brian could offer a course on accountancy – how to keep on the right side of HMRC while offsetting business expenses against income. Grant could do computer instruction and how to protect computers, mobile phones from being hacked. There is plenty of talent here but it's just left to rot.

I see Jim back on the wing. He has just read Jeffrey Archer's *Prison Diary*. According to Jim, Archer quotes prison officers and managers, more than a decade ago, blaming all the problems and bureaucratic stupidities he encountered on staff shortages. In the prison service, the excuses never vary.

Another gym session, this time in the big modern gym. I really do seem to have lost weight and can do all my machines a lot easier than three weeks ago. I do a couple of miles on the running track at a faster speed than when I used to run marathons for charity, more than a decade ago. It's all ill wind.

I watch Ed Miliband making the good point that there are no women beside Cameron on the front bench. Unfortunately the camera shows a beefy Ed Balls sitting grinning beside Ed M. Surely Labour managers could have sandwiched their leader beside women? Alas, Ed has to read out his question. To command the House you have to look up, look out, but not look down at a script.

1215H A real treat. Douggie opens one of his tins of baked beans and we go downstairs to use the microwave and toaster for beans on toast. It's such a change from the soft gummy baguette. Oh boy, it almost feels like being at home.

1535H A prison officer brings up a wodge of mail. One is an official reply to my request to get my suit out of my suitcase, to air and iron it in case I want to wear it when leaving. I suspect the trousers may slip down. I hope so. It was a friendly Irish prisoner officer who said it was normal to allow prisoners access to their good clothes and be neat on leaving. He told me to put in an app.

Now I have a curt reply. 'Your suit will be given to you in Reception on the day you are leaving.' The signature of course is illegible. I don't really care but it shows the petty meanness of the guards. I doubt if Governor Tullett has the faintest idea of what small-rate, sad little bullies they can be.

The guard who brought my mail stops for a chat. Do I know Tony Blair? Yes. 'Well, he should be in prison for going to war in Iraq.'

I have the weary familiar argument about 417 MPs voting for the Iraq invasion. Where has this myth come from that Tony alone, and only Tony, took Britain to war? Rarely has a myth, a lie, become so deeply encrusted in the national mindset.

He says all politicians are the same, all in it just for themselves. I dispossess him of that cliché, though his eyes open in amazement when I describe just how much money some currently very senior MPs and ministers made from the expenses system.

He thinks Brixton is chaos. 'It was chaos when I joined the prison service twenty-six years ago and it's still chaos today.' For once, an honest screw.

1605H I go downstairs to put Simon Gray's *Smoking Diaries* back on the bookshelf. There are four shelves of a cheap imitation brown wood, Ikea-style bookshelf. Three and a half shelves have books, with half a shelf reserved for bibles, one in Greek, and the Book of Mormon.

I notice a book I hadn't seen before, *Tony Blair: A Journey*. Some prisoner must have read it and put it back. His has been the only politician's name I have heard often on the lips of prisoners and screws. Most don't even know the name of the Prime Minister. There is an Iris Murdoch and *Platform* by Michel Houellebecq in a translation by Frank Wynne.

Bill Bryson, Louis de Bernières, Dodie Smith and one Trollope but no Dickens. Michael Dobbs, of course, and Martina Cole for prison and east London crime. George Eliot and Mary Renault and Margaret Drabble span a century or more of serious women novelists. Lots of thrillers of course, and a much better selection than all but the biggest W. H. Smith railway bookstalls.

Various friends here and in America say they go to do writing classes in prison. It sounds terrific. I had visions of a prisoners' newspaper, or maybe a play or revue. But not in Brixton. It is TV or nothing.

1620H Hooray! I have a certificate. It's a general one given to prisoners who make progress in reading and writing. A couple of friends had a spare one and wrote my name in. Like the Straw Man in *The Wizard of Oz* (or is it the Tin Man?), I now have a piece of paper to prove I have gone through this spectacular waste of public money and come out with an official certificate to prove it.

I ask the nurse for an aspirin or Disprin as, again, I have the headache brought on by Brixton Prison's dislike of fresh air. She offers me a paracetamol and refuses me the Disprin that one of her more agreeable colleagues gave me two or three weeks ago. Poor Colostomy Jim is there, begging her to intervene so he can avoid the agony of his burst-apart stomach, caused by the long tramp up to the third floor. He says the prison GP has sent in a recommendation that he be allowed to use a vacant ground-floor cell. He has to be given extra medication to tackle the pain from heaving his body, with its gaping abdomen wound and hernia, up and down stairs.

Then I see the front page of *The Guardian* with Chris Grayling pandering to the right. He wants many more people sent to prison for longer times with cautions replaced by prison sentences. There is no public demand for this that I have noticed. It is pointless atavism, which

Grayling hopes will win him status. Sadiq Khan, his shadow minister, says something about 'hardworking families' in his *Guardian* quote. I don't see the connection. When will anyone protest this lunacy? But then I look at the efforts invested to send me here and I realise I am just a foretaste of this new wave of reactionary prison policy slowly taking shape.

I watch Colostomy Jim bent double in agony as he hobbles upstairs to lie down and try to forget the pain. Chris Grayling probably thinks he is being treated too softly.

1850H I talk to Don Macintyre and alert him to what may happen if I am not out on Friday. I hope it doesn't come to that. But I played by the rules when I trusted people to treat me as other MPs were treated. It was a huge mistake and if I am treated unfairly by Grayling's system and his minions, I shall make my protest and devil take the hindmost.

1920H Paul comes round furious. He shows me a transfer slip to Wandsworth, where he's just come from. No reason is given for this to and fro shuttle. He thinks a bit of paperwork from Wandsworth might have been filled in incorrectly. The cost of transferring a prisoner is about £1,500. It's not permitted to go in a car with handcuffs. Wandsworth is a Category C Prison and Paul has Category D status so he will have to be transferred back here, again at a big cost to the taxpayer. It's something that deserves a Gogol to satirise.

The Nazi Salute Conservative MP, Aidan Burley, is standing down after it was revealed that he provided different stories on the Nazi theme party he organised in a French Alpine resort, close to where Jews were assembled for transfer to Auschwitz. The Conservative Party took no action against him and several Tory MPs defended him and cheered him when he made rabid right-wing speeches in the Commons. At least he isn't in prison.

THURSDAY 6 FEBRUARY 2014

In here I'm the guy who can get things for you … outside all you need is the Yellow Pages. I don't think I could make it.

— *The Shawshank Redemption*, Stephen King

0740H Wake up to poor Crispin Blunt denying the need for an inquiry into the deaths, especially by suicide, in prison. A sad mother recounts the last conversation with her son before he hanged himself. As described by his mother, the boy would have been an obvious target for the uniformed bullies who cannot help themselves when faced with a prisoner they don't like. The boy had a string of minor offences, learning difficulties, attention deficit syndrome; in other words, an eighteen-year-old boy whose 'attitude', as screws like to call it, would have been so in your face he would have suffered the full treatment of humiliation and being abruptly ordered around that the prison service applies to show who's in charge from the moment you arrive.

The rate of suicides in prison is fifteen times higher than in the general population. They are all investigated. In both Belmarsh and Brixton I saw notices left on landing tables naming a prisoner who had killed himself and asking for any information that might be relevant. But it is the system of incarceration – overcrowded, full of sick or harmless non-violent people who do not need to be locked away, and the obsession of judges with sending ever more inside – that is to blame. And who in the Commons or the media cares if some no-good a red dressing gown has sent to Hellmarsh tops himself?

I listen to Crispin Blunt, blathering away about some standing committee chaired by some well-meaning peer who has never experienced prison. There's no need for an inquiry, Blunt insists to the *Today* man.

I like Crispin, who went through an agonising period as an MP and newly appointed Prisons Minister, as he decided about coming out as gay. A former army officer with wife and children, he epitomised the blue-chip Tory MP. We skied together in the parliamentary ski team and found ourselves together in Davos just after he made his announcement he was coming out.

Naturally the *Daily Mail* put a photographer who could ski on the job of hounding and harrying him full-time, so, as I was the better skier, I would scout the pistes from on high and, if I spotted the snapper, would find another way down the mountain. This gave us a chance to talk and I found that Crispin, like most of the former army officer MPs, was a humane, tolerant man, loyal to some Tory nostrums, but with a sense of what it was like to come from, and live on, the other side of the tracks.

Yet as I listen to him waffling on *Today* about his independent inquiry into the appalling rate of suicides and deaths in custody of men aged up to twenty-four, he sounds pure officer class who doesn't need any nosey-parker civilians asking awkward questions.

The problem with Prison Ministers is that they get their ideas from Home Office, or now Justice Ministry officials, who are not the brightest of Whitehall bunnies, or from senior prison service governors and managers, who are the smooth, fluent risers to the top who can do *Guardian*-speak to perfection.

Until you go through the deliberately dehumanising first twenty-four or forty-eight hours in prison – the strip search, the bullying order-barking screw making sure you know who is boss, the lack of communication with family, the worst most tasteless food on the menu, the sight of a stinking toilet as your closest companion, the utter lack of any guidance on what is going to happen or how you are going to survive, it is little wonder that a sense of despair sets in. 'It's prison, get used to it' is the shout you hear from a screw, more than any word of welcome.

It was unpleasant for me in my seventh decade and I had experienced a communist prison in Poland and had spent my life with stupid official-dom. For an eighteen-year-old who had a cock-of-the-walk attitude in his street, who had no idea how poorly equipped his mind and mind-set were for survival in modern Britain, let alone prison, the brutal shock of prison reception must have easily flipped him.

There is no physical duress. No torture. Instead there is a complete deprivation of humanity. The Jesuits said give me a child for forty-eight hours and he will be ours for life. The first forty-eight hours in an English prison are the worst of all the time you will spend inside. They could be the time when everything is explained, when phone calls are encouraged. When cells are visited. When at least one decent meal is offered. When the best and most intelligent of officers and support staff are on duty.

All this may come in due course if a prisoner goes to an intelligently run prison with humane staff. But unless you have gone through it, you will never understand it. That is why nice Crispin Blunt is so wrong. And why our prisons kill so many of our fellow citizens. Two thin green prison sheets and a bar of solid metal are always to hand. Why stay in a world where your humanity is contemptuously denied when an exit door can be opened?

My cellmate, Douggie, who is listening to the *Today* exchange, says he had to deal with a Romanian prisoner who was put in his cell for a night in Wandsworth.

'He was a big beefy guy, as strong as a bear. He just sat there sobbing when they banged him up. His English was terrible but I got out his story as a way of stopping a total breakdown and worse.

'Five years previously on holiday in Ibiza he got into a fight when someone tried to nick his jacket in a club. He was arrested and sent back to Romania. He came to London and, on his way home, he was arrested at the airport by police, saying there was still a warrant out for his arrest from Spain after the Ibiza punch-up.

'No one made any inquries and a judge sent him to Wandsworth. They later found out that the English police had got it all wrong. There was no outstanding warrant from Spain or anywhere else but I really thought he might kill himself as he spent the night sobbing and shaking in the cell.'

Once again a judge who never checks what the police say. Prison first, questions later.

An old friend from university, Jonathon Green, Britain's top slang lexicologist, sends me an email with the admission that no one knows why a cell is called a 'peter' in prison slang.

Peter n   (UK/US Und) 1 [mid-17C – 1930s] (also peeter, petter, pitter) a trunk, a bundle, a bag or parcel of any kind. 2 [late 18C+] a safe or cash-box, a cash register, a till. 3 [mid-19C] (US Und.) a receiver of stolen property. 4 [late 19C] (US tramp) a safebreaker. 5 [late19C+] (Aus) a witness box: thus mount the peter. v. to enter the witness. box 6 [late 19C+] (also pete) a cell, whether in jail, a police station or elsewhere, thus also a prison.

That's as it appears in one of Green's great dictionaries of slang. But he adds, 'You can see the progress. But why "peter" no one seems to know. One thought – but only in the context of a cell – could be peter – rock (see Bible) – stone – cell construction. Any thoughts from your end gratefully received.' I am tempted to go and organise a little seminar on prison slang amongst fellow inmates and still don't know where the term 'bird' for a prison sentence comes from. Del tries to improve my rhyming slang knowledge. I now know what 'deaf and dumb' means though I have yet to experience what is called a cavity search. And I love 'bubble and squeak' for Greek, though how I will explain it to Athenian friends later this year, I do not know.

Norman gives me a copy of the *Prison Service Journal*, in which he has a review of a book by Frankie Owens, *The Little Book of Prison: A Beginner's Guide*. To judge from the review it could be usefully given to every prisoner as soon as he or she begins the walk down from the dock. The review seems very intellectual. One article is entitled 'Thermodynamic, Newtonian Motion, and the Prison: The Effects of Energy, Entropy and Mass on Rehabilitation'. I am sure it is very worthwhile. But somehow I doubt if many of the screws here will be reading it. Britain writes about prisons more than any country. But nothing changes.

I sit quietly reading Houellebecq. Why have I not read him before? Because he is a celebrity author, both in France and internationally. Something puts me off famous novelists. How silly. The book is wonderful, written with a narrative elegance and loads of explanation – a tutorial on this and that in the world.

1120H Paul knocks on the door. He has been sitting quietly downstairs, waiting for his transfer back to Wandsworth. He tells me that they have discovered the missing report on his risk status, duly signed by a Wandworth Prison official. But still he assumed the prison bureaucracy, having listed him for transfer, would carry out this unnecessary procedure. Now he's cheerful. C Wing screws were sympathetic. One told him to throw a sickie as you can buy time by pretending to be ill. But that's not necessary. 'I'm off the bus,' he beams, happy to have someone to tell the news to. I'm glad for him. I wish I knew what was happening to me.

1200H Outside my cell, six black guys are playing Monopoly on the pool table. They make an incredible noise. Sometimes, when they talk fast, I have difficulty in understanding their English. It's lively and musical, a re-ordering of words, different emphases. I love it. Slowly one nation is becoming many. *Ex uno plures.*

Lunch consists of some penne and corn with half a tomato and some lettuce in a plastic box. Nothing to flavour it. I pour a little vinegar and sprinkle salt and pepper on the contents of the box and the small white bag of chips. The apple I have saved up is half rotten and I am able to cut only two small chunks off it.

I go out in a cold drizzle, not heavy but wet, and manage ten minutes of fresh air. One of the more pleasant screws comes in and asks, 'You going home tomorrow?'

I tell her I have no news.

'Oh dear. Normally in prison no news is good news. But this is Brixton.'

Two emails sent yesterday and a letter from David Blunkett, wishing me well and proposing lunch, arrive. My brother and Julia fill their emails with discussions of the wine I'll be drinking tomorrow night. But will I?

I finish the Houellebecq. It's difficult to describe why it's so good. A huge piss-take on the super-rich and their desire for immortality by buying modern art at huge prices. A decent attack on the money-making euthanasia outfit Dignitas in Zurich. But above all, a memorial to the end of France between Napoleon and de Gaulle. France has become a land of tourists and agriculture, not much more. Intense, with neat subplots and characters as well as clever use of real names from the French media world. A truly satisfying novel.

1520H Back after a good gym. My longest run, a decent row, weights and treadmill. I shower and in a bit of mirror see, if not quite Daniel Craig's rippling chest and abs, a torso much slimmer and fitter-looking than at any time in recent years.

I chat to Pete, who walks around with half his teeth out and a neck brace that prevents him from shaving properly. He is serving a short sentence for fraud. He is in Del's cell. Poor Del holds up yet another email from his Essex council, trying to find out when he will get out of prison, as his tag date was sometime last year. There's gentle 74-year-old Brian, whose tag date was more than a month ago but, despite his impeccable middle-class property-owning pillar-of-the-Orpington-bourgeoisie status and style, the taxpayer is still forking out to keep him inside.

Pete says when he transferred to Brixton he had spondylosis – hence the neck brace – cancer of the mouth, which he opens to show scars where the surgeon has done his best, and diabetes.

'All that was on computer at the last nick but can Brixton be arsed to have it transferred to their system? Can they fuck. You're sent to prison for punishment, not to die here,' he says bitterly, a sick old man. He has three months to his tag day and is worried that, as with the no-longer-young Brian and Del, he may be kept beyond it.

'Look at me! Look at Brian! Are we a danger to society? Am I going to go out and attack old ladies?' he says in despair.

I go and make a phone call to my solicitor. This morning I had £40 in phone credit. Now it shows just £0.47. I go to a landing screws' office where two of them are sitting back comfortably and chatting. I politely ask why my phone credit has evaporated.

'They're probably closing down your account because you're going out.'

What! I reel back. I have received no bit of paper, been told nothing. The officer gets up my official prison computer file.

'Look, they're closing down everything and working out how much they have to give you tomorrow when you leave,' he says, as I peer at the columns listing the money I came in with or have 'earned'. I can't quite see all the figures but I may be leaving prison with more money than I came in with. After making no profit from the MP expenses scheme, at last I can pocket a gain.

My heart leaps. Am I really leaving? I go back to my cell and for the first time since Clare was killed, tears well up. Not many, as I so distrust this regime – I won't believe I'm out till I'm out.

But the phone credit signal is positive. I won't need to do my protest hunger strike after all. I feel bad leaving on my tag day when so many cannot. But no one in prison begrudges freedom for a fellow inmate. With only 50p left, I cannot call any of my loved ones to share my elation. That's prison.

I go downstairs and get a Michael Dobbs political parliament thriller from the Maggie era. I just want to relax, and Michael's fiction and faction are always enjoyable. Perhaps I should write a political thriller – a Europe-hating civil servant whose wife sleeps with the Polish plumber. A greedy MP passed over for promotion, jealous of a younger neighbour's swift ascension up the greasy pole. Journalists working for newspapers whose owners are serial tax-dodgers. A publicity-hungry prosecutor and a judge who is in love with prison.

No. Characters like that could never be brought to life and no one would believe that civil servants, MPs, and QCs could ever be so shabby and second-rate. Better stick to writing on Europe and global security.

I get into the Dobbs and hit this line of advice given by a wizened old practitioner to a neophyte: 'Rules are meant for the guidance of the wise and the emasculation of the foolish.' John Lyon CB and Sir Kevin Barron certainly emasculated me as a politician. I hope new generations of MPs take note.

1715H I go round saying goodbye to friends, swapping email addresses. But I still have no confirmation that I am leaving tomorrow. The last dinner is pretty disgusting – a brown sludge of mince with plain boiled rice and diced carrots and swede. What might I eat tomorrow? Or drink? Suddenly the bell rings and a senior officer appears to lock cell doors. I wait nervously and make a quick call to Vicky to say I hope and expect to be out and can she call Sarah to see who might pick me up. The money runs out and the bang-up starts in earnest. The officers say a prisoner needs to go by ambulance to be hospitalised. This requires two escorting screws and we all have to lose ninety minutes of chatting, relaxing, making calls, having a shower, as the system cannot cope with a hospital trip.

It seems the last unpleasantness as a guest of Her Majesty is not even knowing, not being told that I am off tomorrow and not being able to make phone calls to announce it. At least I am going. I say goodbye to Brian and Eamonn. Their tag dates were weeks ago. Brian says glumly, 'You've got powerful friends so you're able to leave on time.' Given what happened to me, the idea I have powerful friends is a generous one. But it is a disgrace, an absolute disgrace that these men who have done their time are still held in prison.

Bill Roache, the *Coronation Street* actor is cleared. Not all of 'Sir' Keir Starmer's celebrity prosecutions have succeeded. Not a single person has been charged over female genital mutilation during his tenure of office. And not a single banker involved in illegal trading in 2008.

1939H My last *EastEnders*. Still no notice I am to leave tomorrow, five days after I have done the time required by the noble Sir Nigel Sweeney.

FRIDAY 7 FEBRUARY 2014

He who has never tasted jail
Lives well within the legal pale,
While he who's served a heavy sentence
Renews the racket, not repentance.

– 'I'm A Stranger Here Myself', Ogden Nash

0645H I get up with Douggie, who was told that he had to be ready to leave for his bakery job at 7 a.m. He teases me with the bacon, eggs and toast breakfast he will enjoy as one of the perks of his prison job. We make tea and coffee, and chat like two old friends, though we only met four weeks ago. I am now well past the halfway stage of the Sweeney sentence. There is no notification that I am leaving. Kenny goes off. I take advantage of the unlocked cell door to have my first early-morning shower since before Christmas.

I put on an old denim Lacoste shirt which over the years had got rather tight. Now it hangs loosely. I make my final muesli. As I am eating it, a screw appears clutching a list.

'MacShane. IT education this morning.'

'Excuse me, sir, but I was led to believe I was leaving this morning.'

'Well, you're down on the list for education.'

Can this be real? I go downstairs and ask another screw. 'There are two lists, one for education and one for discharges. You'll be on both. Just wait in your cell to be called.'

What a shambles. I still cannot call anyone to help with being picked up, as I look at all my books to put in my suitcase.

Other prison friends come up to shake my hand and wish me well. 'You've changed my mind about MPs but I'm still not voting Labour,' says Grant, to whom I will bequeath my trainers.

Brian, the septuagenarian accountant who is now well past his tag date, gives me a letter to forward to his MP, Jo Johnson. Eamonn tells me that despite having been OKed for release last week, he has to stay in for two more weeks. 'They say it's because the reports aren't in. I've talked to my probation officer and they assure me every bit of paper has been sent to Brixton.' Again, sheer incompetence.

I feel slightly ashamed I am leaving only a few days' late, thanks almost certainly to my status. I wonder if anyone will hold Chris Grayling to account for this flagrant waste of public money. I catch the name of the *Desert Island Discs* guest – the elderly DJ Bob Harris. It is time to rejoin the world.

1002H The shout of 'MacShane' comes up from the ground floor. I grab my two plastic bags. It's over. Free. I can have my own name back. I walk with the screw to the reception area. I am in a holding room with four other guys and am the last to leave. The one before me is in his late twenties, pasty-faced and looking sick and nervous. He was in for petty drug dealing. 'My dad died when I was ten, me mum jumped off London Bridge when I was eighteen. I've done a bit of shelf-stacking but this controls me.' He pushes up a sleeve to show a marked, slashed, scarred arm in which he has injected his drugs. 'Now I'll get £46, plus £8 for a tube fare and a telephone number of a homeless hostel. I have no family, nowhere to go. I don't know what I'll do.' He is almost crying with fear and worry at going outside. I know what he'll do. He'll be back.

1059H At last. I get back my suitcase, still with some of the books I was never allowed to bring into prison. I empty the plastic bags of clothes including a prison shirt and all the sheets of paper I have written this on. Now I am going no one is interested in searching me. I get back my wallet, credit and Oyster cards. I sign for the £8 for a tube fare and the £46 discharge allowance. I am temped to sign Ian McShane. The cash comes in the form of crisp £50 notes. I almost feel rich. My money is carefully counted out and I realise I have made a small profit on my stay, or a bigger one if I include the food and everything else I have not had to buy.

I am just another discharged prisoner. I go out the big gate and walk up Jebb Avenue to the barrier. As I leave, I see a prison officer from Wing C going in, cramming a Cornish pasty into his mouth. I am free. He enters prison.

Journalists await. The BBC woman kindly lends me her phone so I can call to get picked up. A *Daily Mirror* reporter gives me a lift down to the Ritzy in Brixton. *Finita la commedia.*

1300H Home for the most enormous fry-up. All the forbidden foods of Belmarsh and Brixton are now waiting in my local Sainsbury. I seem to have lost weight and can fit into clothes that were a tad tight before Christmas. A mountain of mail awaits. Many people just did not know where to write and the National Prison Service never had a 'Denis MacShane' on their books. I was listed by the name they bestowed on me, 'Ian McShane', and anyone who tried to find out which prison I was in was told there wasn't a Denis MacShane anywhere in the prison service.

I am touched by one letter from Nigel Evans, who is going through his own agonies thanks to the CPS love affair with celebrity prosecutions. I have always liked this engaging, slight, cheerful Tory from the wrong side of the tracks in South Wales, who has had a good career as an MP, ending up as Deputy Speaker. Nigel would be blown over by a puff from a rugby player and the idea that he went out raping burly young men in their twenties is absurd. Whatever the outcome of his trial, he will never fully recover, never win back his perch in the Speaker's chair. The CPS surely has to be accountable for destoying people's lives.

1812H The tag team arrive. Actually, it's a kindly lady who fits a grey anklet, which I hardly notice. There is a kind of telephone installed outside the bedroom and I am strictly warned about not going out after seven o'clock. I have tickets for *Rigoletto* at the ENO in a couple of weeks. Can I say I am investigating Italian political and sexual shenanigans to write a piece on Berlusconi and should be allowed out off tag for work reasons? Better not. Perhaps I can send the tickets to John Lyon CB and his wife.

1915H I am already thinking of life after tag. I have an invitation to speak in Canada three days after it comes off and then the following week to Washington for a major economic policy conference. The requests to go to Brussels, Berlin, Geneva, and Zurich stack up. Bits of the self-regarding British establishment treat me a leper. I fear I am about to find out that the idea that serving time wipes clean the slate is a myth. Already the BNP's favourite blogster is busy trolling me but at least he, unlike the prison service, spells my name right.

2010H The first drink since before Christmas. Just a glass of Sancerre, well chilled. I begin arranging a series of tag dinners. MPs, Tory and Labour, journalists and editors, lawyers and judges, novelists and professors all seem keen to accept invitations to entertain me during my home detentions evenings. I can try out some of the recipes I saw on TV in prison. Tonight friends and family come round to celebrate. They listen to my prison stories. I will be dining out on them for the rest of my life.

SATURDAY 8 FEBRUARY

Freedom is not worth having if it does not include the freedom to make mistakes.

– Mahatma Gandhi

0735H The first long run. I go for a good pound round Battersea Park. The anklet chafes a little under the sock but it feels so good to be out in the open air with grass under my feet. I have definitely lost weight. Already, Brixton and Belmarsh fade, as have the BNP and the all the woes and worries of being forced out of Parliament. Like being fired from the BBC, or quitting England to work abroad, or leaving a comfortable job in Geneva and a lovely house under the Jura to become an MP, this caesura in my life somehow makes sense. Time is running out but there is still time to make mistakes and break rules and get into trouble again. I am me, and Lyon CB and Sweeney cannot change that. I feel for the guys I have left behind. There is no need for so many to rot in prison. What can I do to change our useless prison system? Not much.

0900H I thought I had too many letters in prison and lever files fill up with my notes and letters from Belmarsh and Brixton. But there are even more waiting for me as texts, emails and letters. I hope I have tried to help, and lift other horizons, and now it is payback time as there seem to be a load of people expressing solidarity and support. I am tempted to go online with the comments of parliamentarians about my case but chuck it, Denis. Move on. The same for all the hate tweets from BNP and UKIP supporters. If only they knew how they were wasting their time. I like Twitter as a kind of giant comments book you can make any point in. And it keeps me in touch with a hundred and one people and outfits doing things I want to know about. And much cheaper than subscribing to a news wire. I enjoy flinging the odd dart and I like an argument via Twitter. But the sheer ugliness and stupidity of some of the comments, a kind of sub-*Sun* troll language, is charmless and, like urine running down the tweeter's leg, it may make Paul Staines feel warm but no one else cares.

1120H I bike down the Kings Road close to where I live. Just good to pop into shops, see the market, wonder what's on at the Saatchi Gallery.

1420H Skype Laura in Toronto and fix up to see her after talk in Quebec. After all the stress of non-visits over Christmas, it's good to see and talk to children again. She really does not like Judge Meanie, as she calls him. I expect long after all this has faded for me, my nearest and dearest will still be angry over what happened.

1930H A big reunion dinner. Oldest friend from school, climbing partner and No. 10 official, children, brother, partner, mother of my children and her partner, an age range from nineteen to ninety-two, everyone around the big kitchen dining table, drinking champagne, white and red wine or beer, listening to my stories, laughing at the right moments, eating giant roasts of lamb, wanting to know every detail of life inside. I think of all the friends in Belmarsh and Brixton, by now banged up with twelve to fourteen hours before their cell door opens again. Sure, some deserve it. But many don't. I wonder if Britain will reform its prisons before I die.

AFTERWORD

In 1939, Britain had a population of 46 million and we had 11,600 people in prison. Today our population has gone up by 50 per cent to 63 million but we have around 89,000 prisoners in UK prisons. Most of this massive increase has happened in the last twenty years. It was initiated by one politician, Michael Howard, and developed with gusto by his Labour successors at the Home Office and Ministry of Justice.

Sadly, not many MPs take an interest in prison reform or raise a voice about this amazing, barely reported increase in prison numbers. I didn't, and do not, recall any MP who sought to make a name by campaigning against the insatiable demand for sending more and more people to be incarcerated.

Other countries with comparable crime rates and comparable public and media hostility to criminals do not send nearly as many people to prison. In England and Wales there are 148 prisoners per 100,000 citizens. In France, the figure is 83 and Denmark, 73. Why do English judges send so many more people to prison than their French or Danish counterparts?

All crime has fallen in most Western nations in recent years. Britain, despite its enormous prison population, tops or comes close to the top of serious and violent crime league tables in Europe. So judges obsessively sending people to prison does not work.

Prisons are also very costly to the taxpayer. £3.5 billion is spent on prisons each year and £13 billion is the estimated cost of re-offending, as our prisons are simply training schools for crime. Prisons are turntables that send people out only to come back in again, as there is little serious rehabilitation or help to become a better citizen once released. It cost the taxpayer about £7,000 to keep me in prison, and during that time I went on no education courses, and was not asked to do any work. I passed my time talking and writing, as indeed I have passed my life.

I have only recorded what I heard. There are fine books on prison which analyse in detail the statistics and the enormous economic waste, which should engage someone at the Treasury. Vicky Pryce, the government's former joint chief economist, was sentenced to eight months for taking her former husband's speeding points. It was the same judge who sent her to prison who reached out from the Old Bailey and exercised his right to sentence me to a slightly shorter time inside. Ms Pryce's book *Prisonomics* (Biteback Publishing) is a fine, up-to-date guide, both on the hidden scandal of the number of women our largely male judiciary dump into prison for non-violent crimes, and on the wider economic waste that is our prison system.

There is very little writing on prisons in our papers. Ian Katz, when deputy editor at *The Guardian*, encouraged an inmate, Erwin James, sentenced to twenty years for murder in 1984, to write articles. Gathered in a book, *A Life Inside: A Prisoner's Notebook*, they provide a vital insight into prison life in the '90s. David Goodhart, when editor of *Prospect*, published very good columns on prison life by a repeat drug addict offender, Peter Wayne. But on the whole, our press do not take much interest in what is happening inside prisons, save the occasional sensational tabloid story sold by an inmate or prison officer about a notorious prisoner.

I did not read Jeffrey Archer's three volumes of prison diaries until I was out and had finished transcribing this journal. Archer's vivid storytelling style mirrors much of what I experienced in Belmarsh, and it is sad that none of the criticisms he made seem to have been taken on board by the prison service or politicians. If anything, conditions and treatment in prison have worsened since he wrote his prison books more than a decade ago. Unlike Archer, Pryce, and other politician prisoners, I was never sent to an open prison so I cannot report on what happens inside them.

The people who make and execute prison policy – MPs, civil servants, researchers, journalists – never actually experience that which they determine laws and policy on. Unlike other parts of the public realm – the NHS, schools, councils, transport, benefits, police services, the army and so on – where MPs and policy-makers have direct personal experience, no one in the Commons, Whitehall or the media will have been a prisoner.

There are excellent organisations that campaign for prison reform. The Howard League for Penal Reform (www.howardleague.org) was set up in 1866. It is sad that its work is more than ever necessary in the twenty-first century. Other prison reform think tanks and university researchers produce excellent reports and recommendations for reform. The state has three regalien rights. It can remove the citizen's life, liberty and money. Capital punishment is abolished, though the state can send hundreds of young men to be target practice for the Taliban in Afghanistan. We all pay taxes decided by parliament. Wars and taxes are objects of intense political debate and can win or lose elections. But the decisions of the state to remove someone's liberty – by sending citizens to prison – is hardly debated as an issue.

If our hospitals sent 70 per cent of patients out only to see them come straight back in again, or if our schools sent 70 per cent of students out without being able to read or write, there would be an outcry. Yet our prison system is so inefficient that most who enter and then leave are likely to return, as our prison system encourages crime. The treatment of prison-ers as unworthy bad people, by a desperately over-stretched and poorly managed prison staff, turns them into sullen resisters of petty authority.

Home, now Justice, Secretaries come and go. In recent years, and the Labour record is truly shameful, they have sought to profile themselves as being tough with criminals. But beating up men and women behind bars is childish and counter-productive.

Instead, the moment there is an ugly story in a newspaper, ministers start wetting themselves in fear of negative headlines. I have no idea how to overcome this problem. Mrs Thatcher famously never read newspa-pers. In her day, the prison population was under control. Perhaps a ban on politicians and judges reading the press, with its incessant clamour to send people to prison, would help. Our prisons, from my experiences in Belmarsh and Brixton, are hopelessly over-crowded. This is mainly the fault of judges. We do not have a criminal bench with the intellectual self-confidence or better training of other modern democracies, where judges prefer non-custodial but heavily supervised forms of punishment. The man who has done something wrong suffers from being caught, convicted and put before the public in a court. The length of prison sentence hardly matters. The President of the Supreme Court, Lord Neuberger, says that prison sentences of six months or less are pointless. He should go and have lunch with the bewigged and red-robed Old Bailey judges – yes, they really do take their lunch wearing their eighteenth-century clobber – and speak to them.

A former Lord Chancellor assured me that judges were told to act more intelligently on sentences. If so, there is no evidence they are paying any attention, as judges daily decant people into prison as if it was a solution for anything.

But there is no reporting or analysis of what judges do. If you want to hide something, do it public. In their red dressing gowns and white hijabs, judges do their work fully in public. Yet the public, the press and the elected politicians take no interest in what they do. Rotund denunciations, as the clichés roll out in sentencing statements are duly reported as if from Mount Olympus. The occasional judge who shows he is not a prison junkie will be excoriated in the tabloid press. One would hope his fellow judges would show solidarity. Instead they make sure they face no criticism by imposing ever longer and more pointless prison sentences.

I do not have an answer. The CPS and judges are about social order, not justice. No sanction is ever imposed on judges who send innocent people to jail or against CPS prosecutors who yield to fashion and prosecute people with a view to headlines rather than the real crimes, such as rape of women or corruption in the police or crookedness in the banks.

I cannot see the difference between a bottle of vodka and a joint. I have never consumed cocaine but I met plenty of MPs and journalists who did when younger and seemed none the worse for the experience. We live in a prohibition era on recreational drugs. Yes they damage. But nothing like the damage caused by alcohol. In the early twentieth century, the social democrats of Nordic countries and progressive politicians elsewhere insisted on outlawing alcohol and the leftovers of that policy can be seen in state-owned and supervised shops selling alcohol in Sweden or Quebec.

On the whole it was right to give up such prohibitionist policies but they are still applied today against the equivalents of alcohol. The upper and middle classes – the children of judges and civil servants – who smoke a joint or snort a line are never punished. But the men who provide them with these recreational drugs, if caught, are treated as wicked beyond belief. Everyone lives with this hypocrisy but it adds hugely to the prison population and makes prisons less and less efficient.

We are almost all criminals in the sense that there are more than nine million people with a criminal record. I have one. So does Nick Clegg convicted of arson as a young man. A quarter of the UK's working-age population has a criminal record. In 2012, nearly two million people appeared in court to be given a reprimand, a penalty notice or to be sent to prison.

So perhaps we should pat ourselves on the back that there only 89,000 prisoners in Britain. The figure could be so much higher. I can only wish the prison reform lobby all the best as they try and persuade editors and MPs that there are smart alternatives to incarceration.

I am in awe of the wonderful prison charities that do so much work, the good people who visit, the organisations that help ex-prisoners find work, including the Timpson group, who deserve every honour there is for their willingness to allow men and women fresh out of prison a new life.

Banks and insurance companies that treat released prisoners as if they were still active criminals and deny them access to essential financial services are a major problem. My former colleagues in the Commons might find a moment's legislative time to stop the discrimination that ex-prisoners face. As the Swiss Ambassador told me after I was released, 'But, Denis, you have served your time. There is no more problem.' Not for me, perhaps, but for so many of my fellow inmates in Brixton or Belmarsh, the real punishment only begins upon release.

In that sense I hope this journal may provide some guidance. My worries and concerns about our prisons and the criminal justice system that decants so many into prisons are those of a concerned citizen that experienced it.

In Belmarsh and Brixton I found only warmth, friendship and shared solidarity from my fellow prisoners. There was a sense of right and wrong, the difference between truth and mendacity, and a willingness to admit mistakes. In that sense, my time in prison was rather different from my time in the Tea Room of the House of Commons.

The expenses scandal that sent me to prison still lives in the public's mind. Fellow citizens know that many of the pre-2010 generation of MPs profiteered handsomely from the way they submitted expenses claims. Three hundred and seventeen complaints were made against MPs in 2009/10. That a few miscreants such as myself (and I do not deny my fault, and of having made a grievous error) have faced the ultimate sanction of imprisonment. Others have been returned to Cabinet rank after a slap on the wrist.

Hopes that it might be possible to draw the line under the MP expenses scandal have proved an illusion.

Too many MPs still think it is permissible for the taxpayer to pay their wives and children handsome salaries in order to supplement family incomes. The Prime Minister criticised the UKIP-leader Nigel Farage, for 'having his wife on the payroll'. Mr Cameron should look around the Cabinet table, starting with the Justice Secretary, Chris Grayling, whose wife's salary, like that of Mrs Farage, is paid by taxpayers. Too many MPs think it is permissible to trade on their position to earn handsome fees and salaries paid by private firms who want access to law-makers. Too many MPs think it is acceptable to transfer, via their expenses, rental income to their political parties – a taxpayer subsidy that in other democracies would be illegal. Some MPs even think the taxpayer should pay for designer spectacles for their staff. Amongst these MPs are those who serve on the House of Commons Standards Committee, which sits in judgement on MPs.

As long as the memory of what the pre-2010 generation of MPs did exists, and as long as post-2010 MPs continue to assume the taxpayer should pay their family members a salary or pay for expensive designer glasses that their constituents cannot dream of buying, this public dislike of MPs will not go away. I know just how hard MPs work, and how exhausting of family and personal life it is to be a modern British MP. We have leaders of our political parties who are either very rich individually or, in the case of the Leader and Chief Whip of the Opposition Party, enjoy Cabinet-rank salaries which insulate them from the pressures of trying to maintain two residences, a family divided between constituency and Westminster, and incessant demands on time and money that no other public official faces.

None of this is understood, still less sympathised with, by a public whose newspapers, left, liberal and right, as well as vast social media networks, tell them almost daily since 2009 that MPs are conniving, pocket-filling fiddlers.

Unfortunately, when the public reads of the MP who recently claimed £5,000 to pay for electricity for his horses' stables, or another who was paid £90,000 for the costs of a house in which her parents lived and which was then sold for a profit of £1.5 million, or those who still put family members on the taxpayers' payroll, the public contempt gets worse – especially when they see no sanction applied.

I would like to believe that driving me out of the Commons and sending me to Belmarsh would satiate the public desire for the punishment of MPs. But I don't think that is the case. The Commons has less and less authority as more and more power is taken away from democratically elected representatives and transferred to shadowy power-brokers with money, often off-shore, to buy influence and control public debate.

Reforming parliament and restoring trust in politics is a task yet to be undertaken. Meanwhile while we wait for party leaders who understand what needs to be done and set about doing it. I hope that somewhere in the Commons there may be a single MP, better a handful, who will make the reform of our inefficient and malfunctioning prison system a cause they will work for. Britain's prisons are not the best advertisement for our nation. If this journal nudges someone to begin rethinking prison policy, and the reasons why so many are sent without reason and at pointless cost into prison, it will have served a purpose.

This book could not have been brought out so quickly without the help of many people – my friend Iain Dale at Biteback and his editing team under the steady hand of Olivia Beattie. Thanks to Sarah and Laura MacShane, Christine Hotson, and Jack Porteous for help in transcribing. Scarlett McGwire and Clarissa Hyman provided useful comments, mainly telling me to take out references to MPs who thus remain unnamed and unshamed. But they are right.

All faults are mine. I remain, as ever, guilty of whatever you, dear reader, want to find me guilty of.

PRISONER
HM Prison Brixton

P-Nomis	**A7367DC**	CMS URN : **12162**
Surname :	**Mr McShane**	
Forenames :	**IAN**	
Date of Birth	**21/05/1948**	

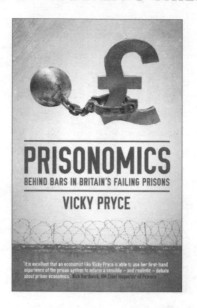

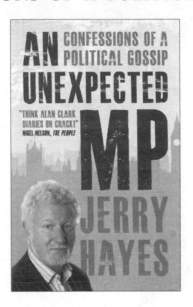

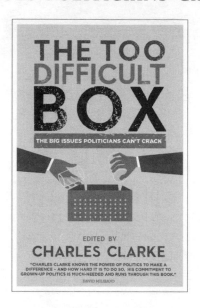

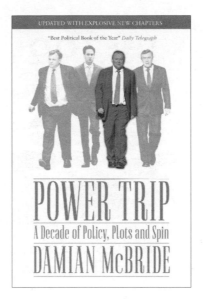